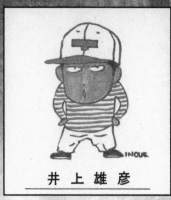

井上雄彦

Takehiko Inoue

I WENT TO THE EAST COAST OF THE U.S. IN
APRIL TO COVER THE NBA. THE BULLS WON THEIR
RECORD 70TH GAME ON THE DAY I GOT THERE.
IN PHILADELPHIA, I GOT TO WATCH THE FINAL
GAME AT THE SPECTRUM. THE PHILADELPHIA
TEAM, THE 76ERS, IS SET TO MOVE INTO A NEW
ARENA NEXT SEASON. IN WASHINGTON, I GOT TO
SEE THE TEAM PLAY AS THE "BULLETS" FOR THE
LAST TIME. THEY'RE CHANGING THEIR NAME TO
THE "WIZARDS" NEXT SEASON (WHAT A STRANGE
NAME). I GOT TO WITNESS A LOT OF HISTORIC
MOMENTS IN ONE TRIP.

Takehiko Inoue's *Slam Dunk* is one of the most
popular manga of all time, having sold over 100
million copies worldwide. He followed that series
up with two titles lauded by critics and fans
alike—*Vagabond*, a fictional account of the life
of Miyamoto Musashi, and *Real*, a manga about
wheelchair basketball.

SLAM DUNK
Vol. 29: Talent

SHONEN JUMP Manga Edition

STORY AND ART BY TAKEHIKO INOUE

English Adaptation/Stan!
Translation/Joe Yamazaki
Touch-up Art & Lettering/James Gaubatz
Cover & Graphic Design/Matt Hinrichs
Editor/Mike Montesa

Printed in Canada

Published by VIZ Media, LLC
P.O. Box 77010
San Francisco, CA 94107

10 9 8 7 6 5 4 3 2 1
First printing, August 2013

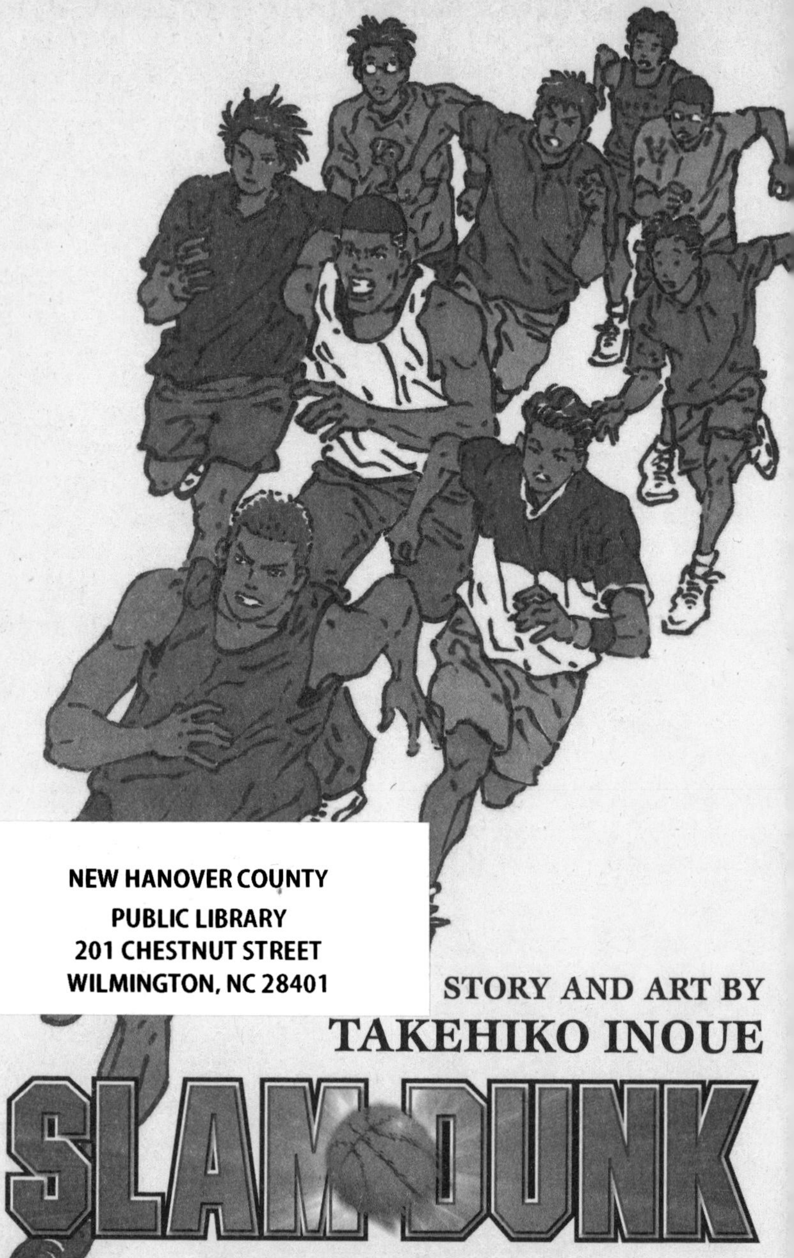

STORY AND ART BY
TAKEHIKO INOUE

SLAM DUNK

Vol. 29: Talent

Character Introduction

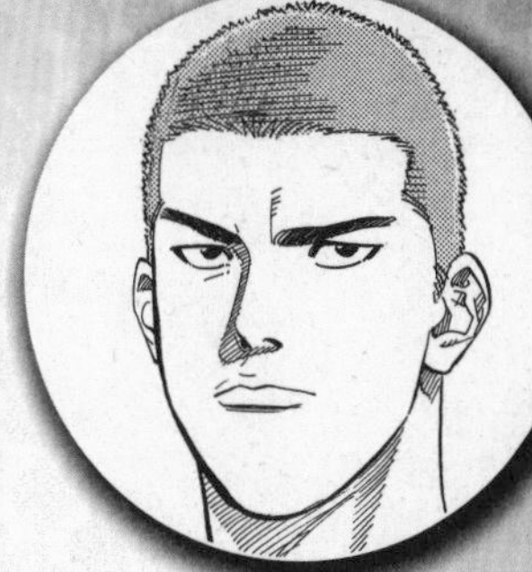

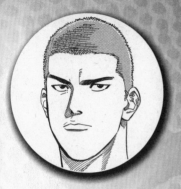

Hanamichi Sakuragi
A first-year at Shohoku High School, Sakuragi is in love with Haruko Akagi.

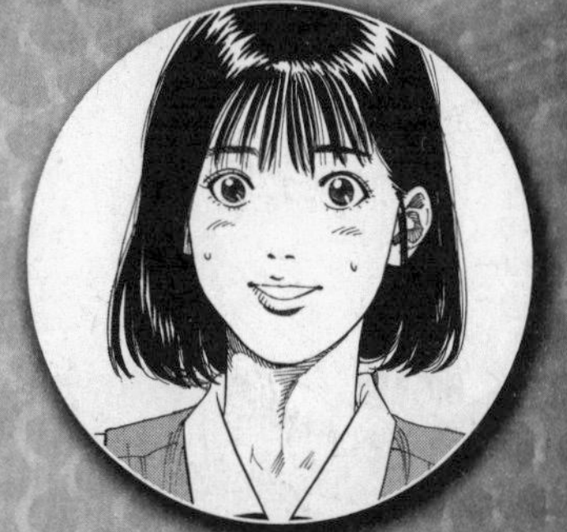

Haruko Akagi
Also a first-year at Shohoku, Takenori Akagi's little sister has a crush on Kaede Rukawa.

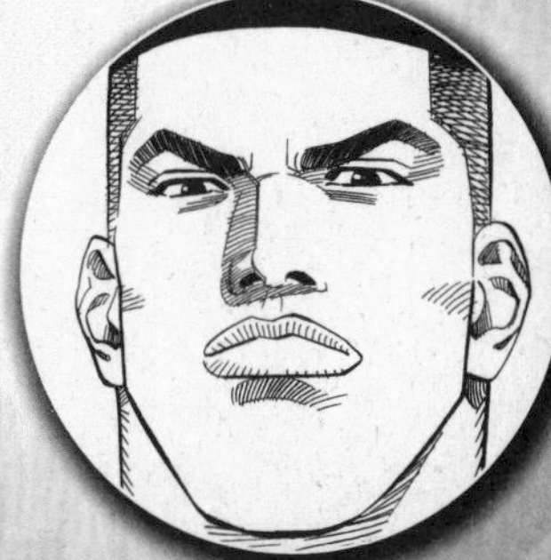

Takenori Akagi
A third-year and the basketball team's captain, Akagi has an intense passion for his sport.

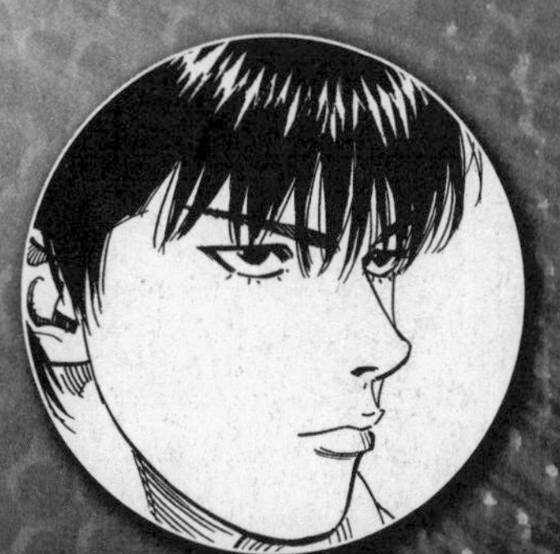

Kaede Rukawa
The object of Haruko's affection (and that of many of Shohoku's female students!), this first-year has been a star player since junior high.

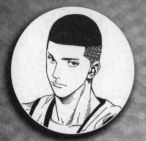

Sawakita

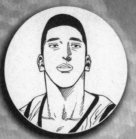

Fukatsu

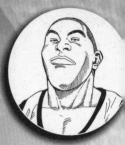

Kawata

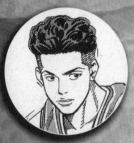

Ryota Miyagi
A problem child with
a thing for Ayako.

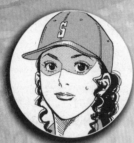

Ayako
Basketball Team
Manager

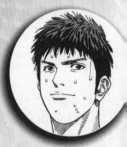

Hisashi Mitsui
An MVP during
junior high.

Our Story Thus Far

Hanamichi Sakuragi is rejected by close to 50 girls during his three years in junior high. He joins the basketball team to be closer to Haruko Akagi, but his frustration mounts when all he does is practice day after day.

Shohoku advances through the Prefectural Tournament and earns a spot in the Nationals.

Shohoku makes it to the second round to face Sannoh Kogyo, last year's national champions and considered by most to be the best team in the country.

Shohoku falls twenty points behind in the second half, but Sakuragi's offensive rebounds help the team regain its rhythm. And then, the game takes a dramatic turn...

Vol. 29:
Talent

Table of Contents

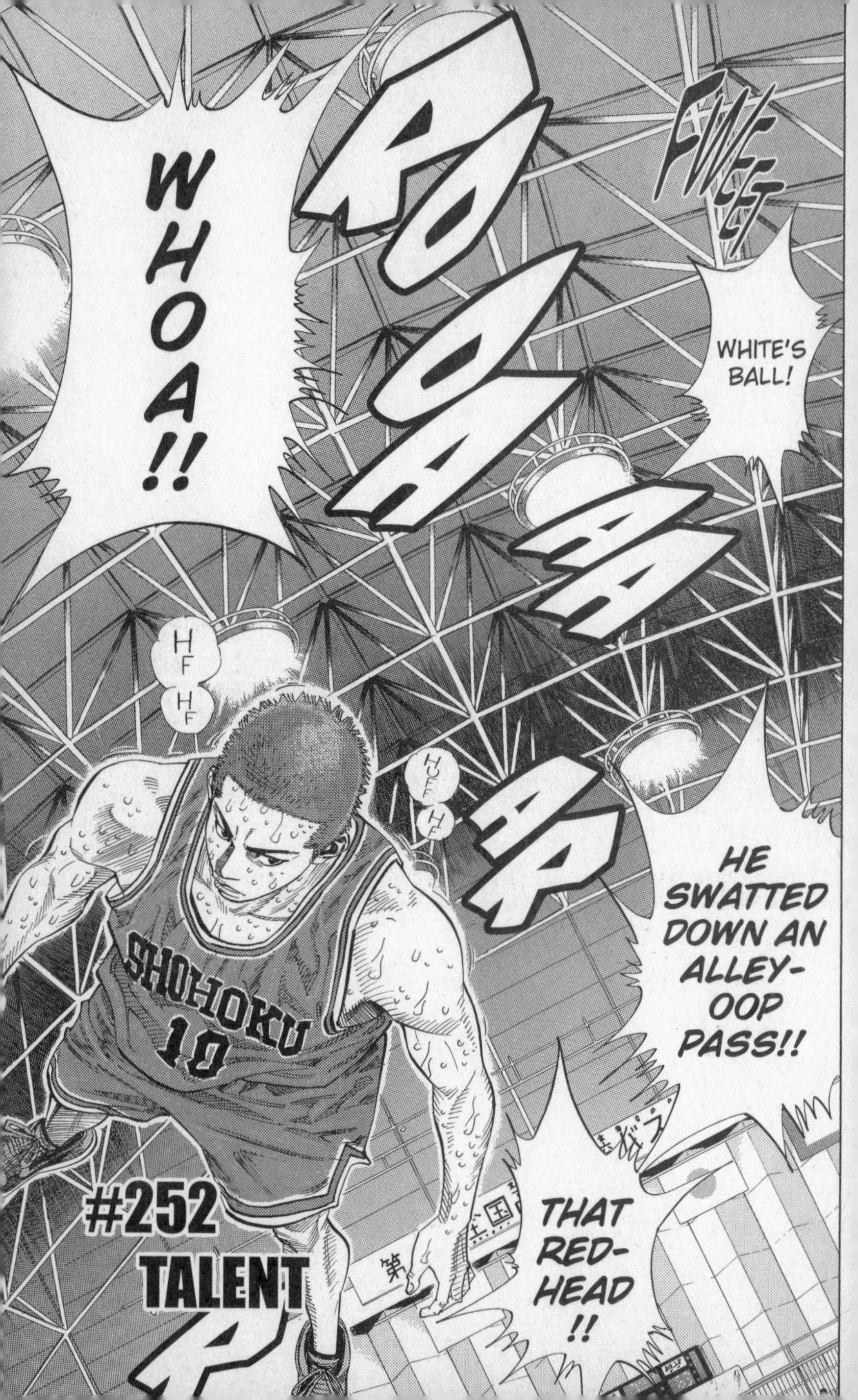
FWEET
WHITE'S BALL!
WHOA!!
HF HF
HUFF HUFF
HE SWATTED DOWN AN ALLEY-OOP PASS!!
THAT RED-HEAD!!
SHOHOKU 10
#252 TALENT

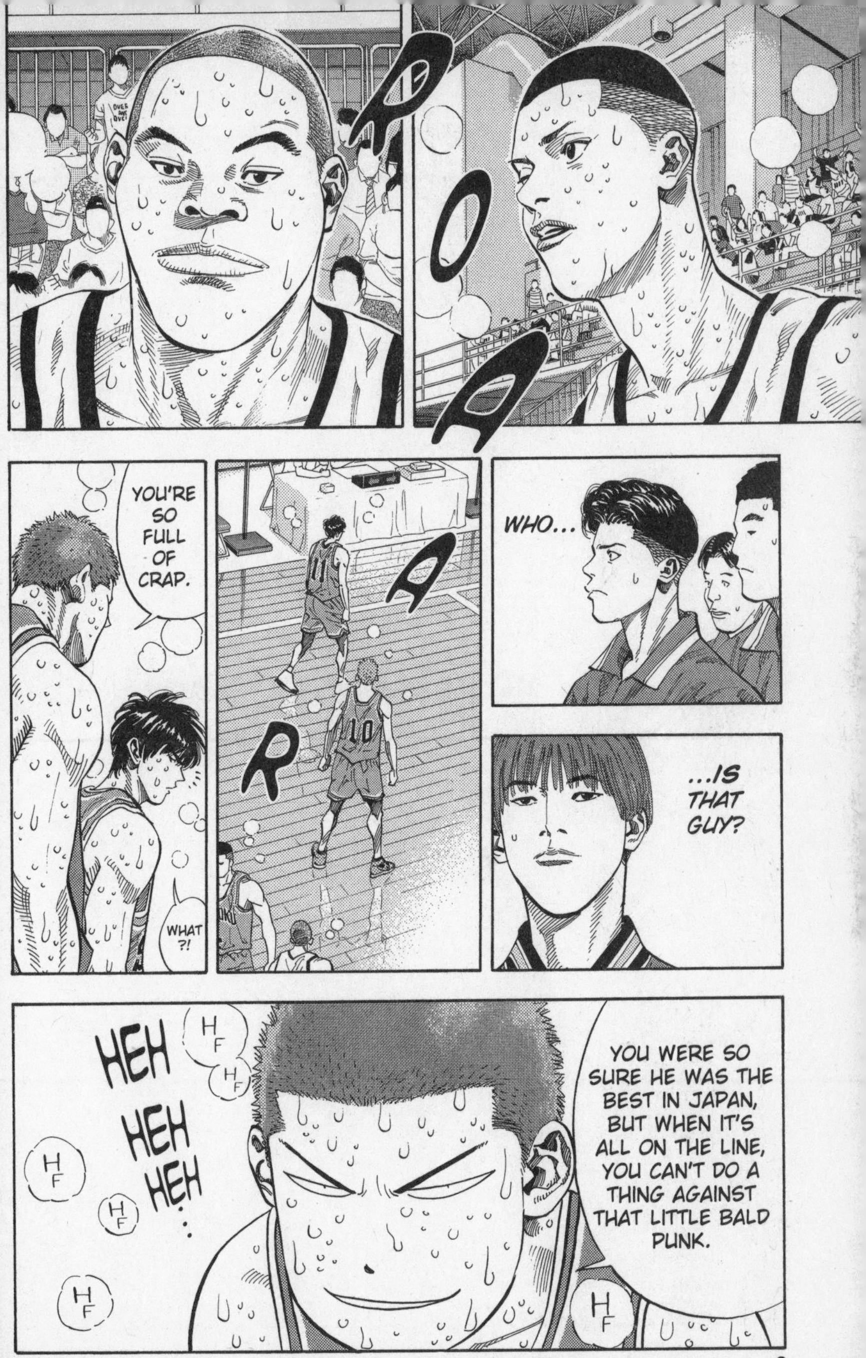
ROAAAR
WHO...
...IS THAT GUY?
YOU'RE SO FULL OF CRAP.
WHAT?!
YOU WERE SO SURE HE WAS THE BEST IN JAPAN, BUT WHEN IT'S ALL ON THE LINE, YOU CAN'T DO A THING AGAINST THAT LITTLE BALD PUNK.
HF HF
HEH HEH HEH...
HF HF HF HF

READ THIS WAY

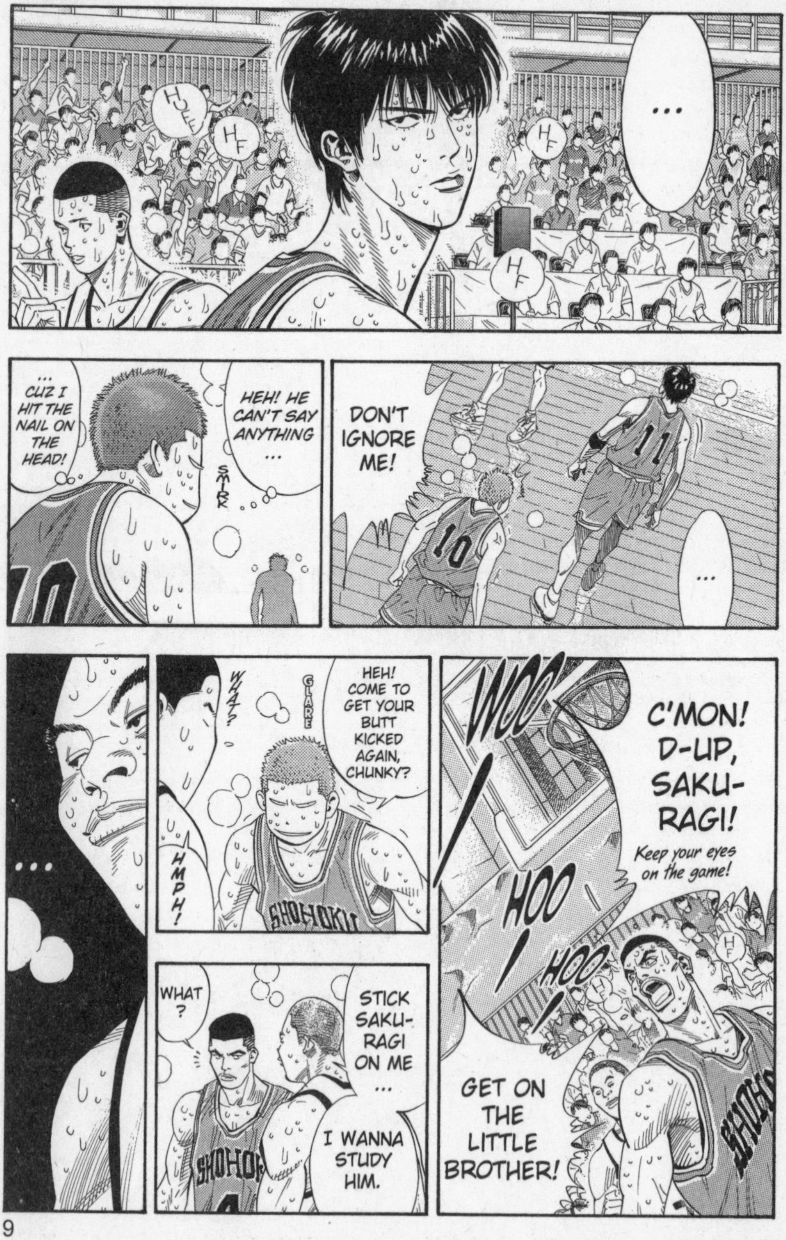
...
HF
HF
HF
HUFF
DON'T IGNORE ME!
...
HEH! HE CAN'T SAY ANYTHING ...
SMIRK
... CUZ I HIT THE NAIL ON THE HEAD!
WOO!
C'MON! D-UP, SAKU-RAGI!
Keep your eyes on the game!
HOO!
HOO!
HF
GET ON THE LITTLE BROTHER!
HEH! COME TO GET YOUR BUTT KICKED AGAIN, CHUNKY?
GLARE
WHAT?
HMPH!
STICK SAKU-RAGI ON ME ...
I WANNA STUDY HIM.
WHAT?
...

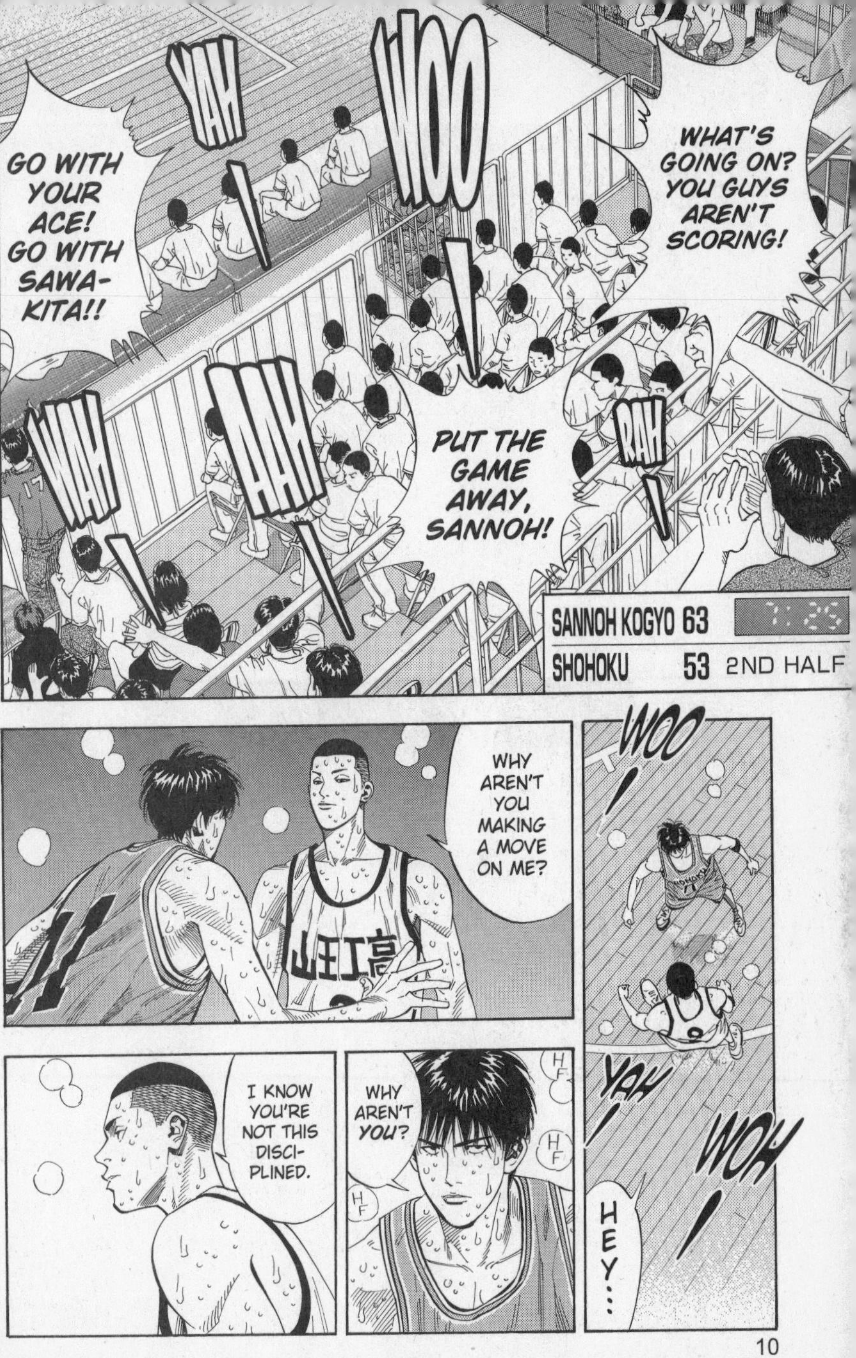
WHAT'S GOING ON? YOU GUYS AREN'T SCORING!
WOO!
YAH!
GO WITH YOUR ACE! GO WITH SAWA-KITA!!
RAH!
PUT THE GAME AWAY, SANNOH!
AAH!
WAH!
SANNOH KOGYO 63 7:25
SHOHOKU 53 2ND HALF
WOO!
YAH!
WOH!
HEY...
WHY AREN'T YOU MAKING A MOVE ON ME?
WHY AREN'T YOU?
HF
HF
HF
I KNOW YOU'RE NOT THIS DISCI-PLINED.

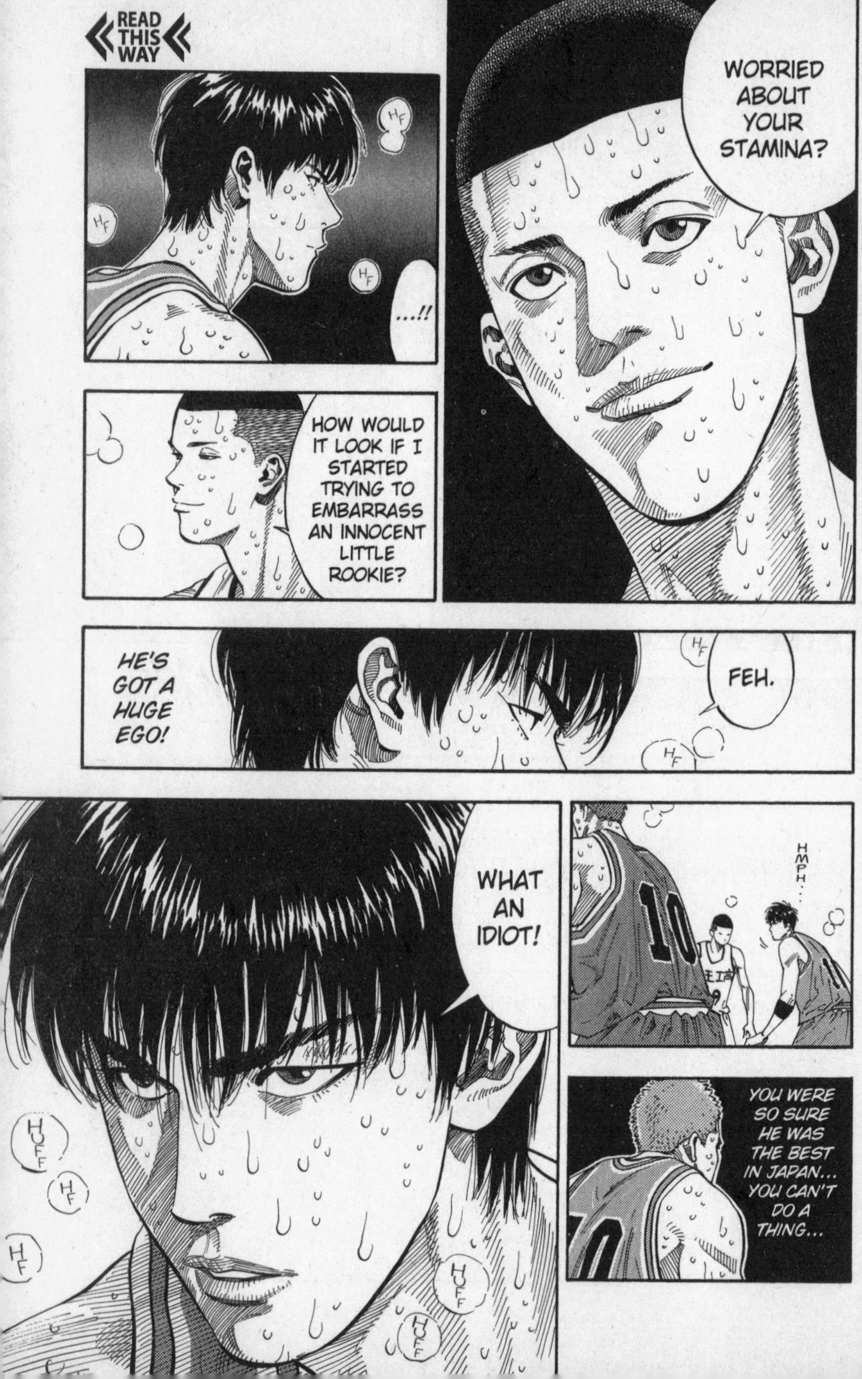
READ THIS WAY
WORRIED ABOUT YOUR STAMINA?
HF
HF
HF
...!!
HOW WOULD IT LOOK IF I STARTED TRYING TO EMBARRASS AN INNOCENT LITTLE ROOKIE?
HF
FEH.
HF
HE'S GOT A HUGE EGO!
HMPH...
YOU WERE SO SURE HE WAS THE BEST IN JAPAN... YOU CAN'T DO A THING...
WHAT AN IDIOT!
HUFF
HUFF
HUFF
HF
HF

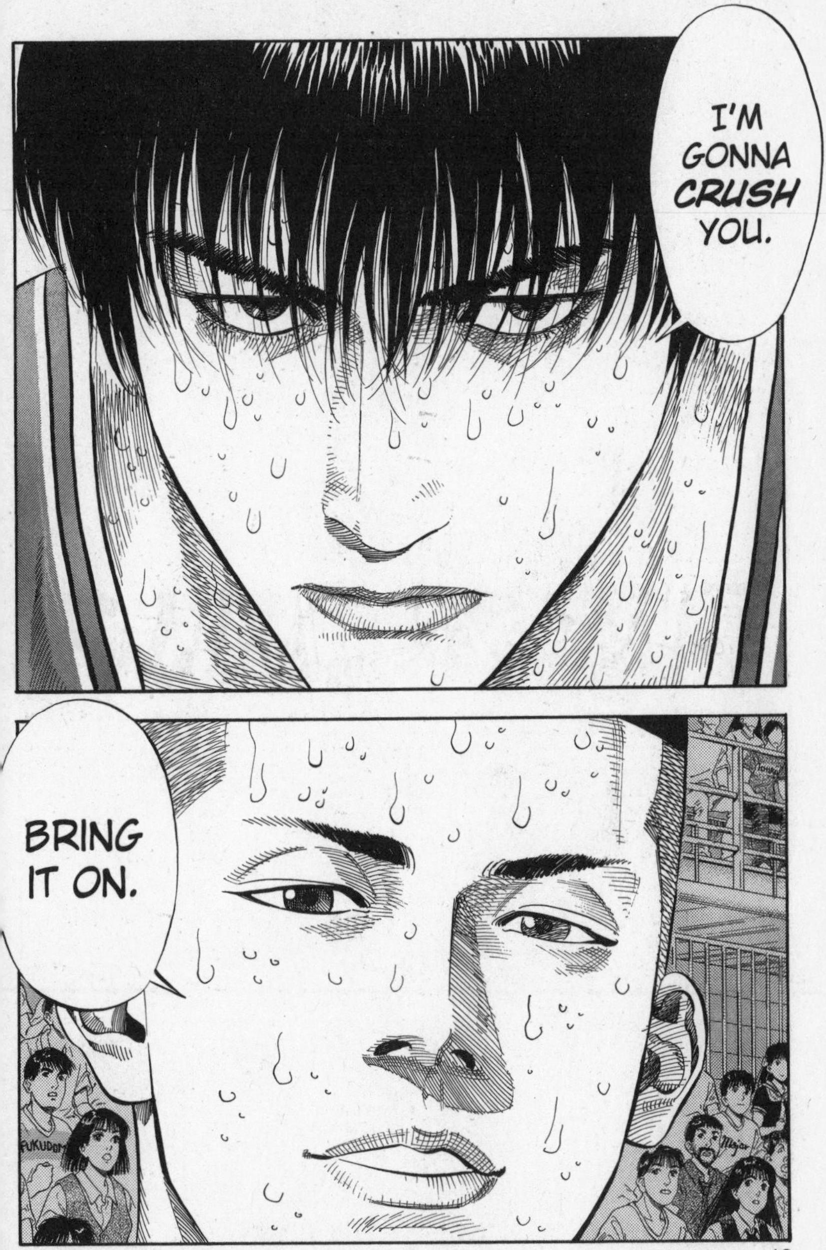
I'M GONNA CRUSH YOU.
BRING IT ON.

READ THIS WAY

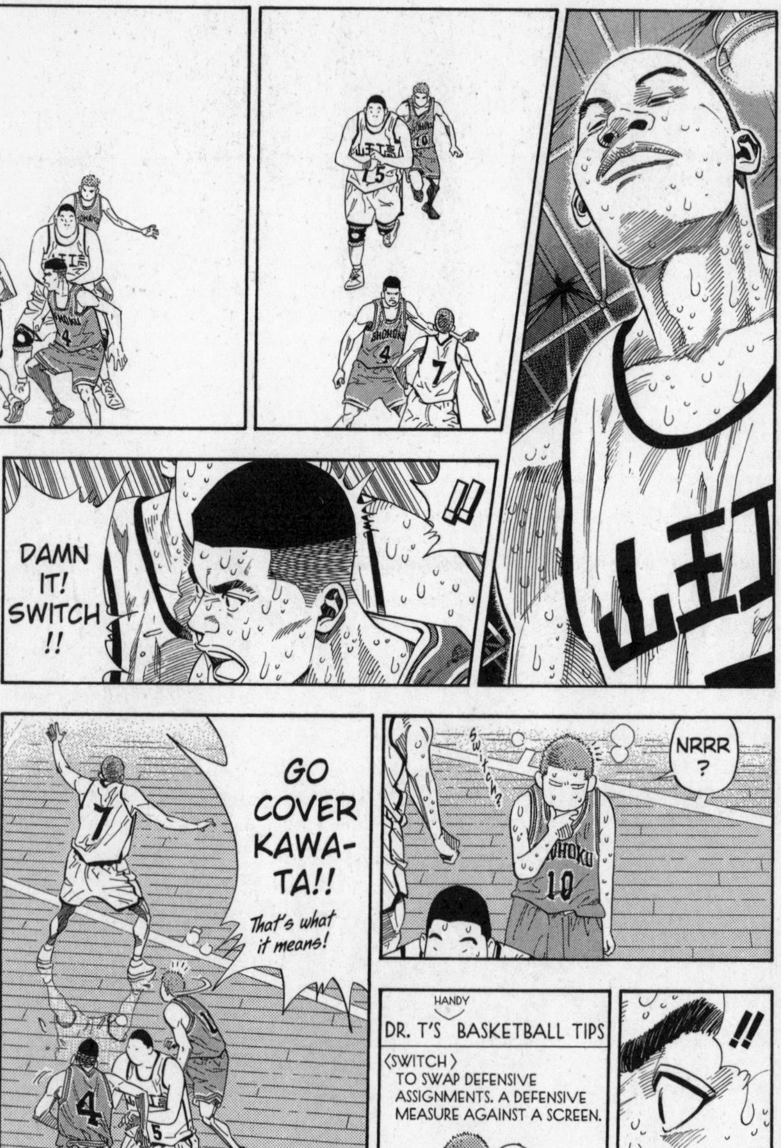

!!
DAMN IT! SWITCH!!
NRRR ?
switch?
GO COVER KAWA-TA!!
That's what it means!
!!
HANDY
DR. T'S BASKETBALL TIPS
〈SWITCH〉
TO SWAP DEFENSIVE ASSIGNMENTS. A DEFENSIVE MEASURE AGAINST A SCREEN.

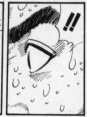

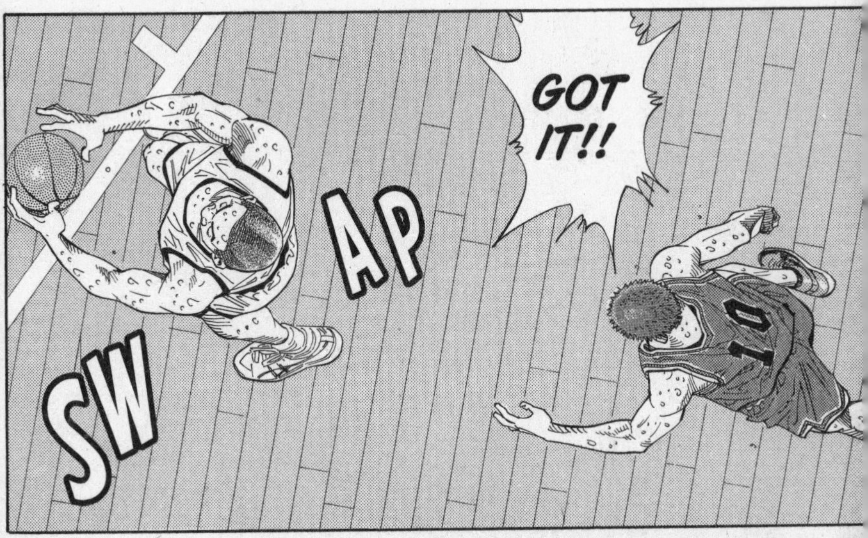
GOT IT!!
SWAP

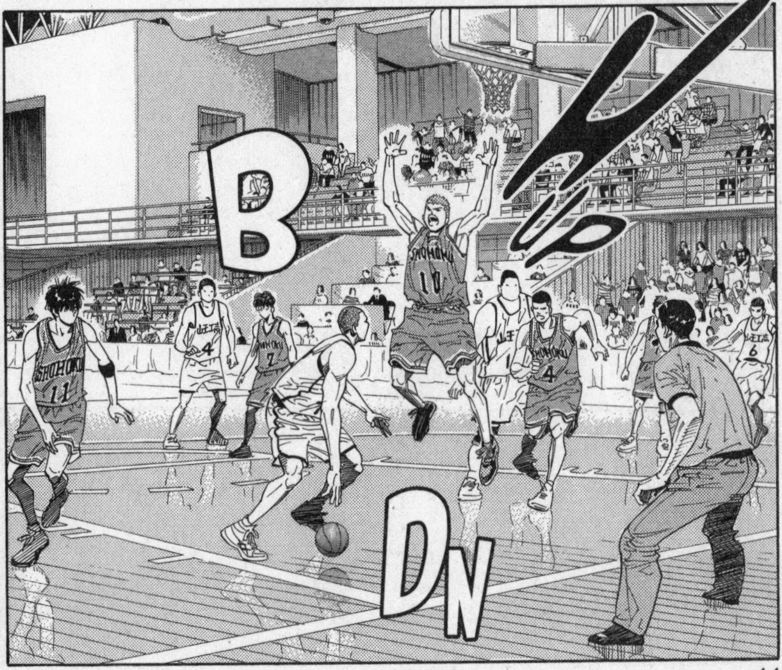
BDN

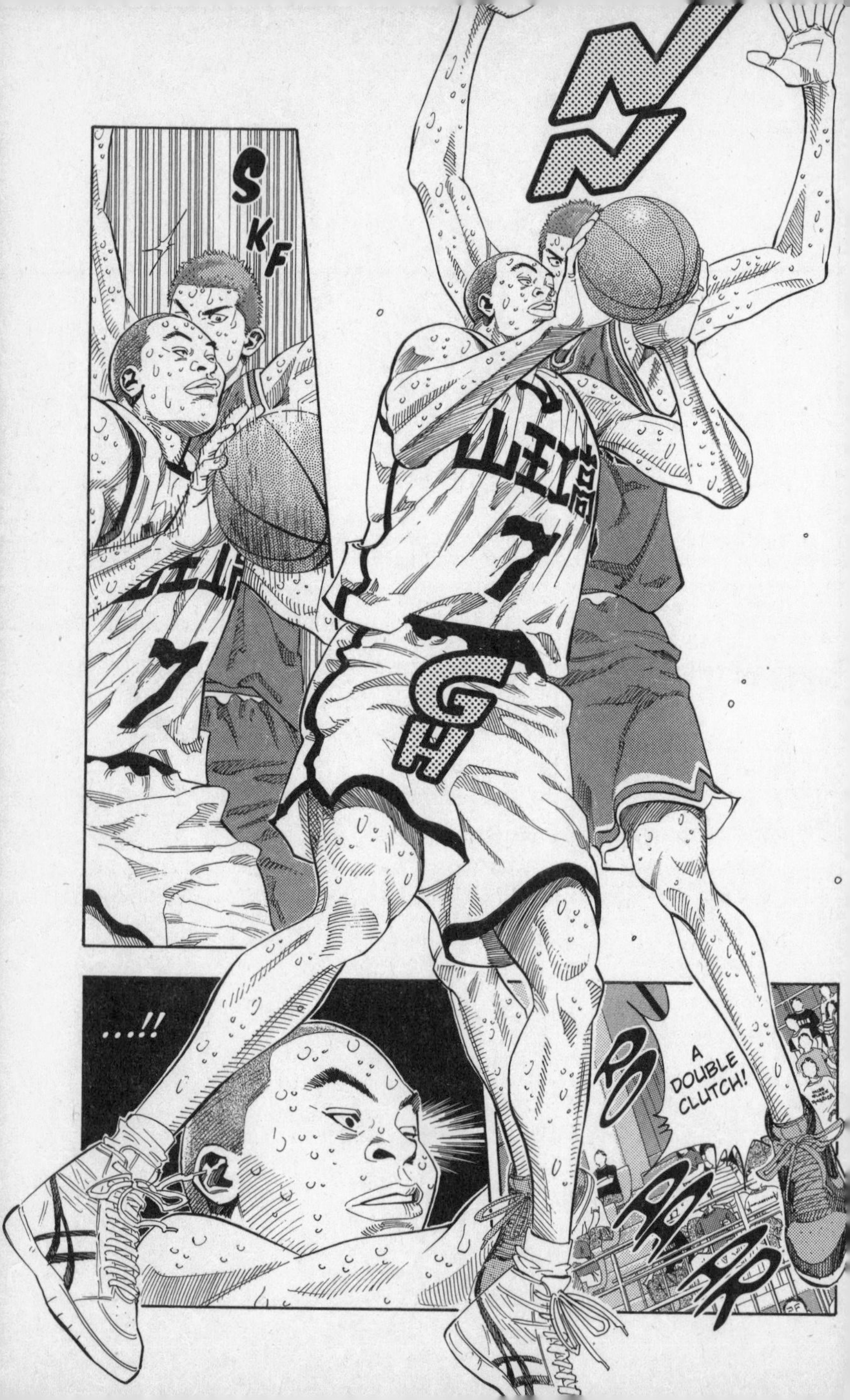
SKF
A DOUBLE CLUTCH!
ROAAARR
...!!

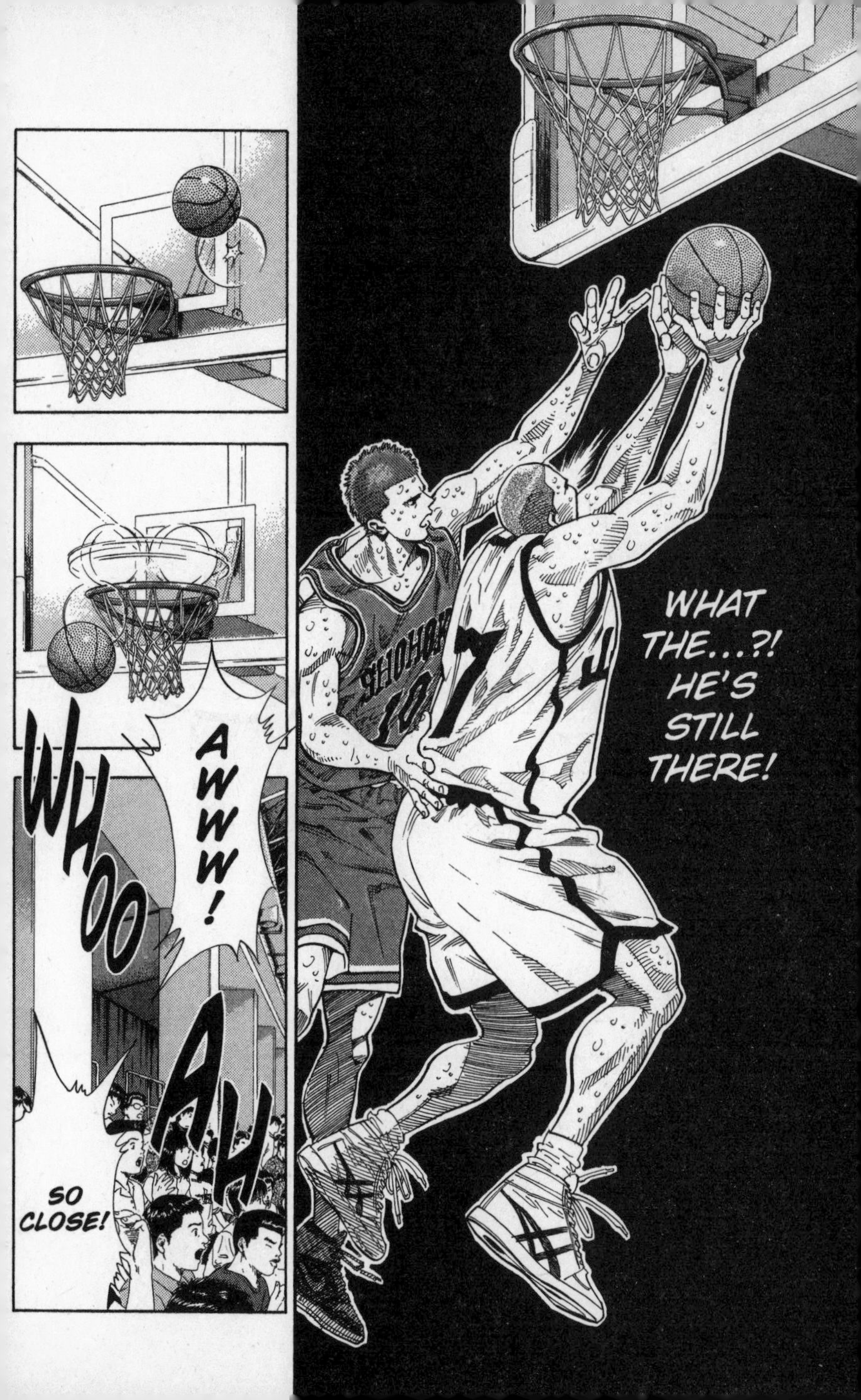
WHAT THE...?! HE'S STILL THERE!
AWWW!
WHOO
AH
SO CLOSE!

READ THIS WAY

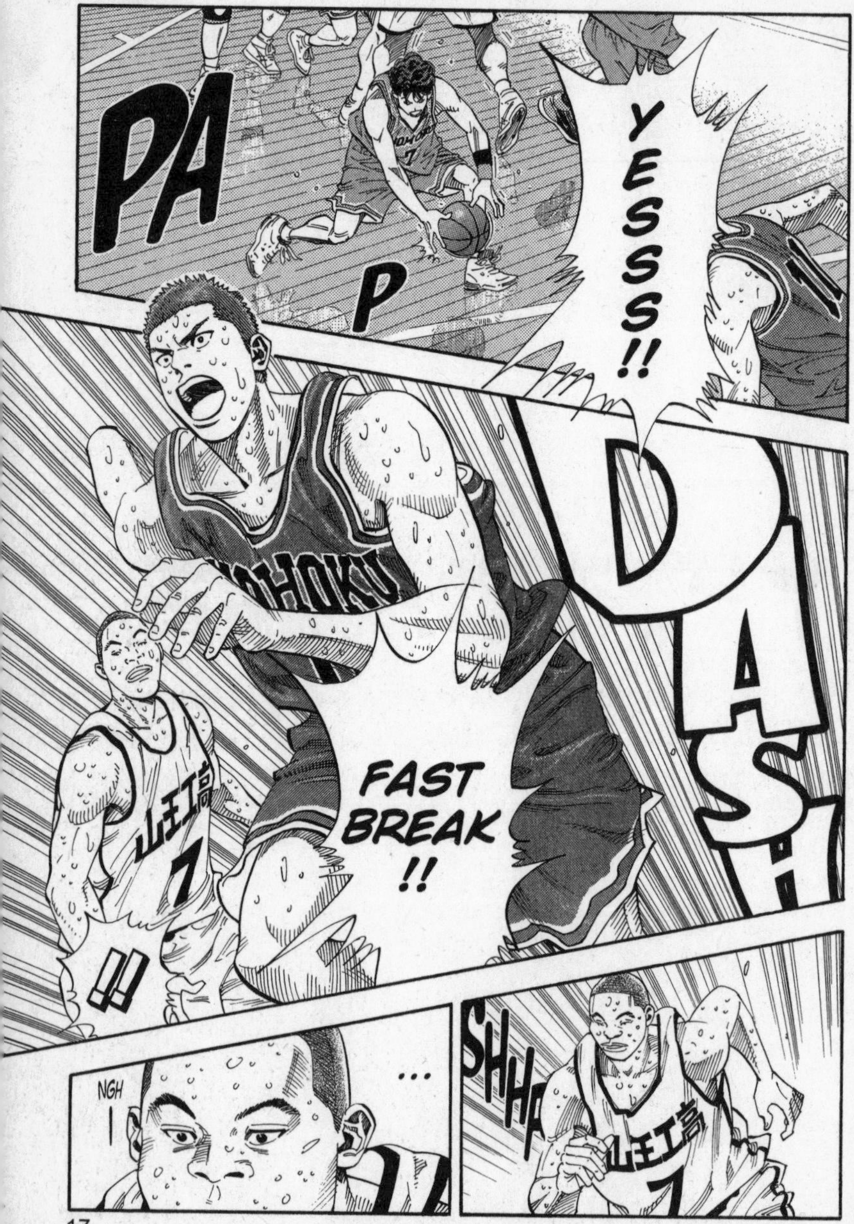

PA
P
YESSSS!!
DASH
FAST BREAK !!
!!
SHHP
...
NGH

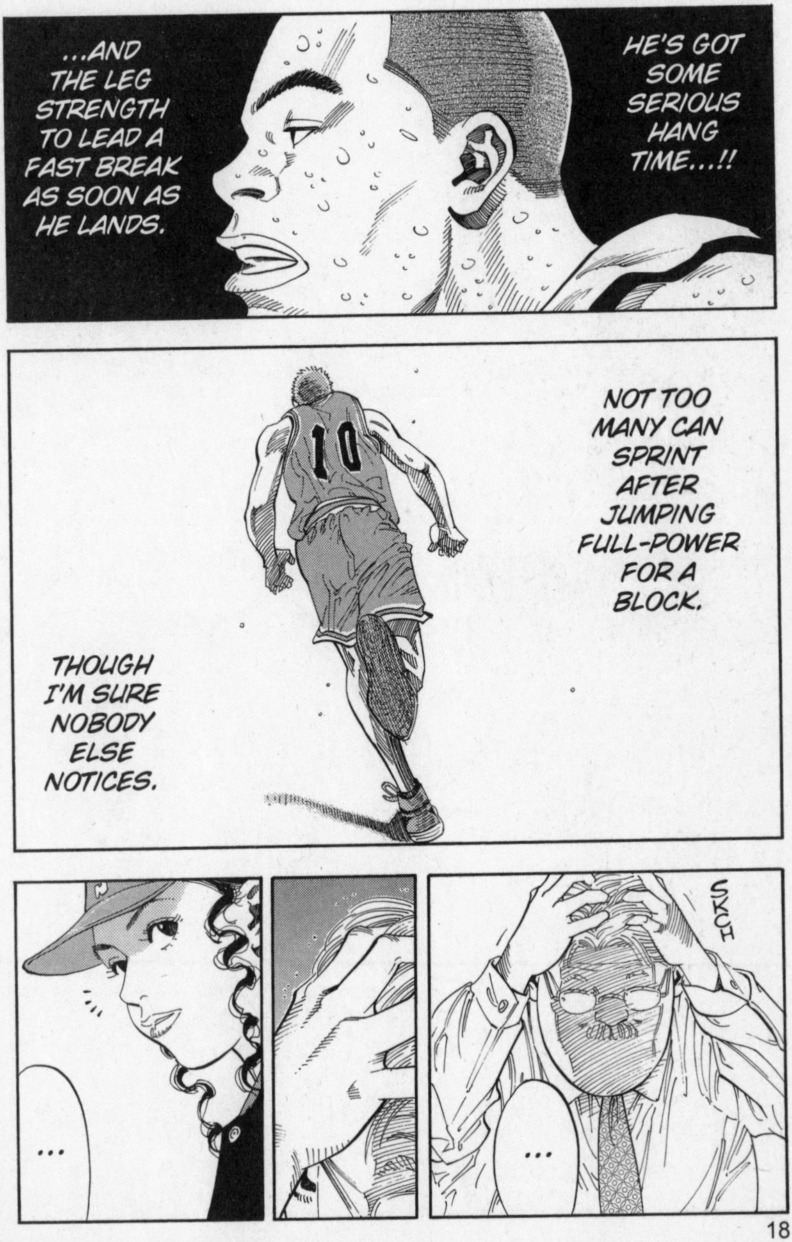
HE'S GOT SOME SERIOUS HANG TIME...!!
...AND THE LEG STRENGTH TO LEAD A FAST BREAK AS SOON AS HE LANDS.
NOT TOO MANY CAN SPRINT AFTER JUMPING FULL-POWER FOR A BLOCK.
THOUGH I'M SURE NOBODY ELSE NOTICES.
SKCH
...
...

READ THIS WAY

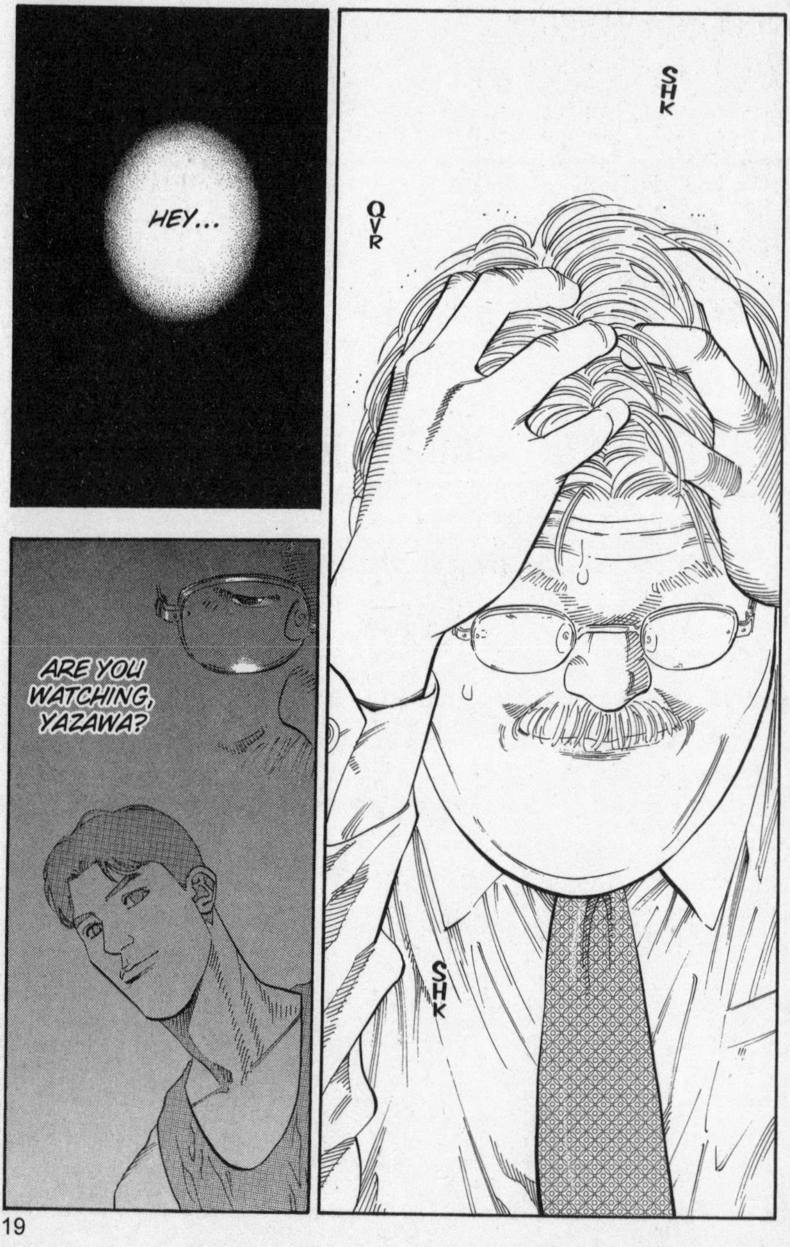
SHK
QVR
SHK
HEY...
ARE YOU WATCHING, YAZAWA?

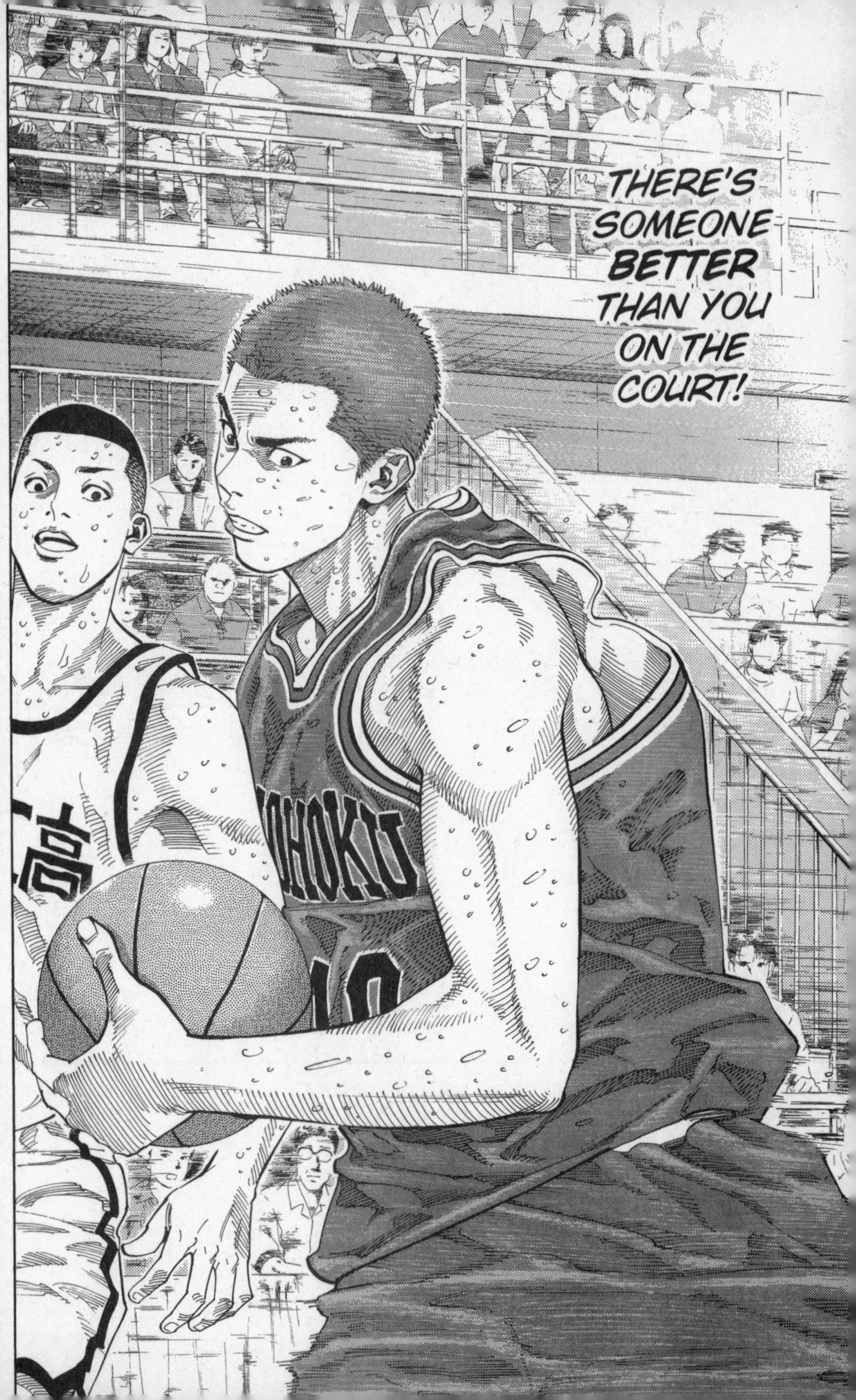
THERE'S SOMEONE BETTER THAN YOU ON THE COURT!
SHOHOKU

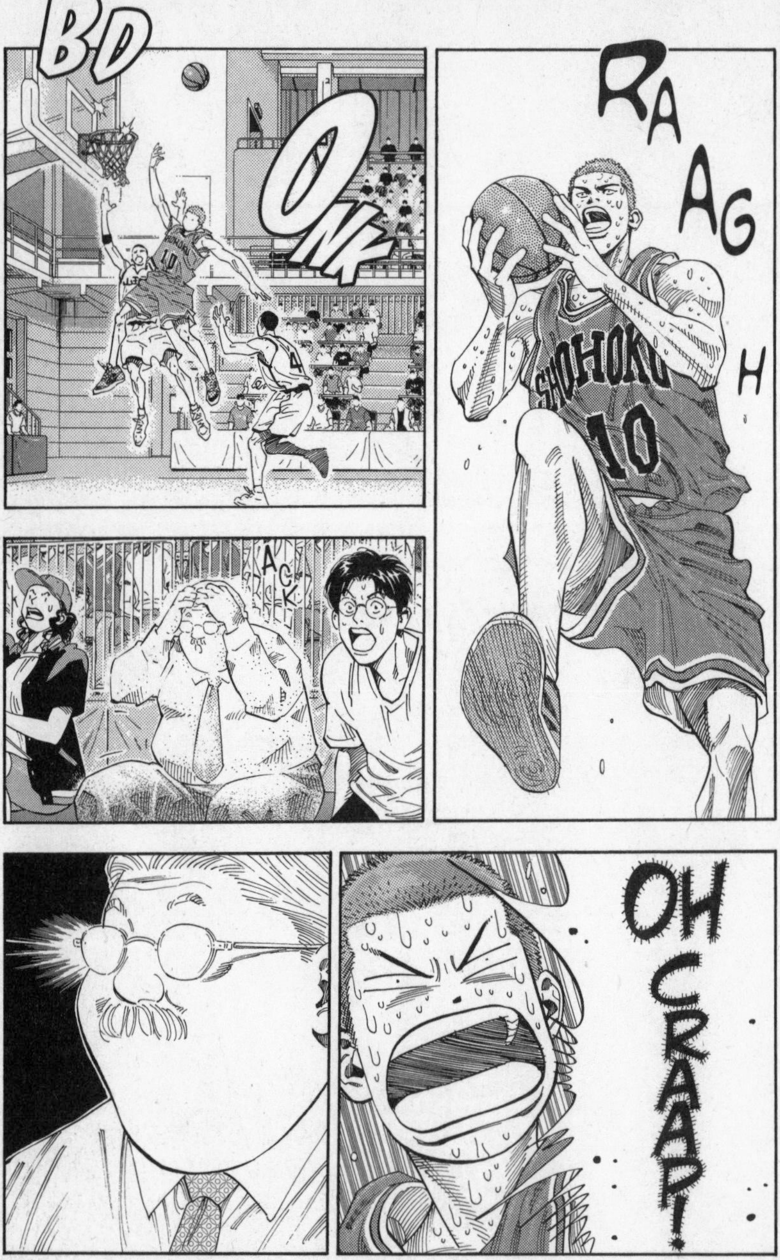
RAAGH
BDONK
ACK
OH CRAP!

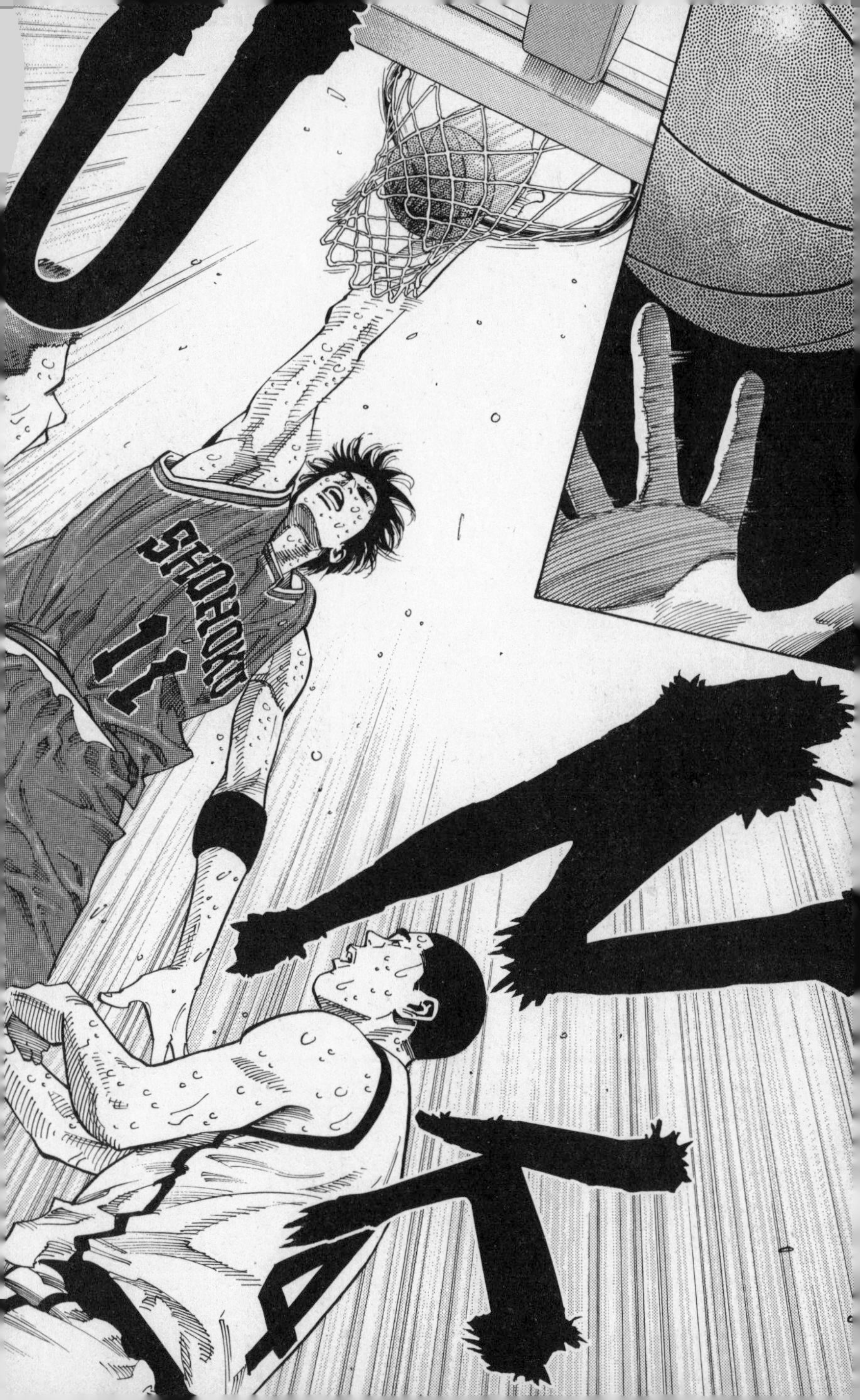
SHOHOKU
11

READ THIS WAY

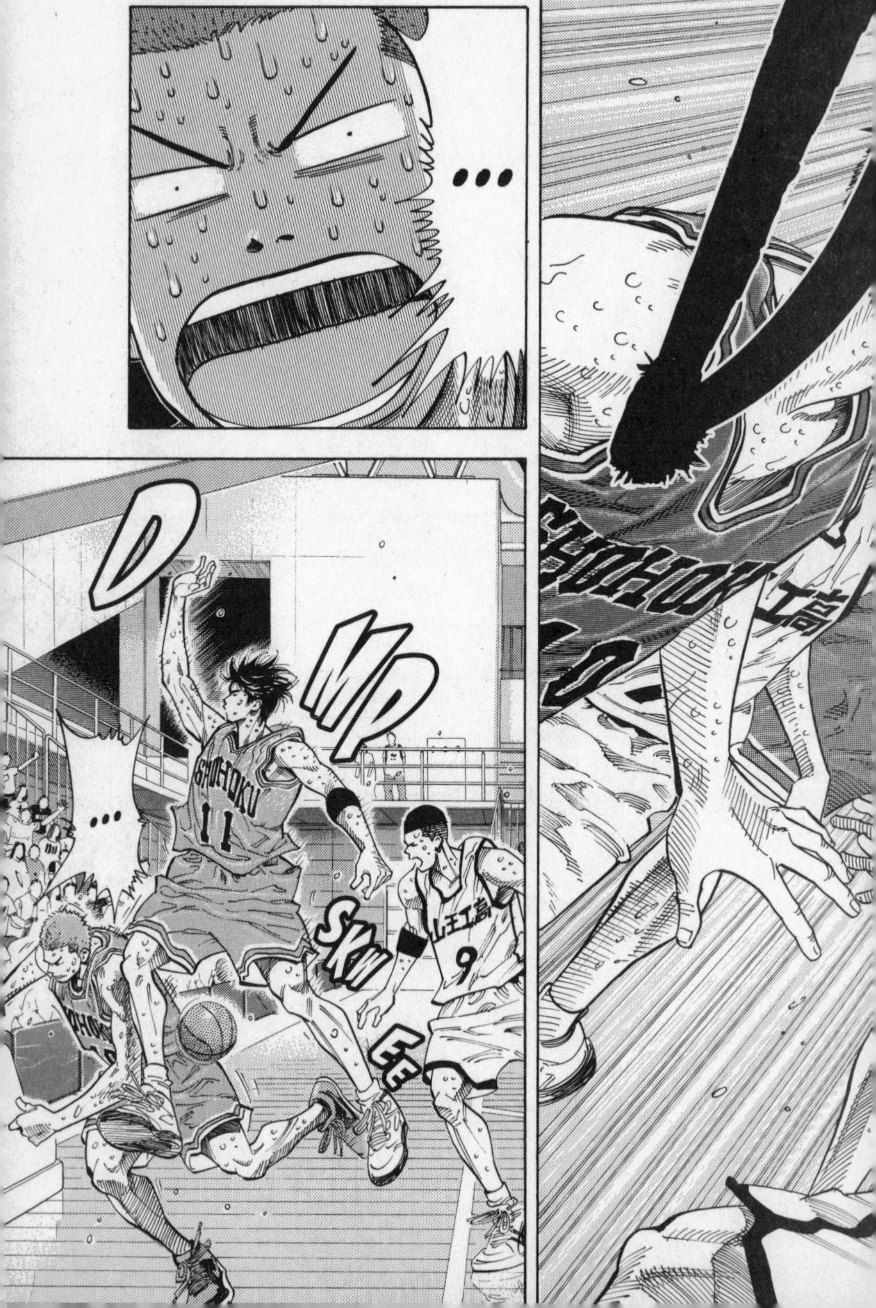
...
D
MP
...
SKW
EE

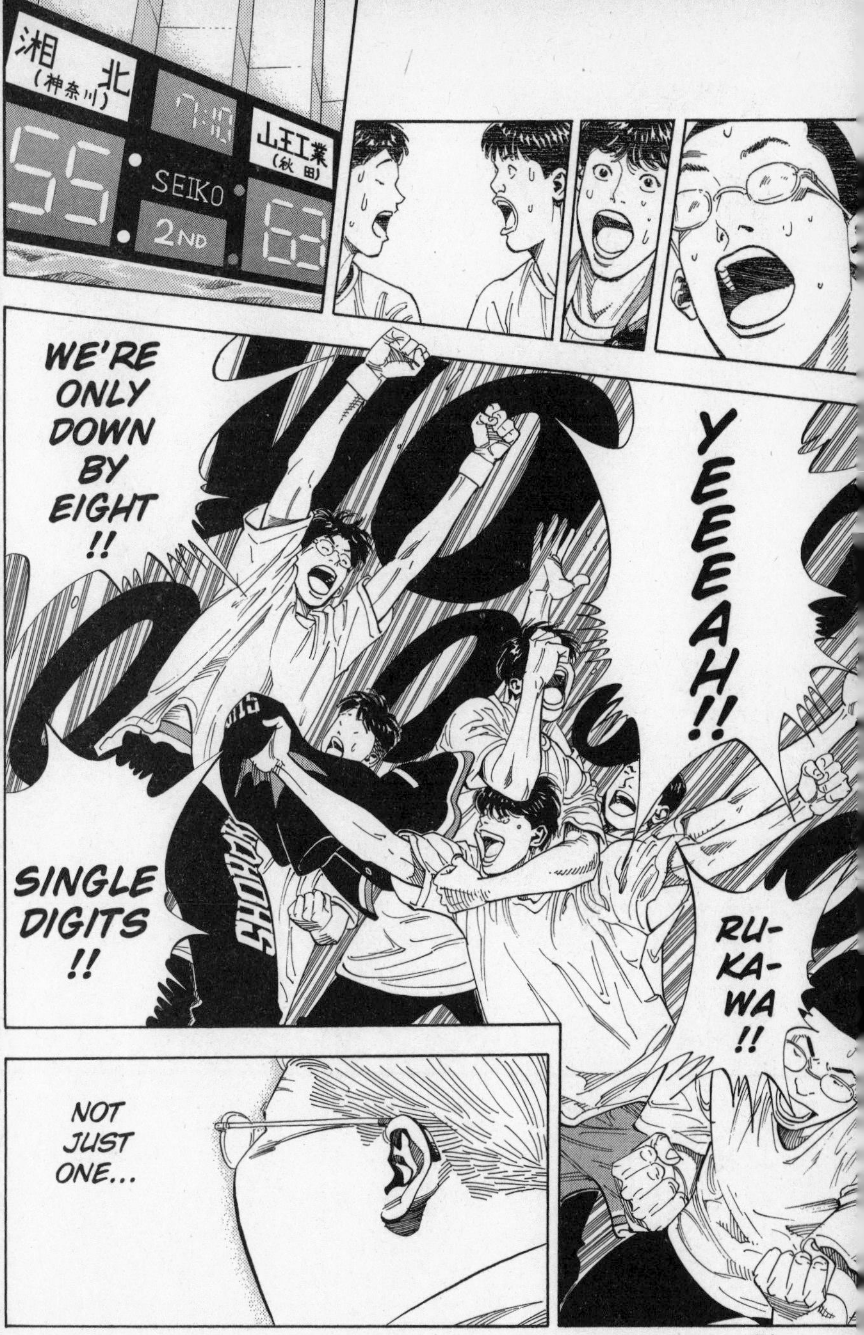
湘北
(神奈川)
55
SEIKO
2ND
山王工業
(秋田)
63
YEEEEAH!!
WE'RE ONLY DOWN BY EIGHT!!
SINGLE DIGITS!!
RU-KA-WA!!
NOT JUST ONE...

READ THIS WAY

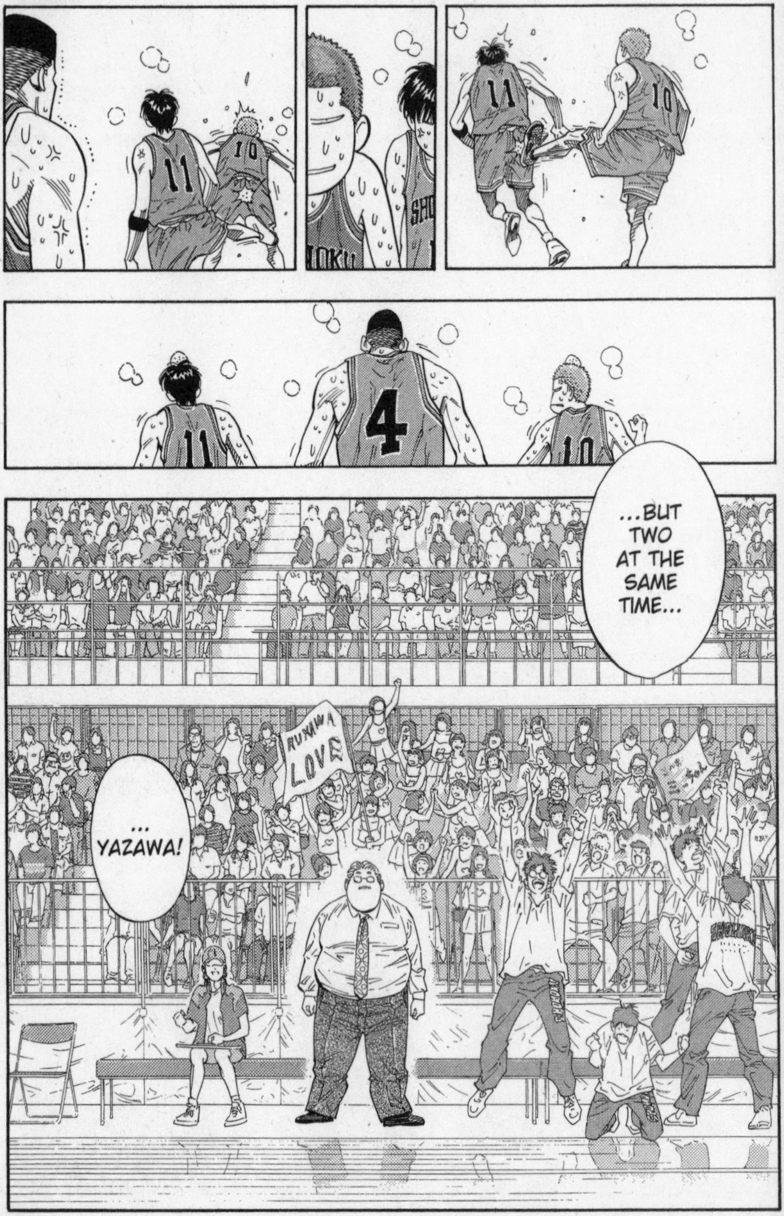
...BUT TWO AT THE SAME TIME...
... YAZAWA!
RUKAWA LOVE

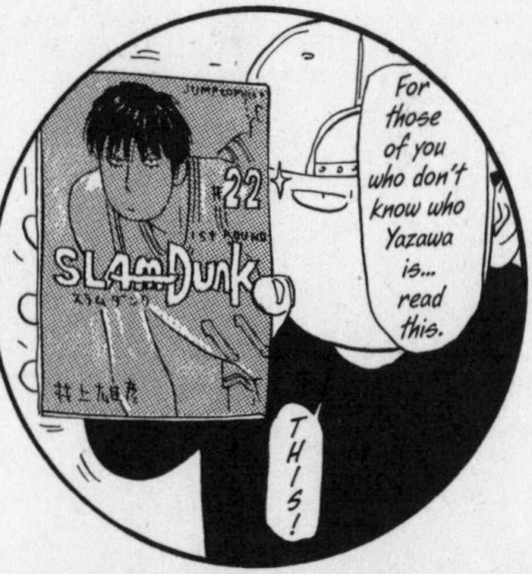
For those of you who don't know who Yazawa is... read this.
THIS!

SLAM DUNK

ACE SAWAKITA STRIKES BACK

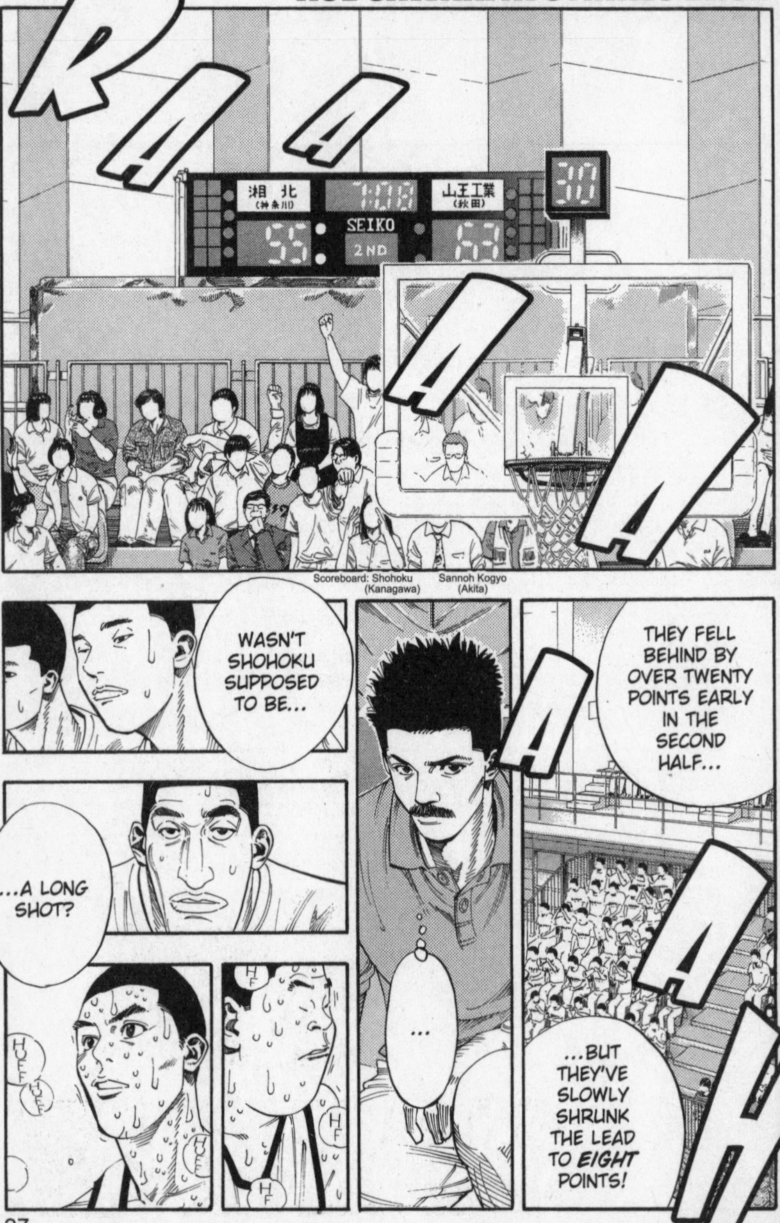
RAAAAAAAH
湘北 (神奈川)
7:08
山王工業 (秋田)
SEIKO
55
2ND
63
30
Scoreboard: Shohoku (Kanagawa) Sannoh Kogyo (Akita)
THEY FELL BEHIND BY OVER TWENTY POINTS EARLY IN THE SECOND HALF...
...BUT THEY'VE SLOWLY SHRUNK THE LEAD TO *EIGHT* POINTS!
...
WASN'T SHOHOKU SUPPOSED TO BE...
...A LONG SHOT?
HF
HF
HF
HUFF
HUFF
HUFF
HUFF

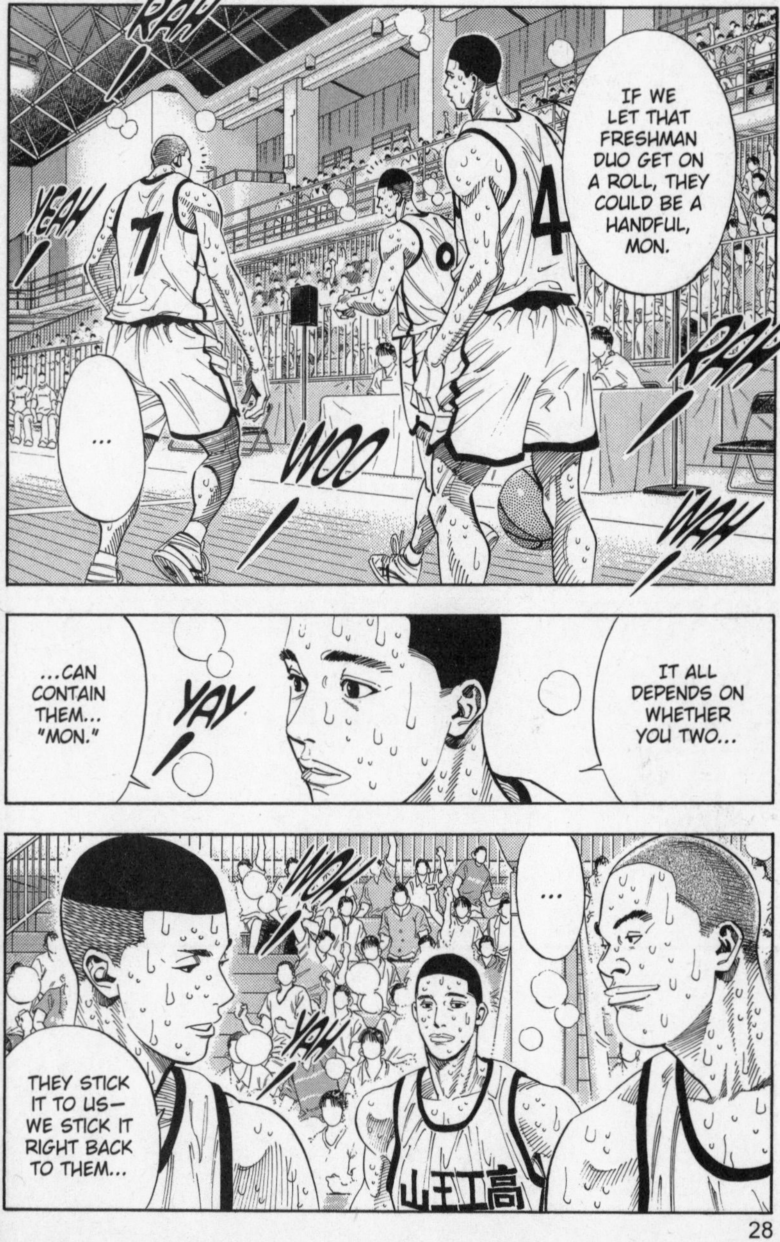
RAH!
IF WE LET THAT FRESHMAN DUO GET ON A ROLL, THEY COULD BE A HANDFUL, MON.
YEAH!
RAH!
WAH!
WOO!
...
IT ALL DEPENDS ON WHETHER YOU TWO...
YAY!
...CAN CONTAIN THEM... "MON."
...
WOH!
YAH!
山王工高
THEY STICK IT TO US— WE STICK IT RIGHT BACK TO THEM...

READ THIS WAY

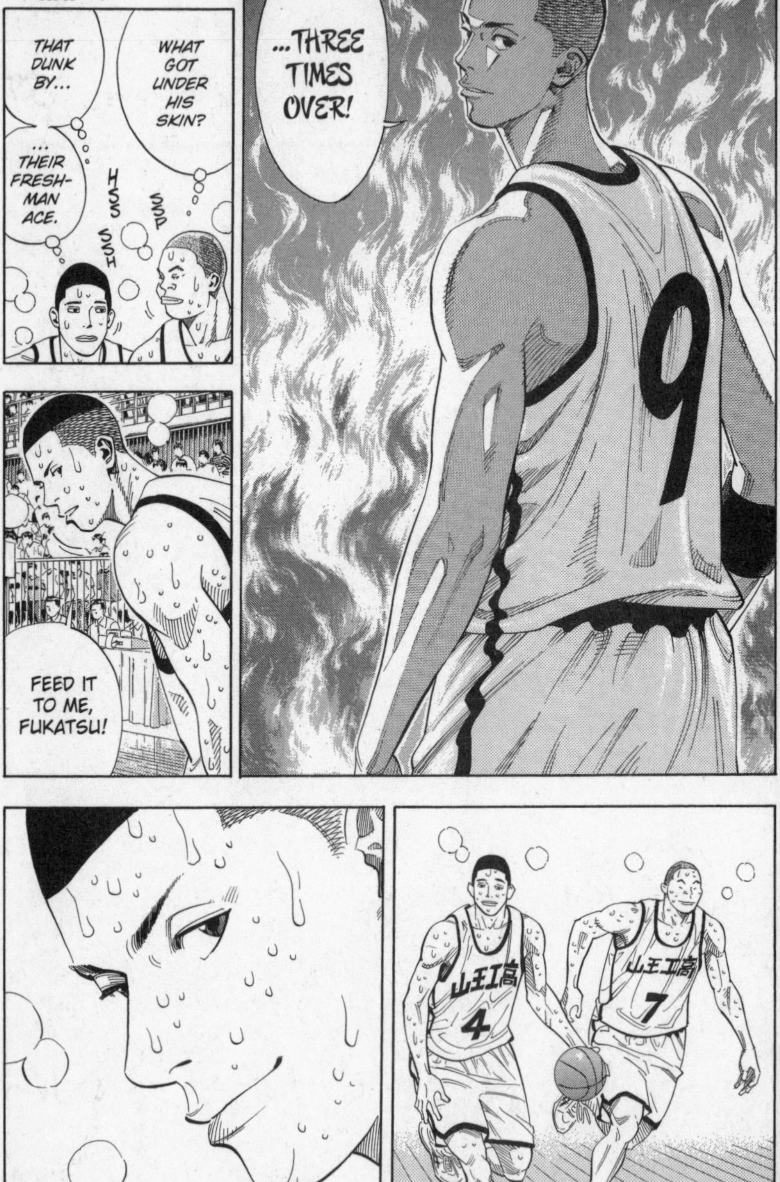
...THREE TIMES OVER!
WHAT GOT UNDER HIS SKIN?
THAT DUNK BY...
...THEIR FRESHMAN ACE.
SSP
HSS
SSH
FEED IT TO ME, FUKATSU!
山王工高
4
山王工高
7

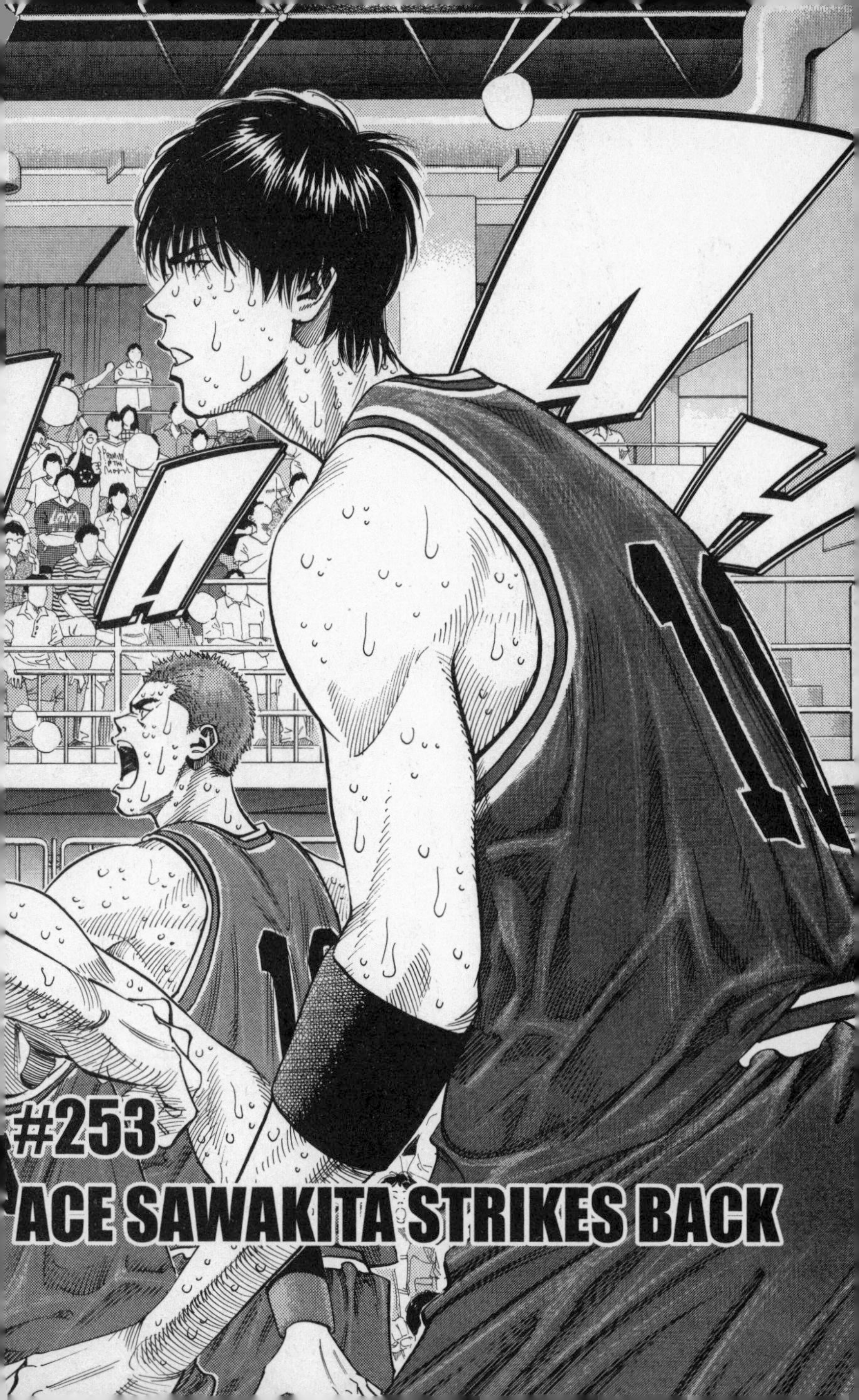
#253
ACE SAWAKITA STRIKES BACK

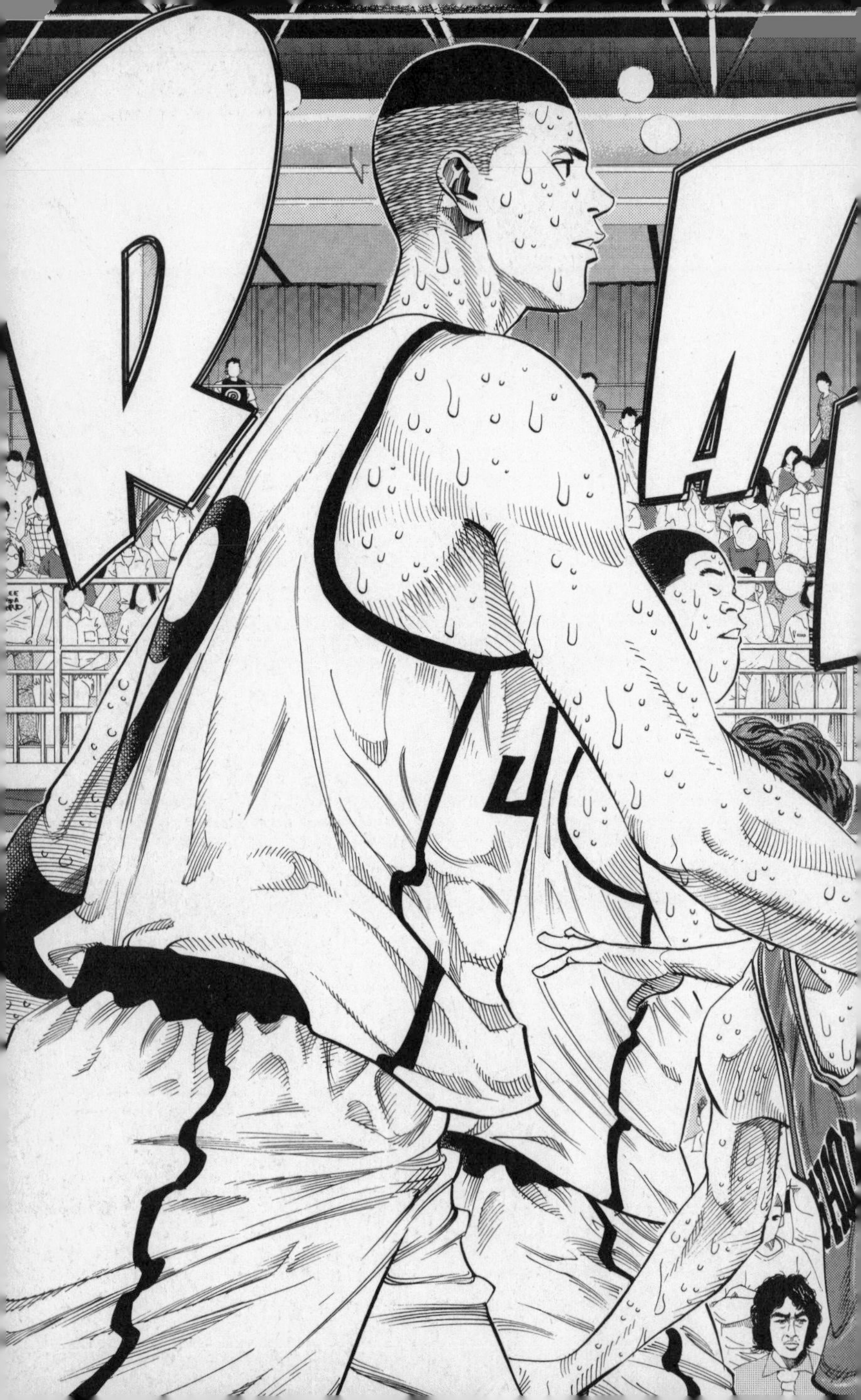

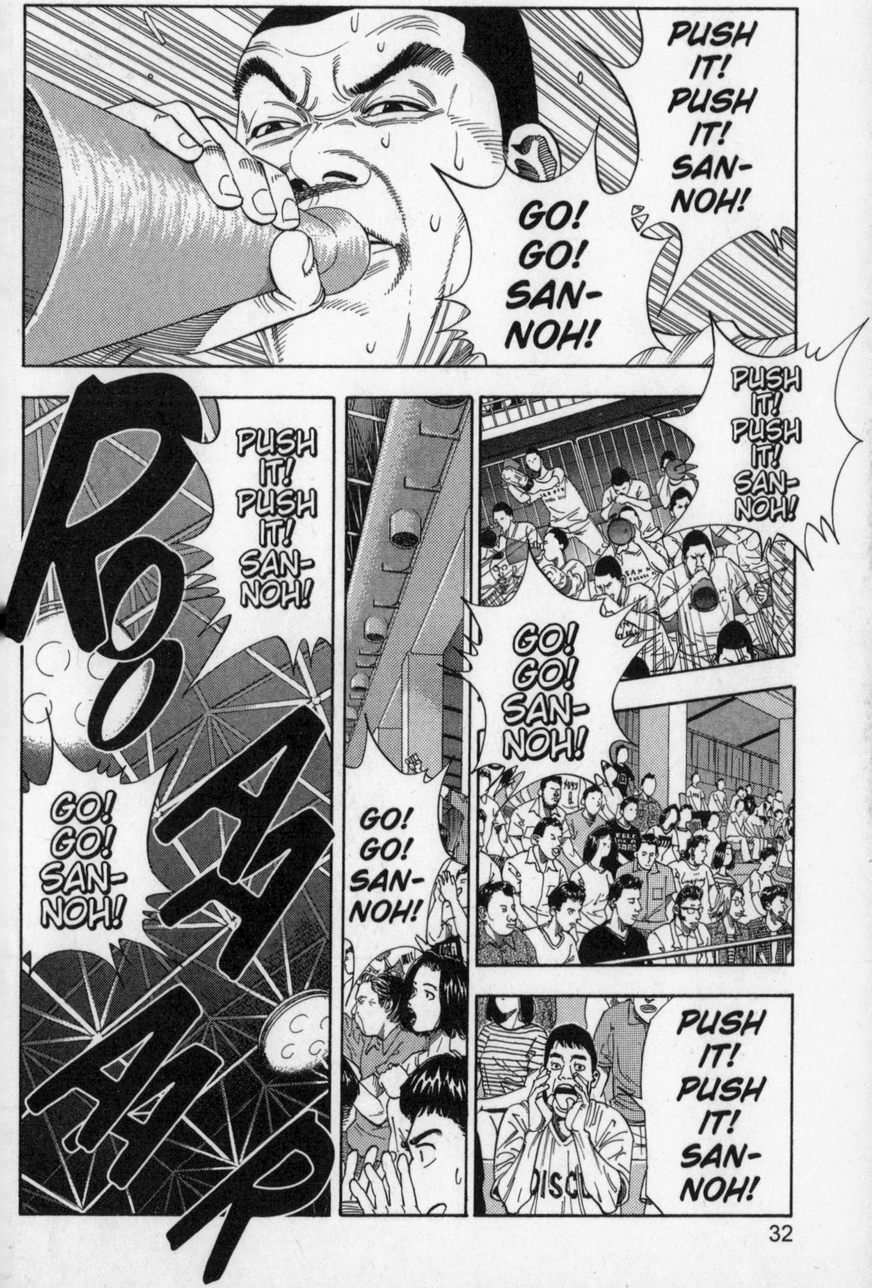
PUSH IT! PUSH IT! SAN-NOH!
GO! GO! SAN-NOH!
PUSH IT! PUSH IT! SAN-NOH!
GO! GO! SAN-NOH!
PUSH IT! PUSH IT! SAN-NOH!
GO! GO! SAN-NOH!
ROAAAR
PUSH IT! PUSH IT! SAN-NOH!
GO! GO! SAN-NOH!

READ THIS WAY

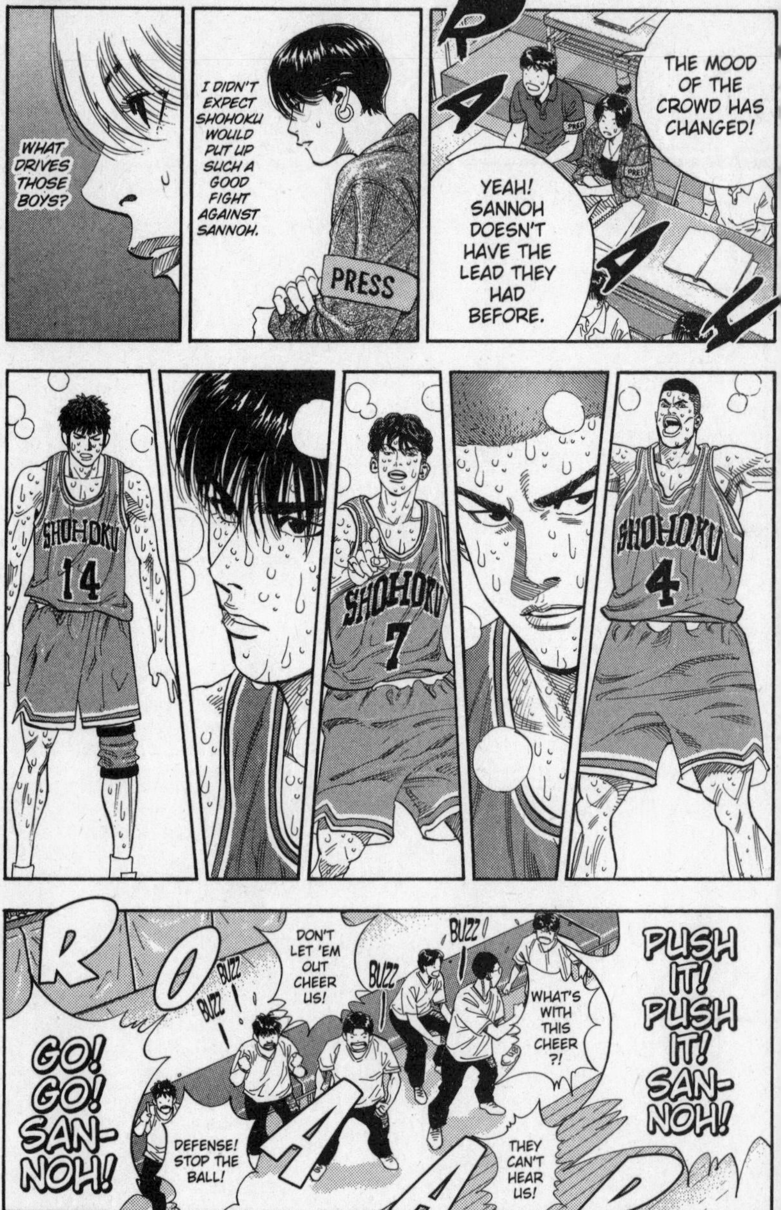
THE MOOD OF THE CROWD HAS CHANGED!
YEAH! SANNOH DOESN'T HAVE THE LEAD THEY HAD BEFORE.
PRESS
PRESS
I DIDN'T EXPECT SHOHOKU WOULD PUT UP SUCH A GOOD FIGHT AGAINST SANNOH.
WHAT DRIVES THOSE BOYS?
SHOHOKU 4
SHOHOKU 7
SHOHOKU 14
PUSH IT! PUSH IT! SAN-NOH!
ROAAR
BUZZ
WHAT'S WITH THIS CHEER?!
BUZZ
DON'T LET 'EM OUT CHEER US!
BUZZ BUZZ
THEY CAN'T HEAR US!
DEFENSE! STOP THE BALL!
GO! GO! SAN-NOH!

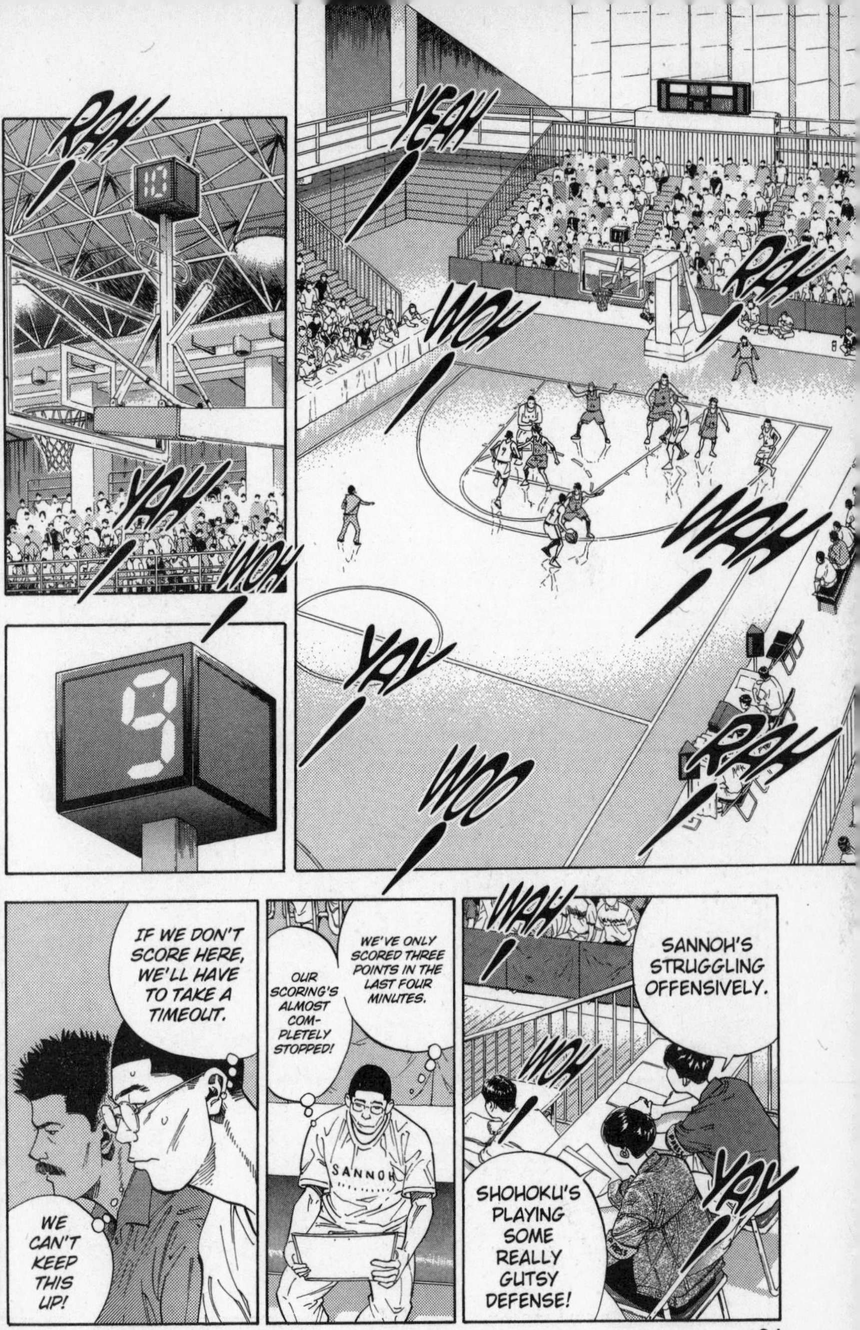
YEAH
RAH
WOH
WAH
YAY
RAH
WOO
RAH
YAH
WOH
WAH
SANNOH'S STRUGGLING OFFENSIVELY.
WOH
YAY
SHOHOKU'S PLAYING SOME REALLY GUTSY DEFENSE!
WE'VE ONLY SCORED THREE POINTS IN THE LAST FOUR MINUTES.
OUR SCORING'S ALMOST COM-PLETELY STOPPED!
IF WE DON'T SCORE HERE, WE'LL HAVE TO TAKE A TIMEOUT.
WE CAN'T KEEP THIS UP!

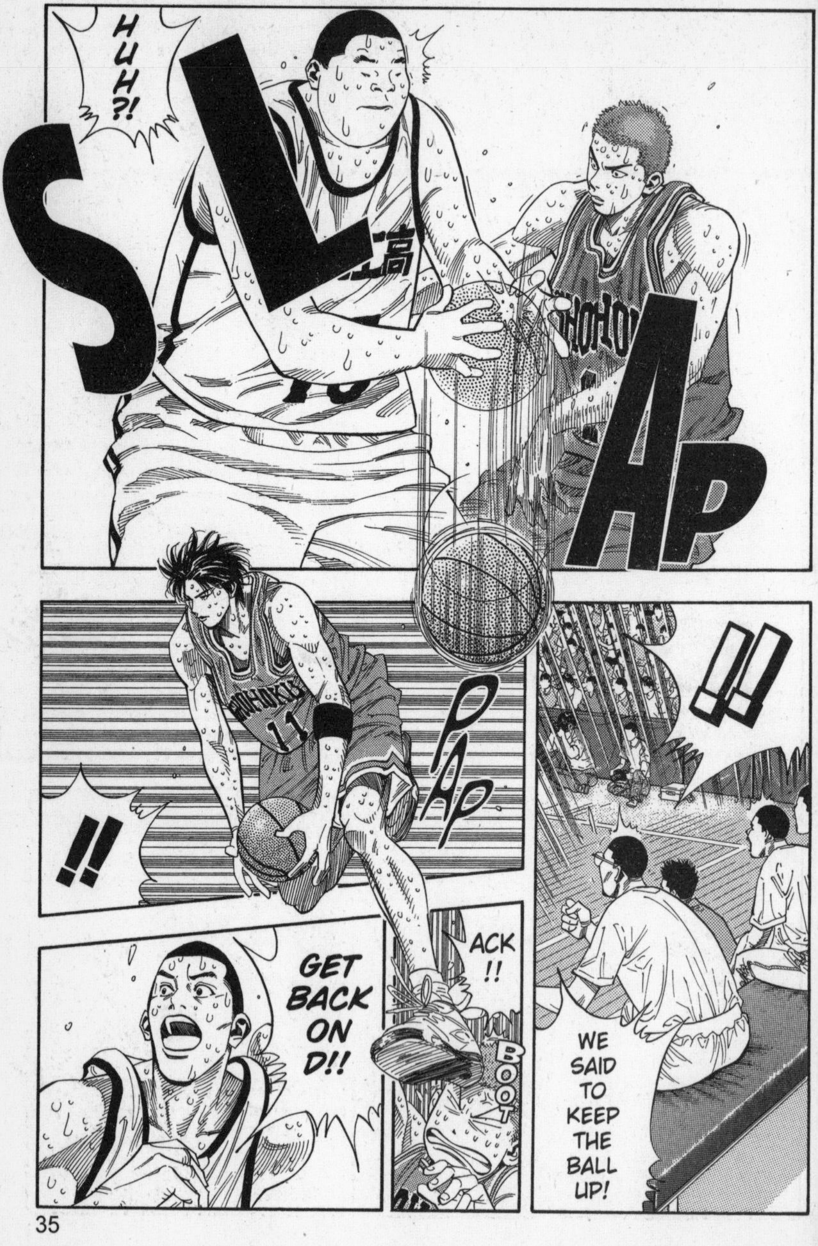
SLAP
HUH?!
!!
WE SAID TO KEEP THE BALL UP!
PAP
!!
ACK!!
BOOT
GET BACK ON D!!

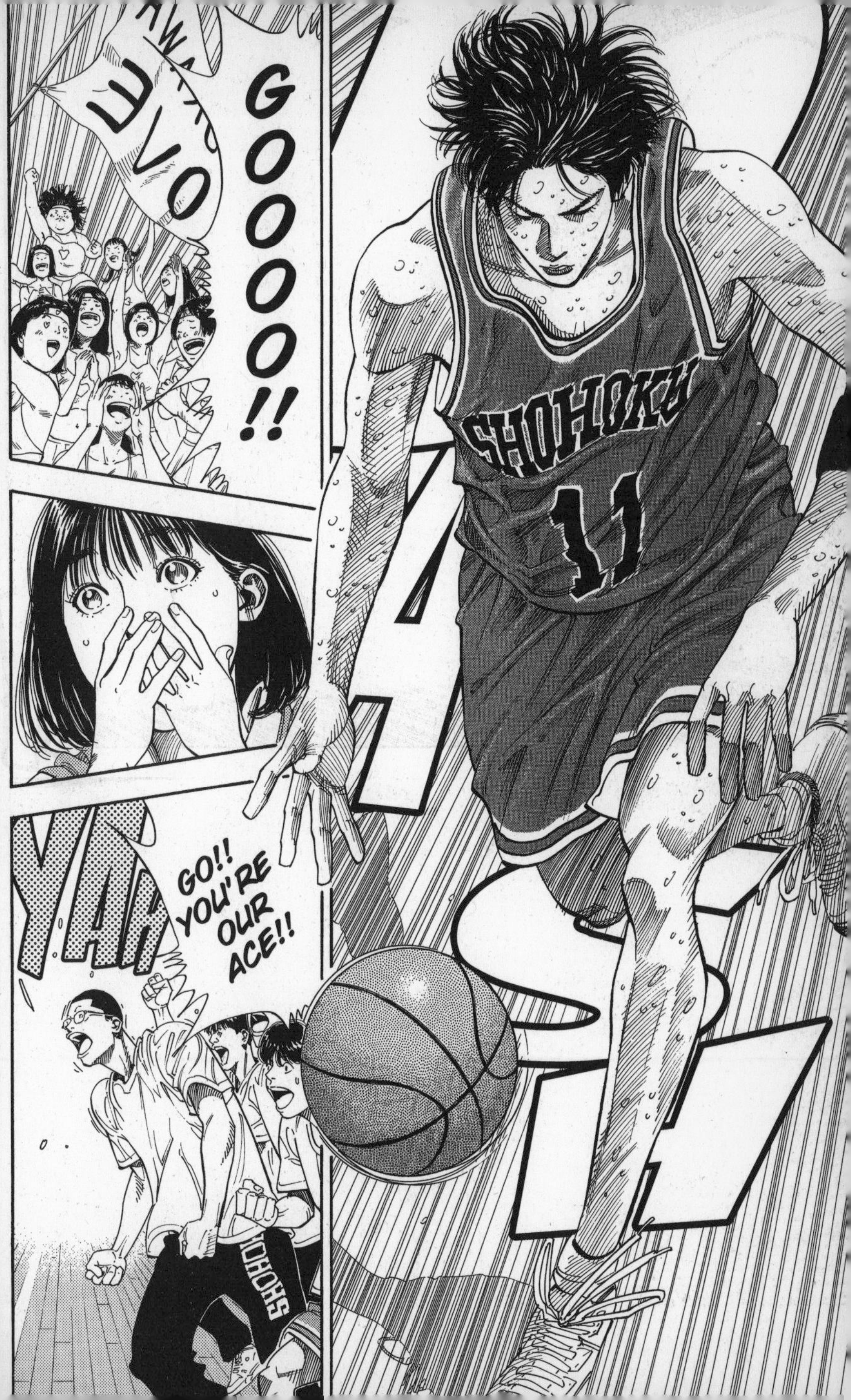
GOOOO!!
YAA
GO!! YOU'RE OUR ACE!!

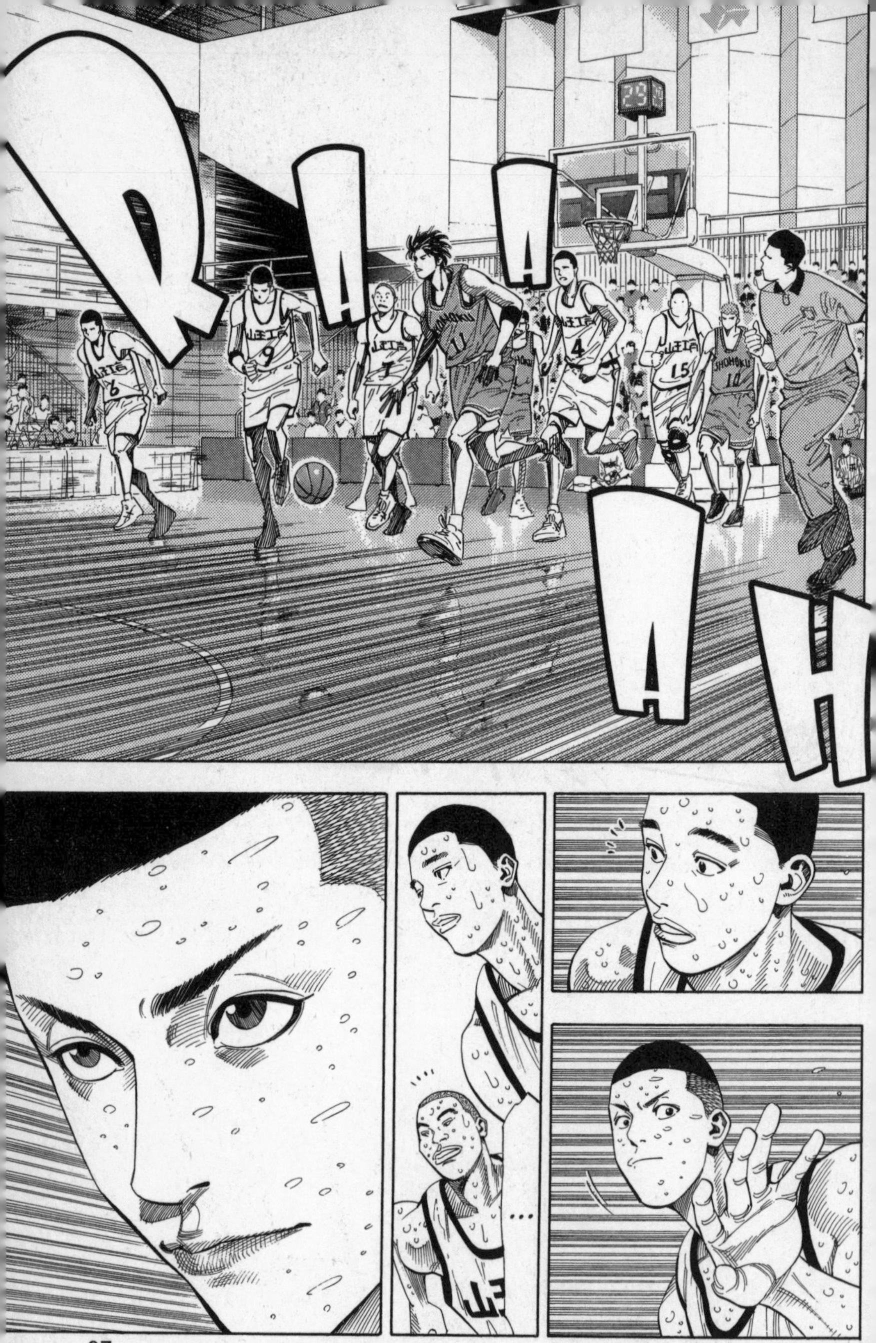
RAAAH
...

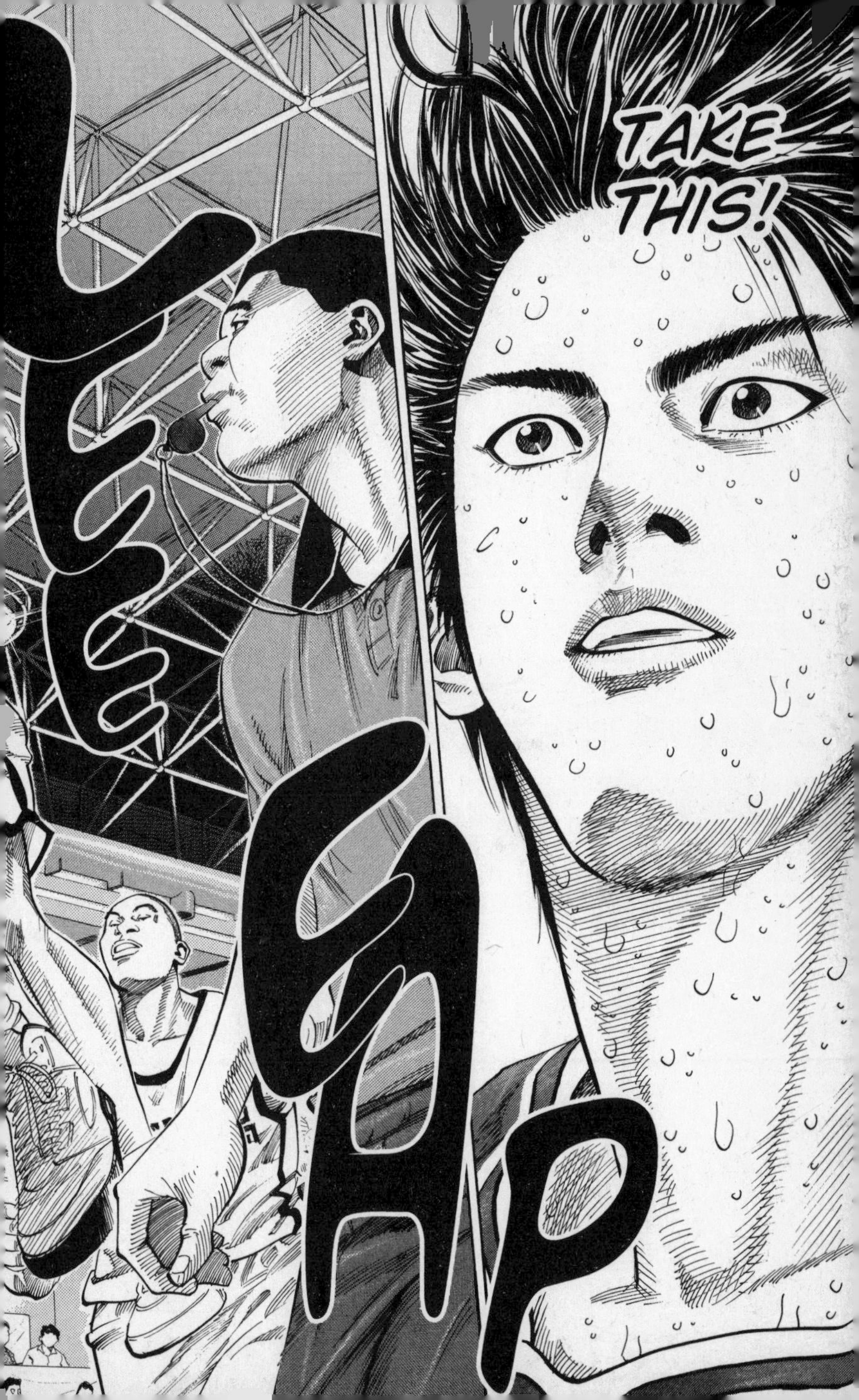
TAKE THIS!

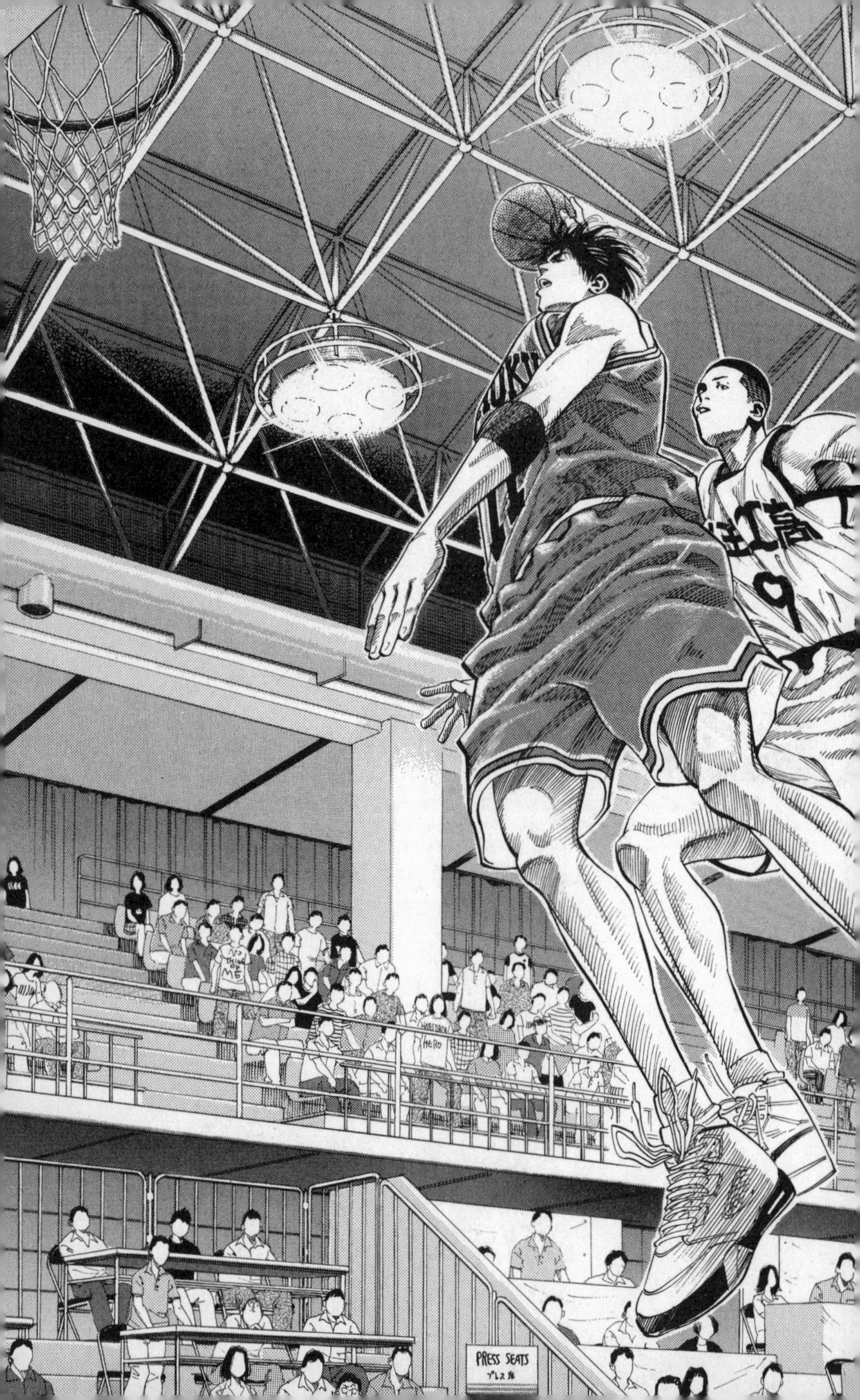
PRESS SEATS
プレス席

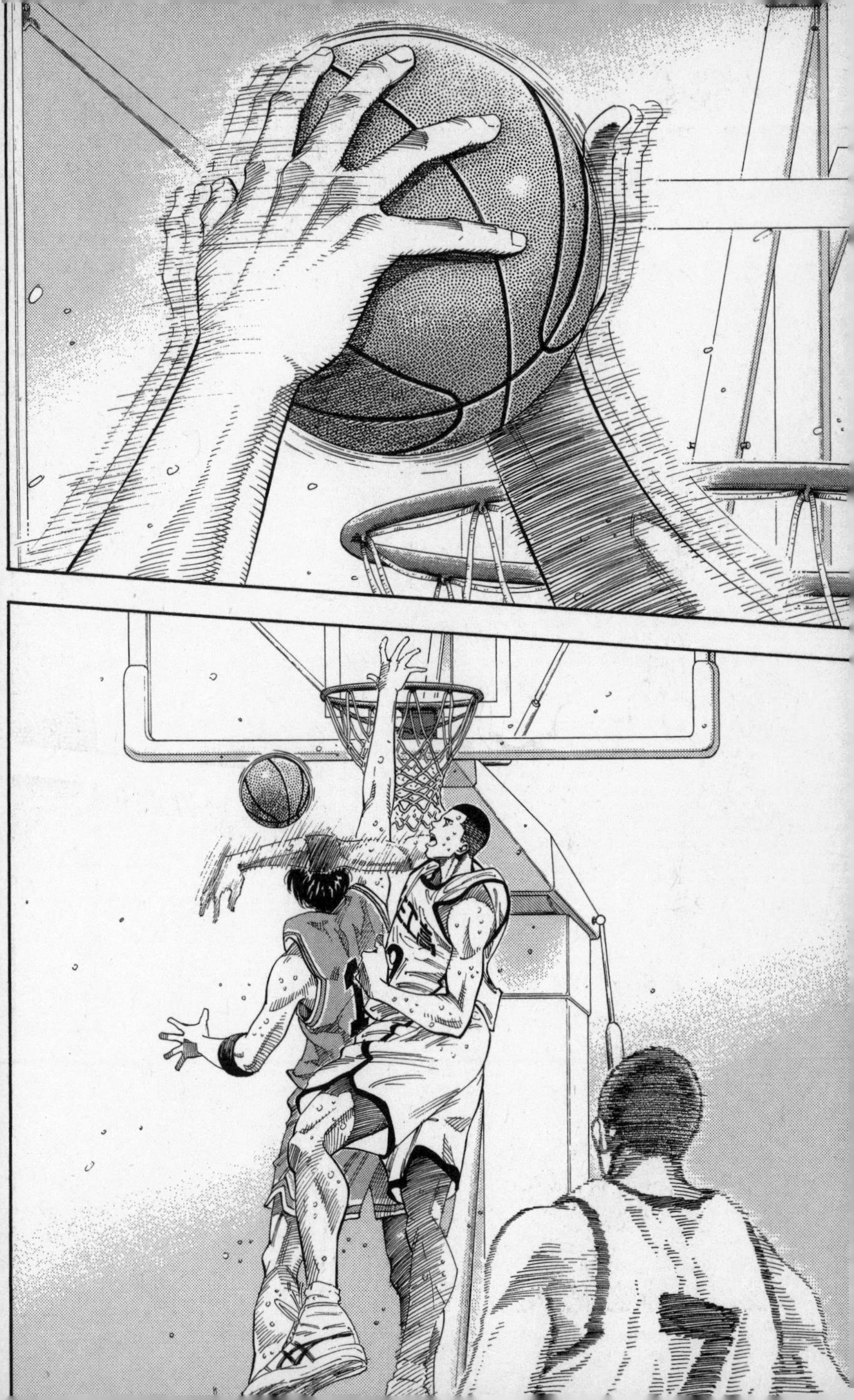

READ THIS WAY

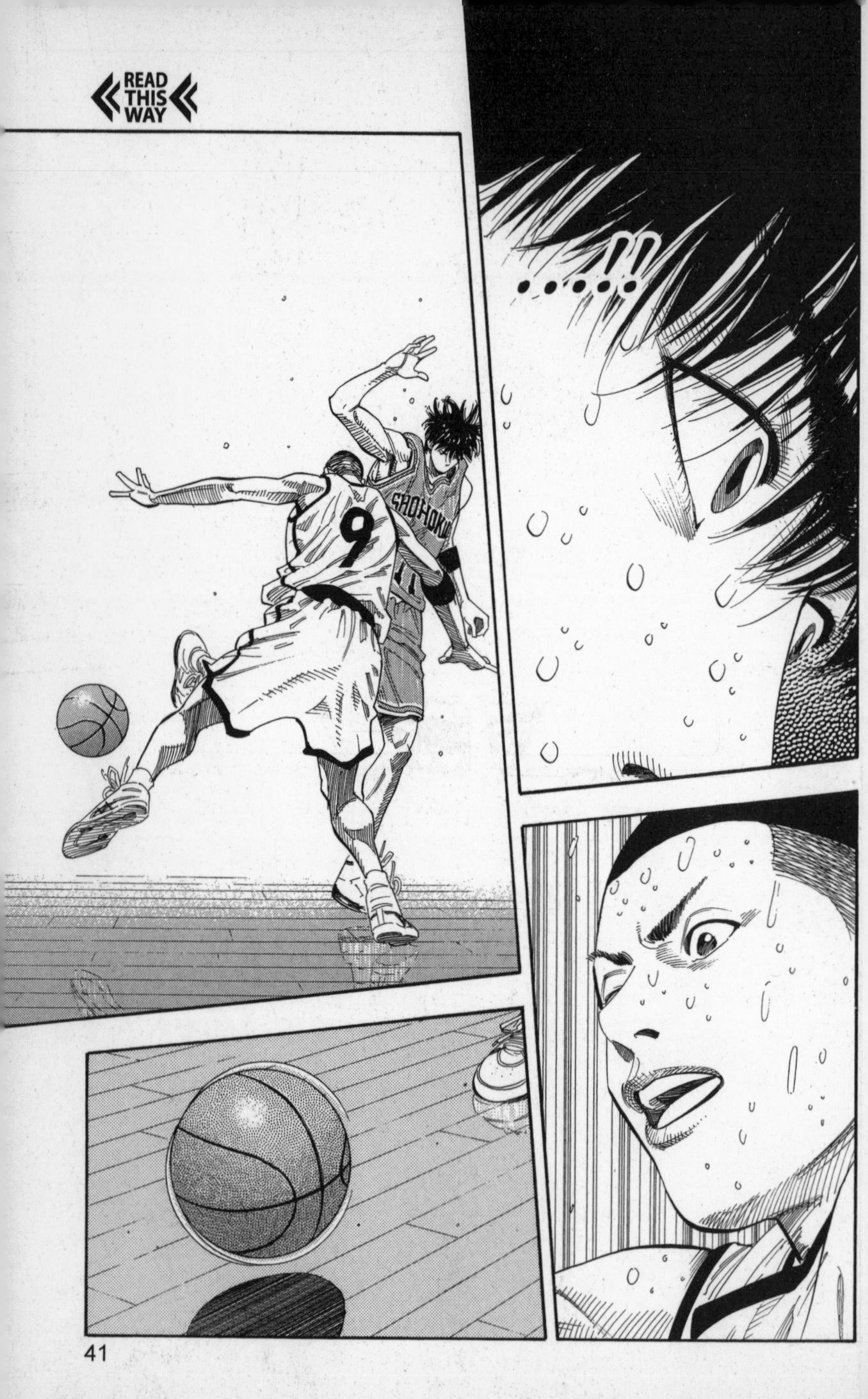

....!!
SHOHOKU
9

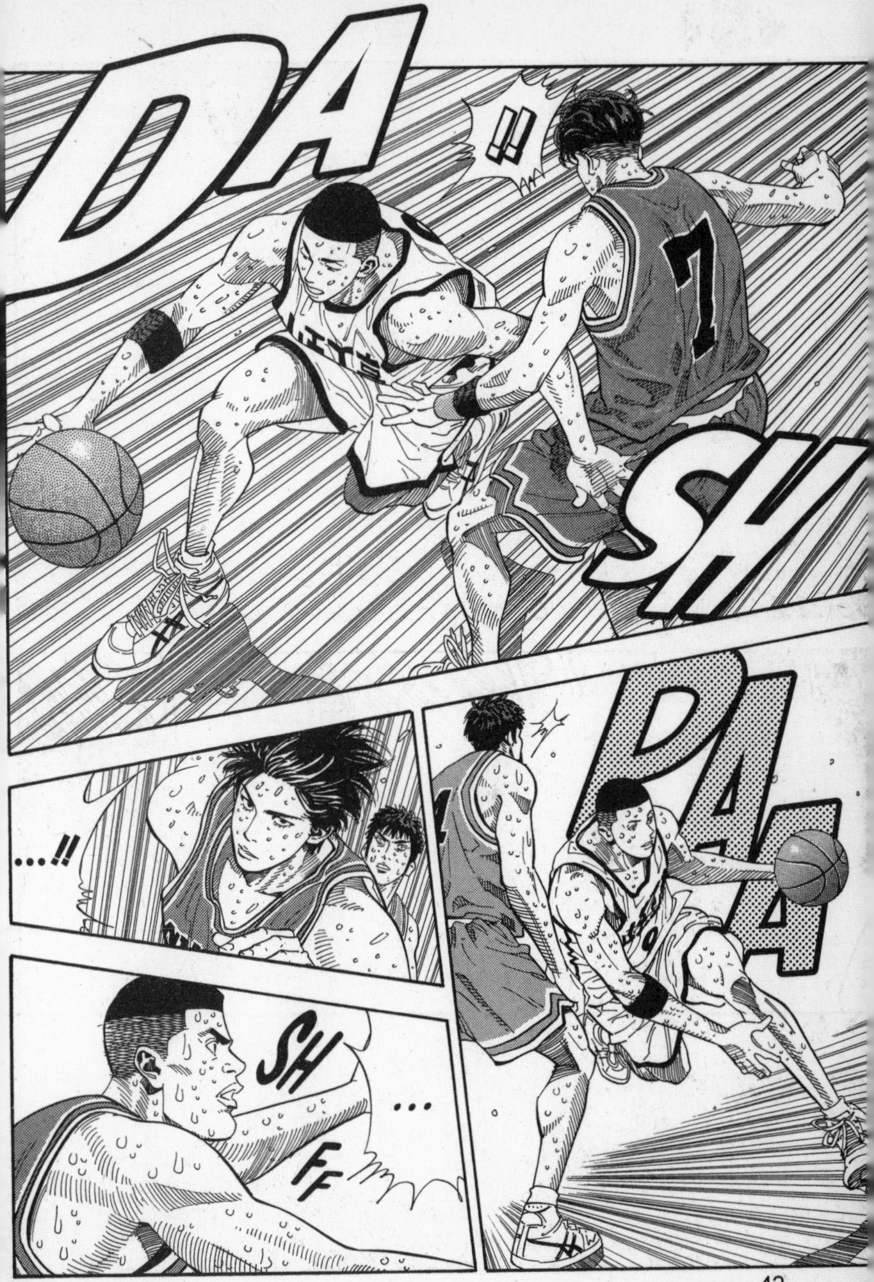
DA
!!
SH
DAA
...!!
SH
...
FF

READ THIS WAY

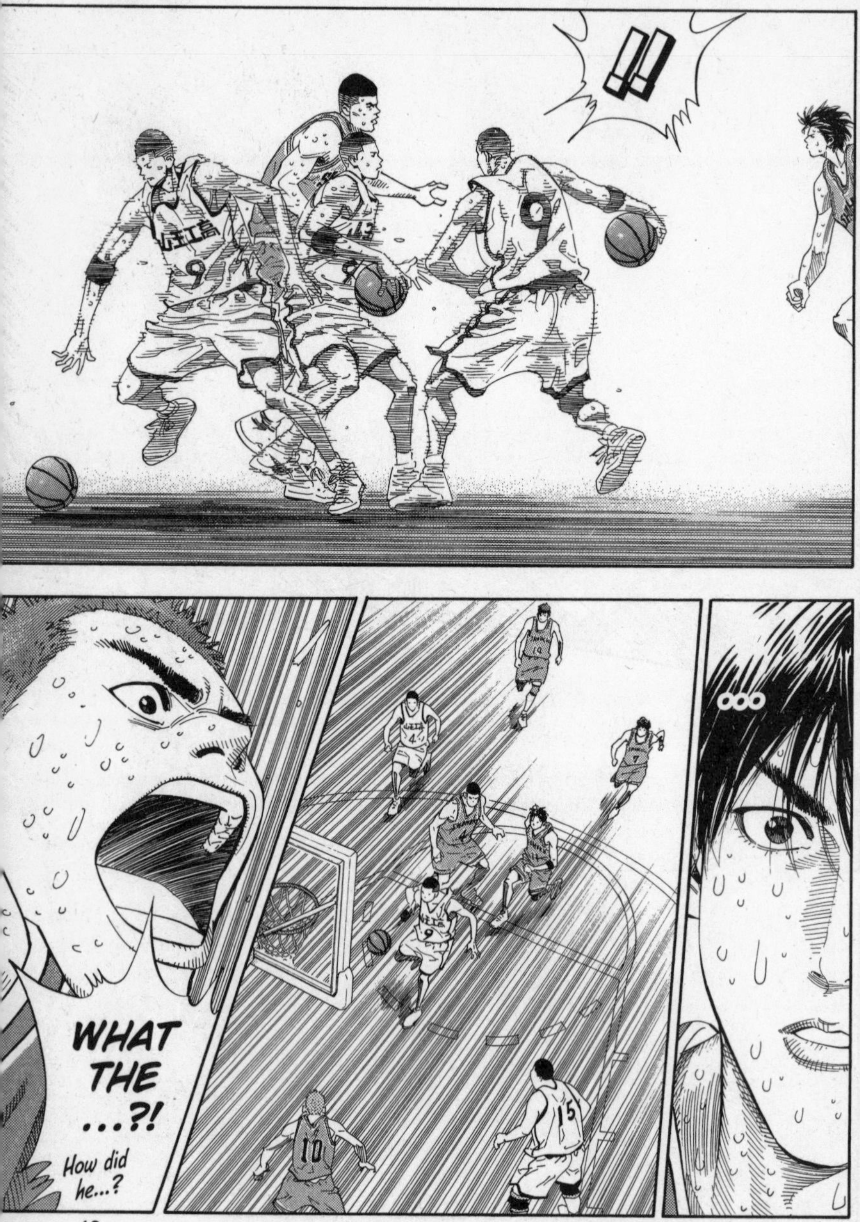
!!
...
WHAT THE ...?!
How did he...?

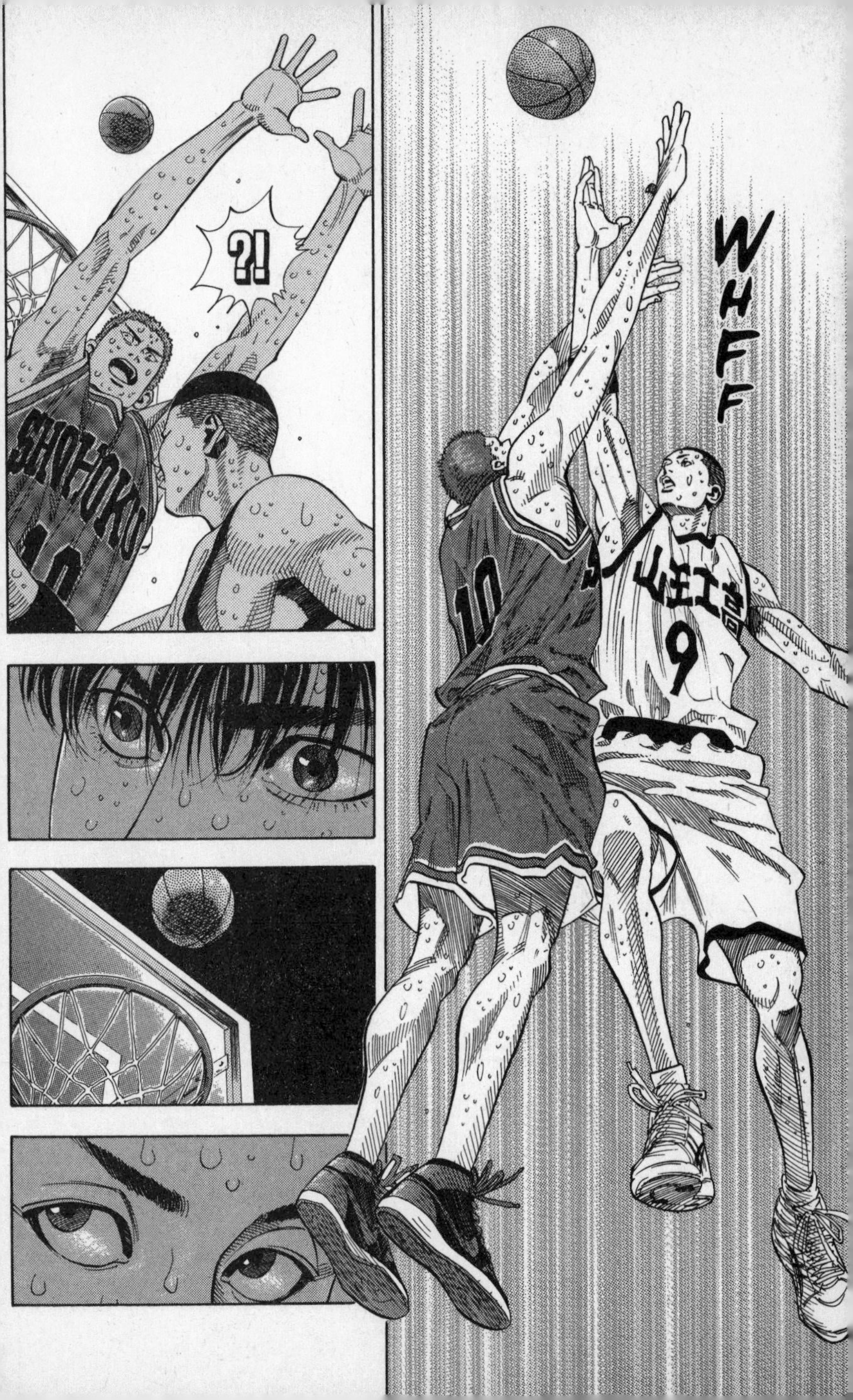
WHFF
?!

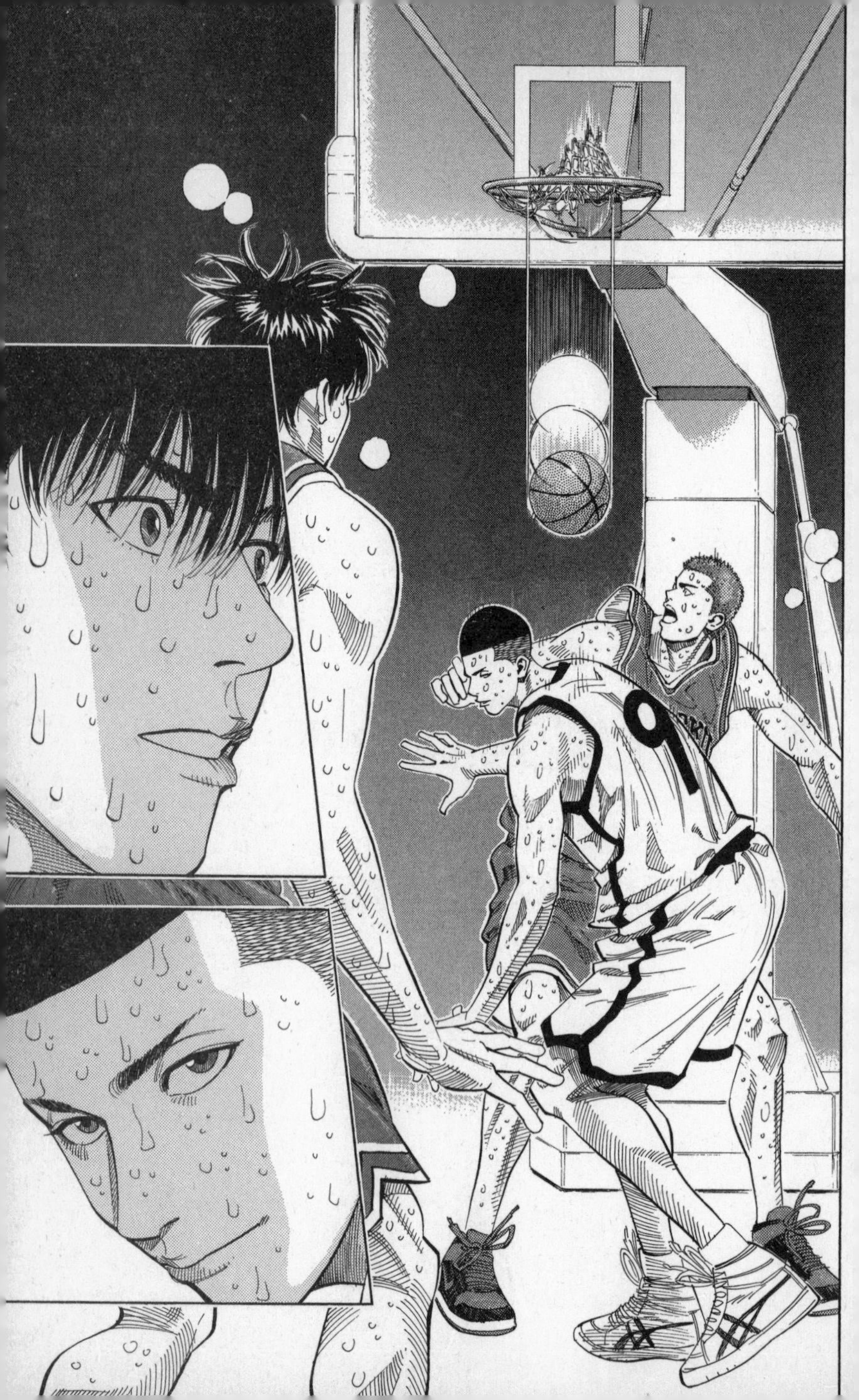

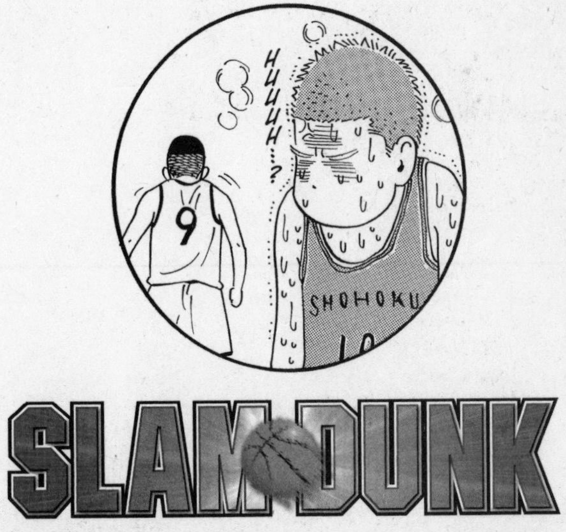
HUUUH...?
9
SHOHOKU

SLAM DUNK

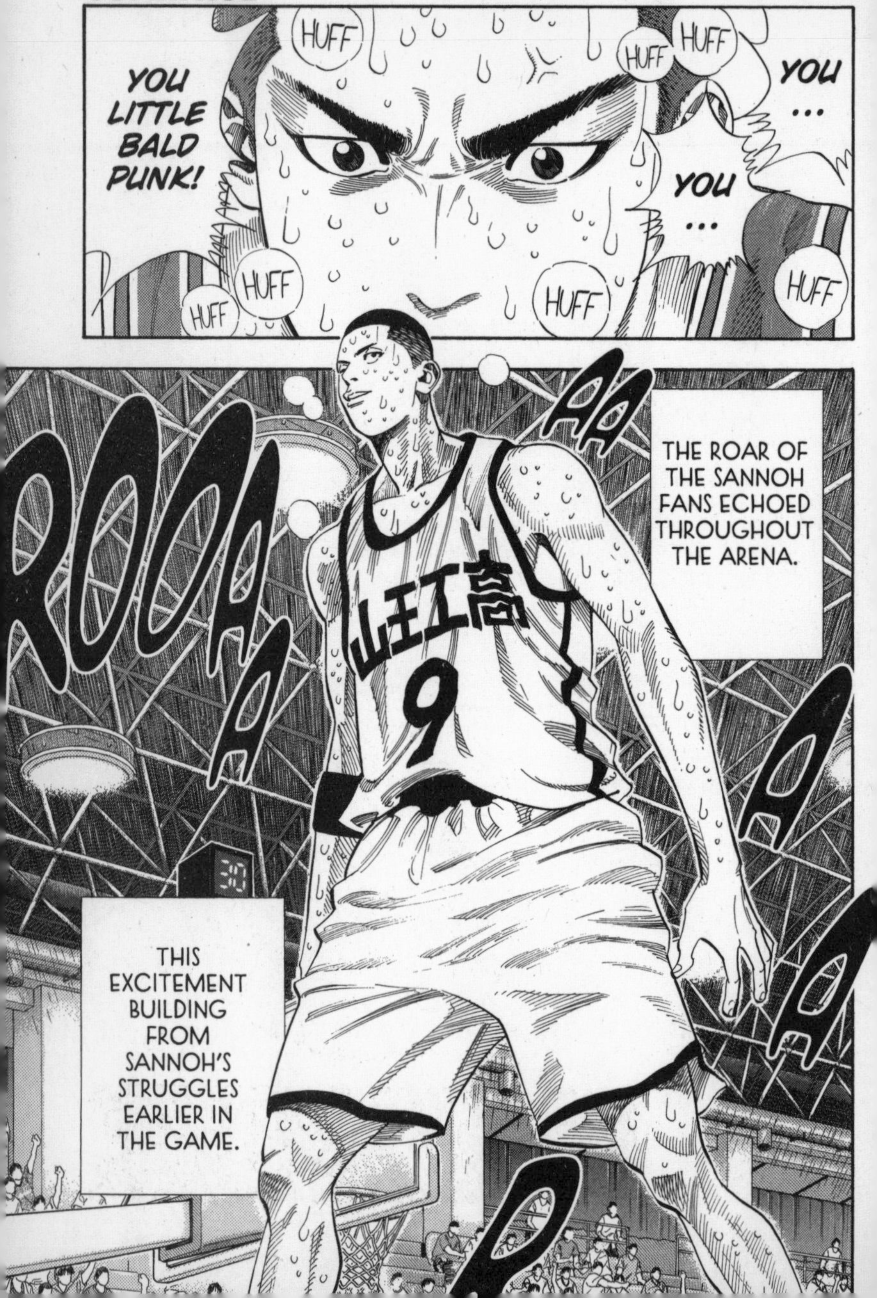
HUFF
HUFF
YOU ...
YOU ...
HUFF
HUFF
HUFF
HUFF
YOU LITTLE BALD PUNK!
THE ROAR OF THE SANNOH FANS ECHOED THROUGHOUT THE ARENA.
AAAAAAA
ROOOAAA
山王工高
9
THIS EXCITEMENT BUILDING FROM SANNOH'S STRUGGLES EARLIER IN THE GAME.

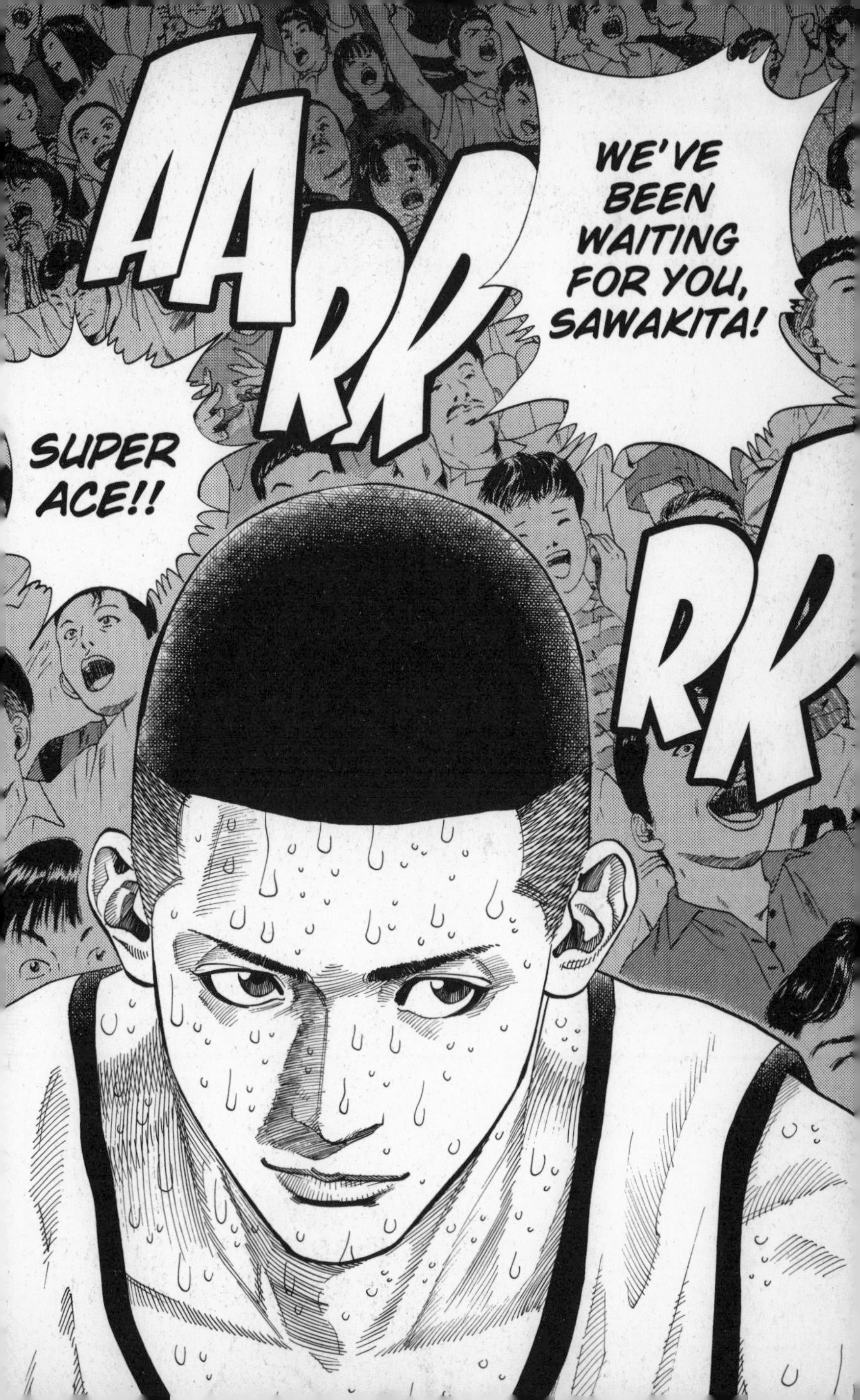
WE'VE BEEN WAITING FOR YOU, SAWAKITA!
AARK
RK
SUPER ACE!!

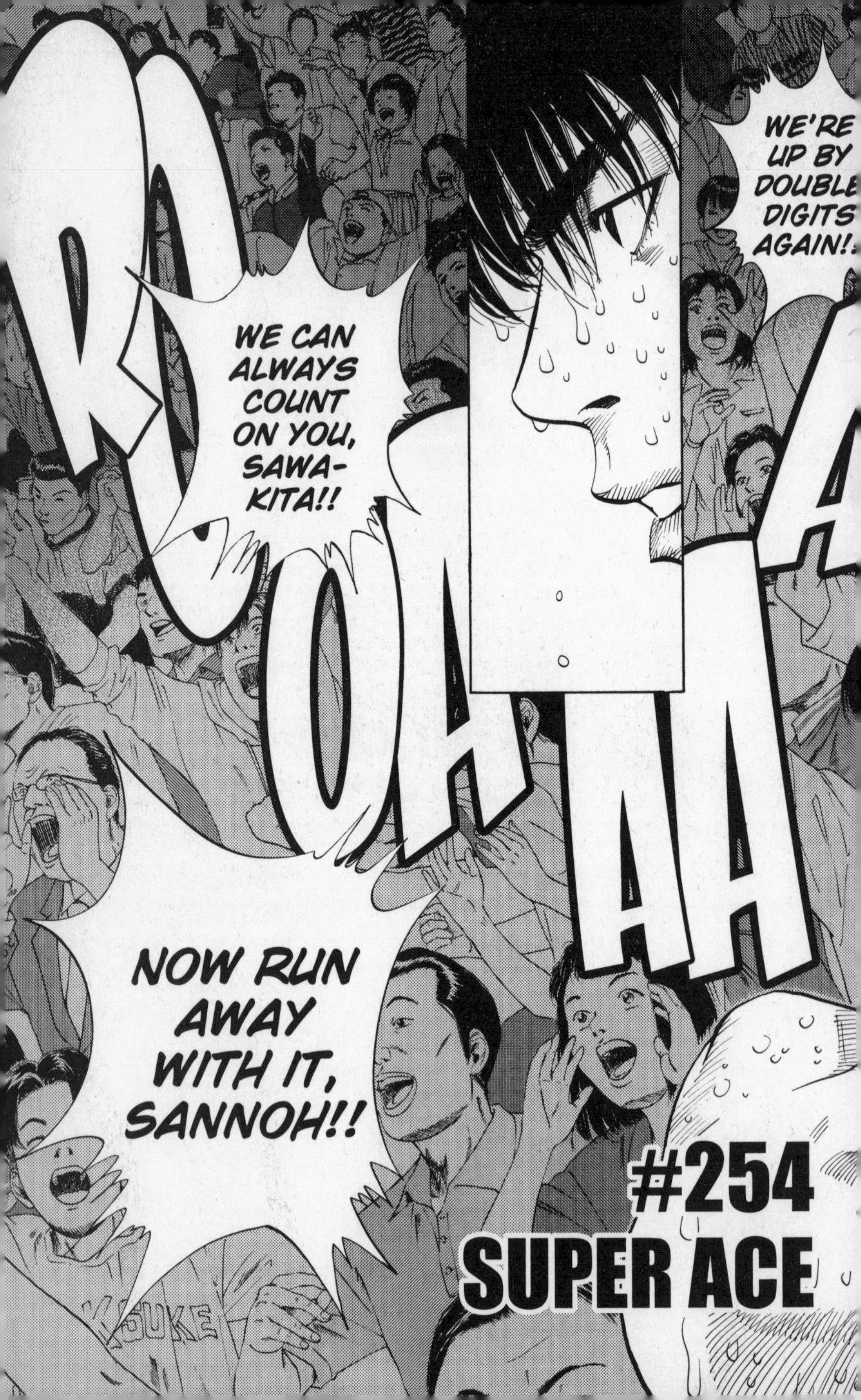
WE'RE UP BY DOUBLE DIGITS AGAIN!!
ROOAAAA
WE CAN ALWAYS COUNT ON YOU, SAWA-KITA!!
NOW RUN AWAY WITH IT, SANNOH!!
#254
SUPER ACE

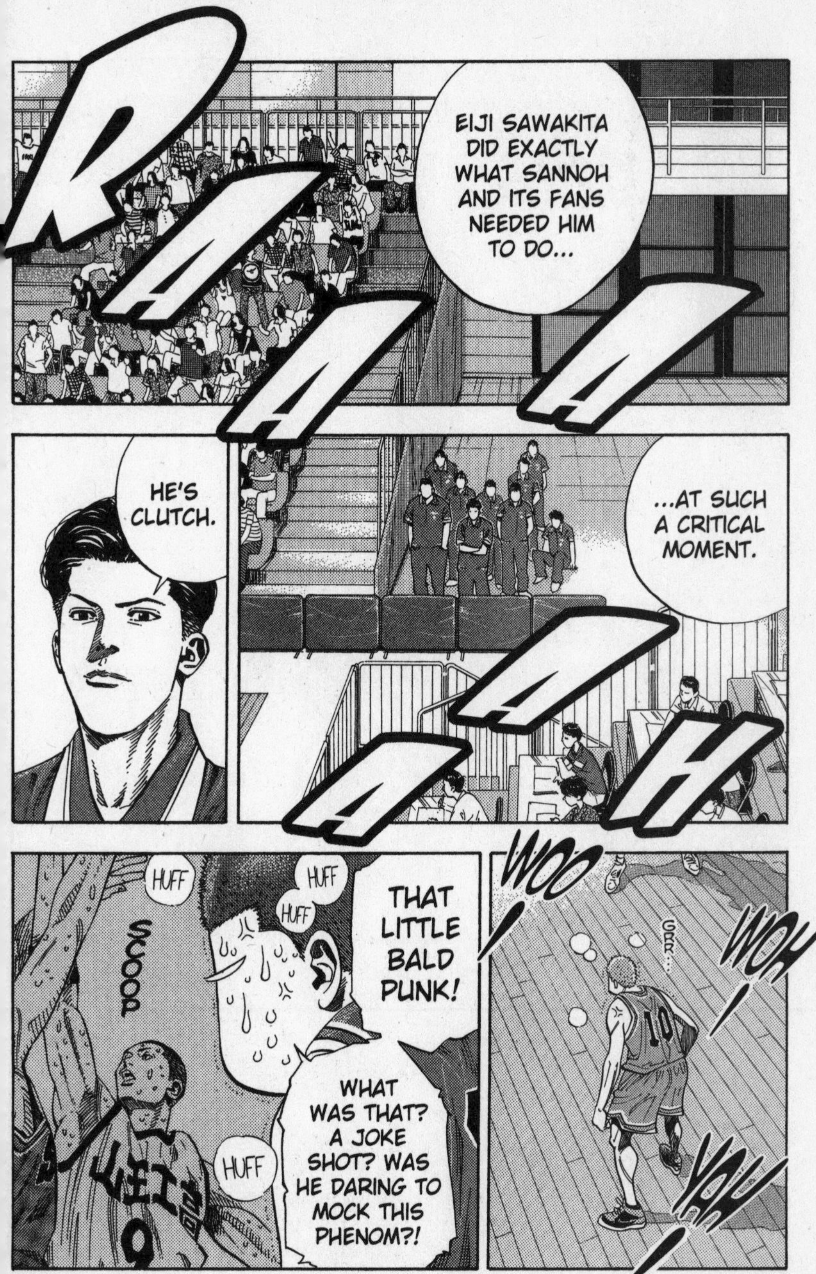
RAAAAAH
EIJI SAWAKITA DID EXACTLY WHAT SANNOH AND ITS FANS NEEDED HIM TO DO...
...AT SUCH A CRITICAL MOMENT.
HE'S CLUTCH.
WOO!
WOH!
YAH!
GRR...
HUFF
HUFF
HUFF
THAT LITTLE BALD PUNK!
WHAT WAS THAT? A JOKE SHOT? WAS HE DARING TO MOCK THIS PHENOM?!
SCOOP
HUFF

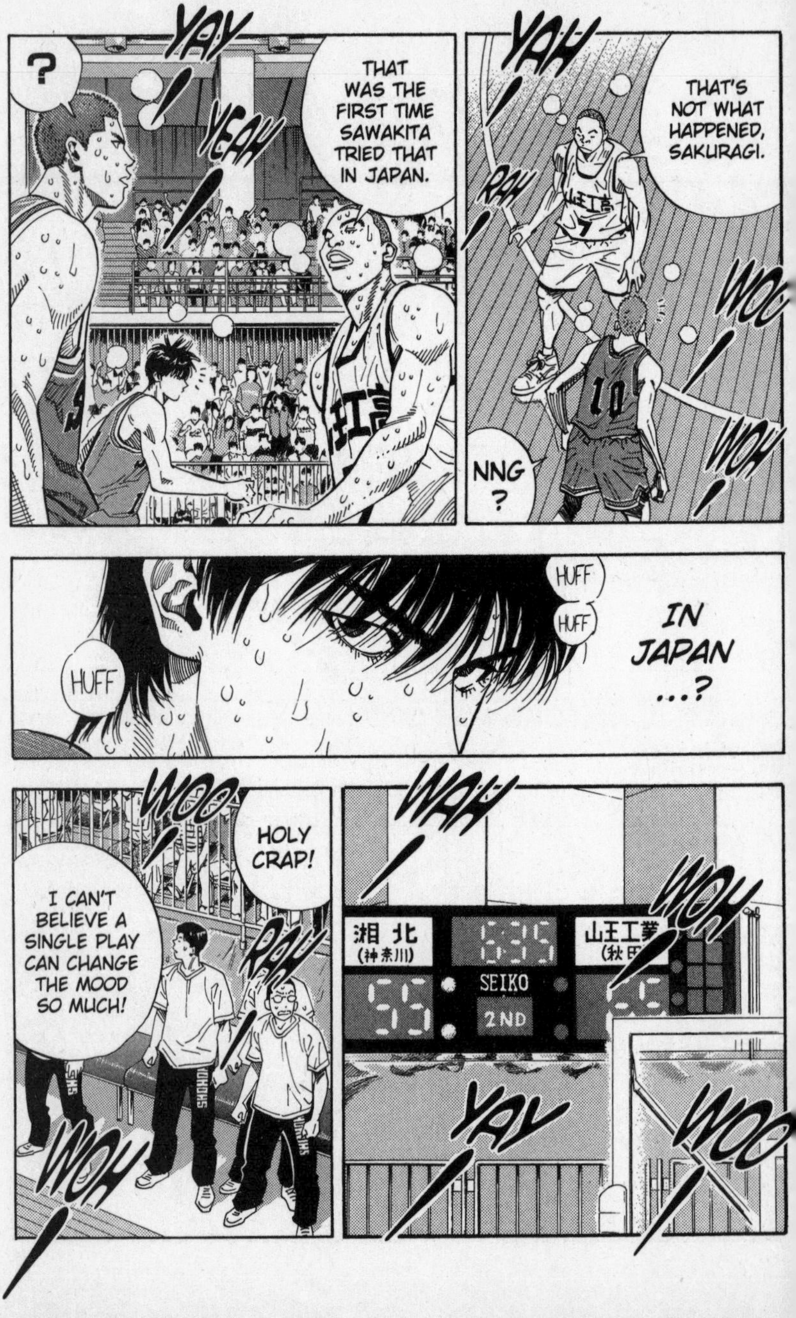
YAH
RAH
THAT'S NOT WHAT HAPPENED, SAKURAGI.
WOO
WOH
NNG?
YAY
YEAH
THAT WAS THE FIRST TIME SAWAKITA TRIED THAT IN JAPAN.
?
IN JAPAN ...?
HUFF
HUFF
HUFF
WAH
WOH
湘北
(神奈川)
6:35
山王工業
SEIKO
55
2ND
YAY
WOO
WOO
HOLY CRAP!
I CAN'T BELIEVE A SINGLE PLAY CAN CHANGE THE MOOD SO MUCH!
RAH
WOH

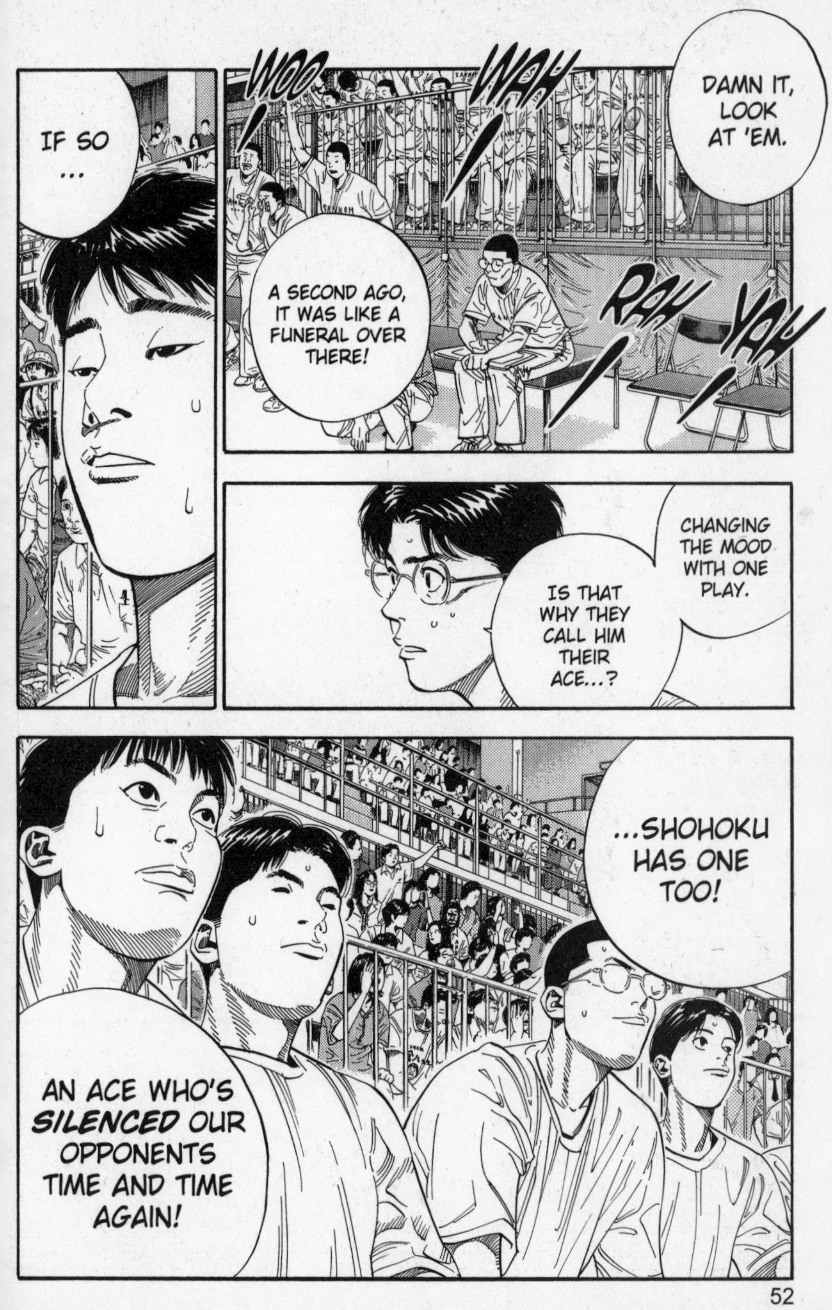
DAMN IT, LOOK AT 'EM.
WAH!
WOO!
A SECOND AGO, IT WAS LIKE A FUNERAL OVER THERE!
RAH YAH!
CHANGING THE MOOD WITH ONE PLAY.
IS THAT WHY THEY CALL HIM THEIR ACE...?
IF SO ...
...SHOHOKU HAS ONE TOO!
AN ACE WHO'S *SILENCED* OUR OPPONENTS TIME AND TIME AGAIN!

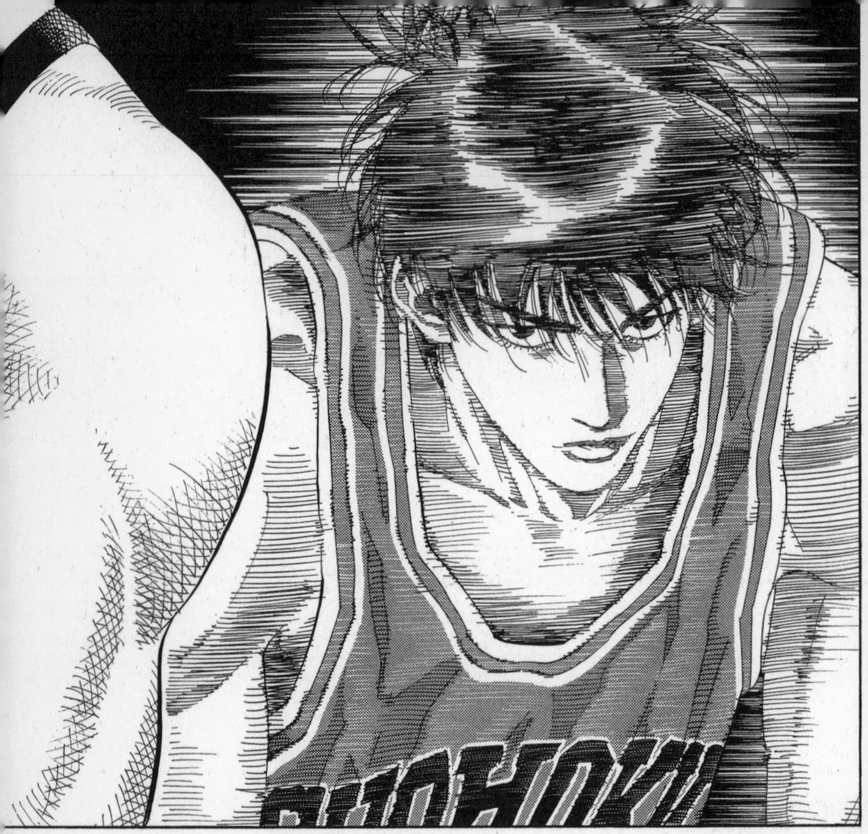

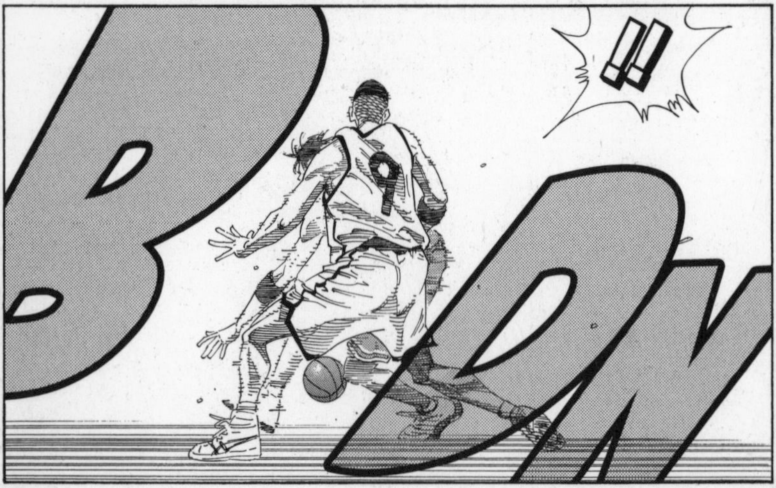
!!

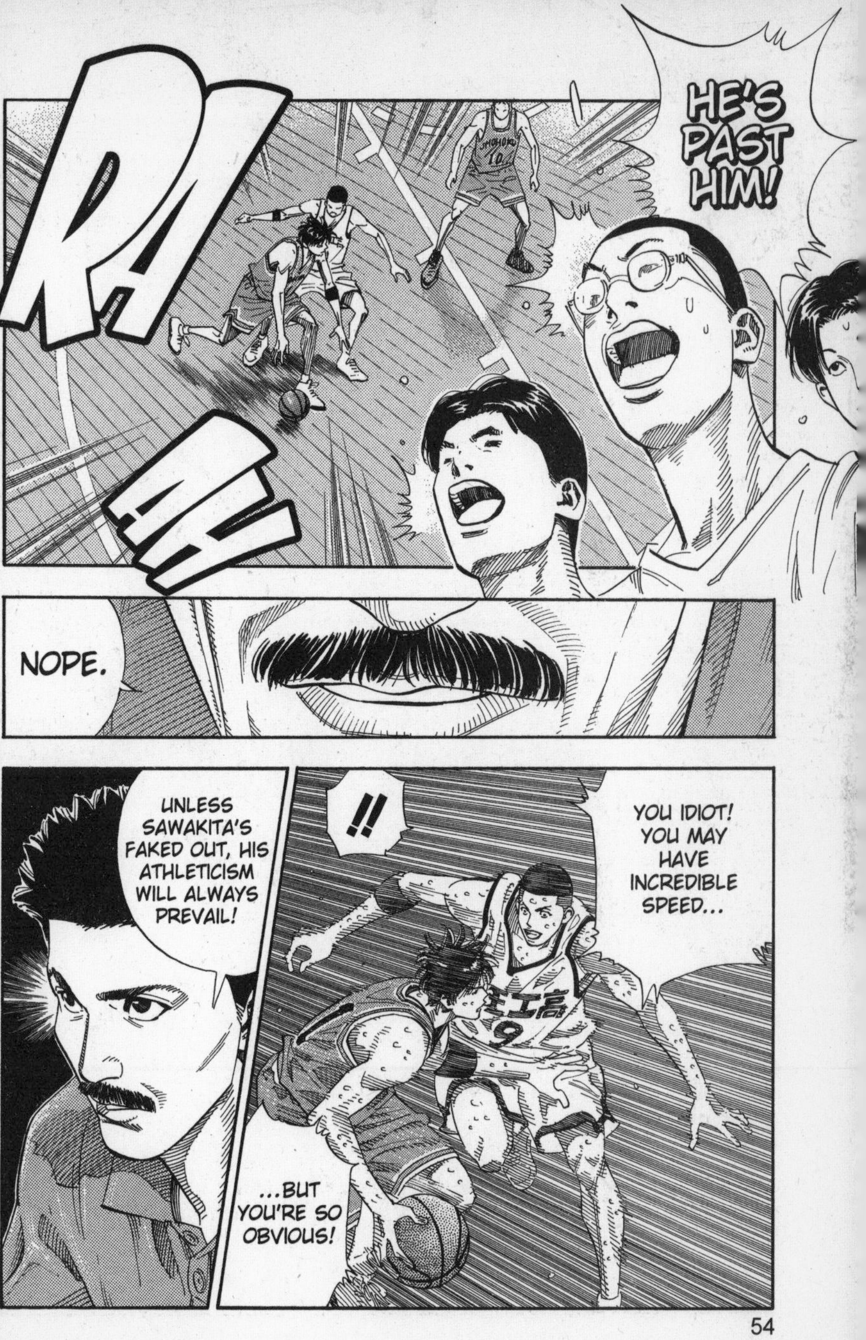
HE'S PAST HIM!
DA
SH
NOPE.
YOU IDIOT! YOU MAY HAVE INCREDIBLE SPEED...
!!
...BUT YOU'RE SO OBVIOUS!
UNLESS SAWAKITA'S FAKED OUT, HIS ATHLETICISM WILL ALWAYS PREVAIL!

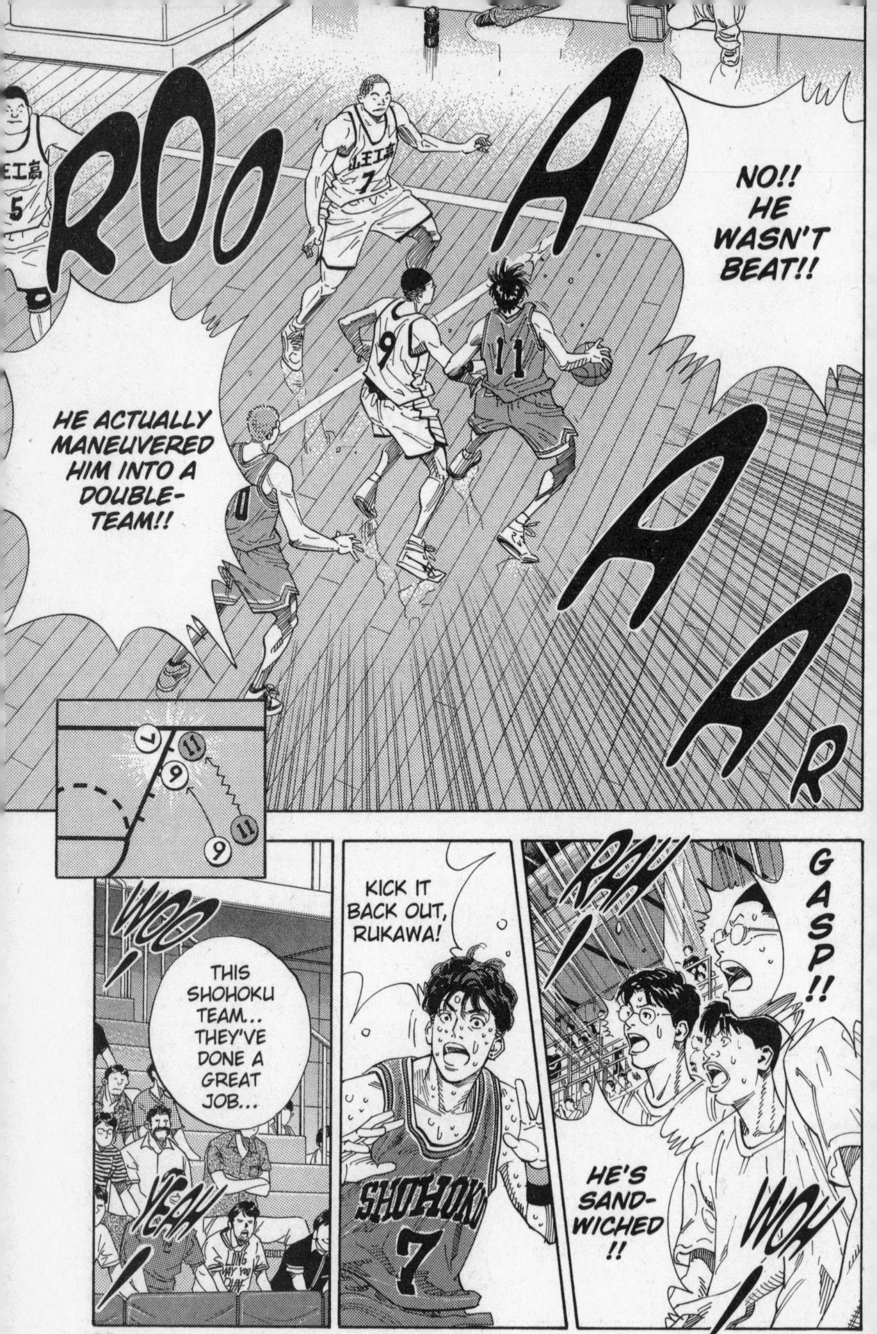
ROOOAAAAR
NO!! HE WASN'T BEAT!!
HE ACTUALLY MANEUVERED HIM INTO A DOUBLE-TEAM!!
GASP!!
RAH!
HE'S SANDWICHED!!
WOH!
KICK IT BACK OUT, RUKAWA!
SHOHOKU
7
WOO!
THIS SHOHOKU TEAM... THEY'VE DONE A GREAT JOB...
YEAH!

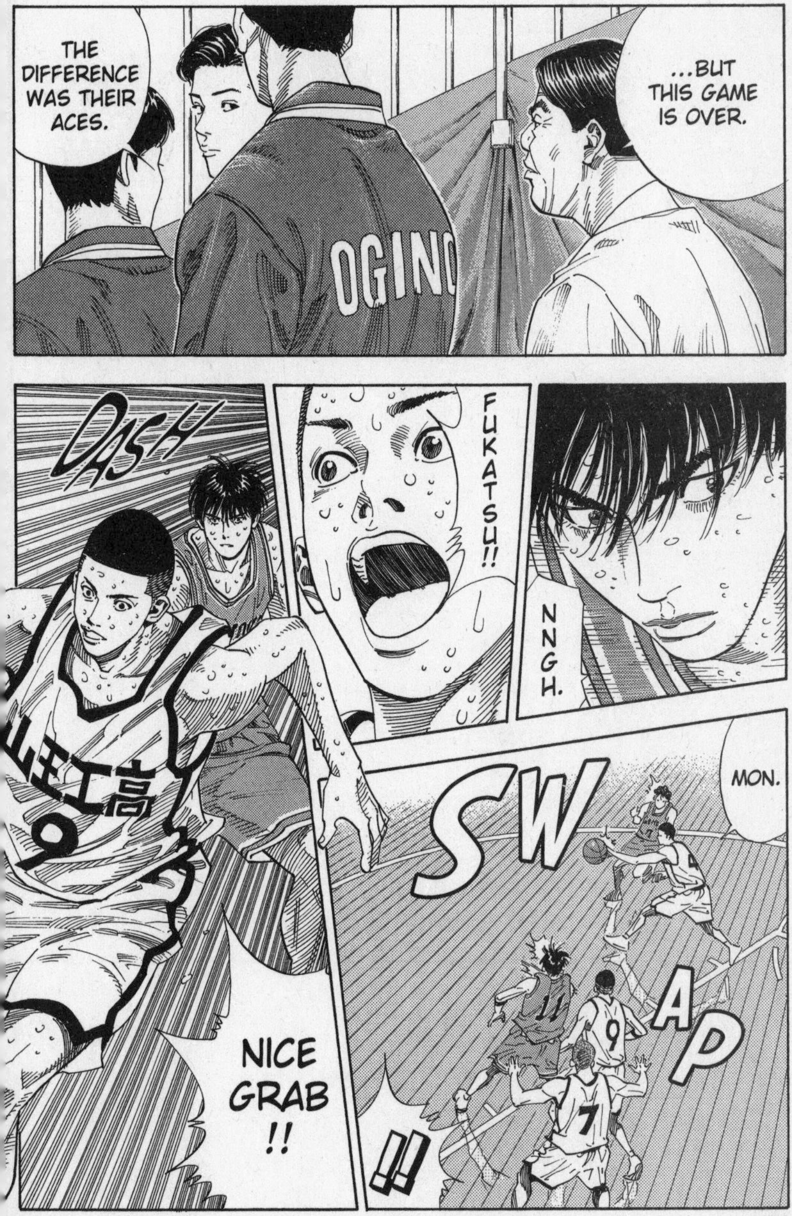
...BUT THIS GAME IS OVER.
THE DIFFERENCE WAS THEIR ACES.
OGINO
NNGH.
FUKATSU!!
MON.
SWAP
!!
DASH
NICE GRAB !!

READ THIS WAY

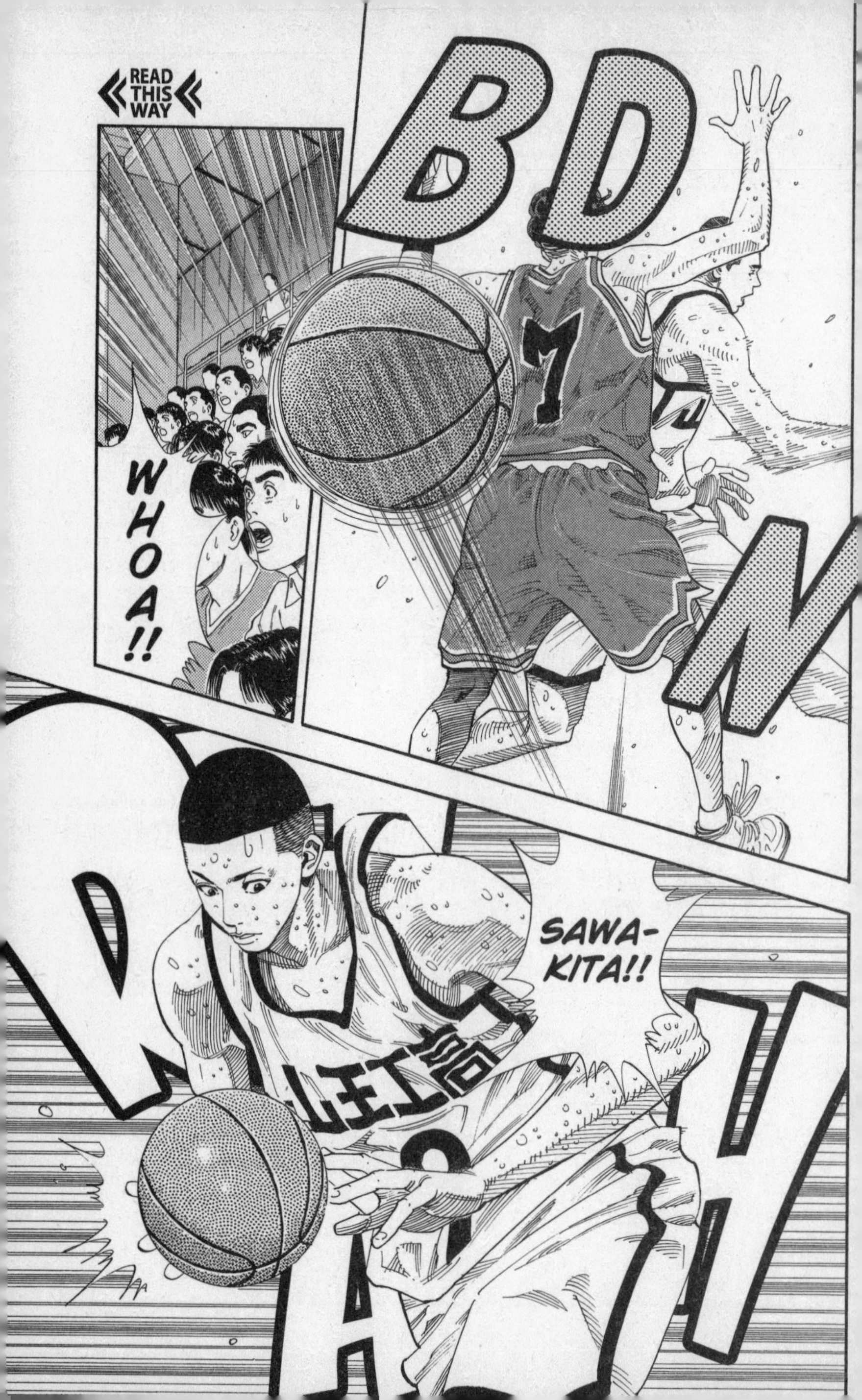
BDN
WHOA!!
SAWA-KITA!!

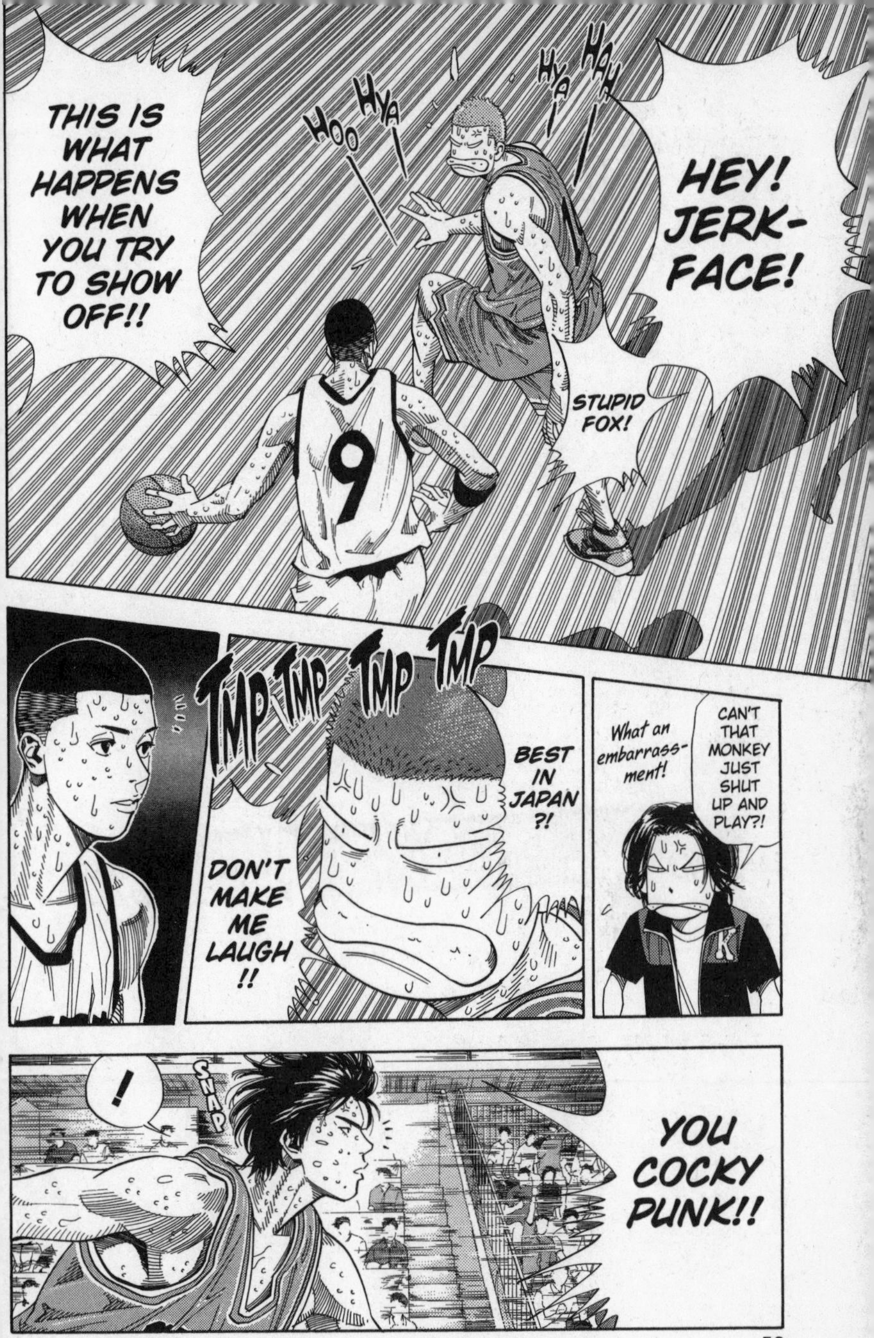
HYA HAH
HEY! JERK-FACE!
HOO HYA
THIS IS WHAT HAPPENS WHEN YOU TRY TO SHOW OFF!!
STUPID FOX!
CAN'T THAT MONKEY JUST SHUT UP AND PLAY?!
What an embarrass-ment!
TMP TMP TMP TMP
BEST IN JAPAN ?!
DON'T MAKE ME LAUGH !!
YOU COCKY PUNK!!
SNAP
!

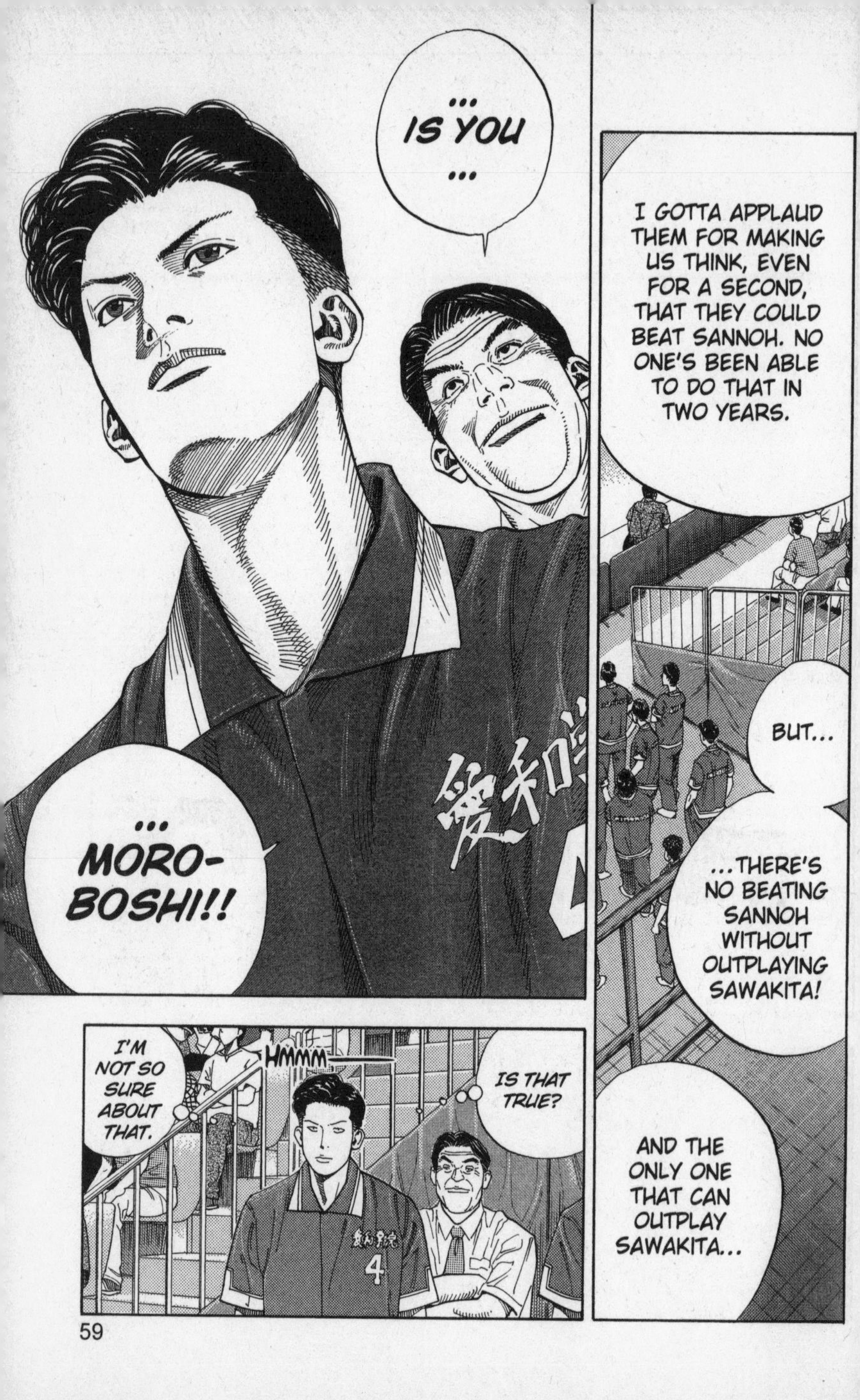
I GOTTA APPLAUD THEM FOR MAKING US THINK, EVEN FOR A SECOND, THAT THEY COULD BEAT SANNOH. NO ONE'S BEEN ABLE TO DO THAT IN TWO YEARS.
BUT...
...THERE'S NO BEATING SANNOH WITHOUT OUTPLAYING SAWAKITA!
AND THE ONLY ONE THAT CAN OUTPLAY SAWAKITA...
... IS YOU ...
... MORO-BOSHI!!
IS THAT TRUE?
HMMM
I'M NOT SO SURE ABOUT THAT.

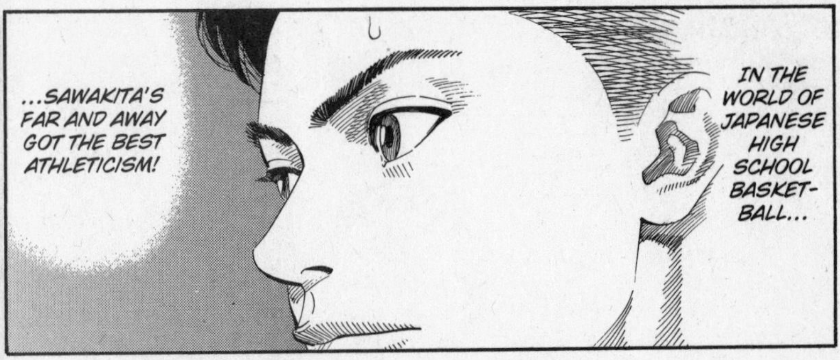
IN THE WORLD OF JAPANESE HIGH SCHOOL BASKET-BALL...
...SAWAKITA'S FAR AND AWAY GOT THE BEST ATHLETICISM!

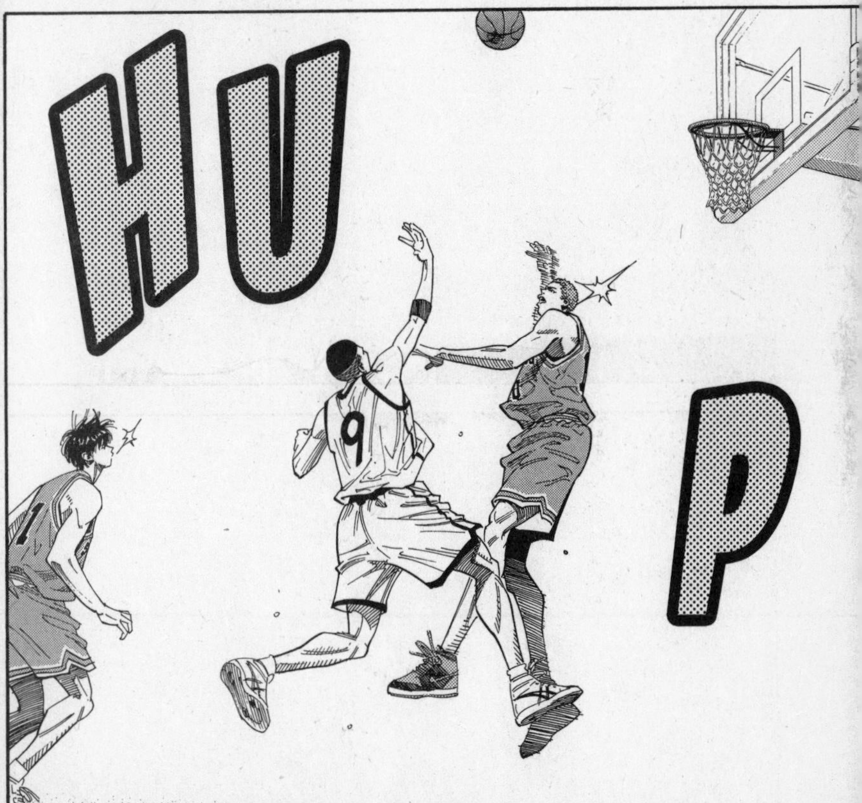
HUP

READ THIS WAY

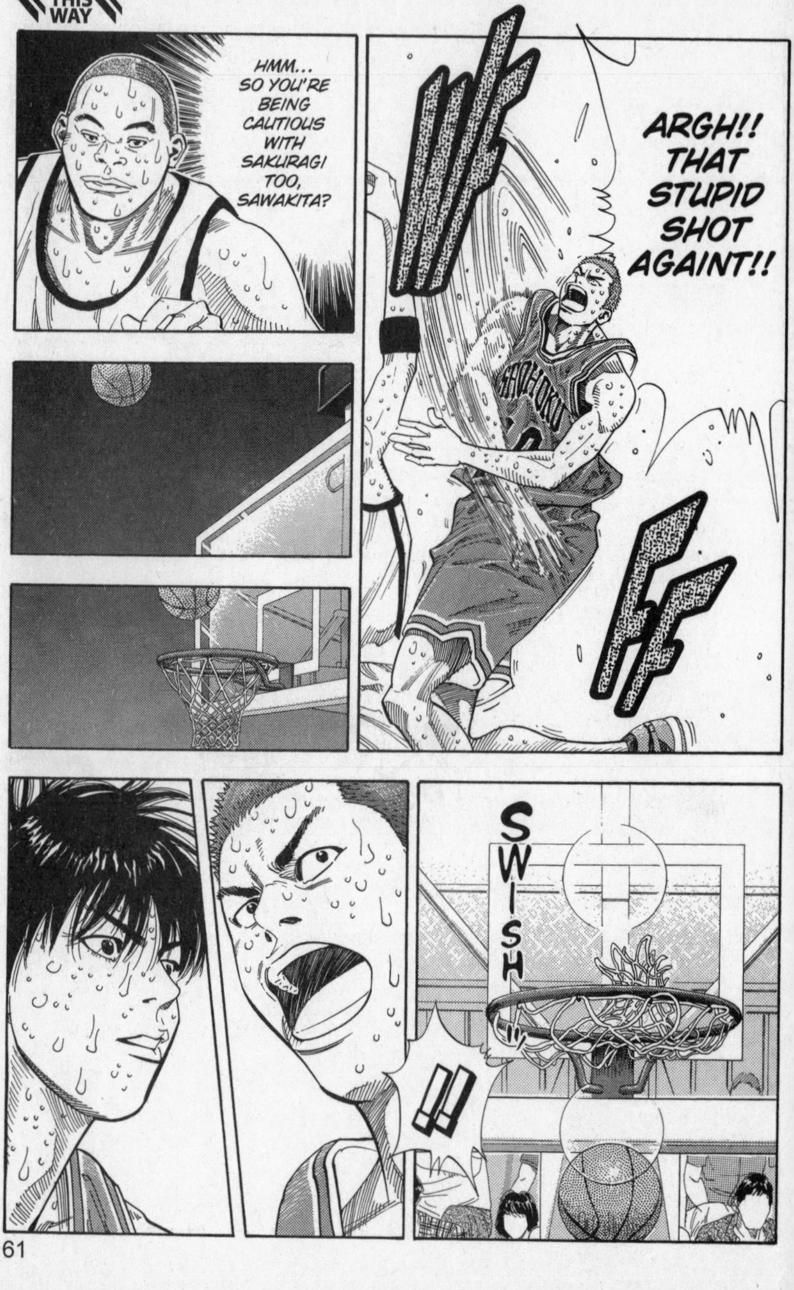

ARGH!! THAT STUPID SHOT AGAINT!!
HMM... SO YOU'RE BEING CAUTIOUS WITH SAKURAGI TOO, SAWAKITA?
SWISH
!!

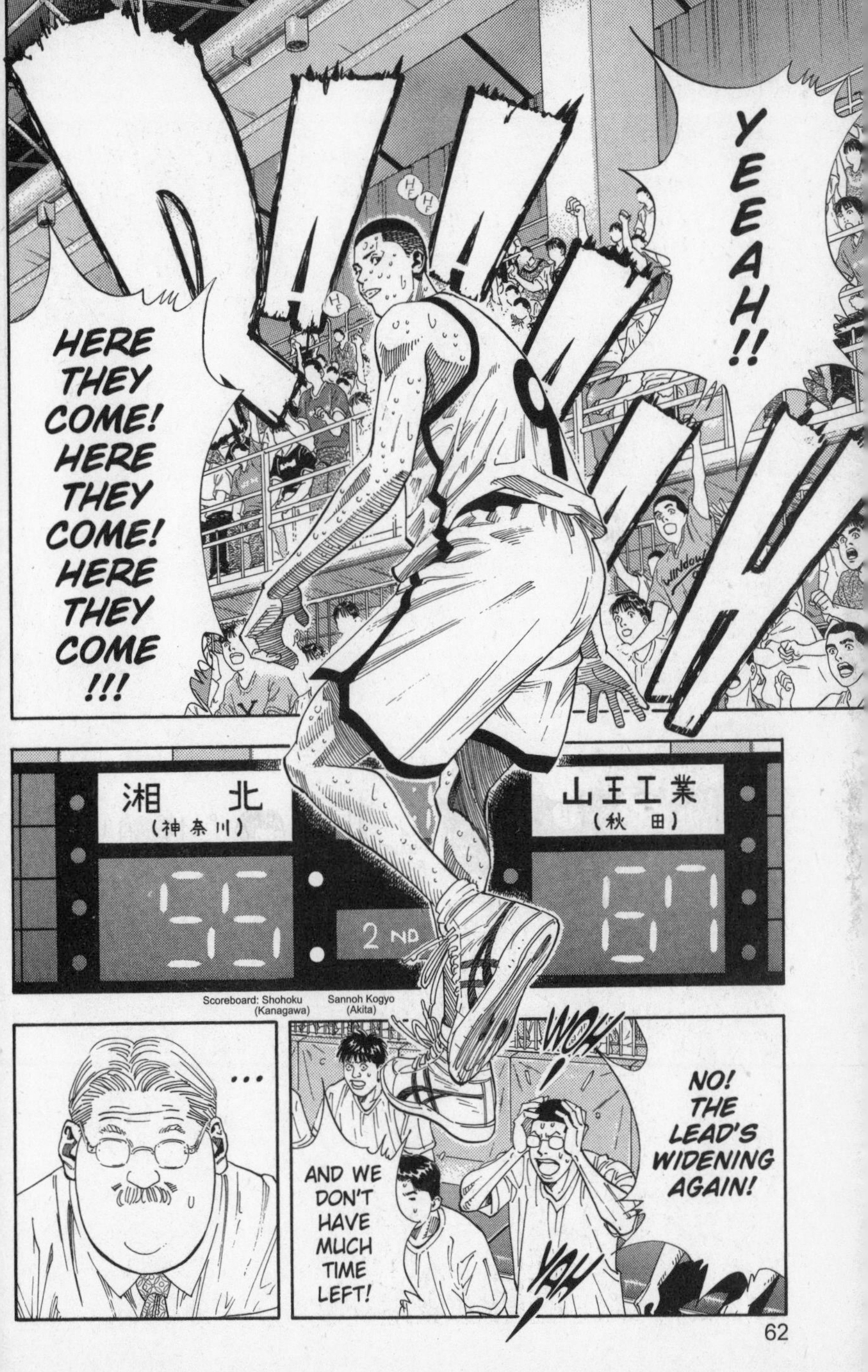
YEEEAH!!
HERE THEY COME! HERE THEY COME! HERE THEY COME!!!
H F
H F
H F
湘北
(神奈川)
山王工業
(秋田)
2ND
WOH!
NO! THE LEAD'S WIDENING AGAIN!
AND WE DON'T HAVE MUCH TIME LEFT!
YAH!
...
Scoreboard: Shohoku (Kanagawa) Sannoh Kogyo (Akita)

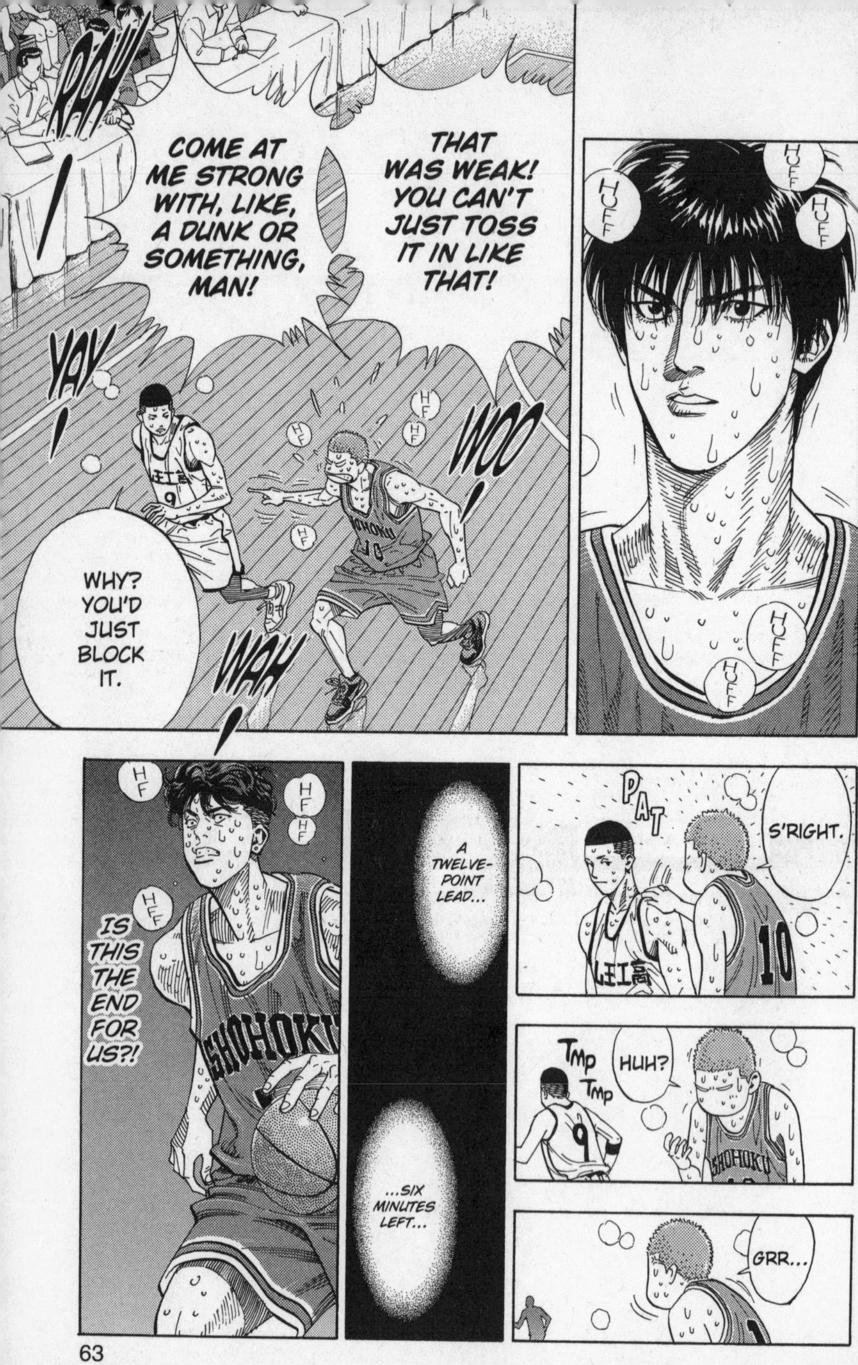
HUFF
HUFF
HUFF
HUFF
HUFF
RAAH!
THAT WAS WEAK! YOU CAN'T JUST TOSS IT IN LIKE THAT!
COME AT ME STRONG WITH, LIKE, A DUNK OR SOMETHING, MAN!
YAY!
WOO!
HF
HF
HF
HF
WHY? YOU'D JUST BLOCK IT.
WAH!
S'RIGHT.
PAT
HUH?
Tmp Tmp
GRR...
A TWELVE-POINT LEAD...
...SIX MINUTES LEFT...
HF
HF
HF
HFF
IS THIS THE END FOR US?!

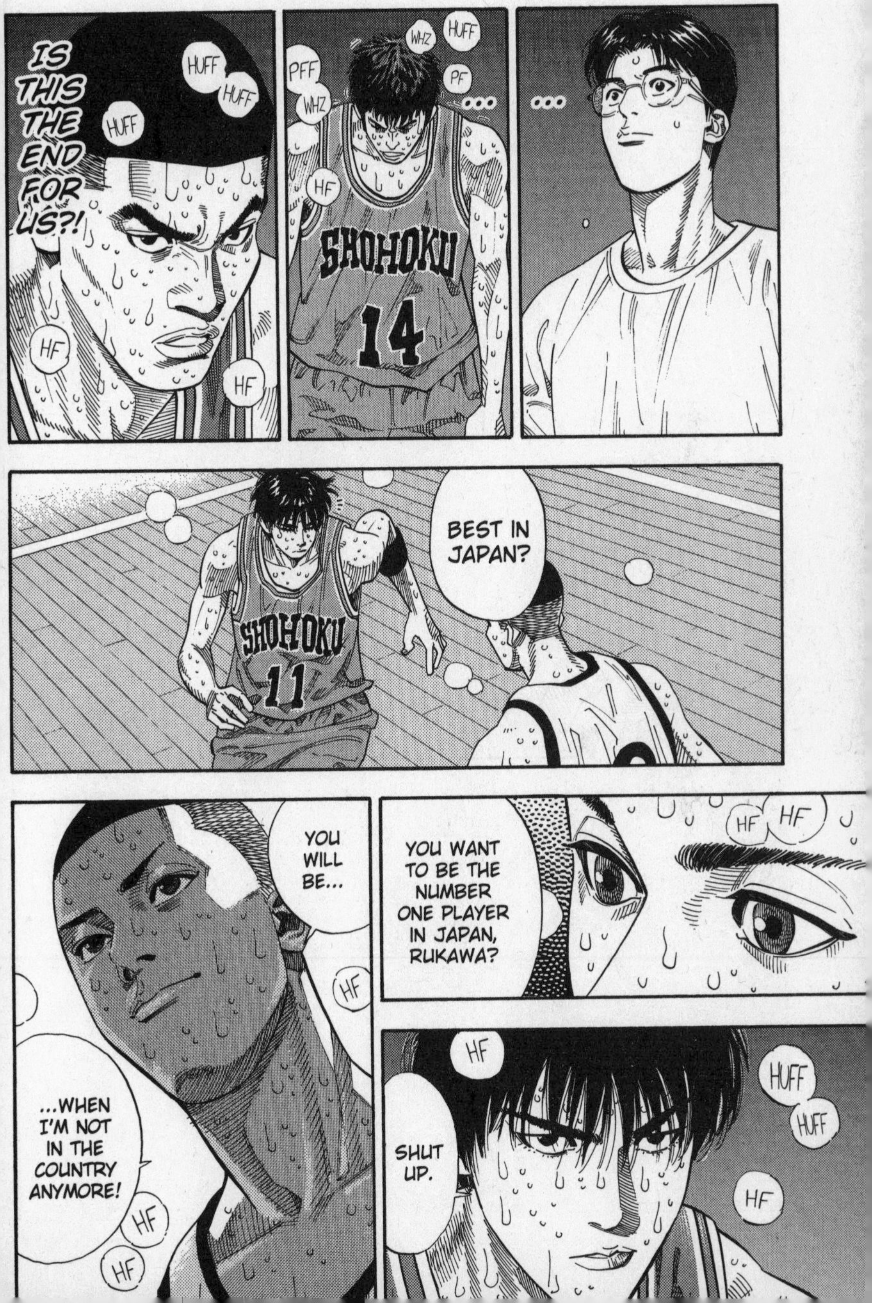

...
HUFF
WHZ
PF
PFF
WHZ
...
HF
IS THIS THE END FOR US?!
HUFF
HUFF
HUFF
HF
HF
BEST IN JAPAN?
HF
HF
YOU WANT TO BE THE NUMBER ONE PLAYER IN JAPAN, RUKAWA?
HF
HUFF
HUFF
SHUT UP.
HF
YOU WILL BE...
HF
...WHEN I'M NOT IN THE COUNTRY ANYMORE!
HF
HF

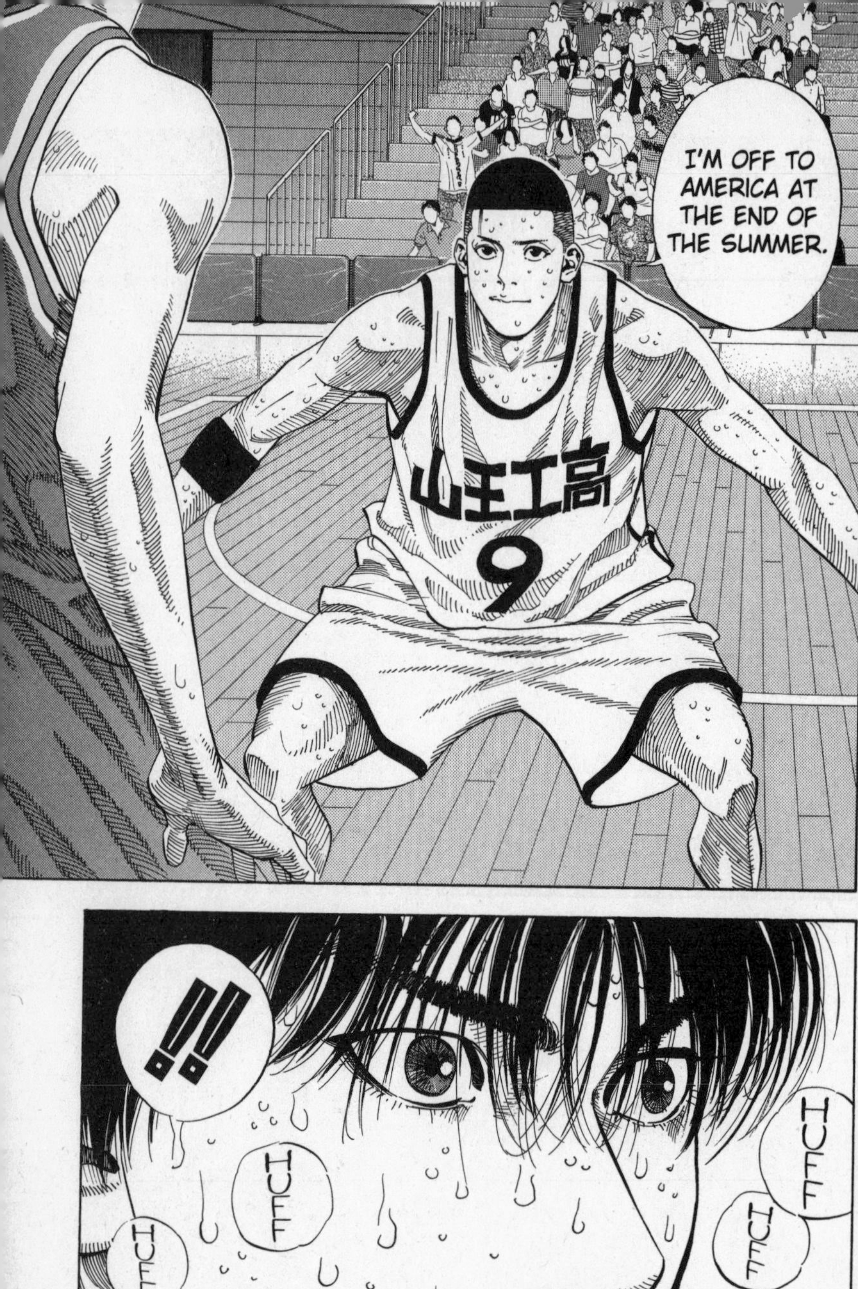
I'M OFF TO AMERICA AT THE END OF THE SUMMER.
!!
HUFF
HUFF
HUFF
HUFF

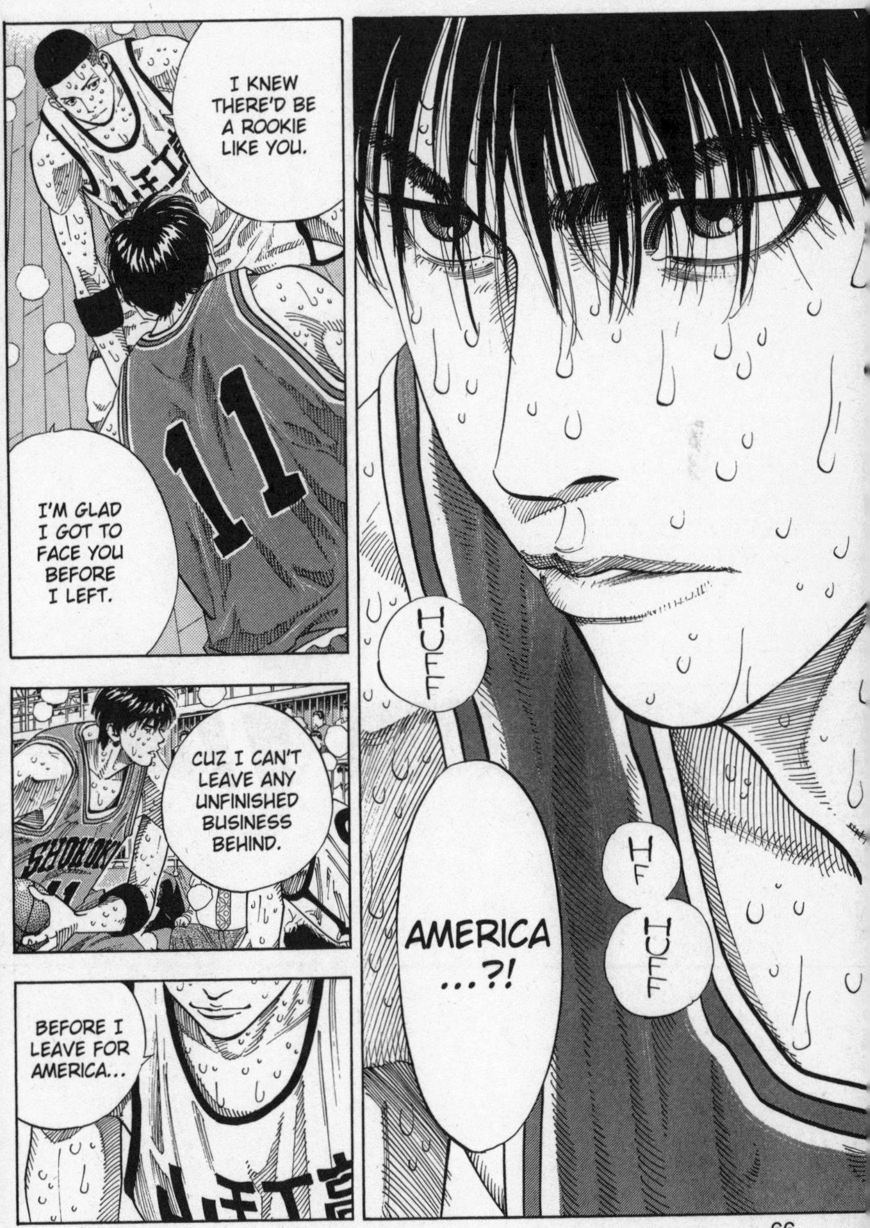
I KNEW THERE'D BE A ROOKIE LIKE YOU.
I'M GLAD I GOT TO FACE YOU BEFORE I LEFT.
CUZ I CAN'T LEAVE ANY UNFINISHED BUSINESS BEHIND.
BEFORE I LEAVE FOR AMERICA...
HUFF
HF
HUFF
AMERICA ...?!

#255 SAWAKITA

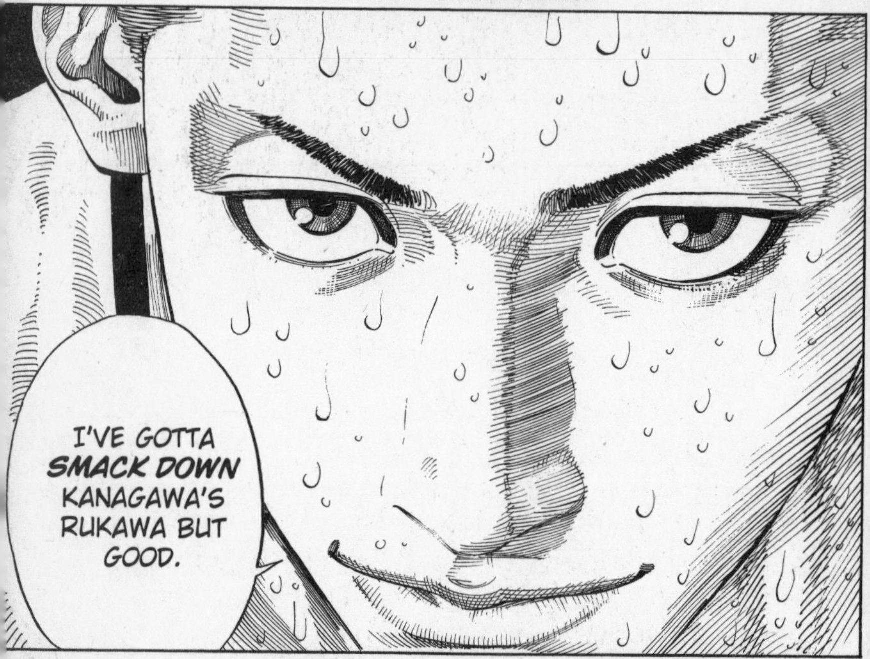
I'VE GOTTA SMACK DOWN KANAGAWA'S RUKAWA BUT GOOD.

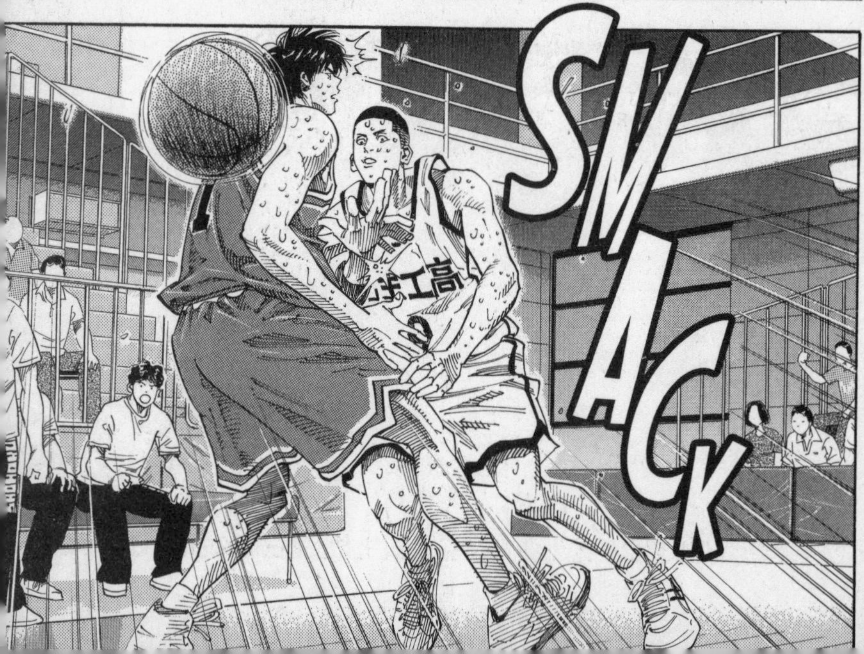
SMACK

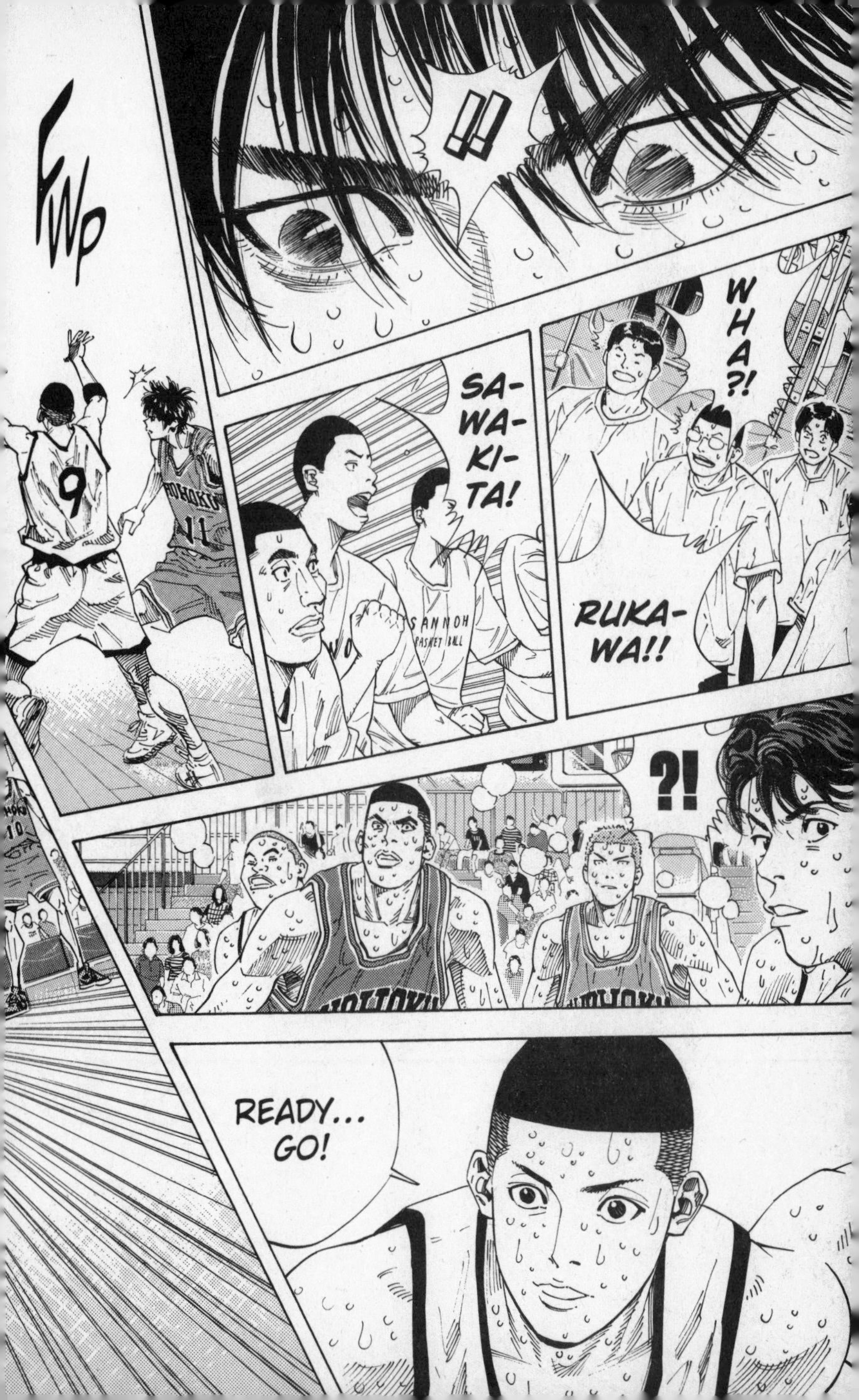
!!
WHA?!
RUKA-WA!!
SA-WA-KI-TA!
FWP
?!
READY... GO!

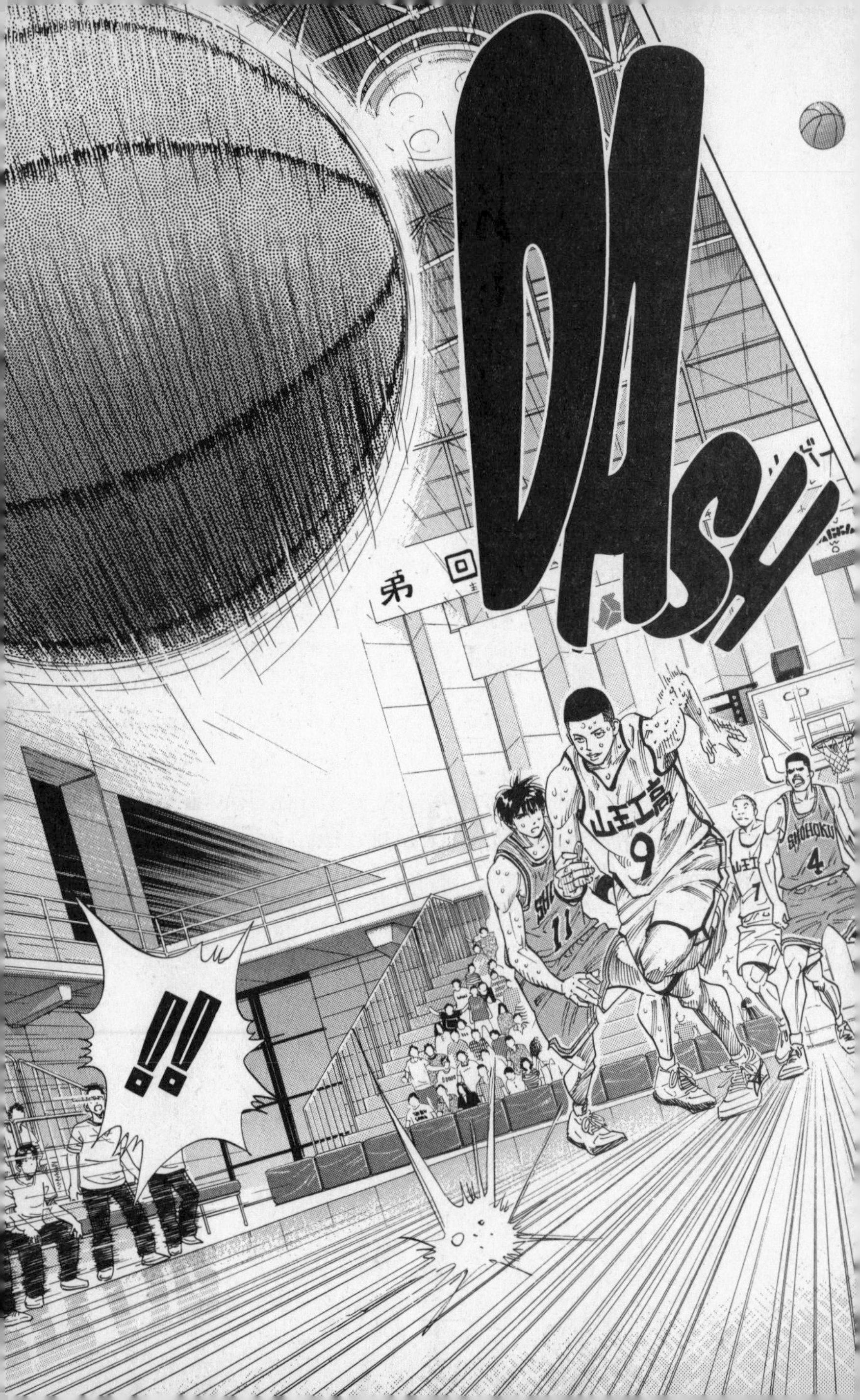
DASH
!!

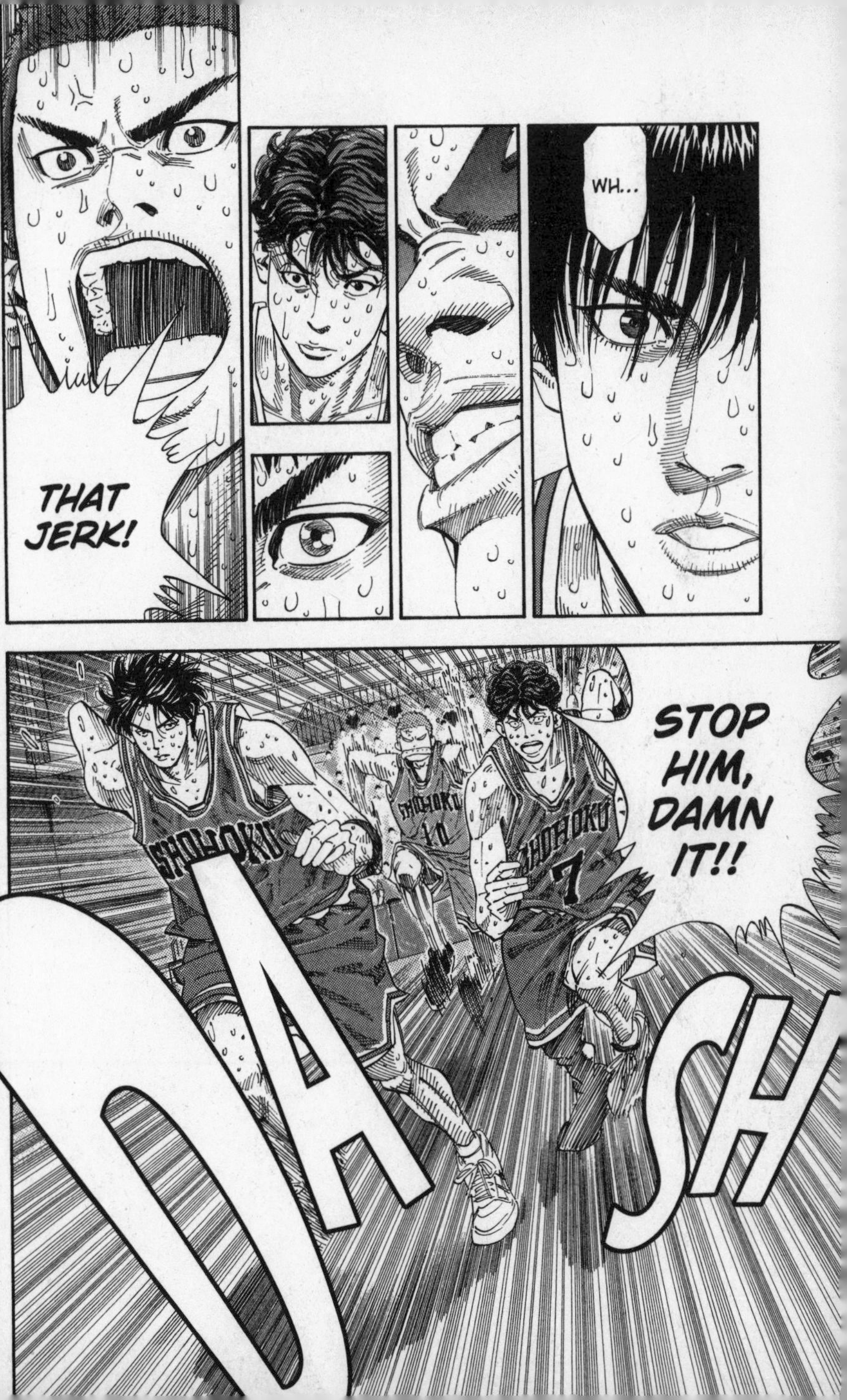
WH...
THAT JERK!
STOP HIM, DAMN IT!!
DASH

READ THIS WAY

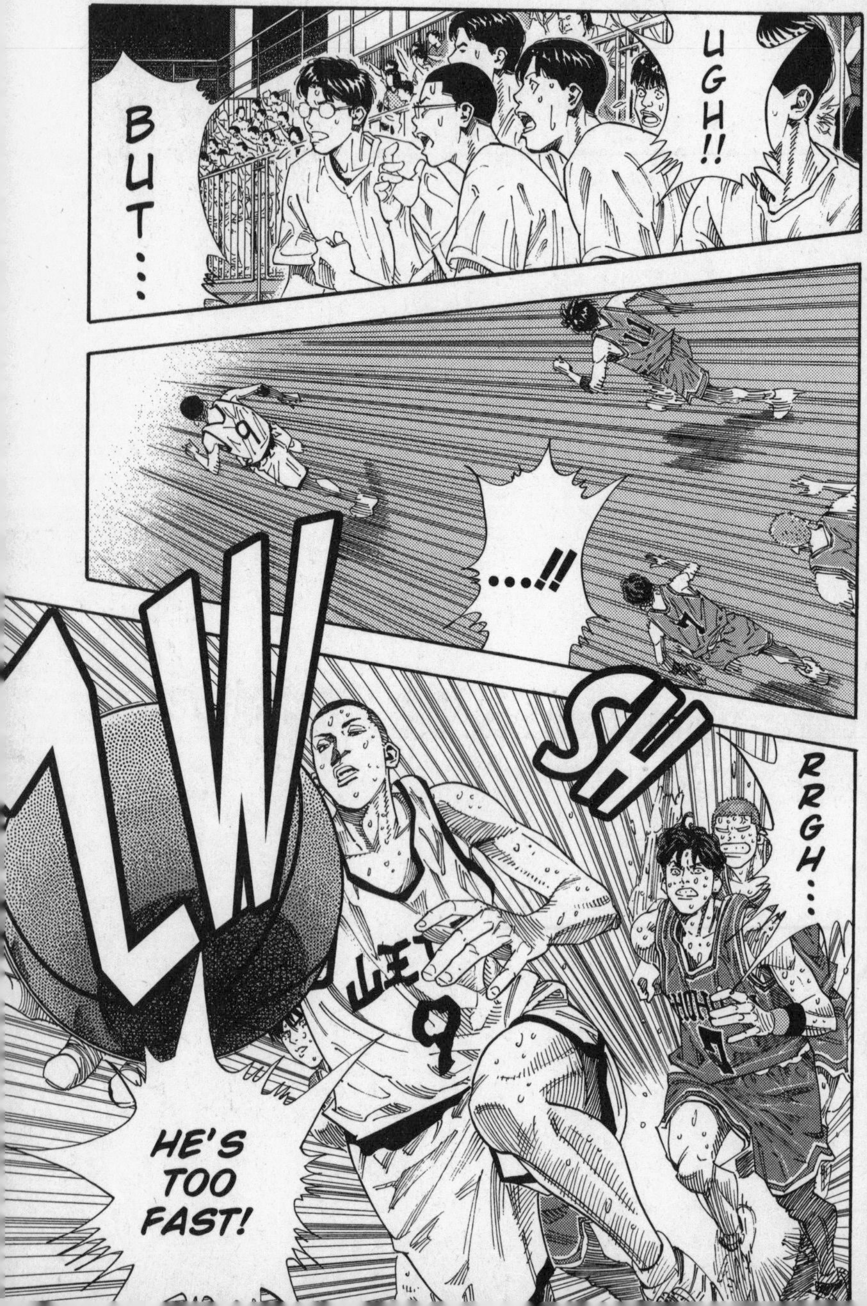
UGH!!
BUT...
...!!
SH
RRGH...
HE'S TOO FAST!

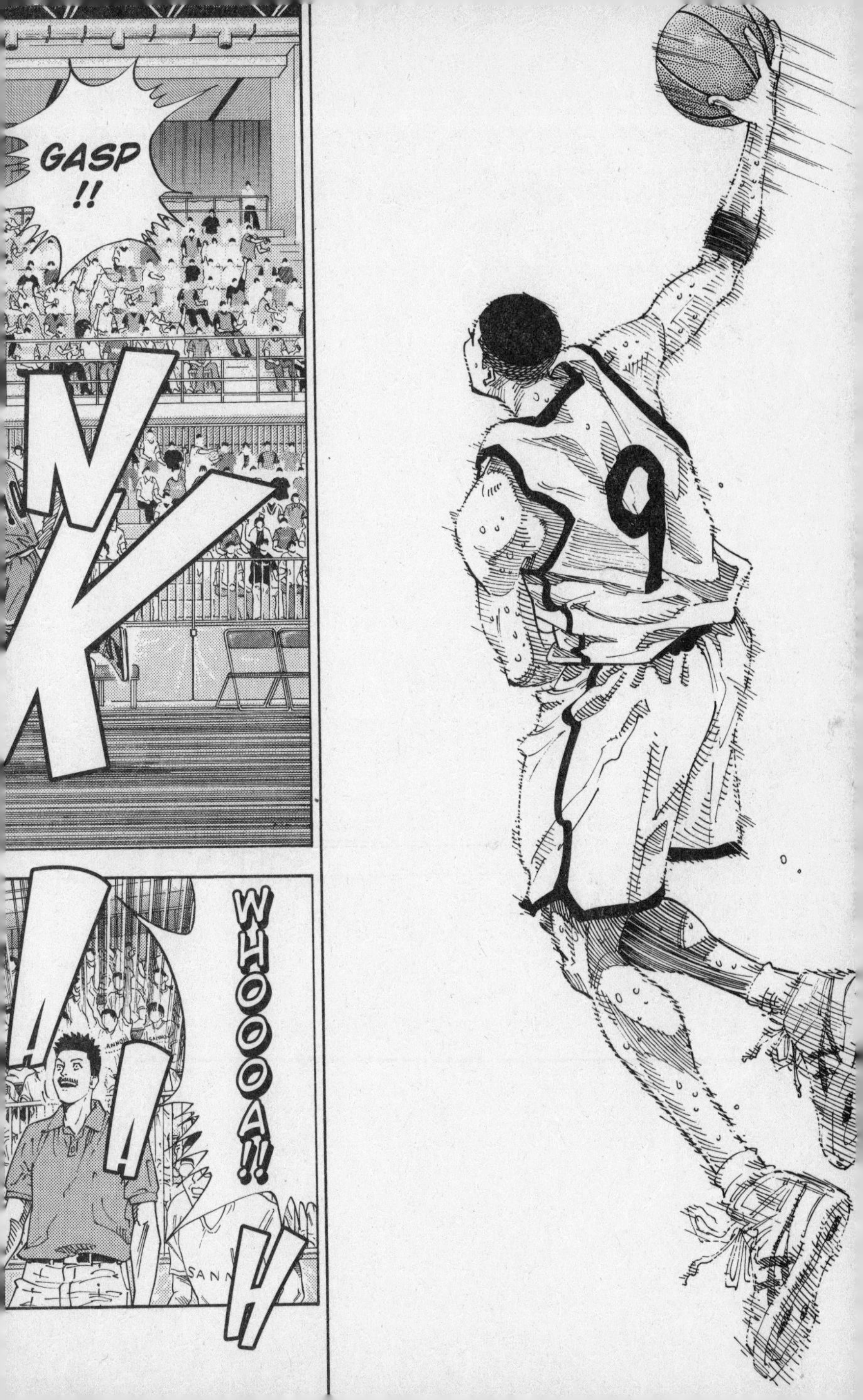
GASP !!
NK
WHOOOOA!!

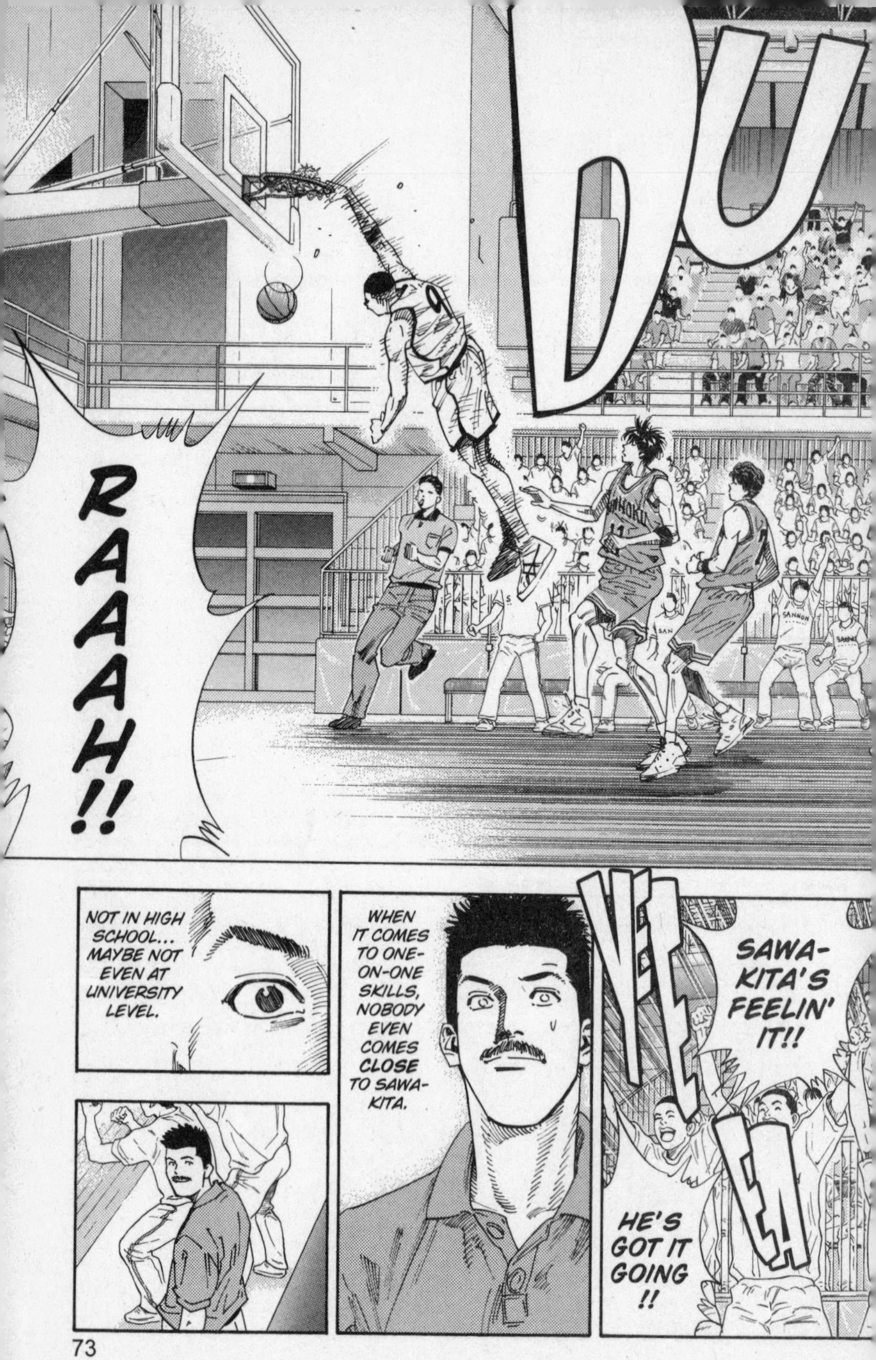
DU
RAAAAH!!
SAWA-KITA'S FEELIN' IT!!
HE'S GOT IT GOING !!
WHEN IT COMES TO ONE-ON-ONE SKILLS, NOBODY EVEN COMES CLOSE TO SAWA-KITA.
NOT IN HIGH SCHOOL... MAYBE NOT EVEN AT UNIVERSITY LEVEL.

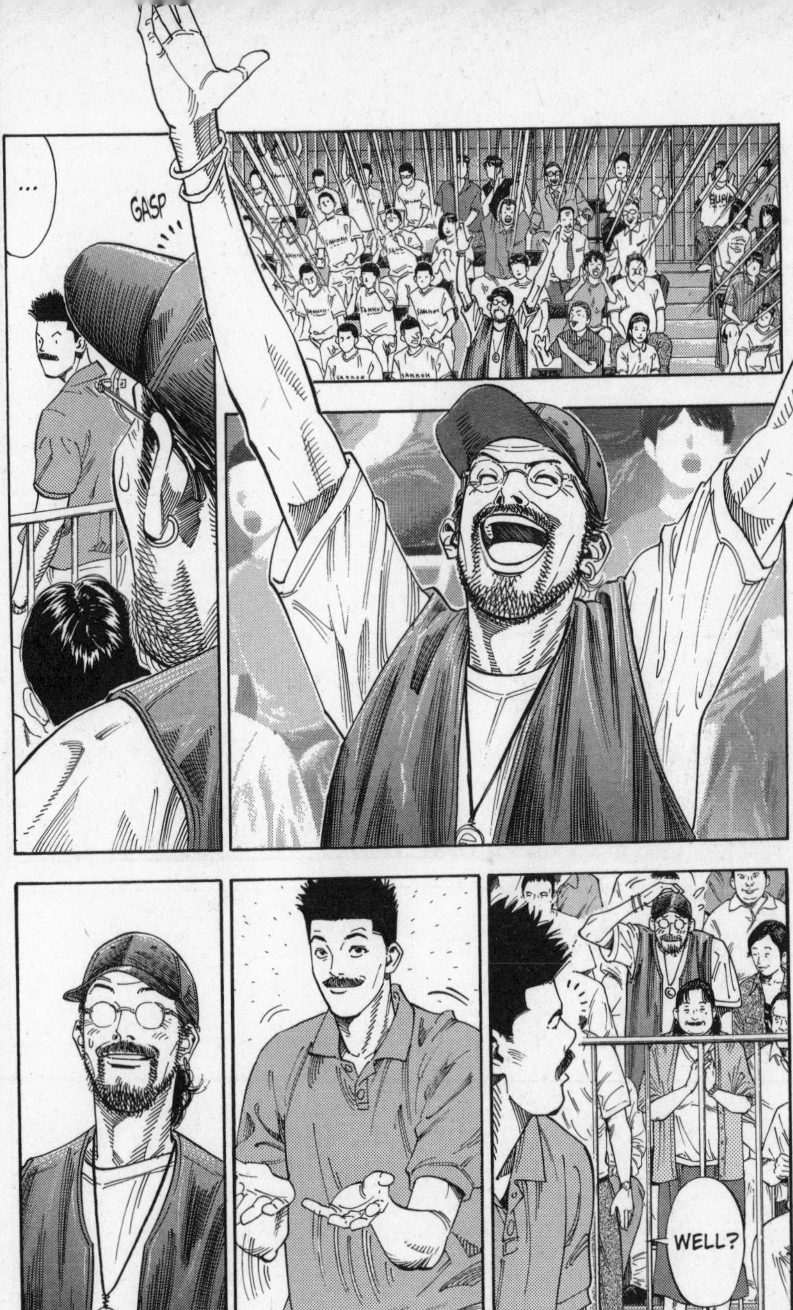
...
GASP
WELL?

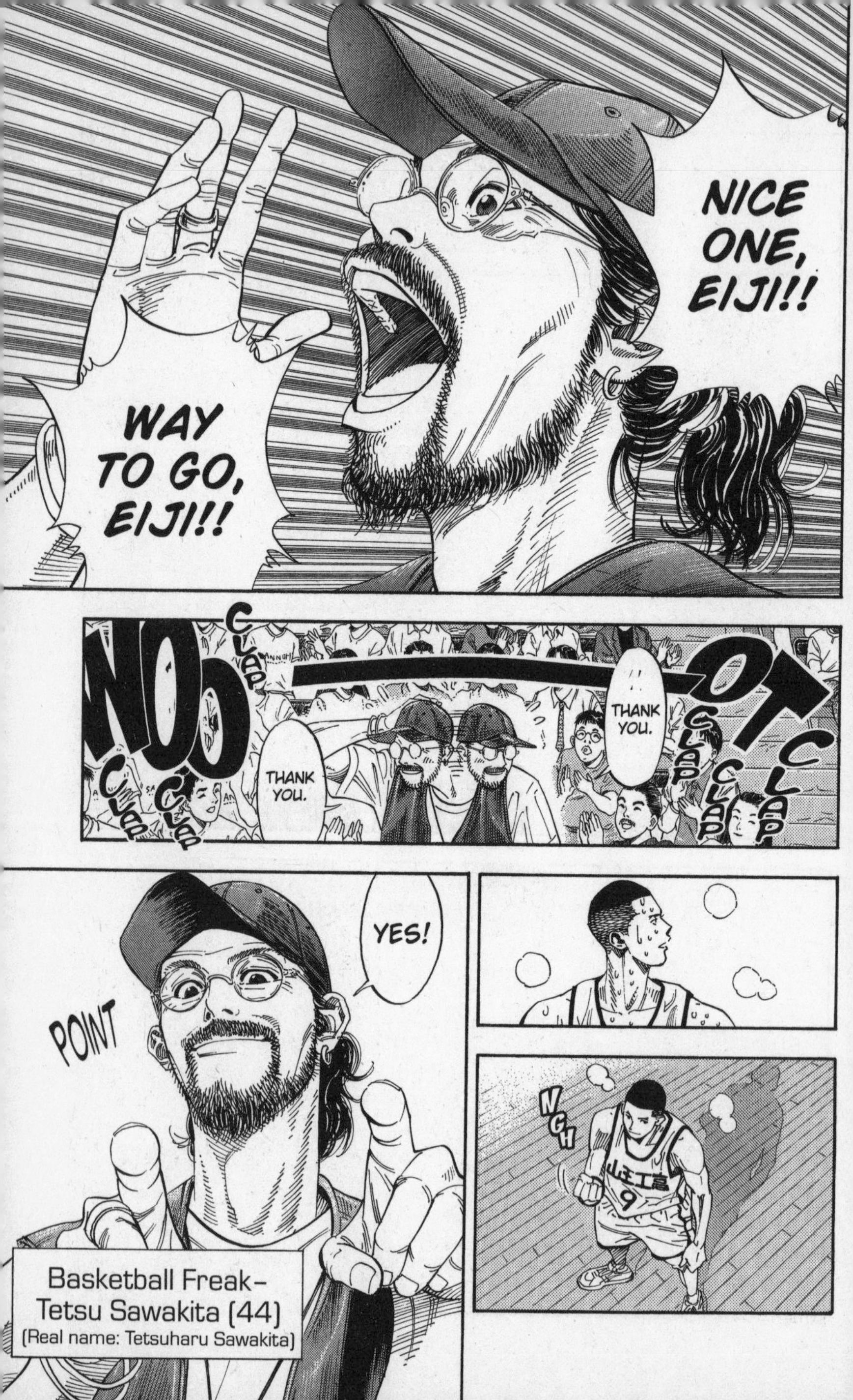
NICE ONE, EIJI!!
WAY TO GO, EIJI!!
WOO—OT
CLAP CLAP CLAP
THANK YOU.
THANK YOU.
CLAP CLAP CLAP
NGH
YES!
POINT
Basketball Freak– Tetsu Sawakita (44)
(Real name: Tetsuharu Sawakita)

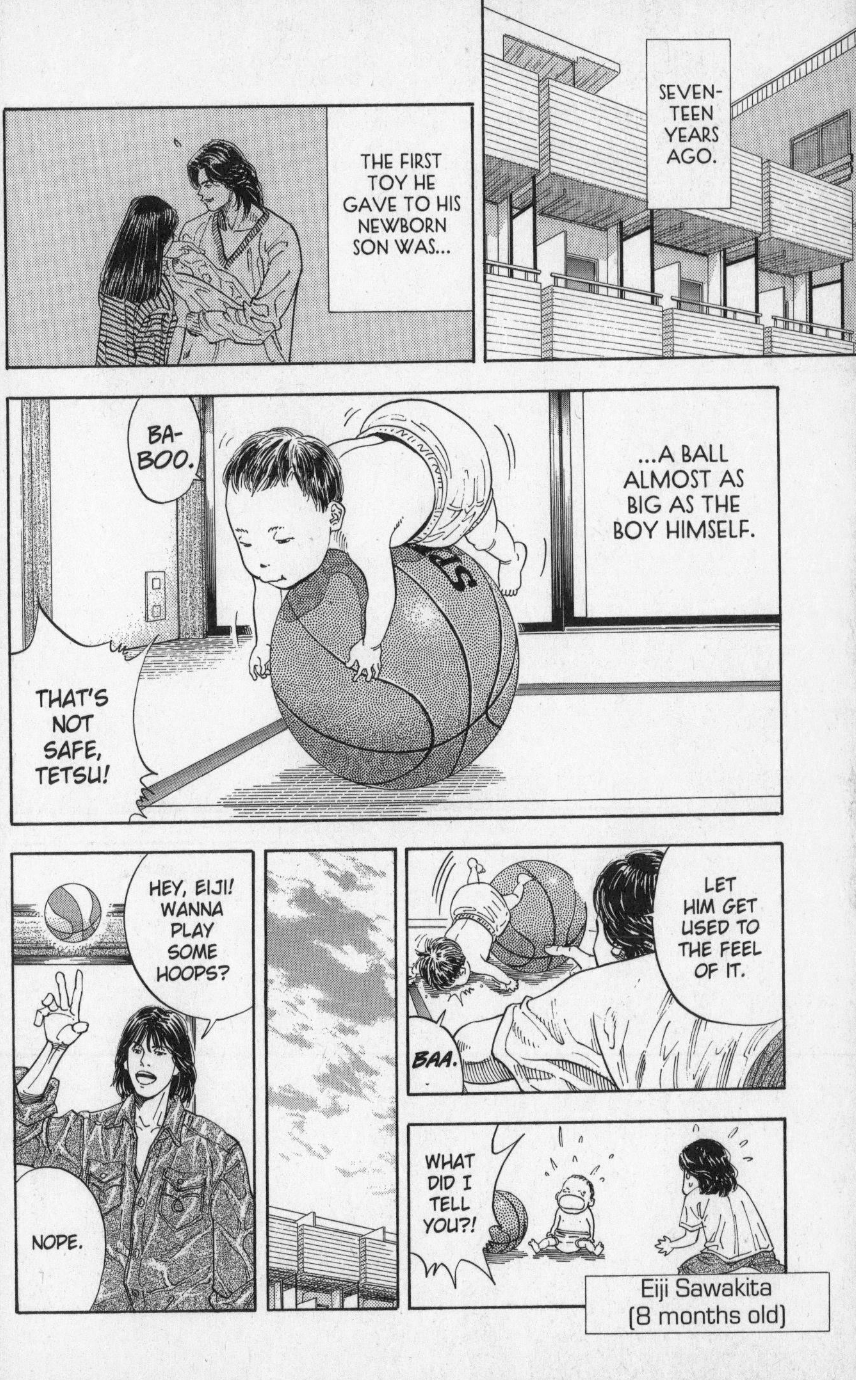
SEVEN-TEEN YEARS AGO.
THE FIRST TOY HE GAVE TO HIS NEWBORN SON WAS...
...A BALL ALMOST AS BIG AS THE BOY HIMSELF.
BA-BOO.
THAT'S NOT SAFE, TETSU!
LET HIM GET USED TO THE FEEL OF IT.
BAA.
WHAT DID I TELL YOU?!
Eiji Sawakita (8 months old)
HEY, EIJI! WANNA PLAY SOME HOOPS?
NOPE.

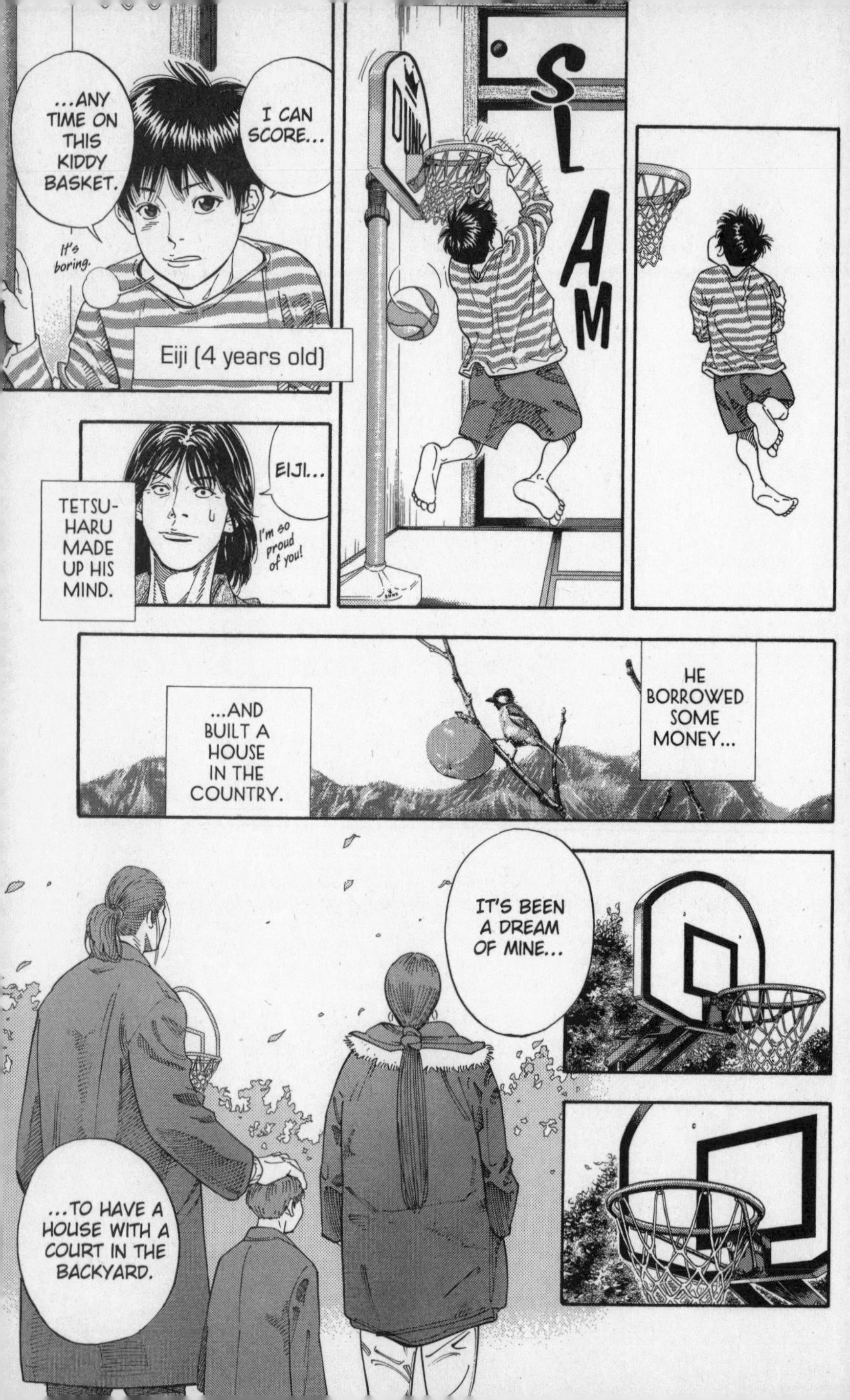
SLAM
I CAN SCORE...
...ANY TIME ON THIS KIDDY BASKET.
It's boring.
Eiji (4 years old)
EIJI...
I'm so proud of you!
TETSU-HARU MADE UP HIS MIND.
HE BORROWED SOME MONEY...
...AND BUILT A HOUSE IN THE COUNTRY.
IT'S BEEN A DREAM OF MINE...
...TO HAVE A HOUSE WITH A COURT IN THE BACKYARD.

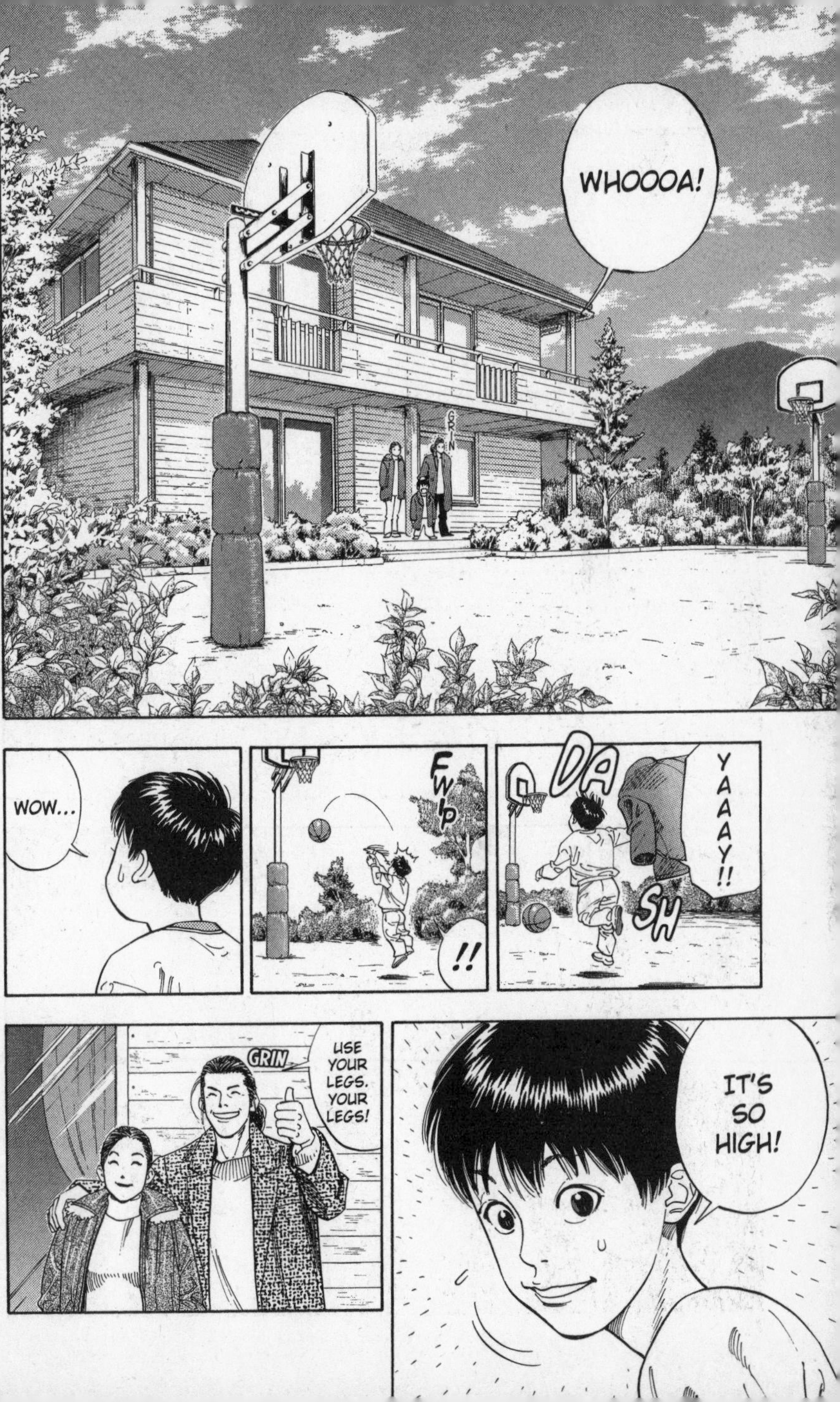
WHOOOA!
GRIN
YAAAAY!!
DA
SH
FWIP
!!
WOW...
IT'S SO HIGH!
USE YOUR LEGS. YOUR LEGS!
GRIN

READ THIS WAY

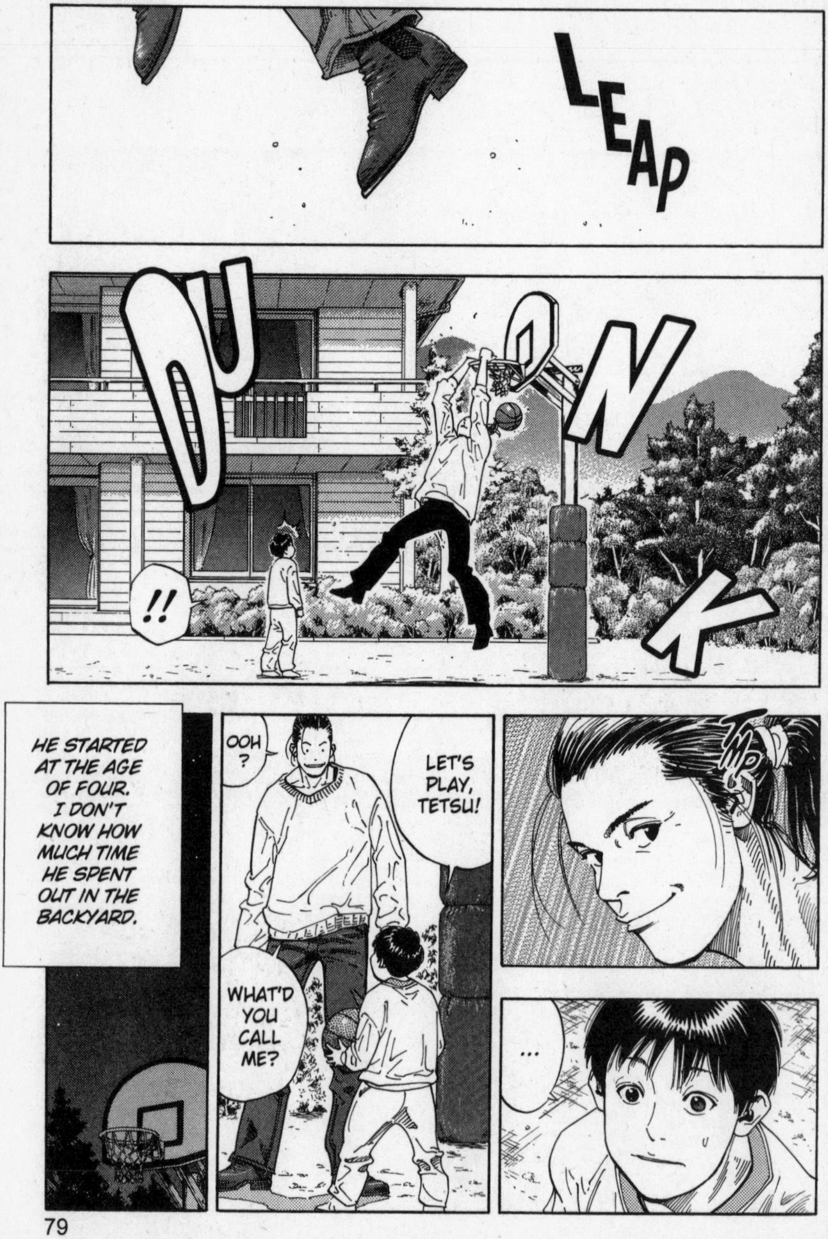
LEAP
DUNK
!!
...
LET'S PLAY, TETSU!
OOH ?
WHAT'D YOU CALL ME?
HE STARTED AT THE AGE OF FOUR. I DON'T KNOW HOW MUCH TIME HE SPENT OUT IN THE BACKYARD.

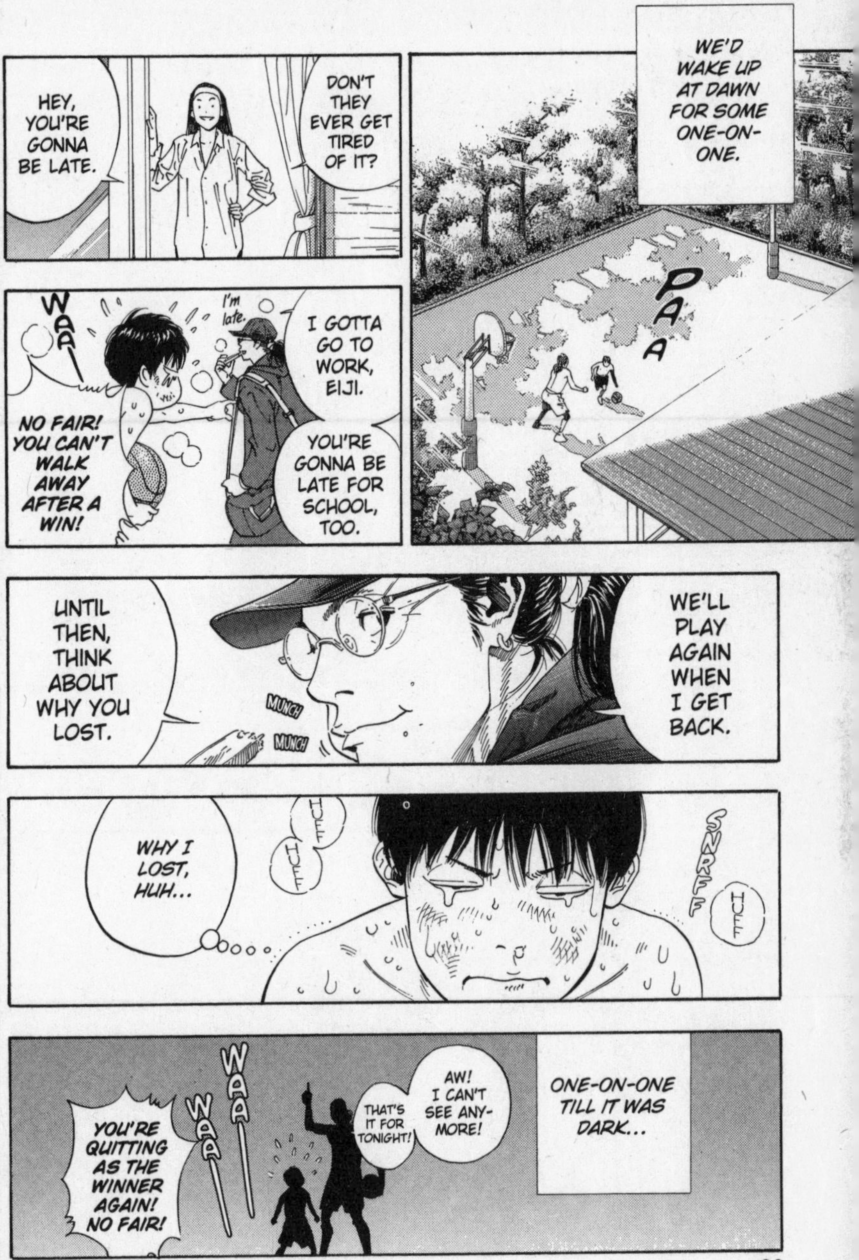

WE'D WAKE UP AT DAWN FOR SOME ONE-ON-ONE.
PAA
DON'T THEY EVER GET TIRED OF IT?
HEY, YOU'RE GONNA BE LATE.
I GOTTA GO TO WORK, EIJI.
YOU'RE GONNA BE LATE FOR SCHOOL, TOO.
I'm late.
WAA
NO FAIR! YOU CAN'T WALK AWAY AFTER A WIN!
WE'LL PLAY AGAIN WHEN I GET BACK.
UNTIL THEN, THINK ABOUT WHY YOU LOST.
MUNCH
MUNCH
SNRFF
HUFF
HUFF
HUFF
WHY I LOST, HUH...
ONE-ON-ONE TILL IT WAS DARK...
AW! I CAN'T SEE ANY-MORE!
THAT'S IT FOR TONIGHT!
WAA
WAA
YOU'RE QUITTING AS THE WINNER AGAIN! NO FAIR!

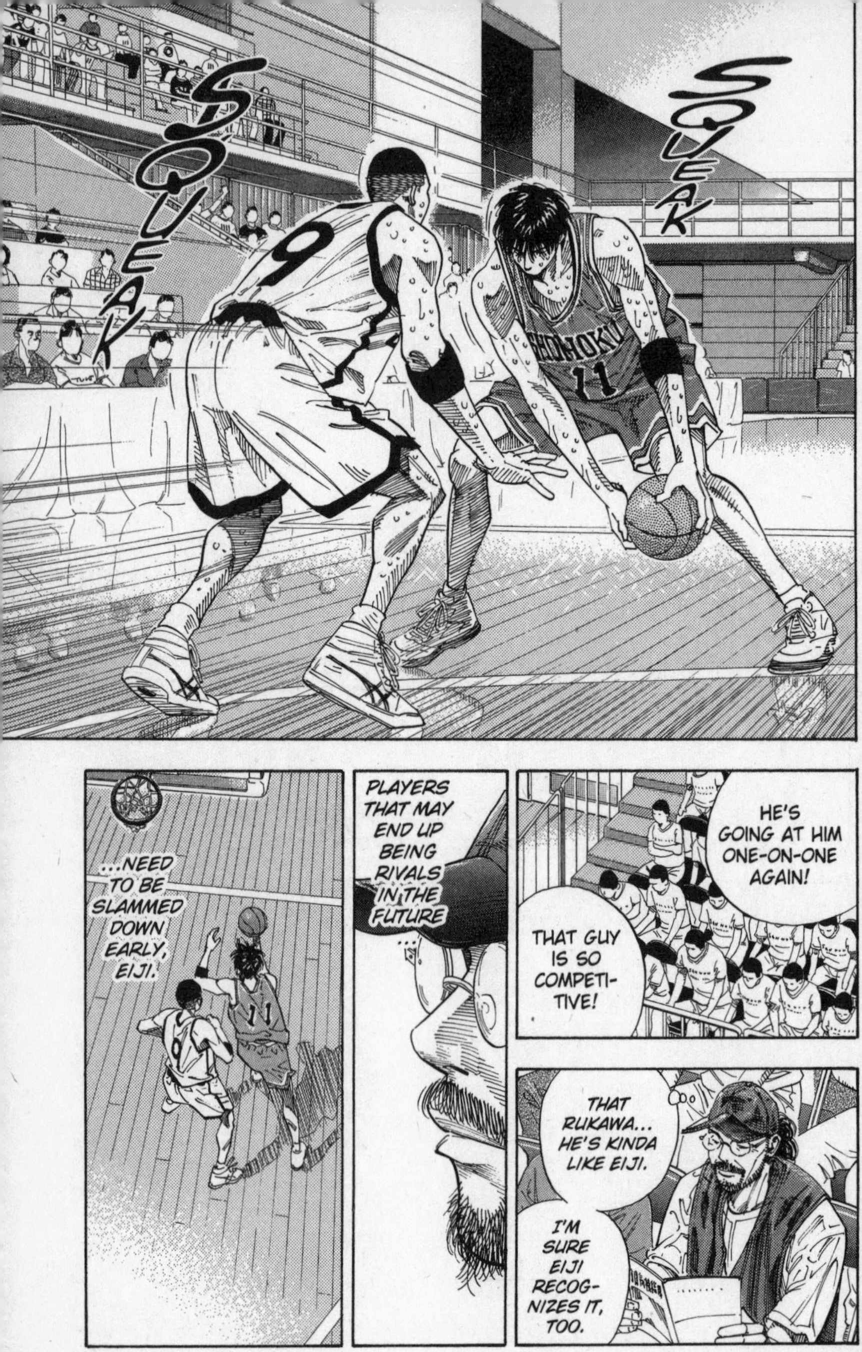
SQUEAK
SQUEAK
HE'S GOING AT HIM ONE-ON-ONE AGAIN!
THAT GUY IS SO COMPETI-TIVE!
THAT RUKAWA... HE'S KINDA LIKE EIJI.
I'M SURE EIJI RECOG-NIZES IT, TOO.
PLAYERS THAT MAY END UP BEING RIVALS IN THE FUTURE...
...NEED TO BE SLAMMED DOWN EARLY, EIJI.

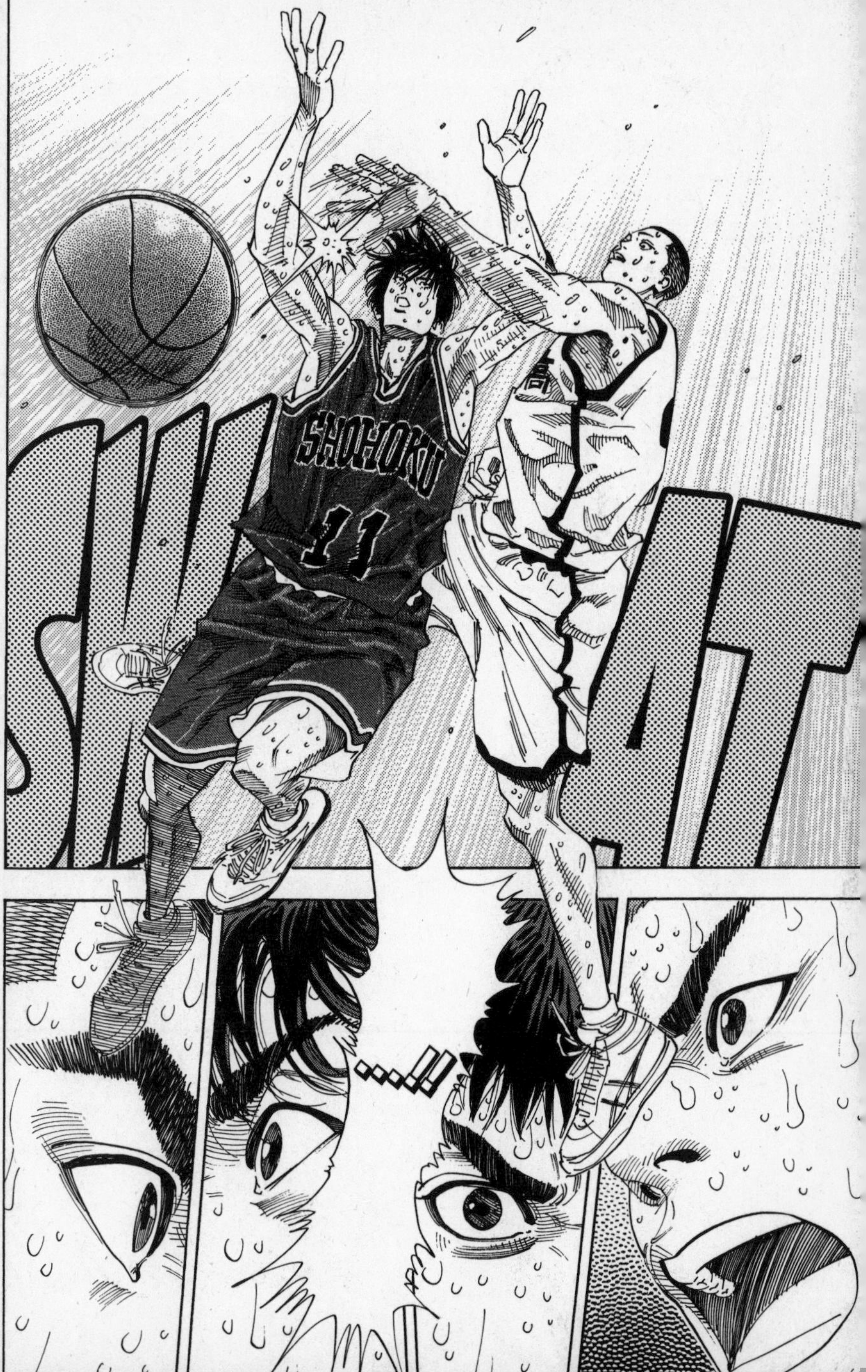
....!!

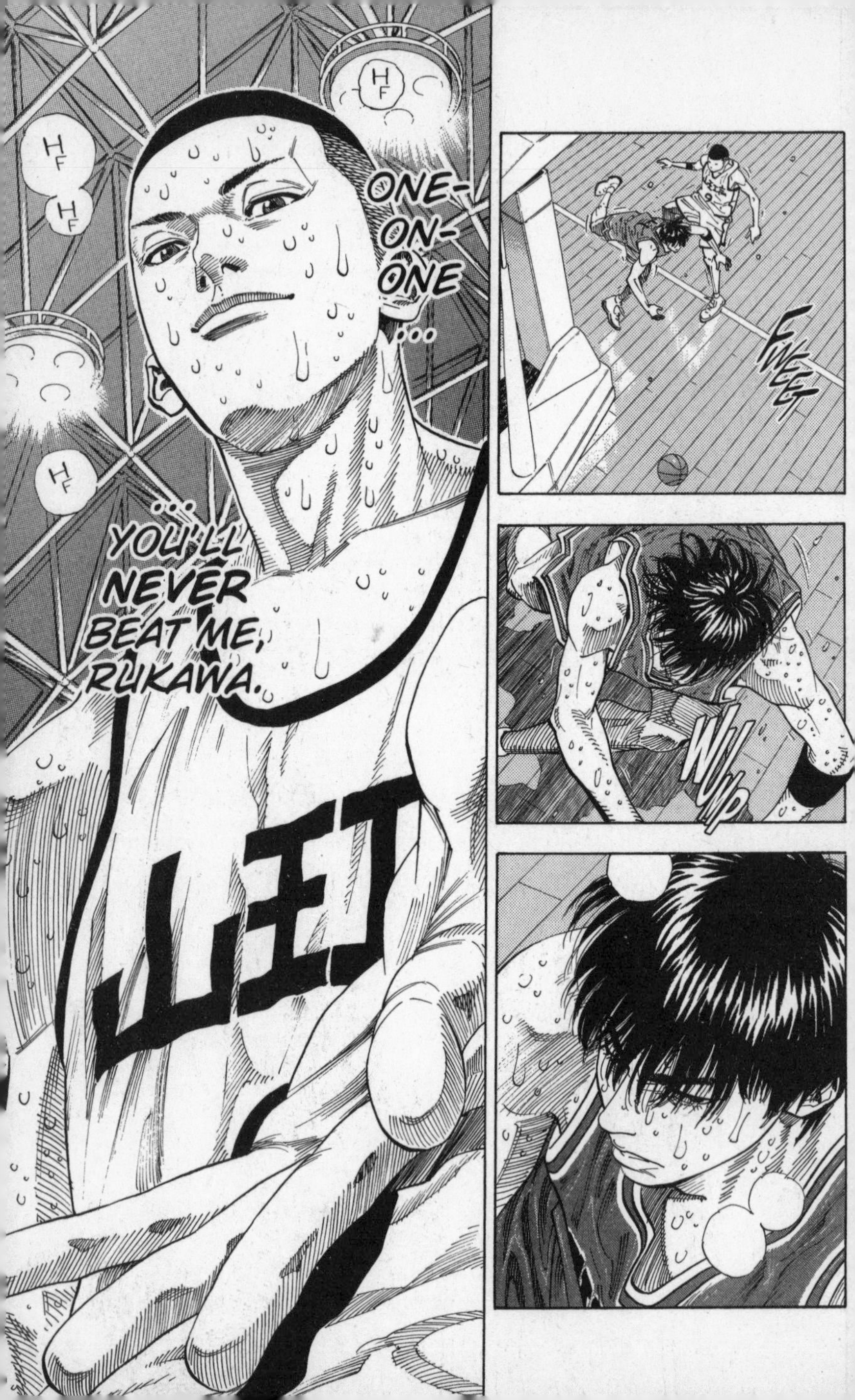
FWEET
WHIP
HF
HF
HF
HF
ONE-ON-ONE...
...YOU'LL NEVER BEAT ME, RUKAWA.

AGE 17
AGE 13
AGE 4

SLAM DUNK

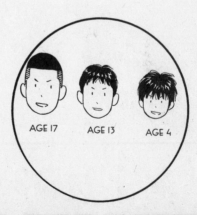

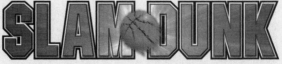

#256 CHALLENGE

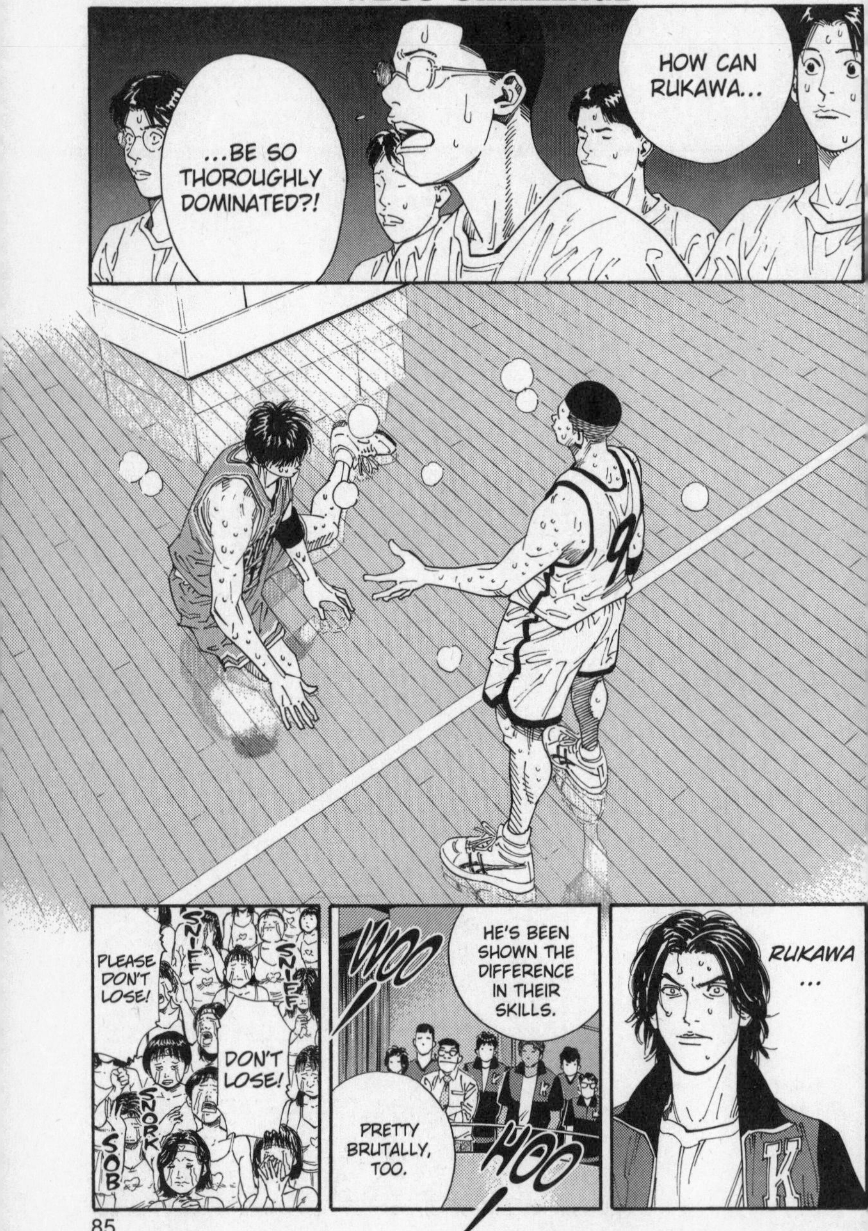

HOW CAN RUKAWA...
...BE SO THOROUGHLY DOMINATED?!
RUKAWA ...
HE'S BEEN SHOWN THE DIFFERENCE IN THEIR SKILLS.
WOO
PRETTY BRUTALLY, TOO.
WOO
SNIFF
PLEASE DON'T LOSE!
SNIFF
DON'T LOSE!
SNORK
SOB

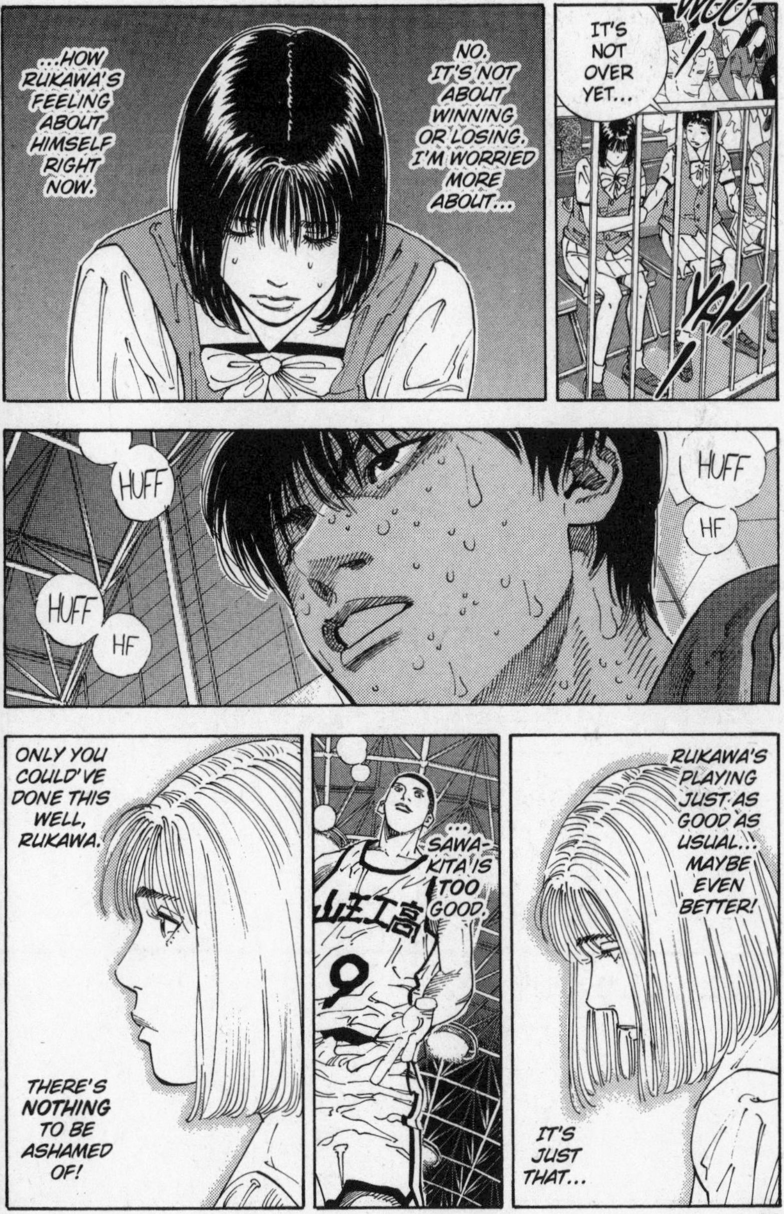
WOO
IT'S NOT OVER YET...
YAH!
NO. IT'S NOT ABOUT WINNING OR LOSING. I'M WORRIED MORE ABOUT...
...HOW RUKAWA'S FEELING ABOUT HIMSELF RIGHT NOW.
HUFF
HF
HUFF
HUFF
HF
RUKAWA'S PLAYING JUST AS GOOD AS USUAL... MAYBE EVEN BETTER!
IT'S JUST THAT...
...SAWAKITA IS TOO GOOD.
山王工高
9
ONLY YOU COULD'VE DONE THIS WELL, RUKAWA.
THERE'S NOTHING TO BE ASHAMED OF!

READ THIS WAY

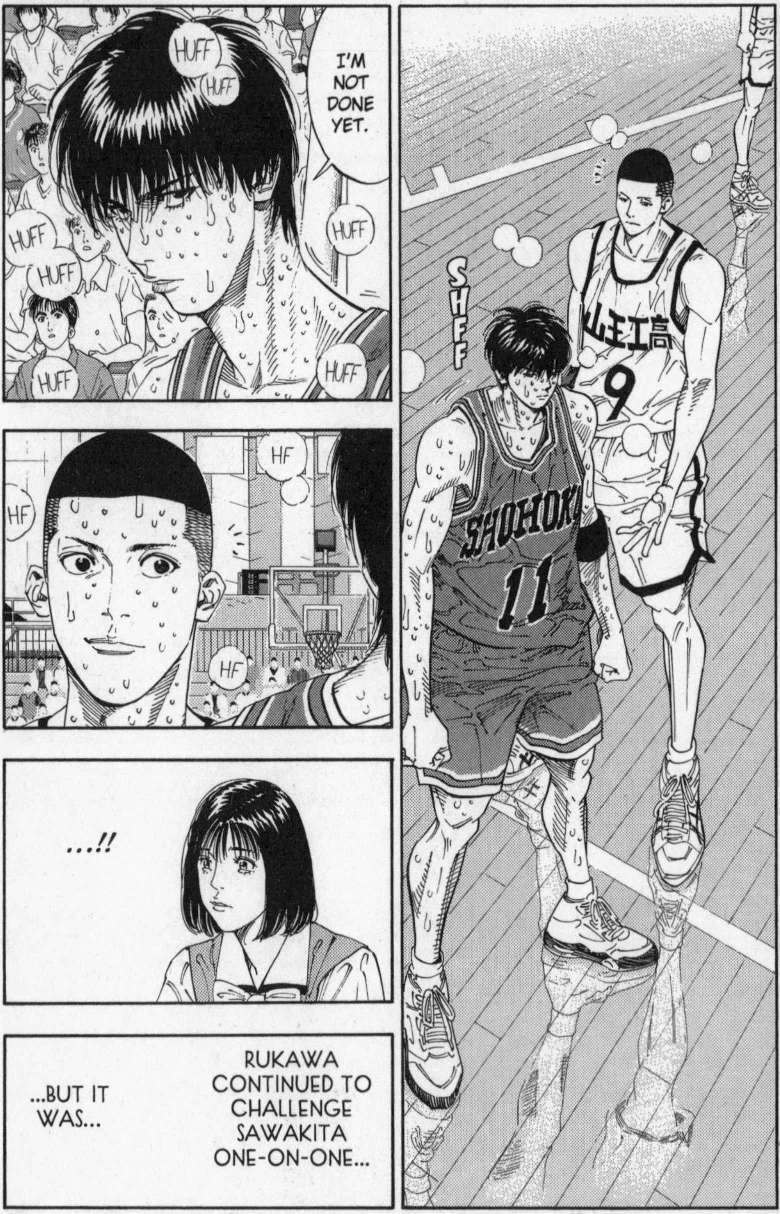
SHFF
山王工高
HUFF
HUFF
I'M NOT DONE YET.
HUFF
HUFF
HUFF
HUFF
HUFF
HF
HF
HF
...!!
RUKAWA CONTINUED TO CHALLENGE SAWAKITA ONE-ON-ONE...
...BUT IT WAS...

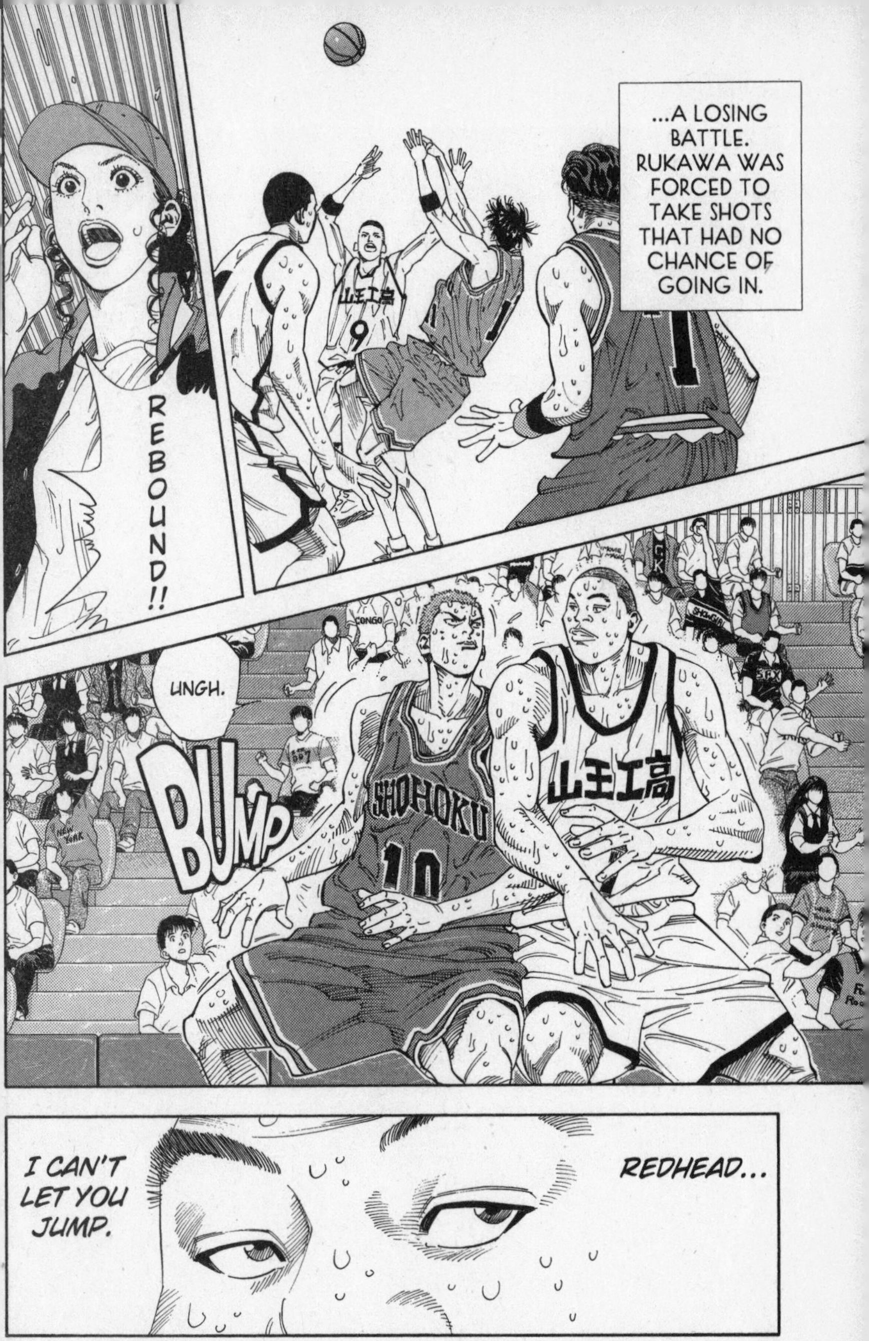
...A LOSING BATTLE. RUKAWA WAS FORCED TO TAKE SHOTS THAT HAD NO CHANCE OF GOING IN.
REBOUND!!
UNGH.
BUMP
REDHEAD...
I CAN'T LET YOU JUMP.

READ THIS WAY

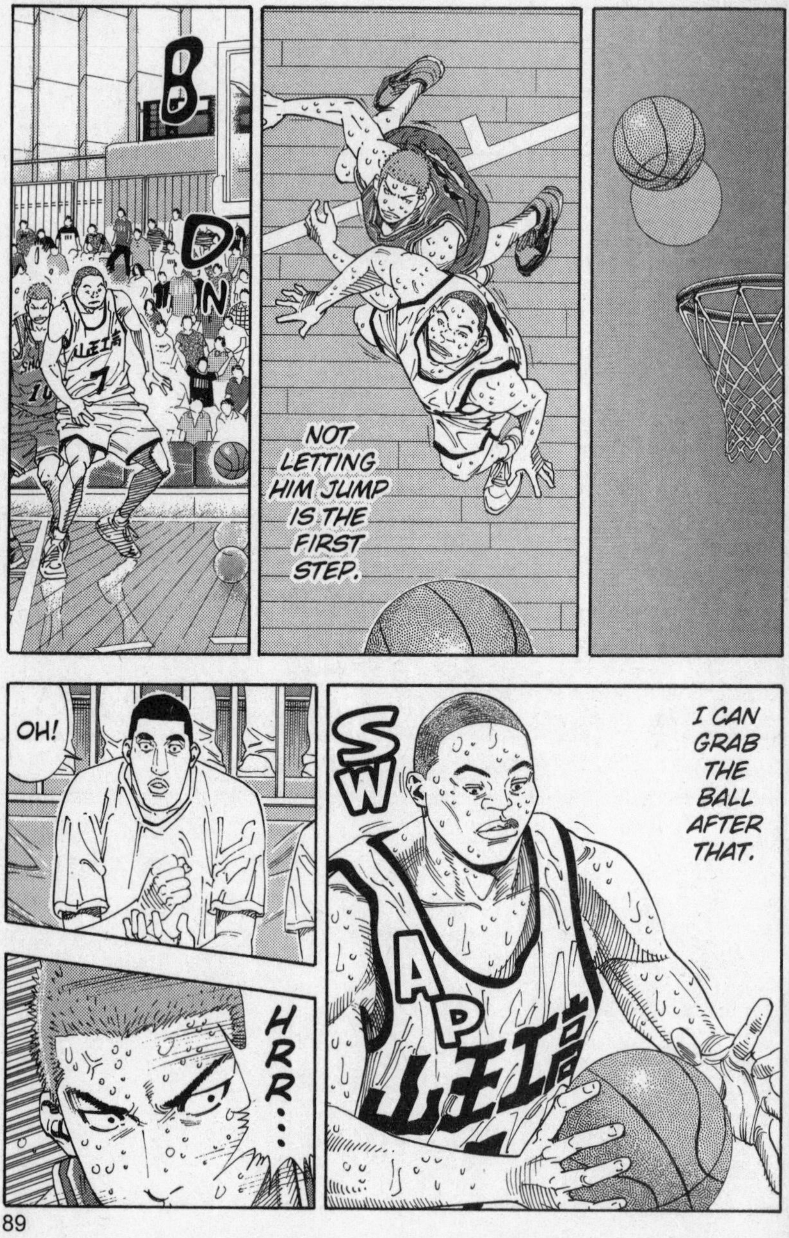
NOT LETTING HIM JUMP IS THE FIRST STEP.
BDN
I CAN GRAB THE BALL AFTER THAT.
SW
AP
OH!
HRR...

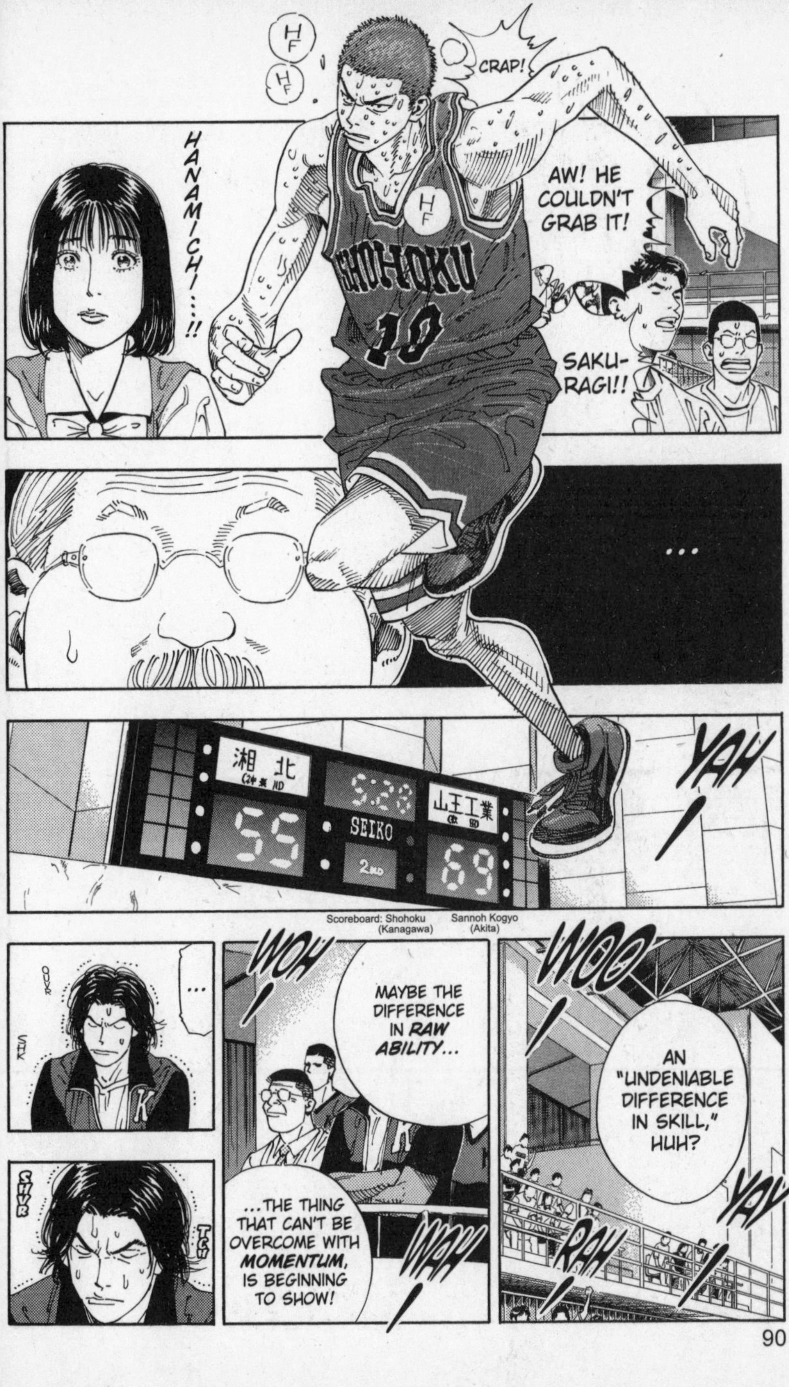
HF
HF
HF
CRAP!
HF
AW! HE COULDN'T GRAB IT!
SAKU-RAGI!!
HANAMICHI...!!
...
YAH!
湘北
SEIKO
山王工業
Scoreboard: Shohoku (Kanagawa) Sannoh Kogyo (Akita)
WOO!
AN "UNDENIABLE DIFFERENCE IN SKILL," HUH?
YAY!
RAH!
WOH!
MAYBE THE DIFFERENCE IN *RAW ABILITY*...
...THE THING THAT CAN'T BE OVERCOME WITH *MOMENTUM*, IS BEGINNING TO SHOW!
WAH!
...
SHK
SHVR
TCH

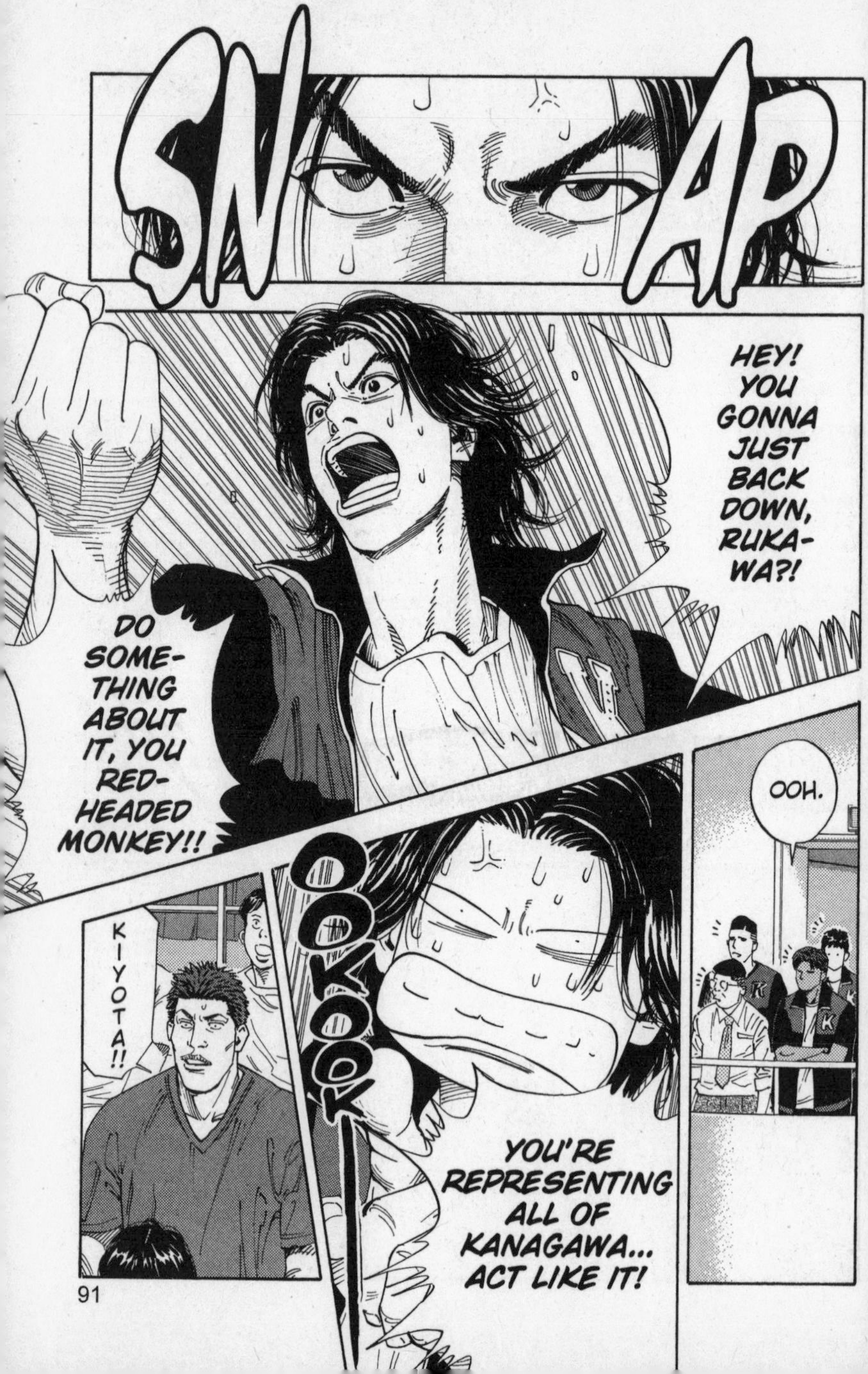
SNAP
HEY! YOU GONNA JUST BACK DOWN, RUKAWA?!
DO SOMETHING ABOUT IT, YOU RED-HEADED MONKEY!!
OOH.
OOKOOK
YOU'RE REPRESENTING ALL OF KANAGAWA... ACT LIKE IT!
KIYOTA!!

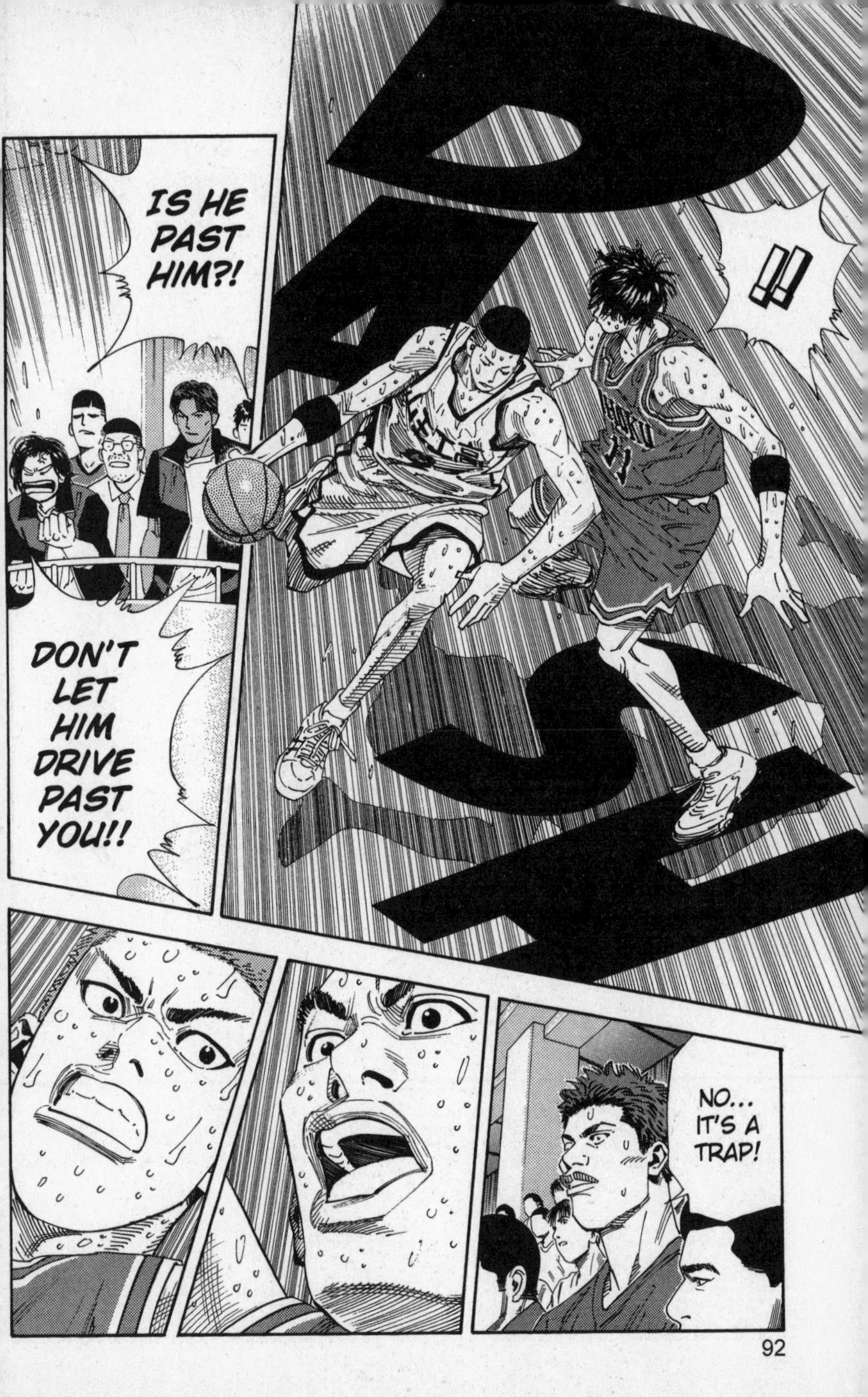
DASH
!!
IS HE PAST HIM?!
DON'T LET HIM DRIVE PAST YOU!!
NO... IT'S A TRAP!

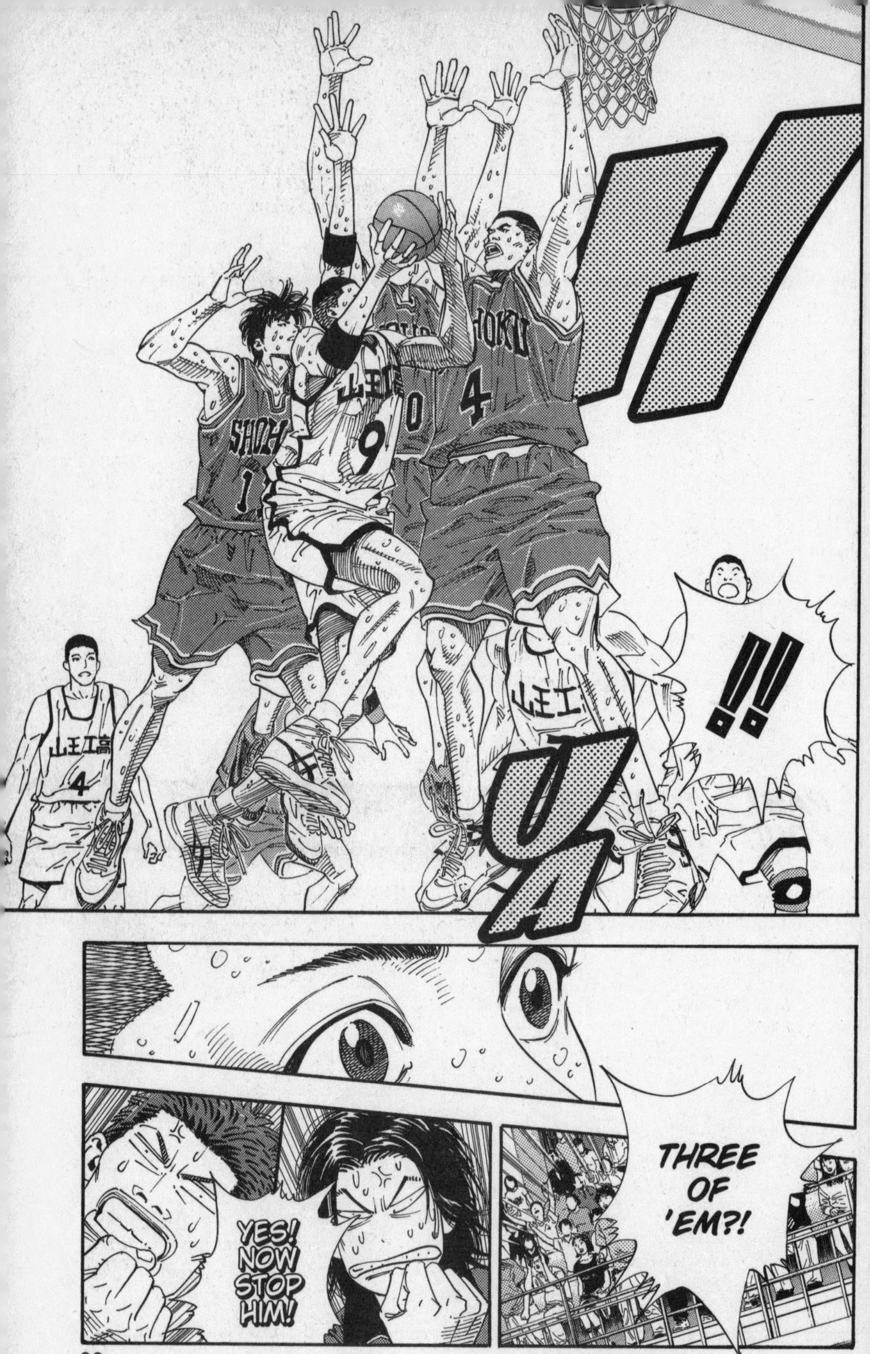
HU
!!
THREE OF 'EM?!
YES! NOW STOP HIM!

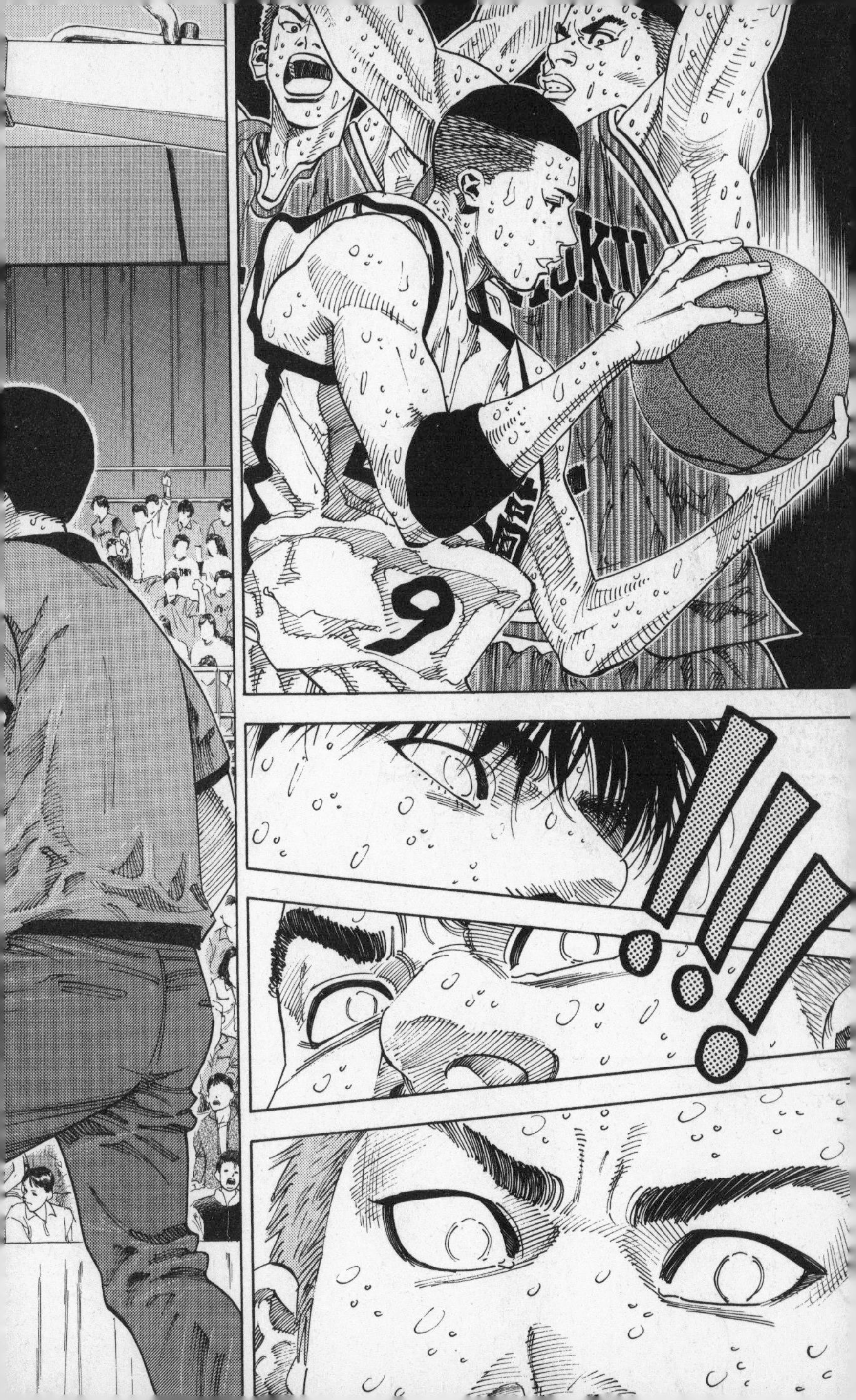

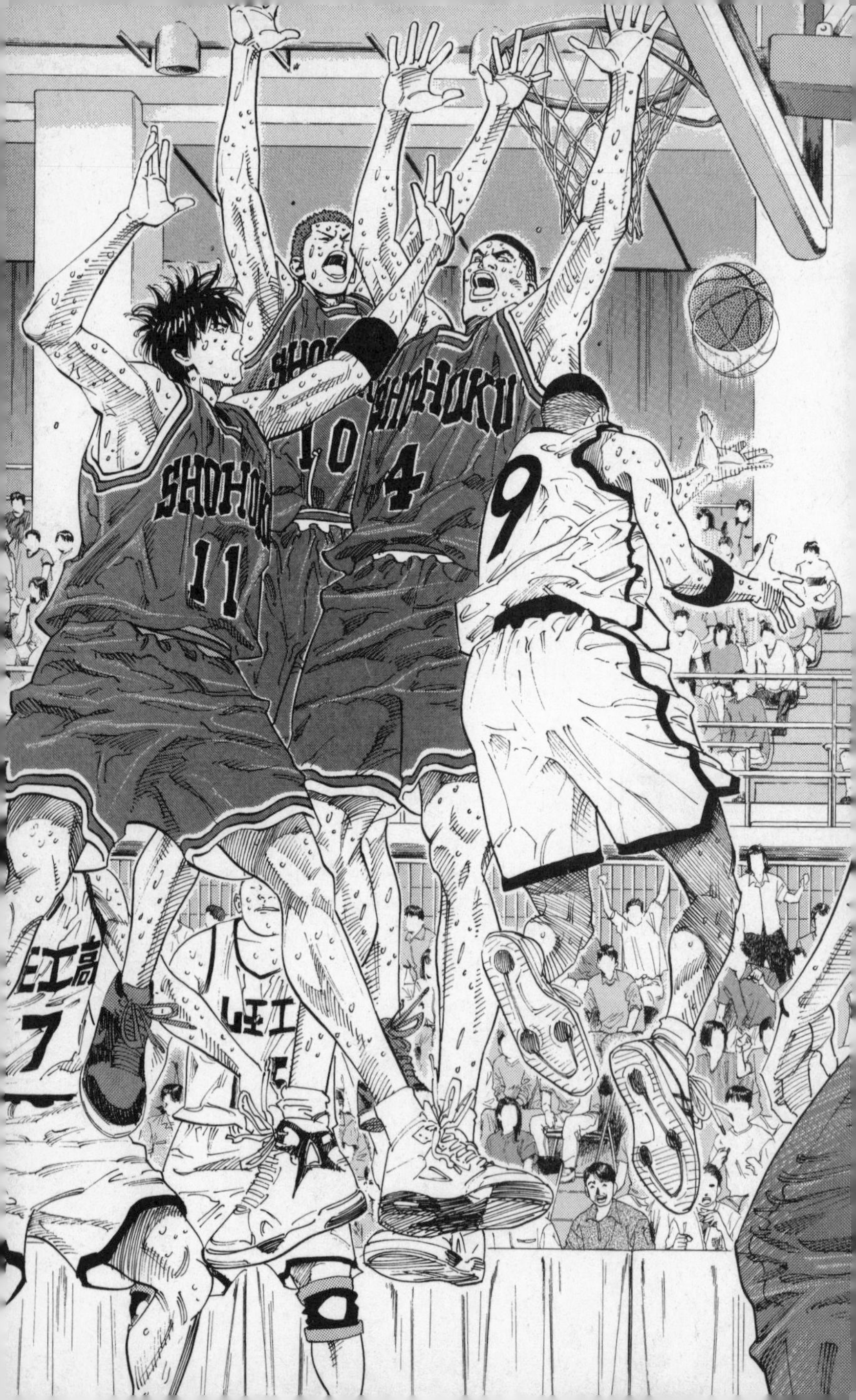

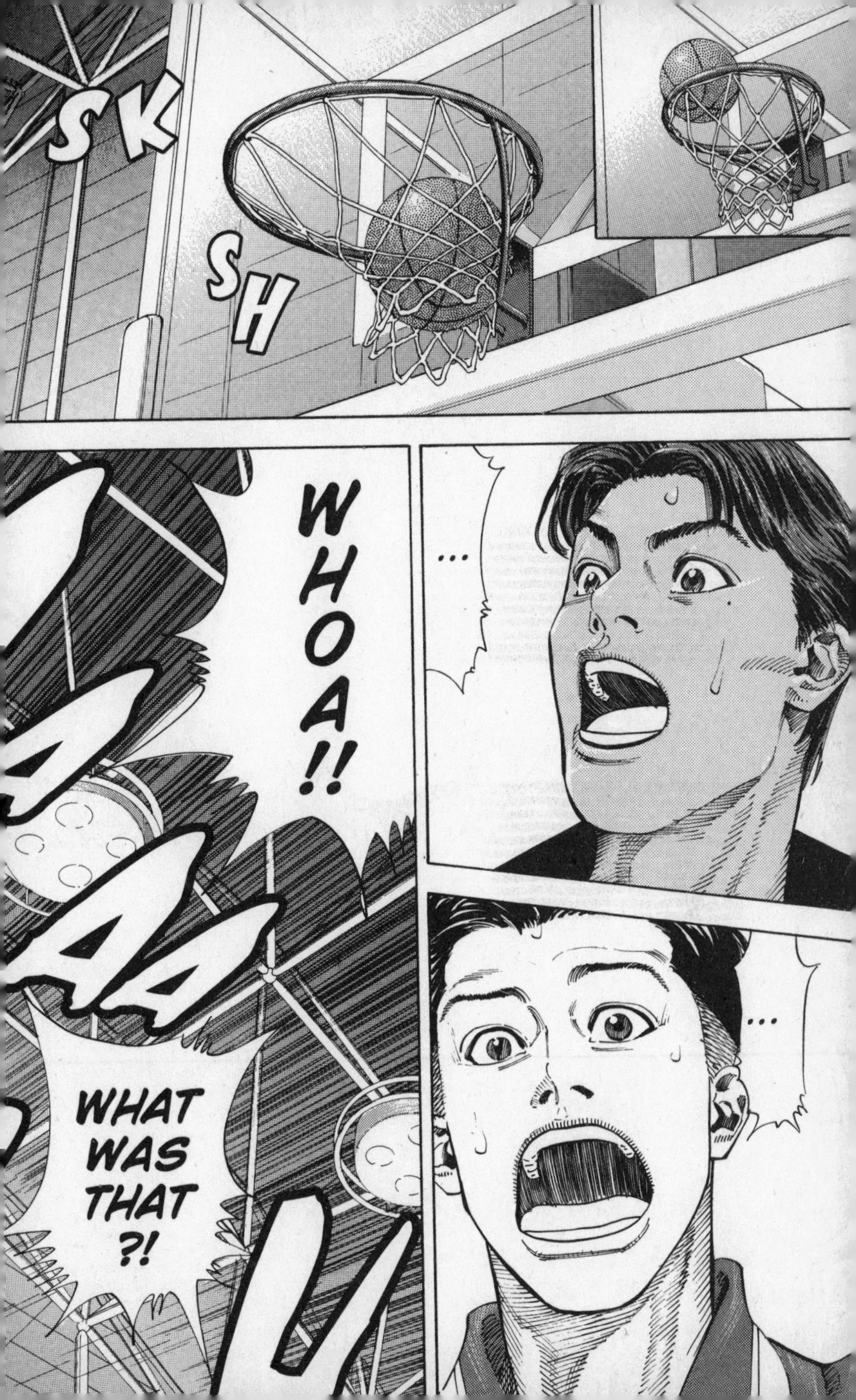
SK
SH
...
...
WHOA!!
WHAT WAS THAT?!

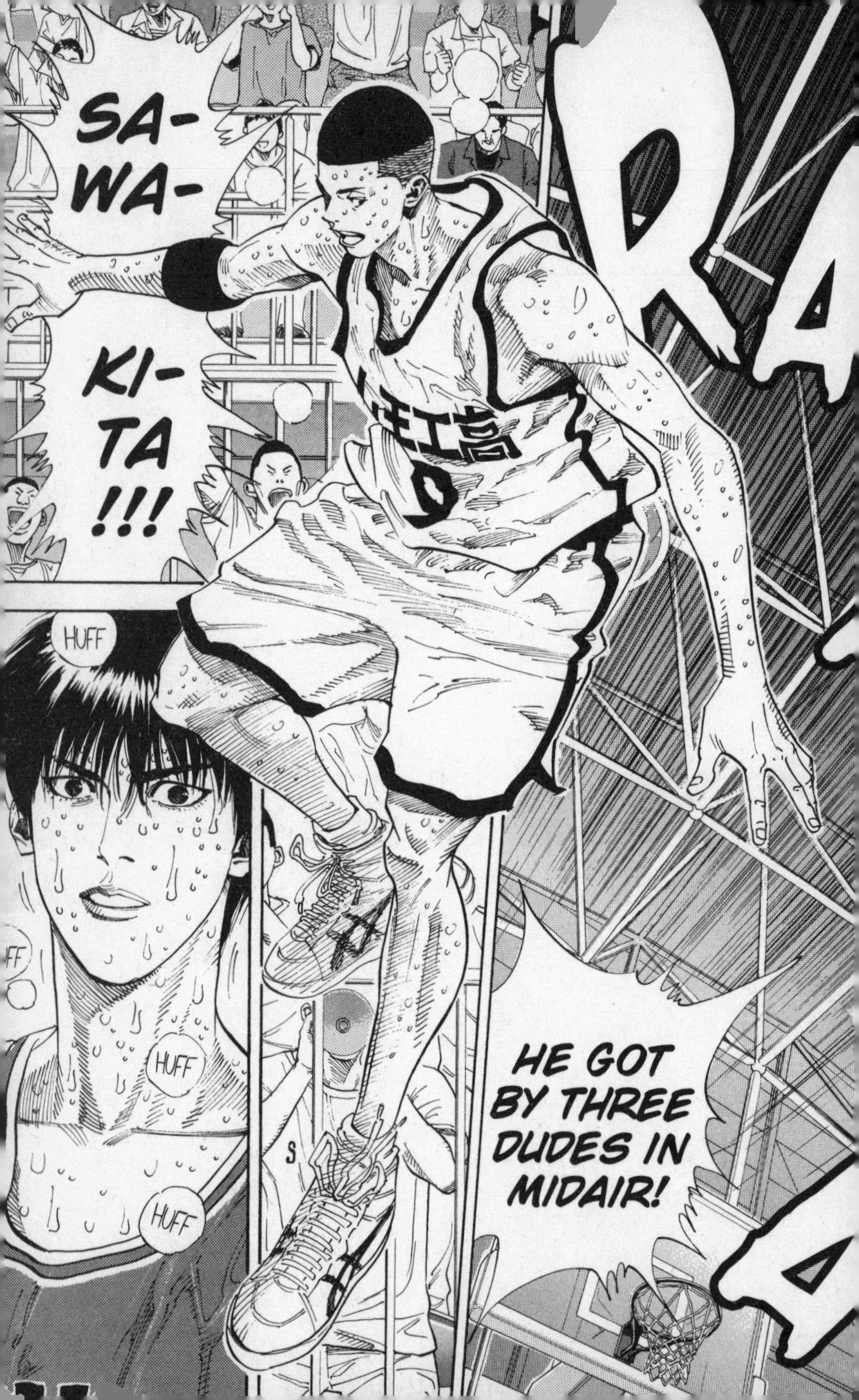
SA-WA-KI-TA!!!
HE GOT BY THREE DUDES IN MIDAIR!
HUFF
HUFF
HUFF

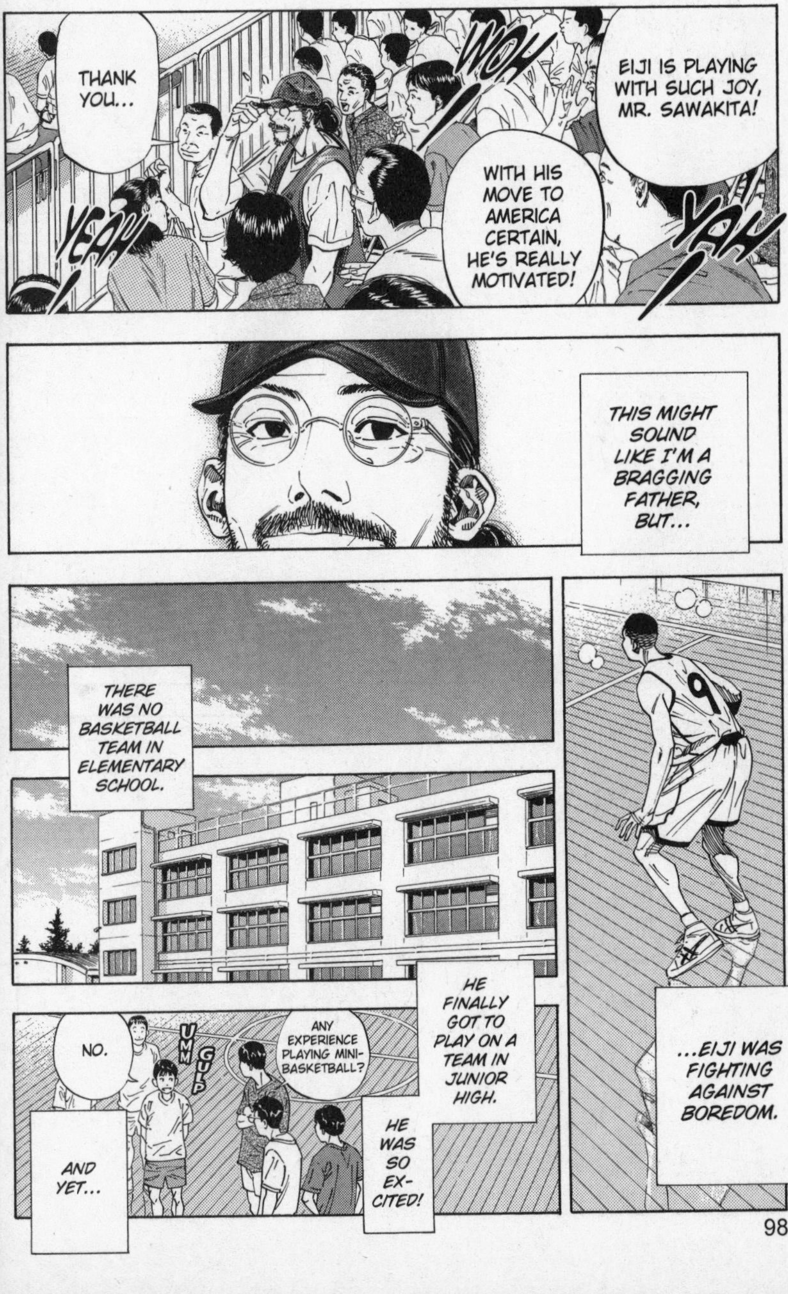
EIJI IS PLAYING WITH SUCH JOY, MR. SAWAKITA!
YAH
WOH
WITH HIS MOVE TO AMERICA CERTAIN, HE'S REALLY MOTIVATED!
THANK YOU...
YEAH
THIS MIGHT SOUND LIKE I'M A BRAGGING FATHER, BUT...
...EIJI WAS FIGHTING AGAINST BOREDOM.
THERE WAS NO BASKETBALL TEAM IN ELEMENTARY SCHOOL.
HE FINALLY GOT TO PLAY ON A TEAM IN JUNIOR HIGH.
HE WAS SO EX-CITED!
ANY EXPERIENCE PLAYING MINI-BASKETBALL?
UMM
GULP
NO.
AND YET...

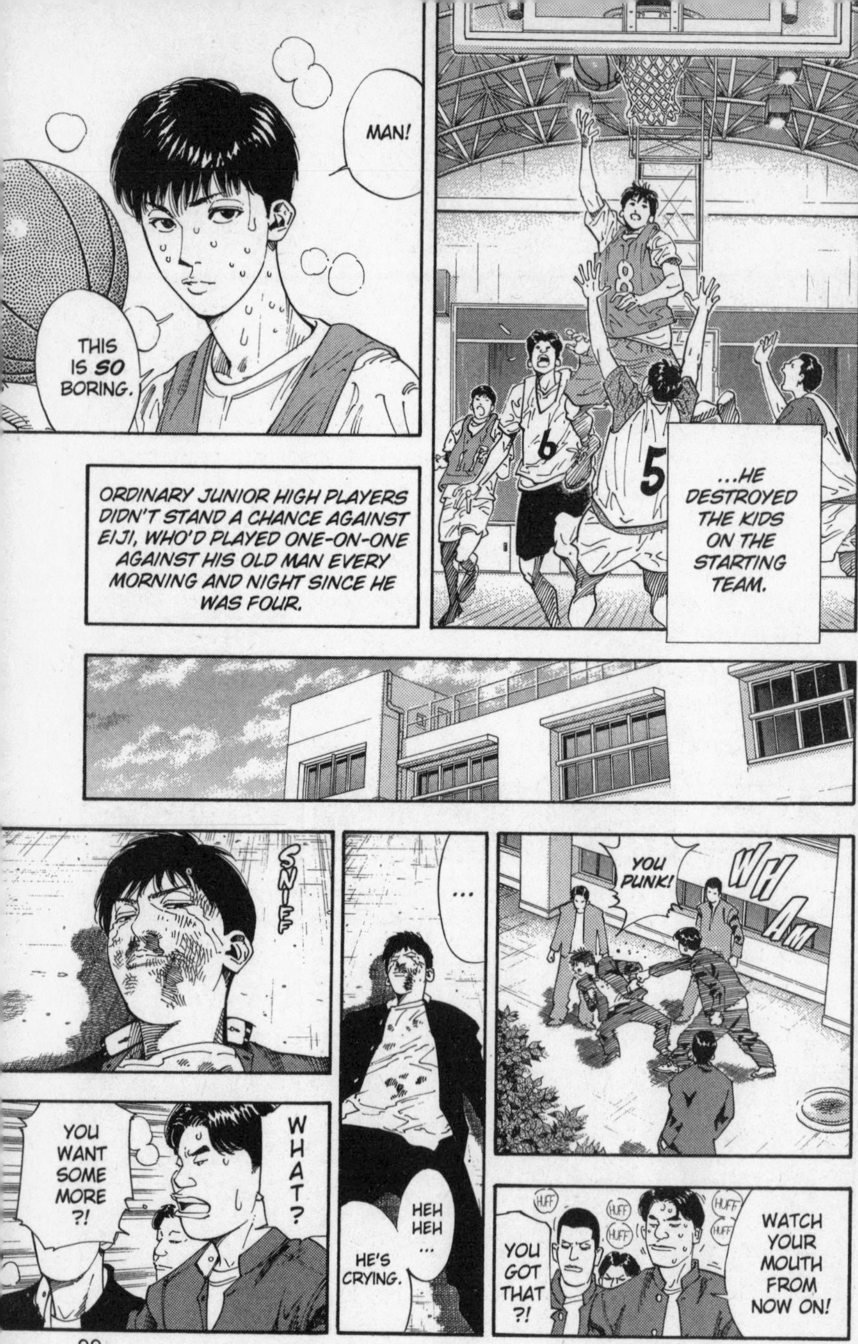
...HE DESTROYED THE KIDS ON THE STARTING TEAM.
MAN!
THIS IS SO BORING.
ORDINARY JUNIOR HIGH PLAYERS DIDN'T STAND A CHANCE AGAINST EIJI, WHO'D PLAYED ONE-ON-ONE AGAINST HIS OLD MAN EVERY MORNING AND NIGHT SINCE HE WAS FOUR.
WHAM
YOU PUNK!
WATCH YOUR MOUTH FROM NOW ON!
HUFF
HUFF
HUFF
HUFF
HUFF
YOU GOT THAT ?!
...
HEH HEH ...
HE'S CRYING.
SNIFF
WHAT?
YOU WANT SOME MORE ?!

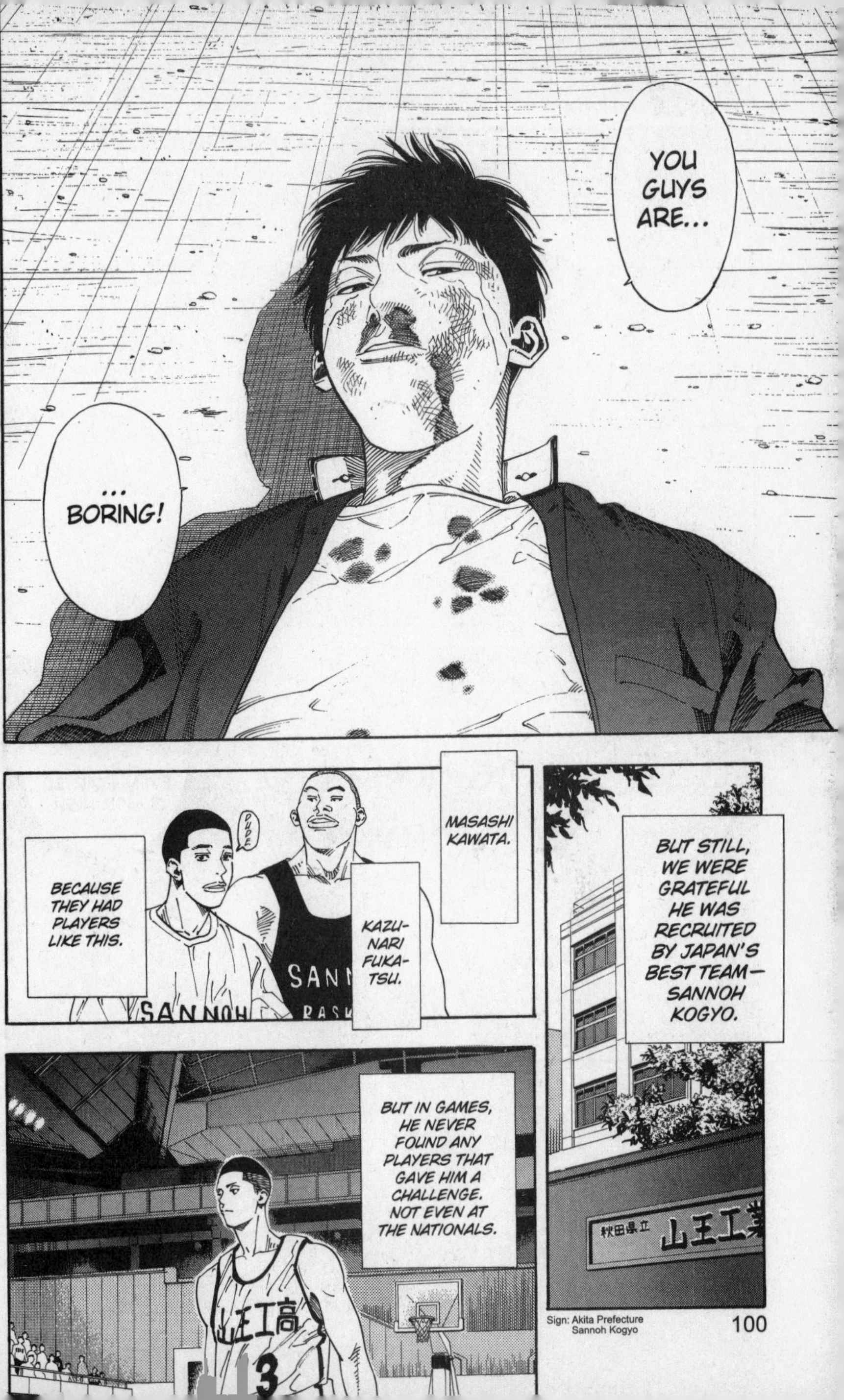
YOU GUYS ARE...
...BORING!
BUT STILL, WE WERE GRATEFUL HE WAS RECRUITED BY JAPAN'S BEST TEAM—SANNOH KOGYO.
秋田県立
MASASHI KAWATA.
DUDE
KAZUNARI FUKATSU.
BECAUSE THEY HAD PLAYERS LIKE THIS.
BUT IN GAMES, HE NEVER FOUND ANY PLAYERS THAT GAVE HIM A CHALLENGE. NOT EVEN AT THE NATIONALS.
山王工高
Sign: Akita Prefecture Sannoh Kogyo

READ THIS WAY

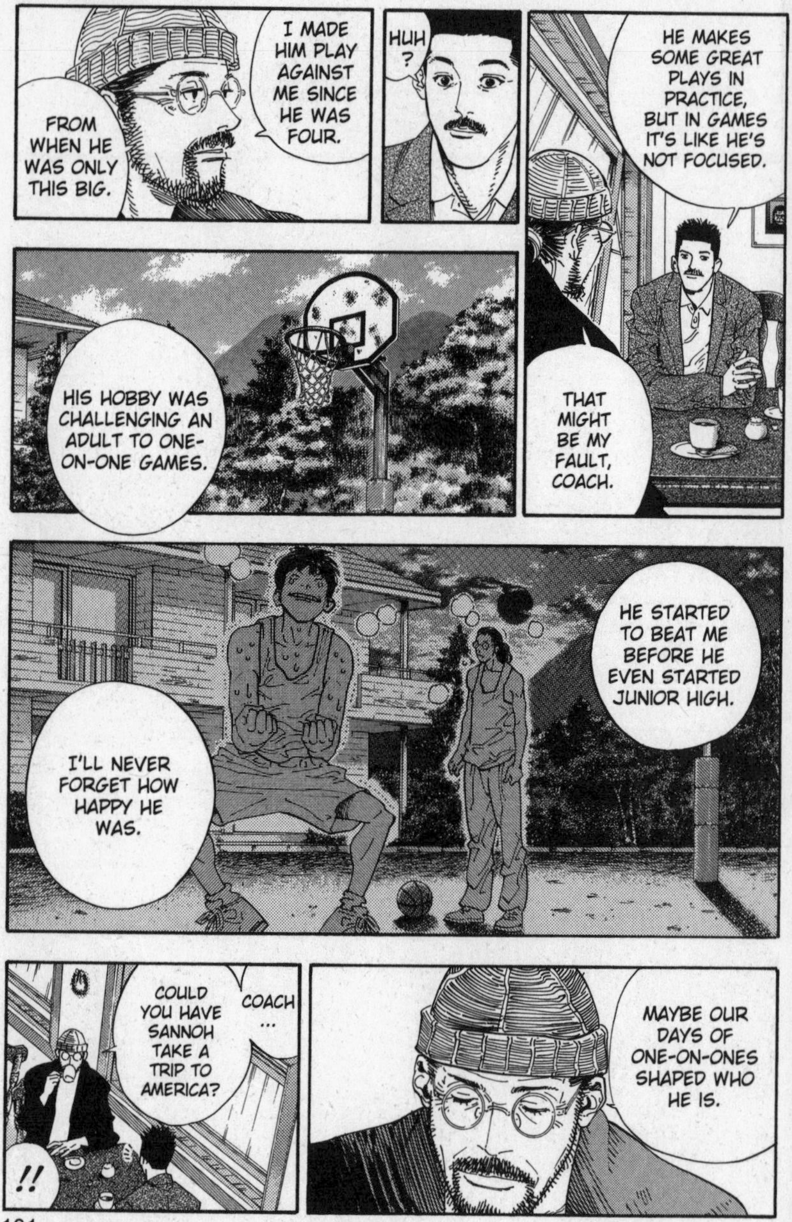
HE MAKES SOME GREAT PLAYS IN PRACTICE, BUT IN GAMES IT'S LIKE HE'S NOT FOCUSED.
THAT MIGHT BE MY FAULT, COACH.
HUH?
I MADE HIM PLAY AGAINST ME SINCE HE WAS FOUR.
FROM WHEN HE WAS ONLY THIS BIG.
HIS HOBBY WAS CHALLENGING AN ADULT TO ONE-ON-ONE GAMES.
HE STARTED TO BEAT ME BEFORE HE EVEN STARTED JUNIOR HIGH.
I'LL NEVER FORGET HOW HAPPY HE WAS.
MAYBE OUR DAYS OF ONE-ON-ONES SHAPED WHO HE IS.
COACH ...
COULD YOU HAVE SANNOH TAKE A TRIP TO AMERICA?
!!

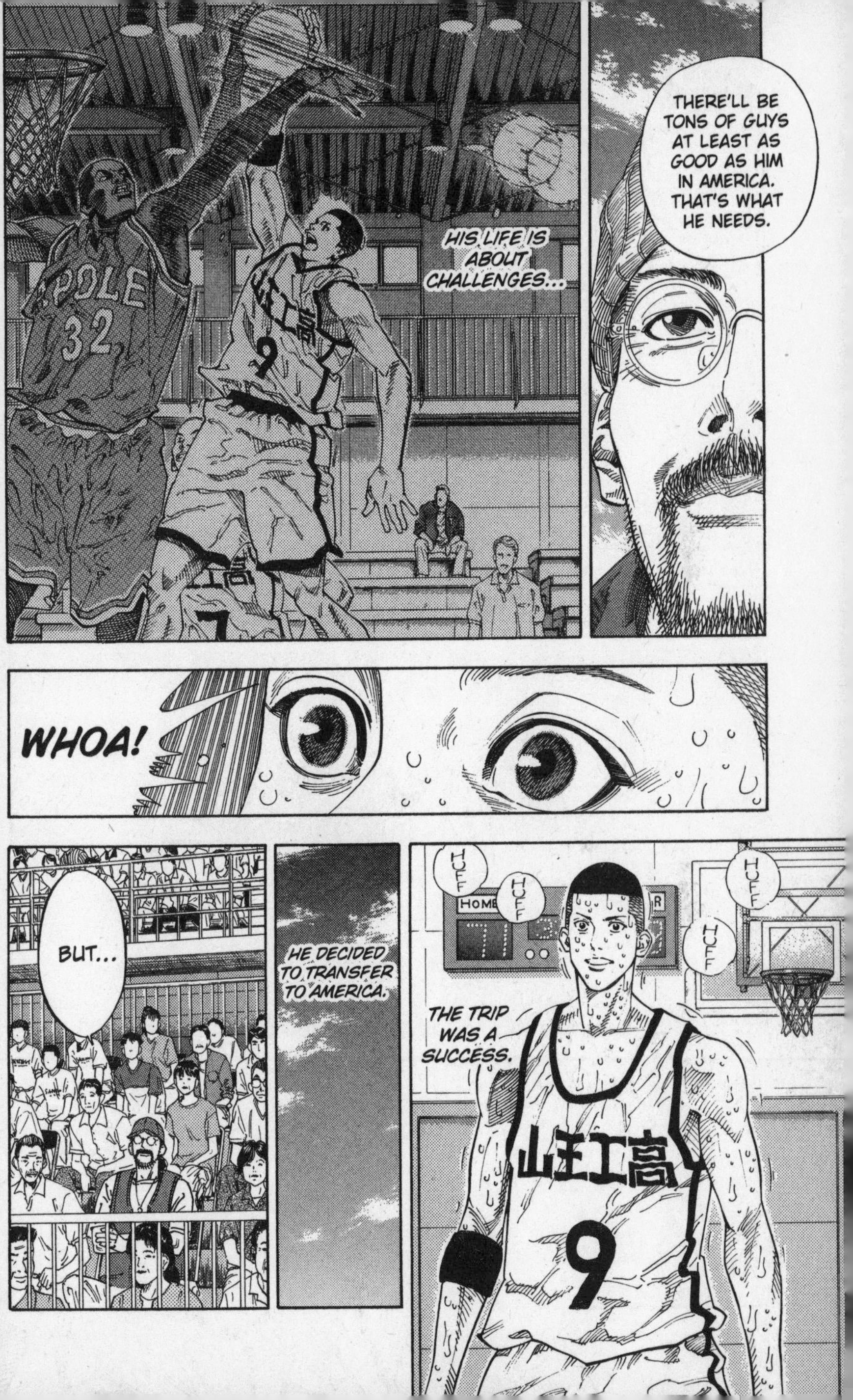
THERE'LL BE TONS OF GUYS AT LEAST AS GOOD AS HIM IN AMERICA. THAT'S WHAT HE NEEDS.
HIS LIFE IS ABOUT CHALLENGES...
WHOA!
HUFF
HUFF
HUFF
HUFF
THE TRIP WAS A SUCCESS.
山王工高
HE DECIDED TO TRANSFER TO AMERICA.
BUT...

READ THIS WAY

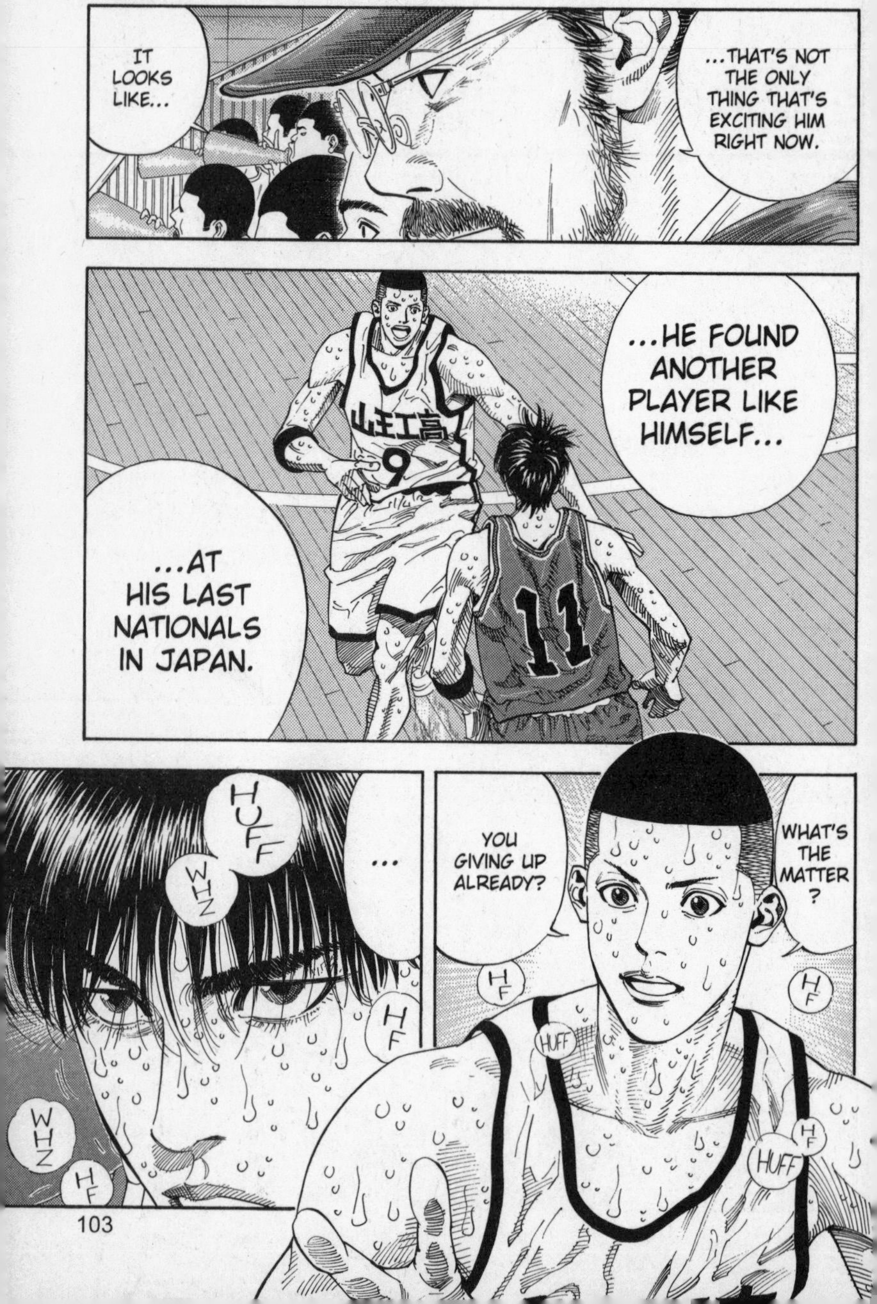
IT LOOKS LIKE...
...THAT'S NOT THE ONLY THING THAT'S EXCITING HIM RIGHT NOW.
...HE FOUND ANOTHER PLAYER LIKE HIMSELF...
...AT HIS LAST NATIONALS IN JAPAN.
WHAT'S THE MATTER?
YOU GIVING UP ALREADY?
HF
HF
HUFF
HF
HUFF
...
HUFF
WHZ
HF
WHZ
HF

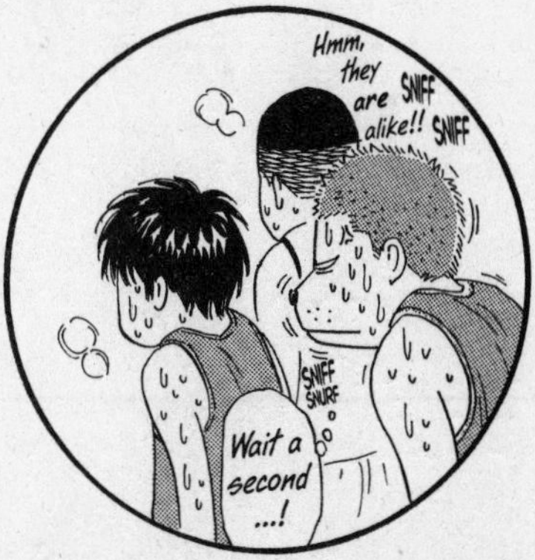
Hmm, they are alike!!
SNIFF
SNIFF
SNIFF
SNURF
Wait a second ....!

SLAM DUNK

#257 CHALLENGE 2

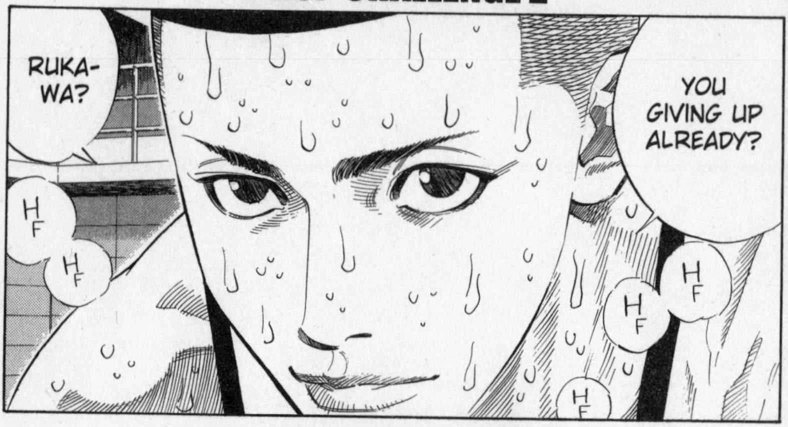
YOU GIVING UP ALREADY?
HF
HF
HF
RUKA-WA?
HF
HF

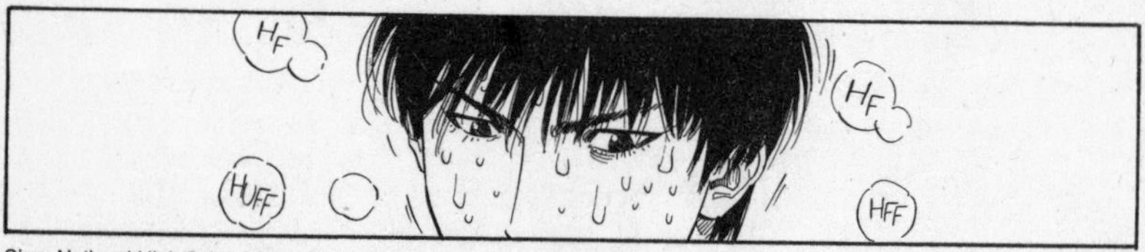
HF
HFF
HF
HUFF

Sign: National High School Basketball Championship Tournament

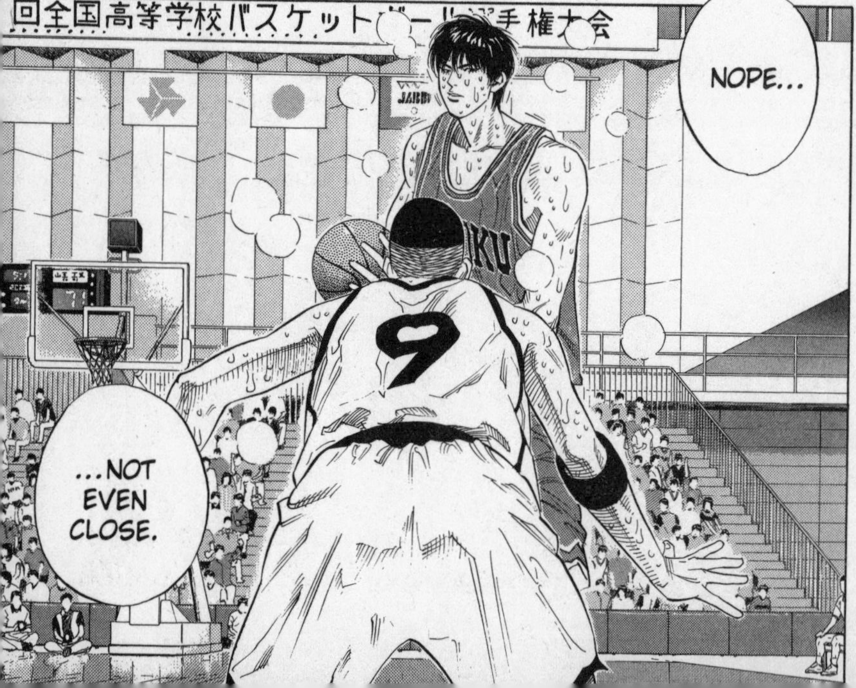
NOPE...
...NOT EVEN CLOSE.

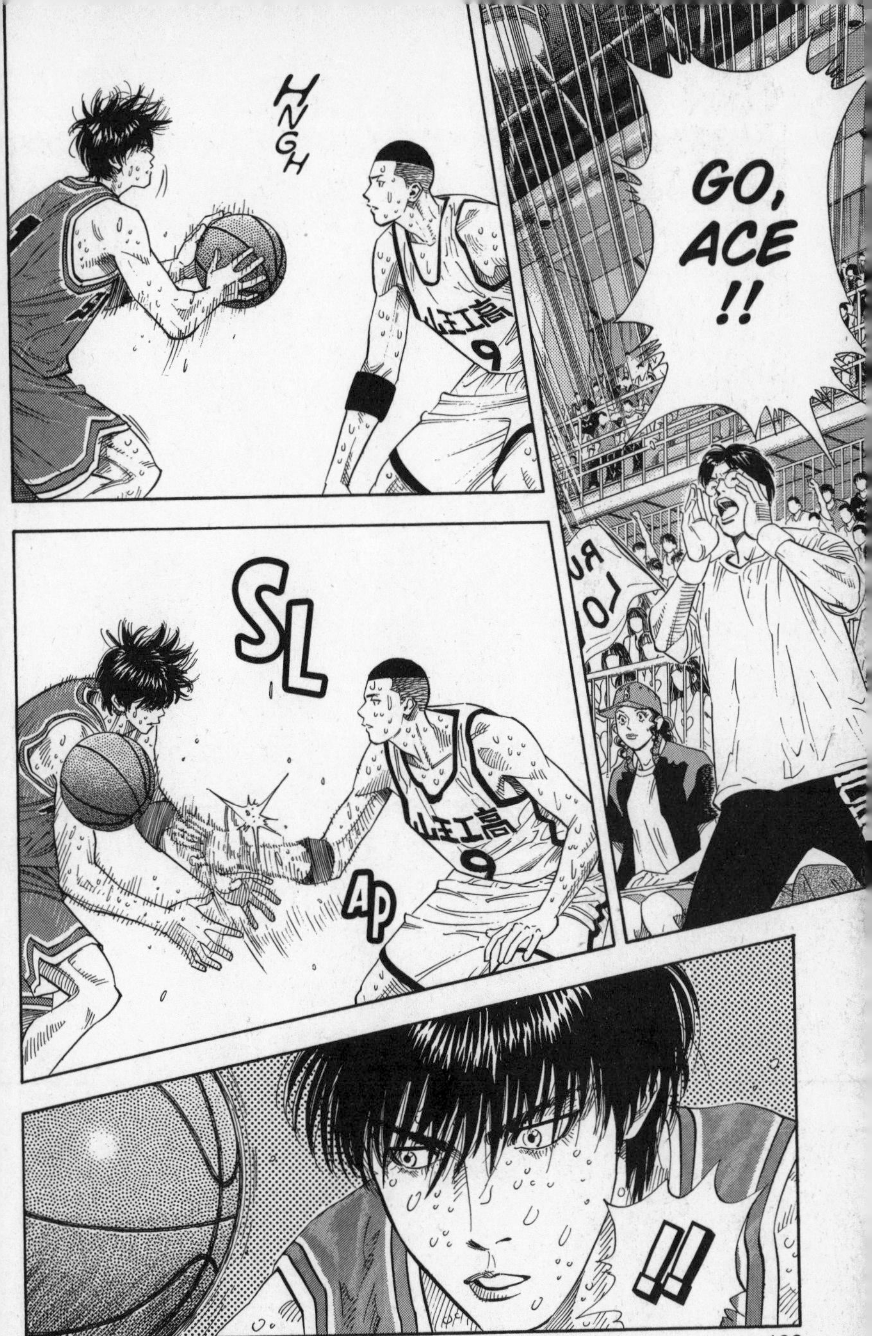
GO, ACE !!
HNGH
SL
AP
!!

READ THIS WAY

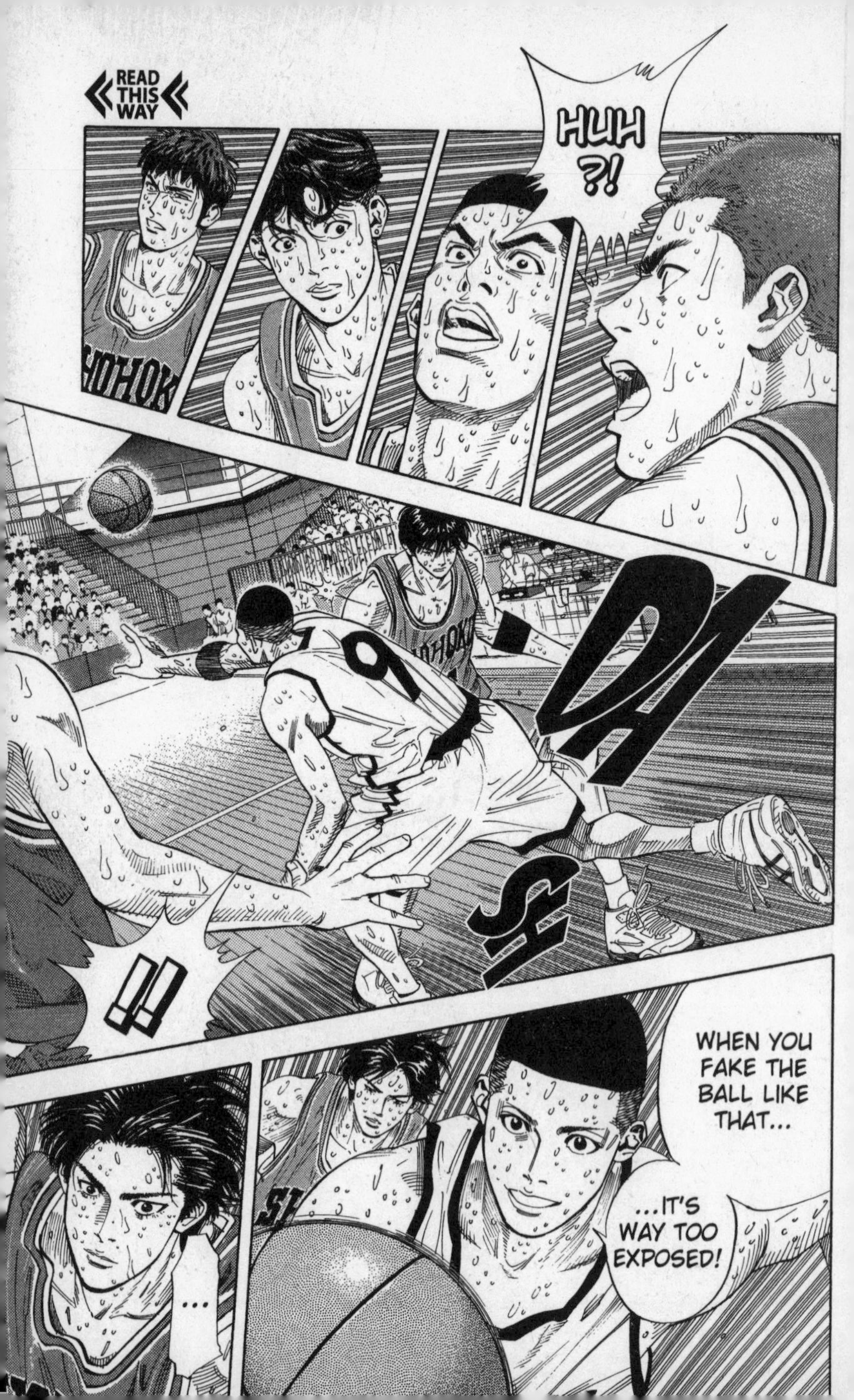
HUH ?!
DASH
!!
WHEN YOU FAKE THE BALL LIKE THAT...
...IT'S WAY TOO EXPOSED!
...

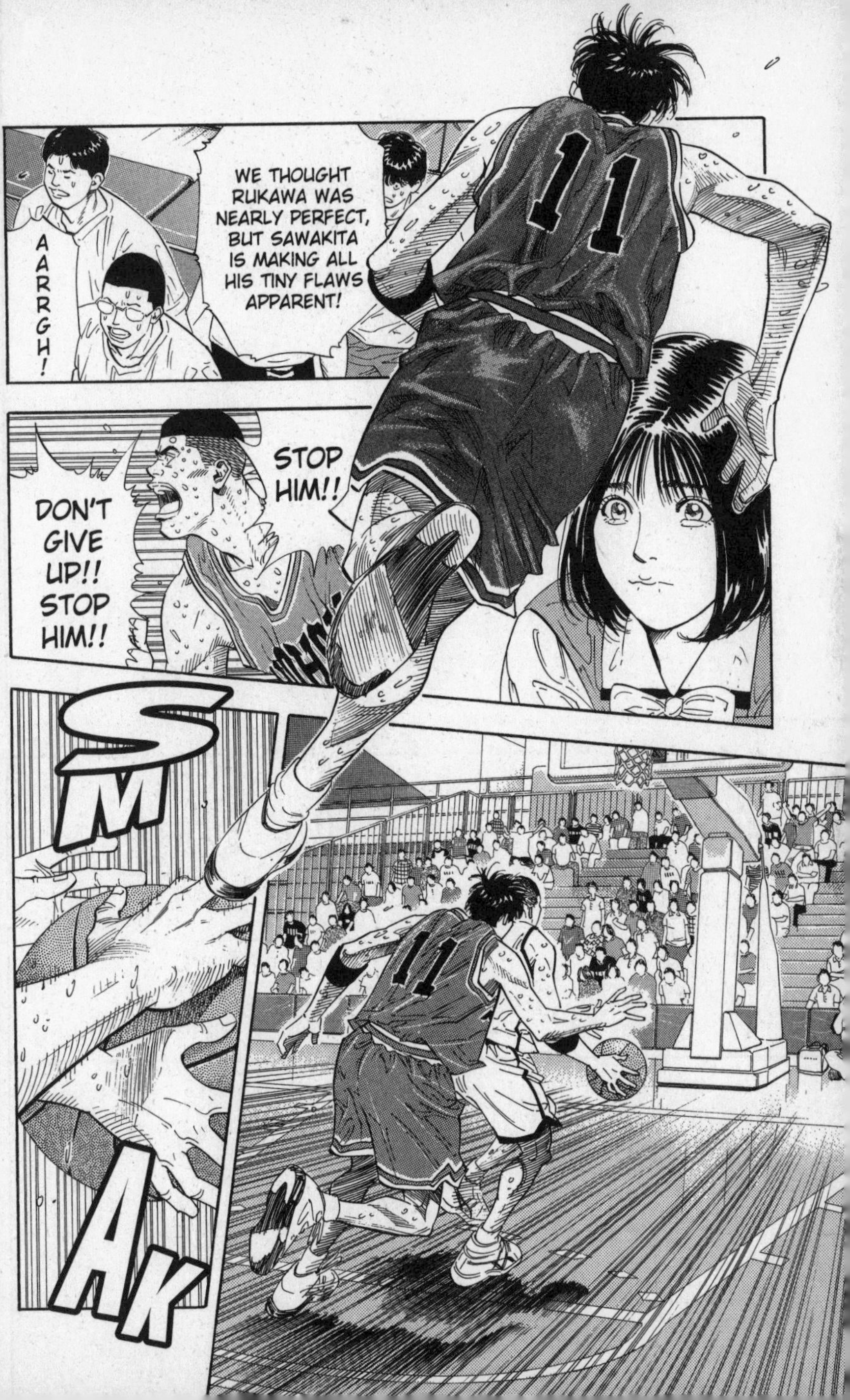
WE THOUGHT RUKAWA WAS NEARLY PERFECT, BUT SAWAKITA IS MAKING ALL HIS TINY FLAWS APPARENT!
AARRGH!
STOP HIM!!
DON'T GIVE UP!! STOP HIM!!
SMACK

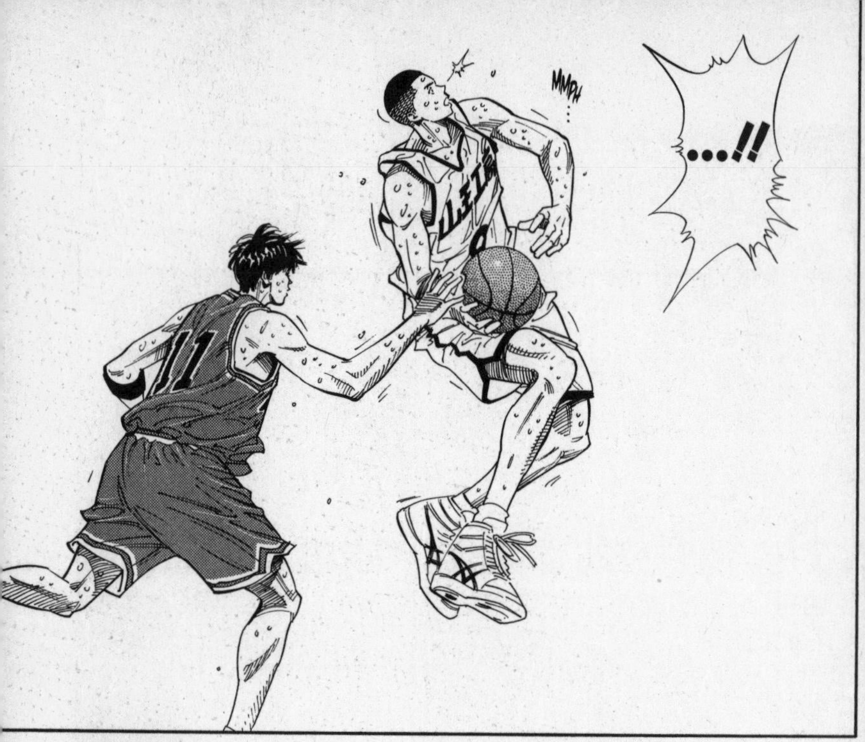
...!!
MMPH...
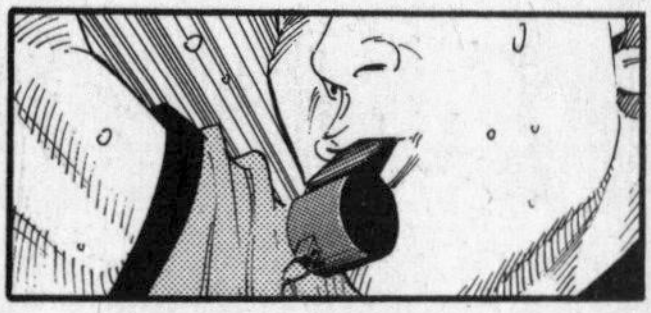
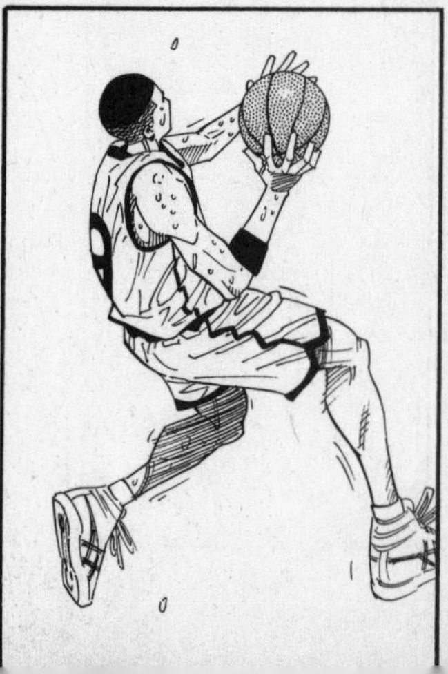
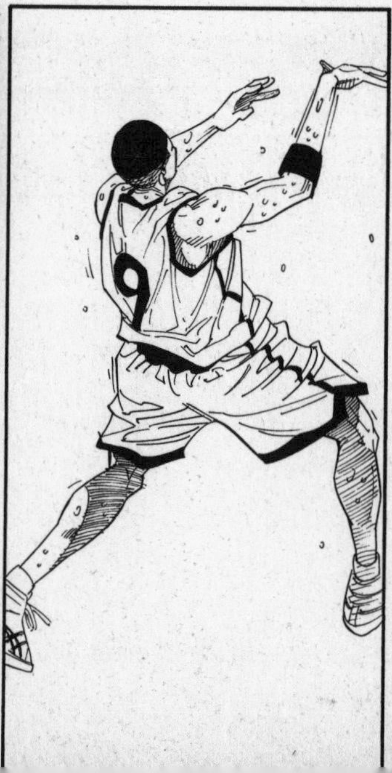
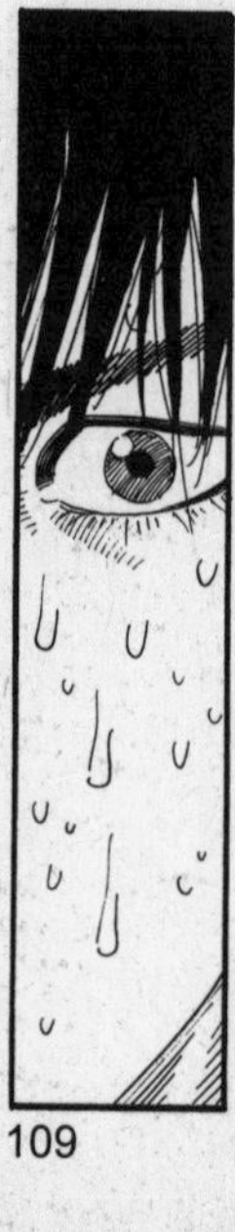

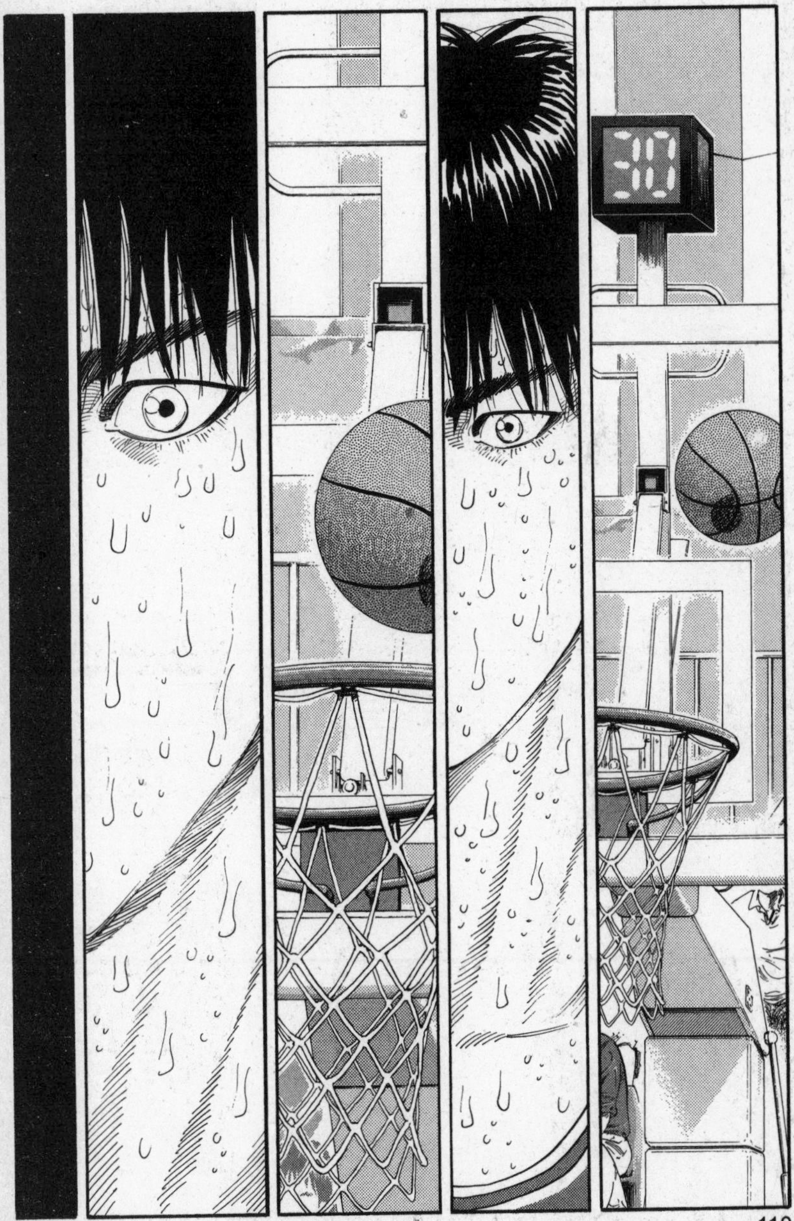
30

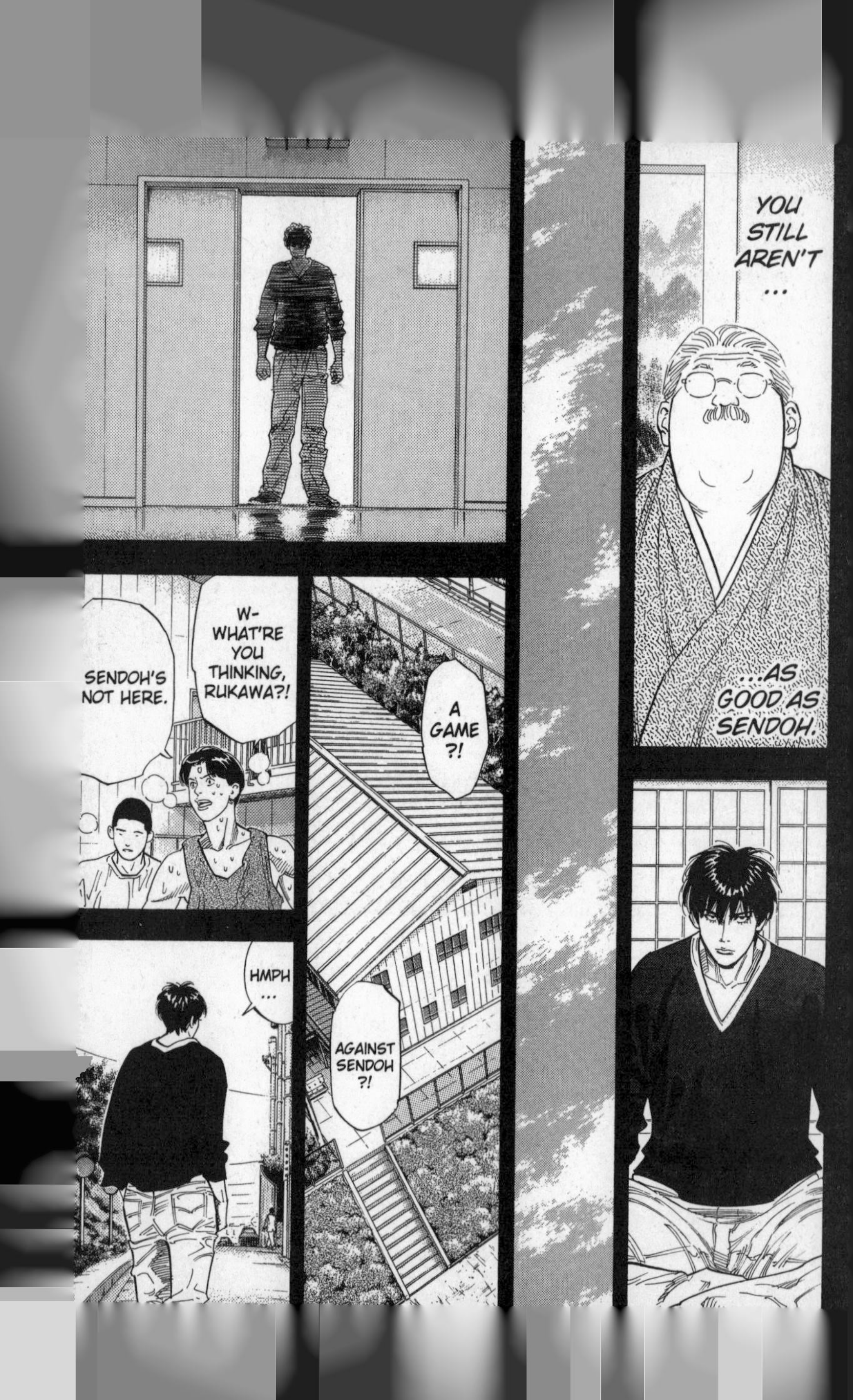
YOU STILL AREN'T ...
...AS GOOD AS SENDOH.
A GAME ?!
AGAINST SENDOH ?!
W-WHAT'RE YOU THINKING, RUKAWA?!
SENDOH'S NOT HERE.
HMPH ...

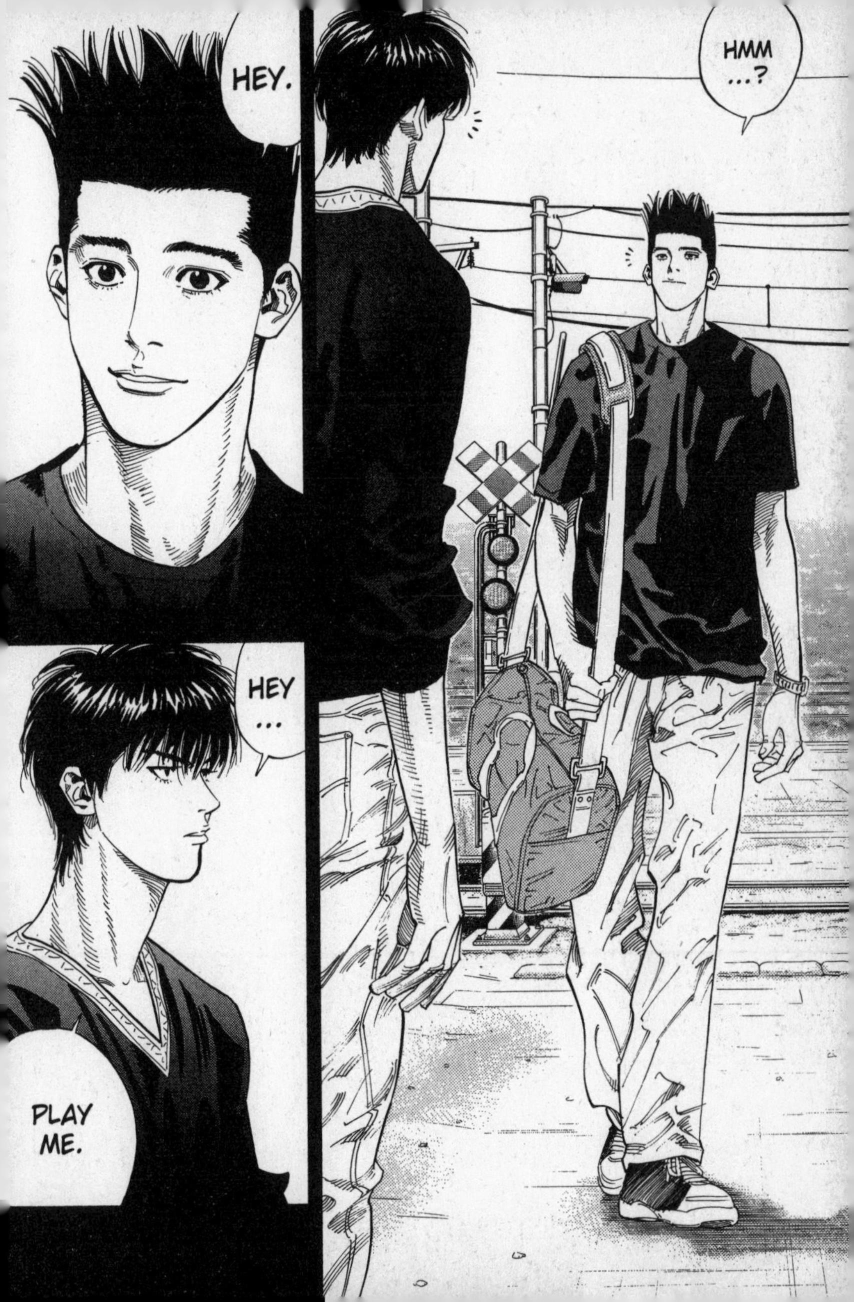
HMM ...?
HEY.
HEY ...
PLAY ME.

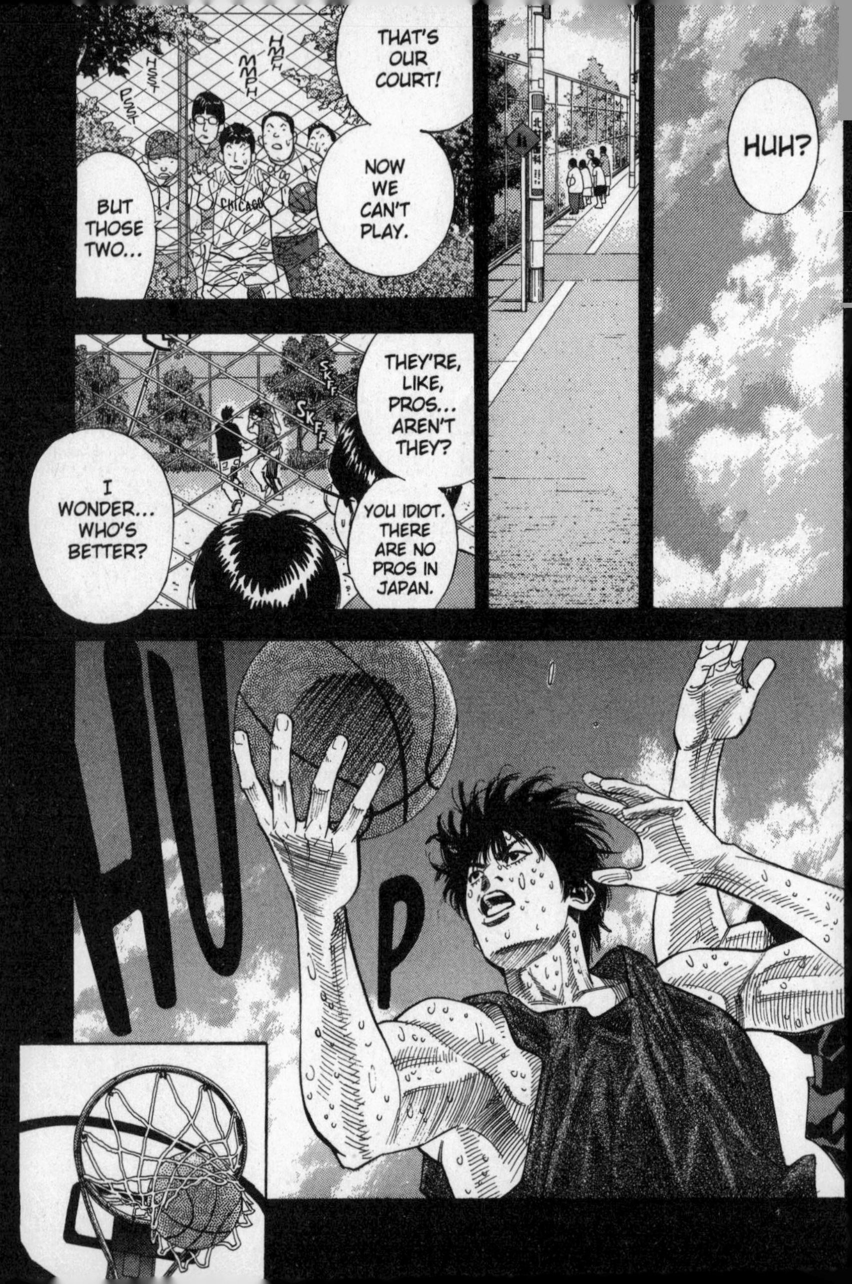
HUH?
THAT'S OUR COURT!
HMMPH
MMPH
NOW WE CAN'T PLAY.
HSST
PSST
BUT THOSE TWO...
THEY'RE, LIKE, PROS... AREN'T THEY?
SKFF
SKFF
YOU IDIOT. THERE ARE NO PROS IN JAPAN.
I WONDER... WHO'S BETTER?
HUP

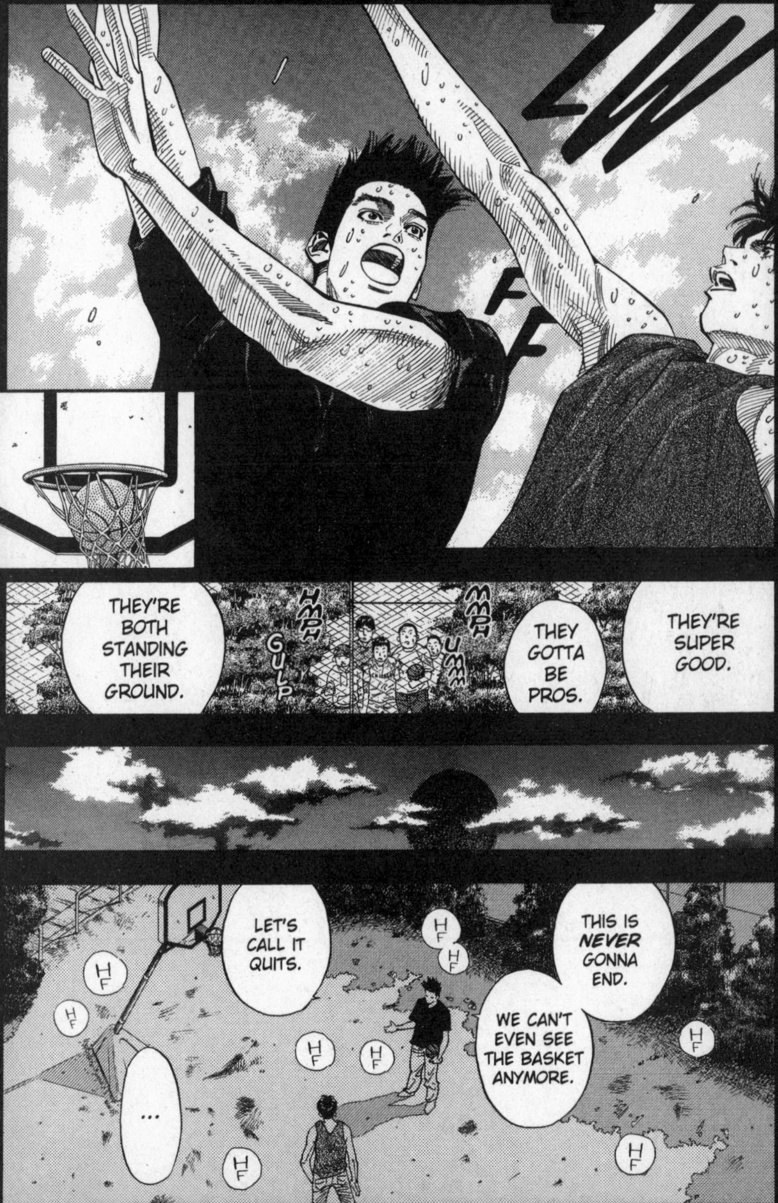

THEY'RE SUPER GOOD.
THEY GOTTA BE PROS.
MMPH
UMMM
HMPH
GULP
THEY'RE BOTH STANDING THEIR GROUND.
HF
HF
THIS IS *NEVER* GONNA END.
WE CAN'T EVEN SEE THE BASKET ANYMORE.
LET'S CALL IT QUITS.
HF
HF
HF
HF
HF
HF
...
HF

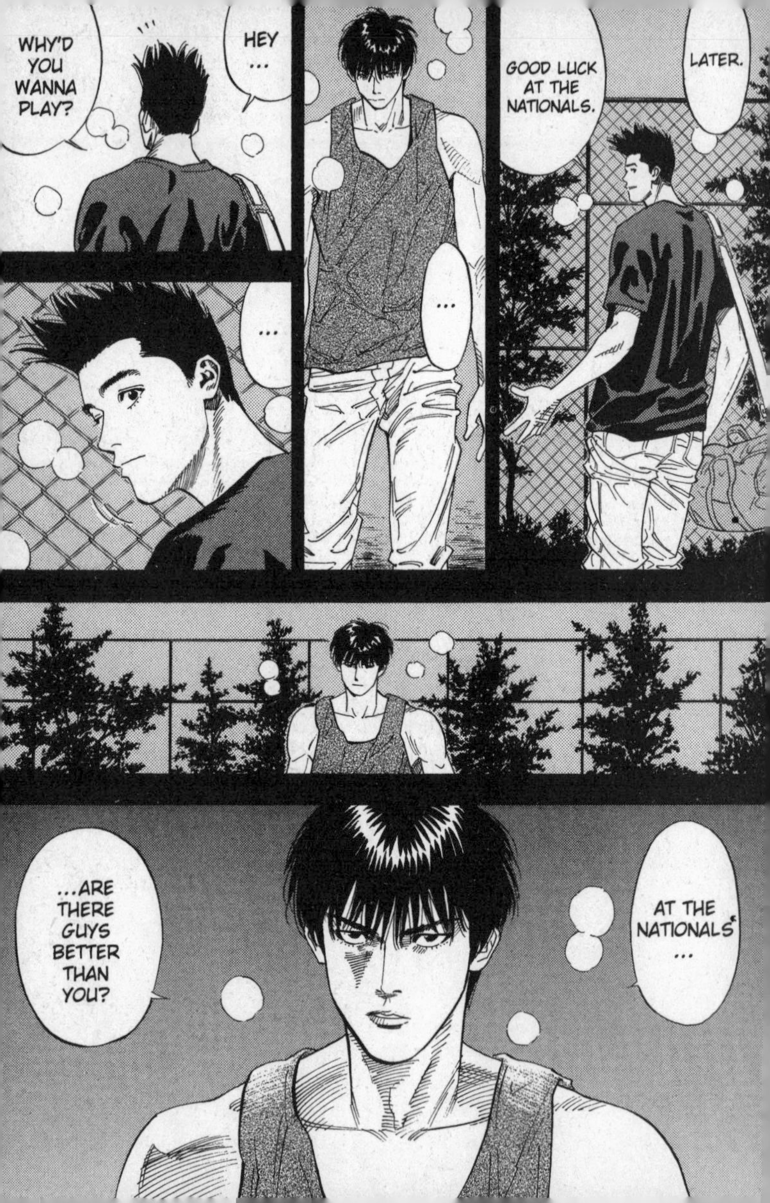
LATER.
GOOD LUCK AT THE NATIONALS.
...
HEY ...
WHY'D YOU WANNA PLAY?
...
AT THE NATIONALS ...
...ARE THERE GUYS BETTER THAN YOU?

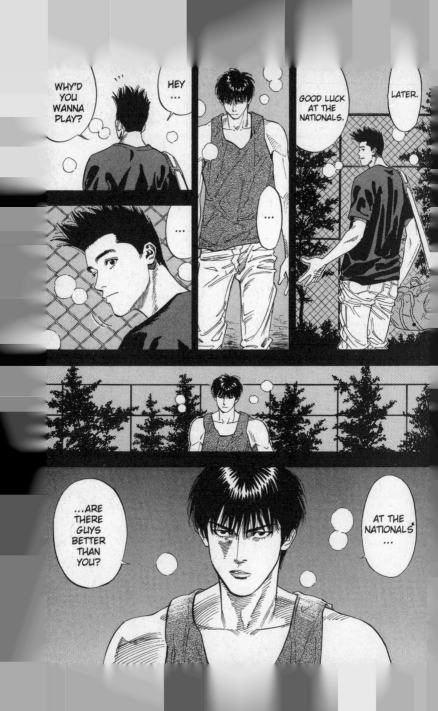

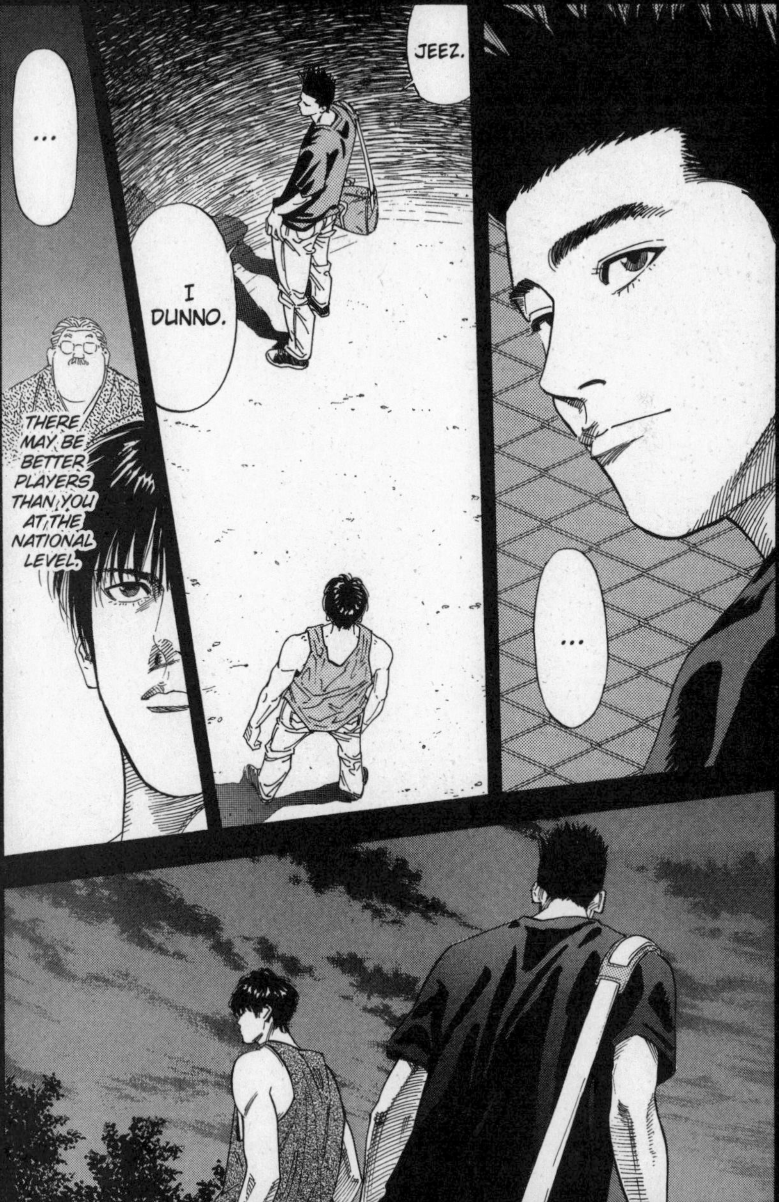
...
JEEZ.
I DUNNO.
...
THERE MAY BE BETTER PLAYERS THAN YOU AT THE NATIONAL LEVEL.

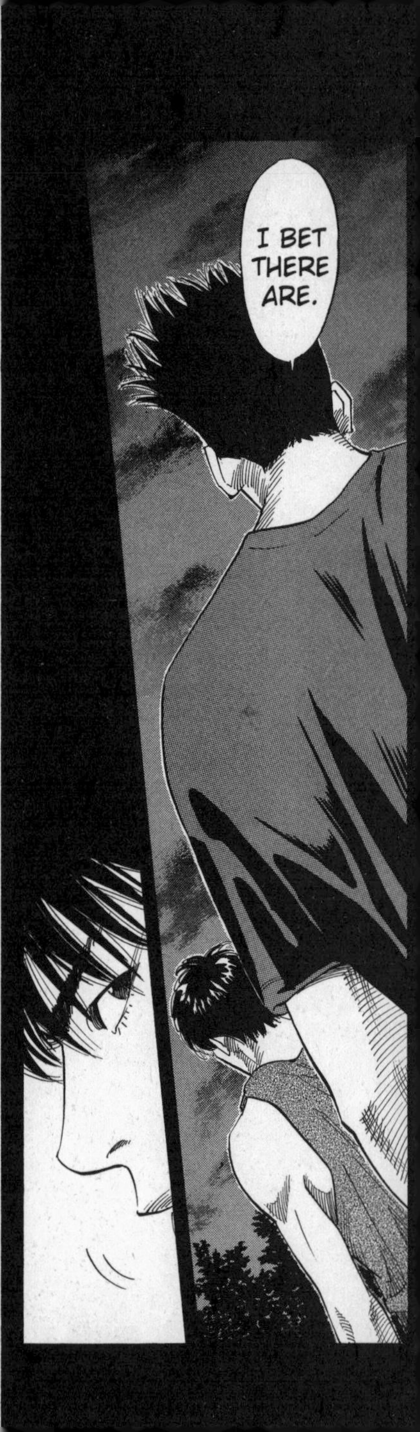
I BET THERE ARE.
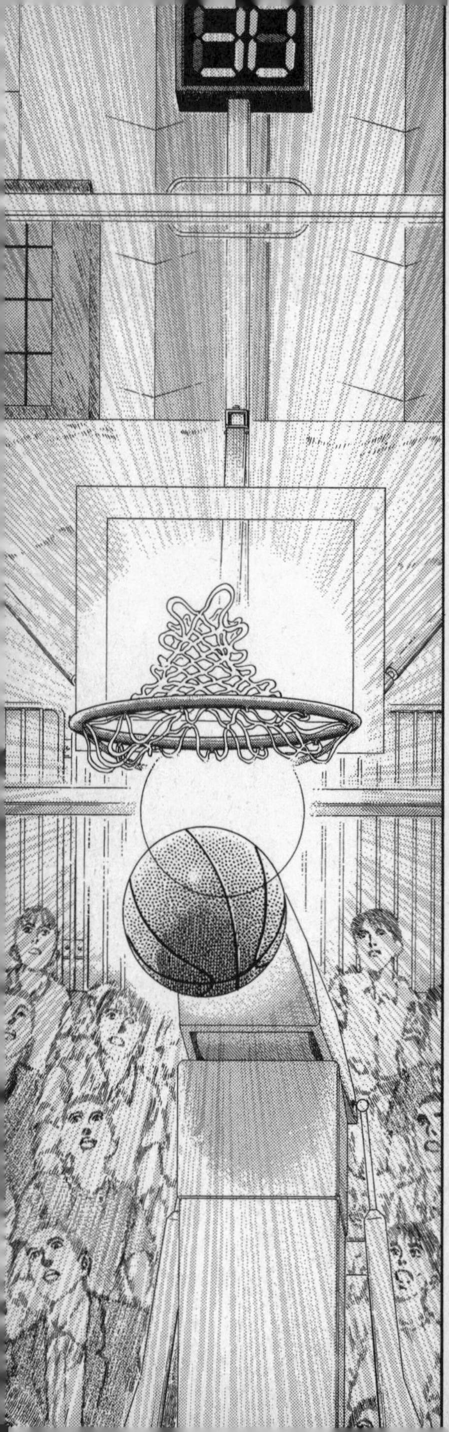

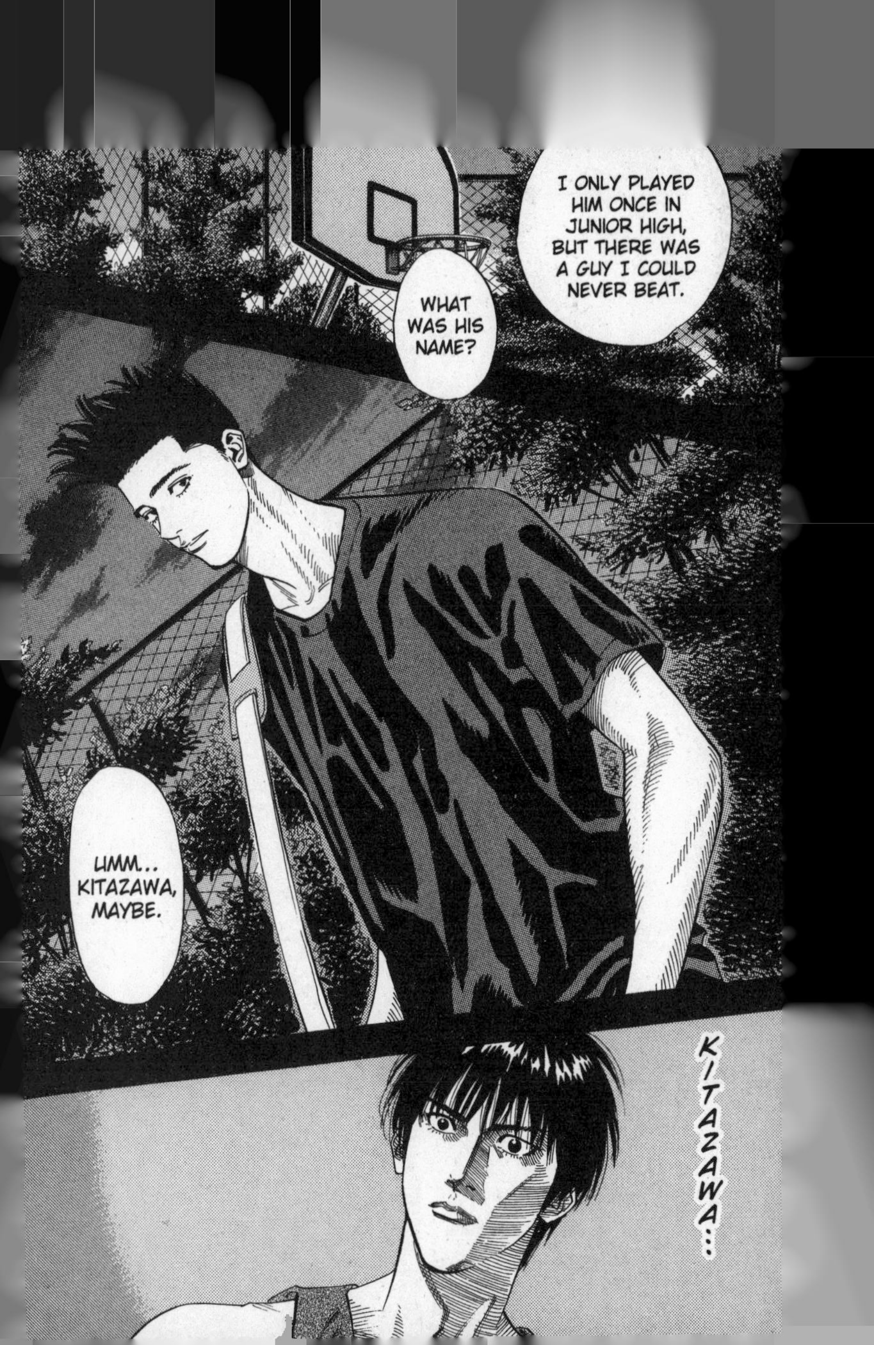
I ONLY PLAYED HIM ONCE IN JUNIOR HIGH, BUT THERE WAS A GUY I COULD NEVER BEAT.
WHAT WAS HIS NAME?
UMM... KITAZAWA, MAYBE.
KITAZAWA...

READ THIS WAY

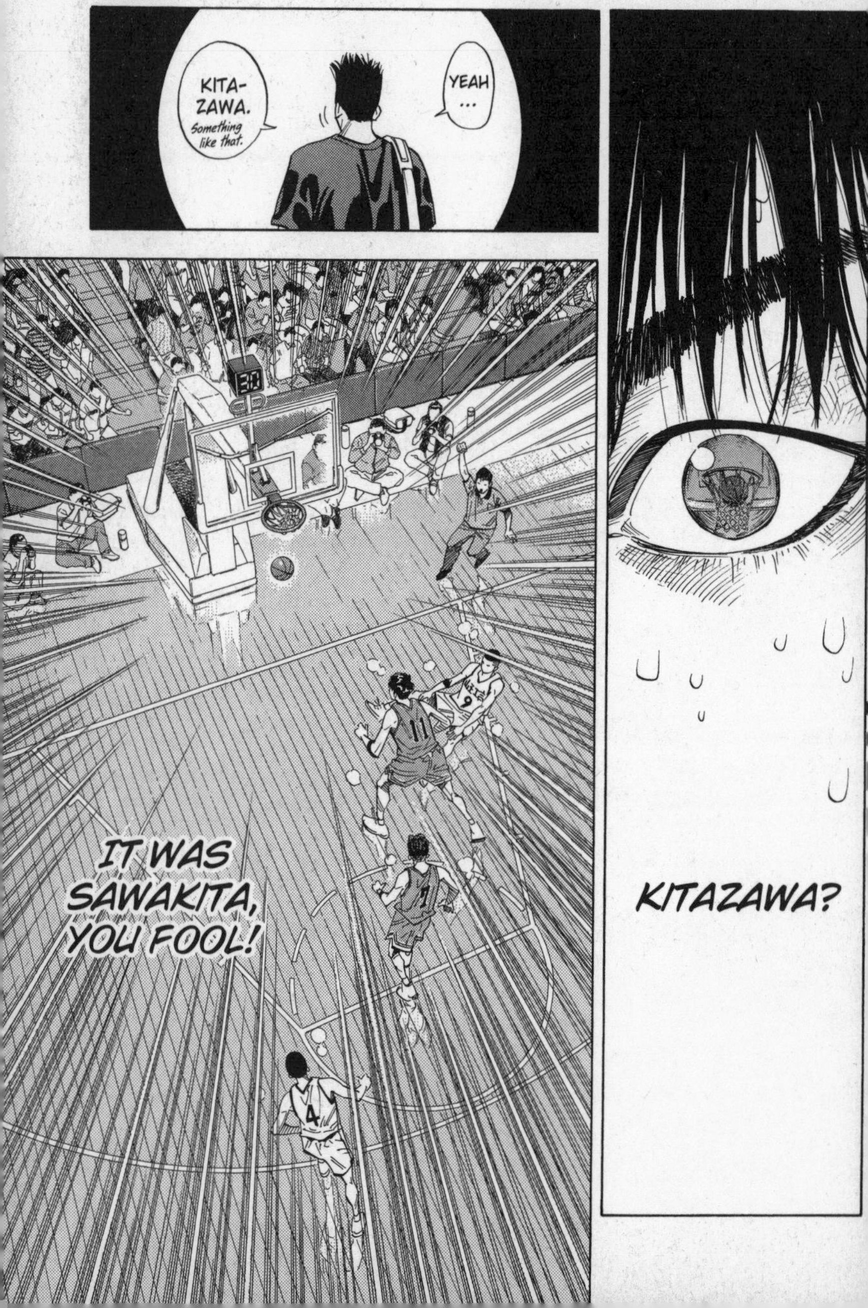
KITAZAWA?
KITA-ZAWA. Something like that.
YEAH ...
IT WAS SAWAKITA, YOU FOOL!

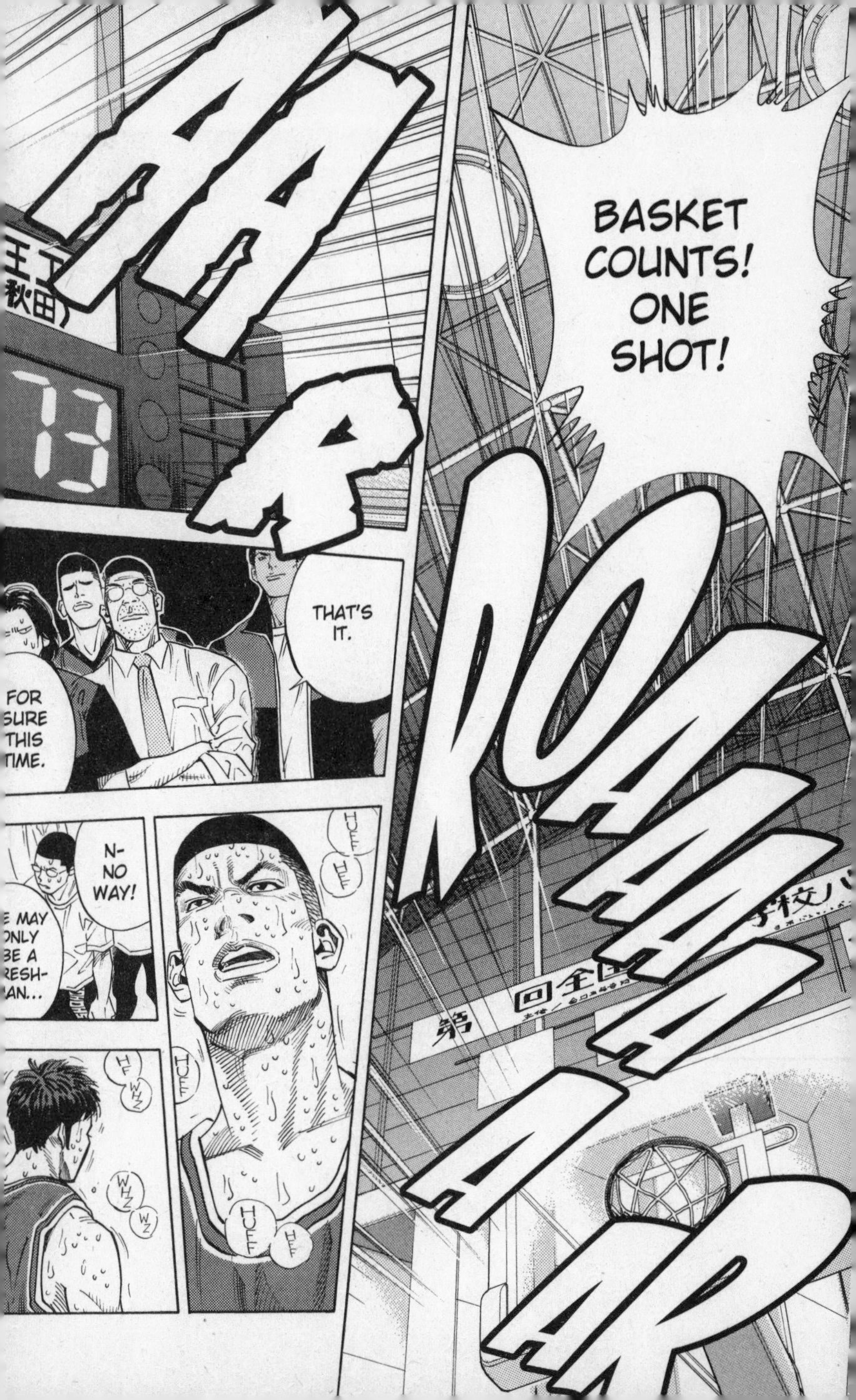
BASKET COUNTS! ONE SHOT!
73
THAT'S IT.
FOR SURE THIS TIME.
HUFF HUFF
HUFF
HUFF HF
N-NO WAY!
E MAY ONLY BE A RESH-AN...
HF WHZ
WHZ WZ

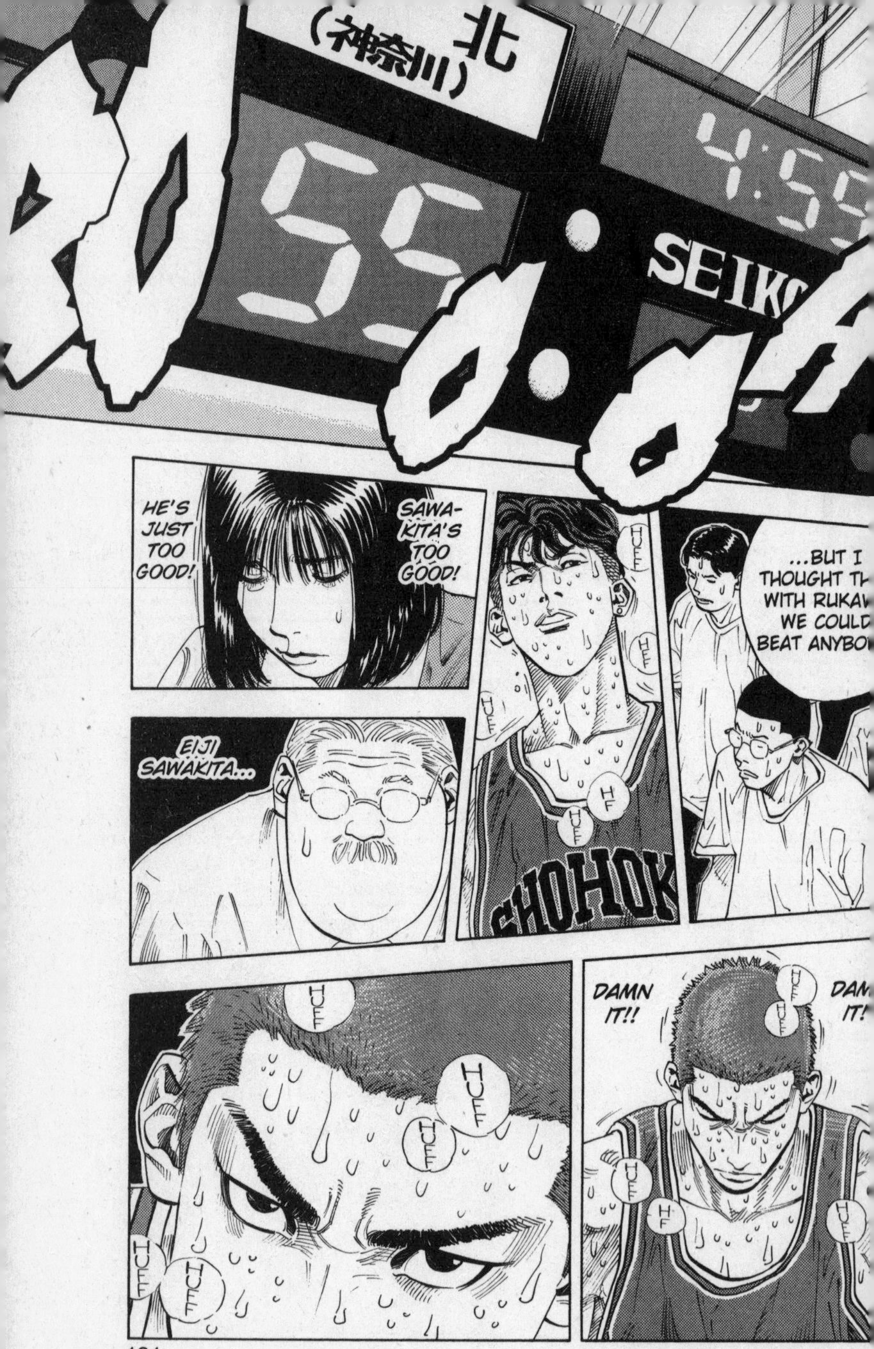

北
(神奈川)
55
SEIKO
...BUT I THOUGHT TH WITH RUKAW WE COULD BEAT ANYBO
HUFF
HF
HF
SHOHOK
SAWA-KITA'S TOO GOOD!
HE'S JUST TOO GOOD!
EIJI SAWAKITA...
DAM IT!
DAMN IT!!
HUFF
HF
HUFF
HUFF
HUFF

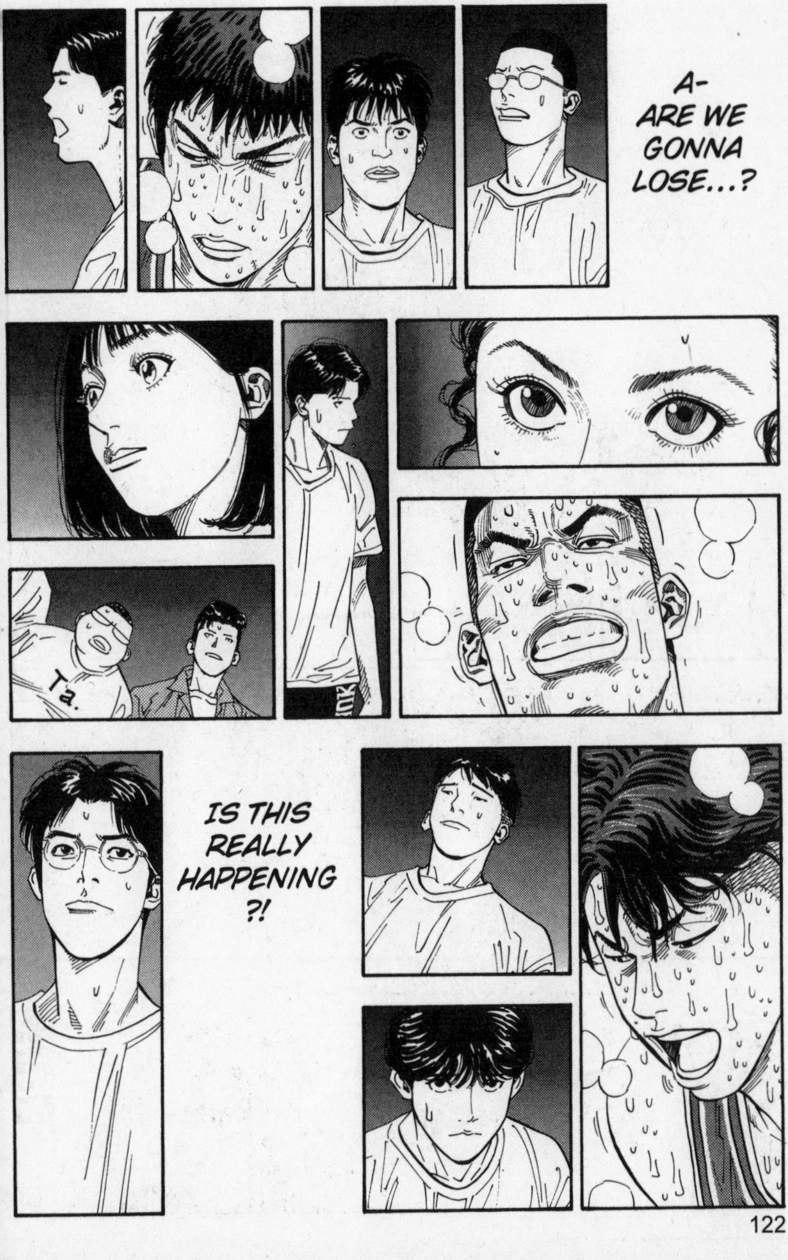
A-
ARE WE GONNA LOSE...?
Ta.
IS THIS REALLY HAPPENING ?!

READ THIS WAY

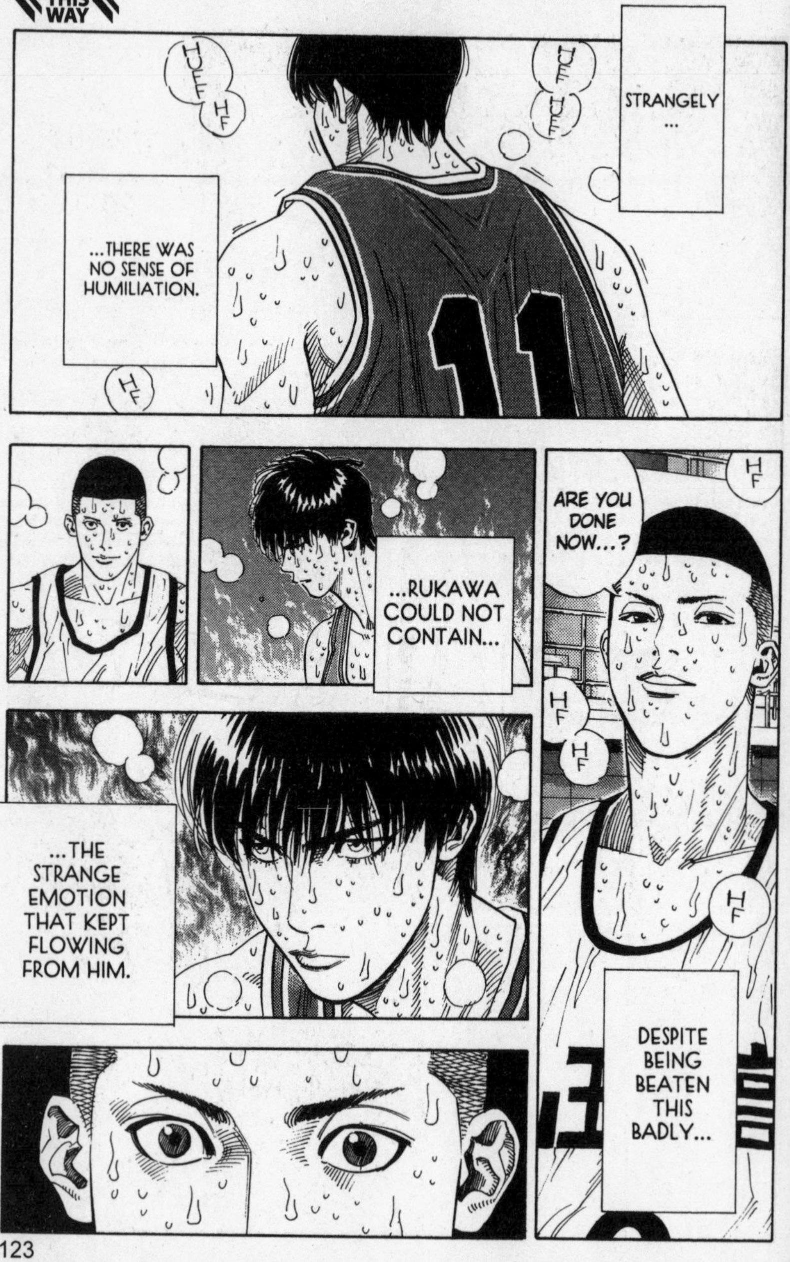

STRANGELY ...
HUF HUF
HUFF HF
...THERE WAS NO SENSE OF HUMILIATION.
HF
HF
ARE YOU DONE NOW...?
HF
HF
HF
DESPITE BEING BEATEN THIS BADLY...
...RUKAWA COULD NOT CONTAIN...
...THE STRANGE EMOTION THAT KEPT FLOWING FROM HIM.

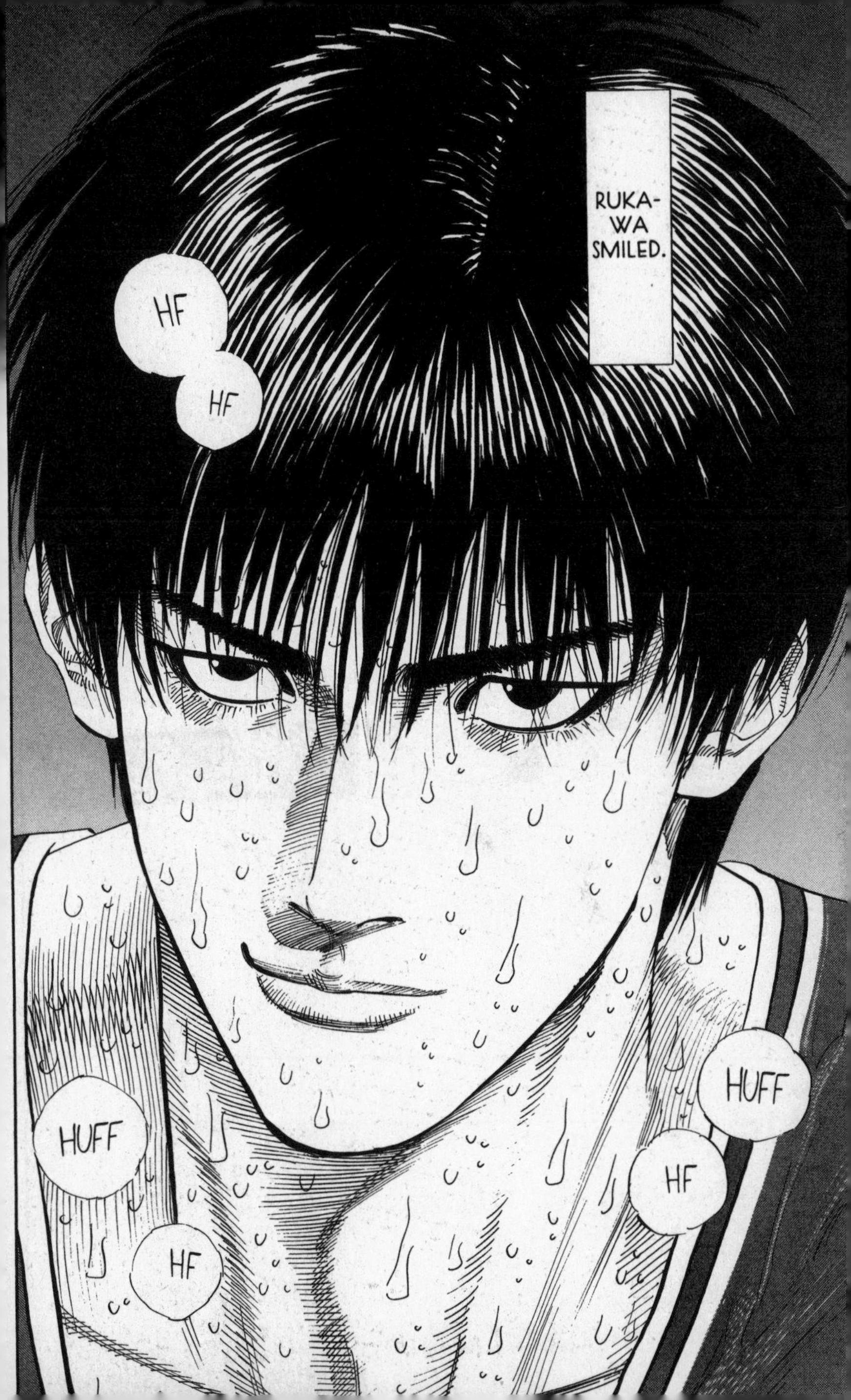
RUKA-
WA
SMILED.
HF
HF
HUFF
HF
HUFF
HF

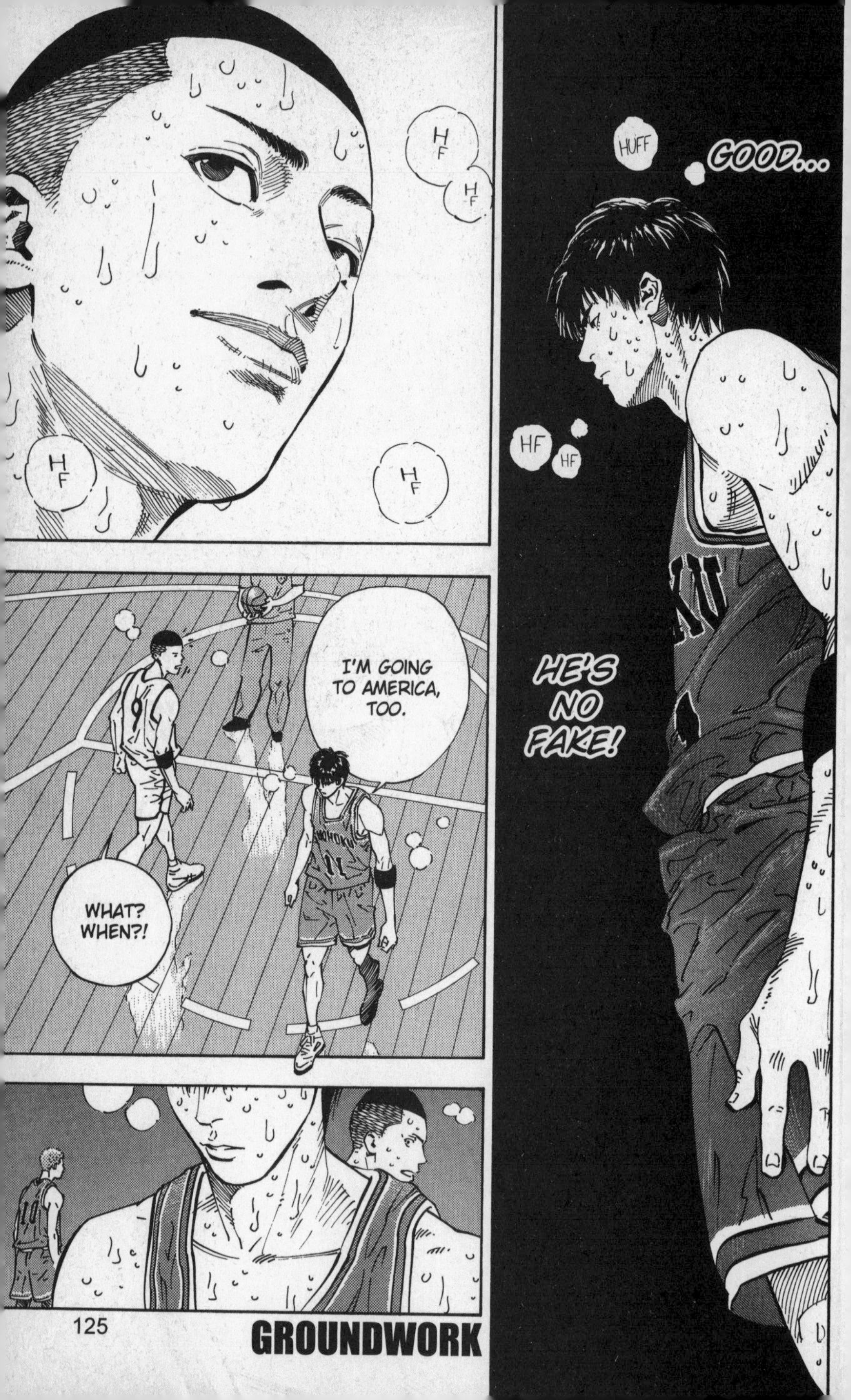
HUFF
GOOD...
HF
HF
HE'S NO FAKE!
HF
HF
HF
HF
I'M GOING TO AMERICA, TOO.
WHAT? WHEN?!

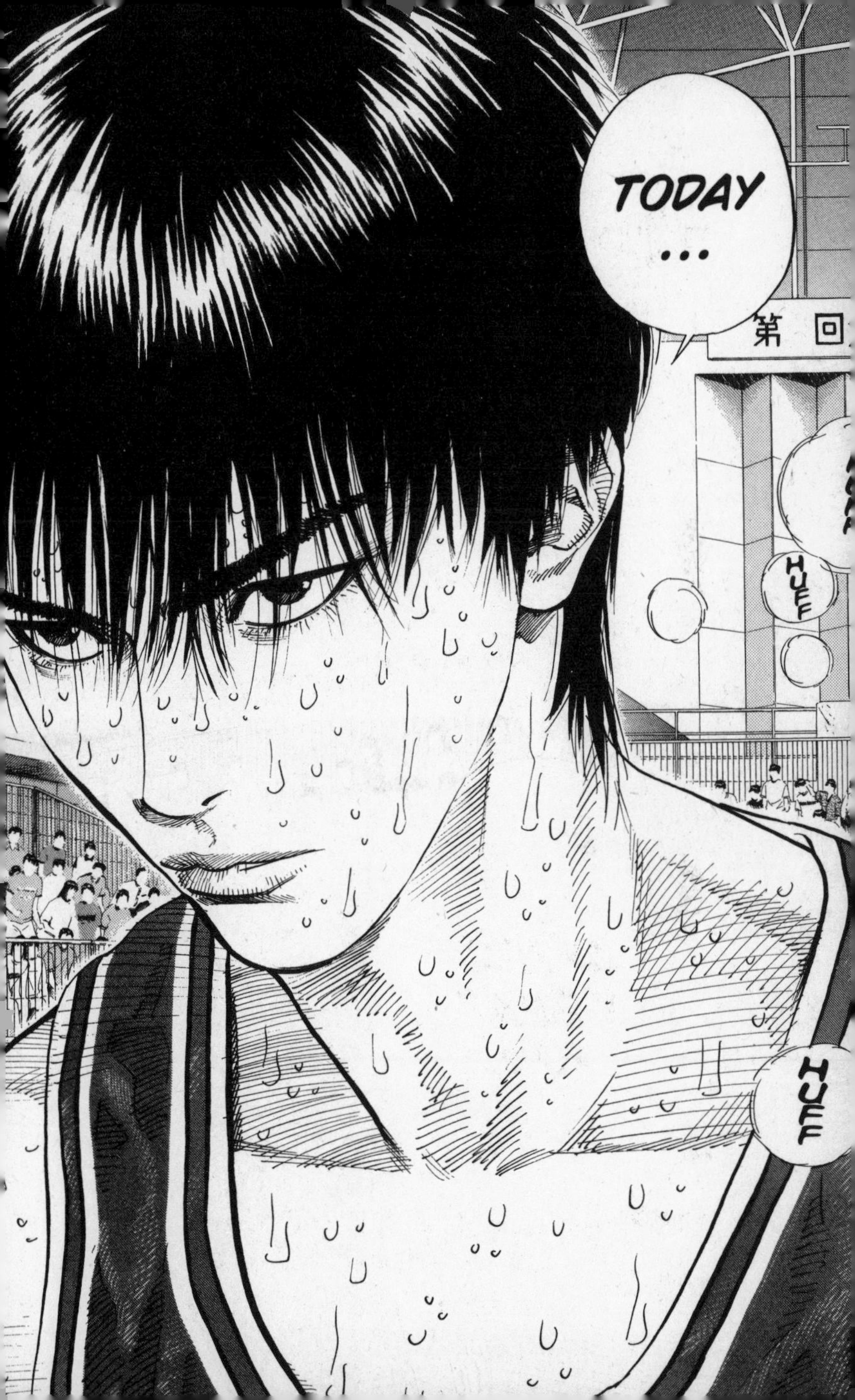
TODAY ...
第 回
HUFF
HUFF

#258 GROUNDWORK

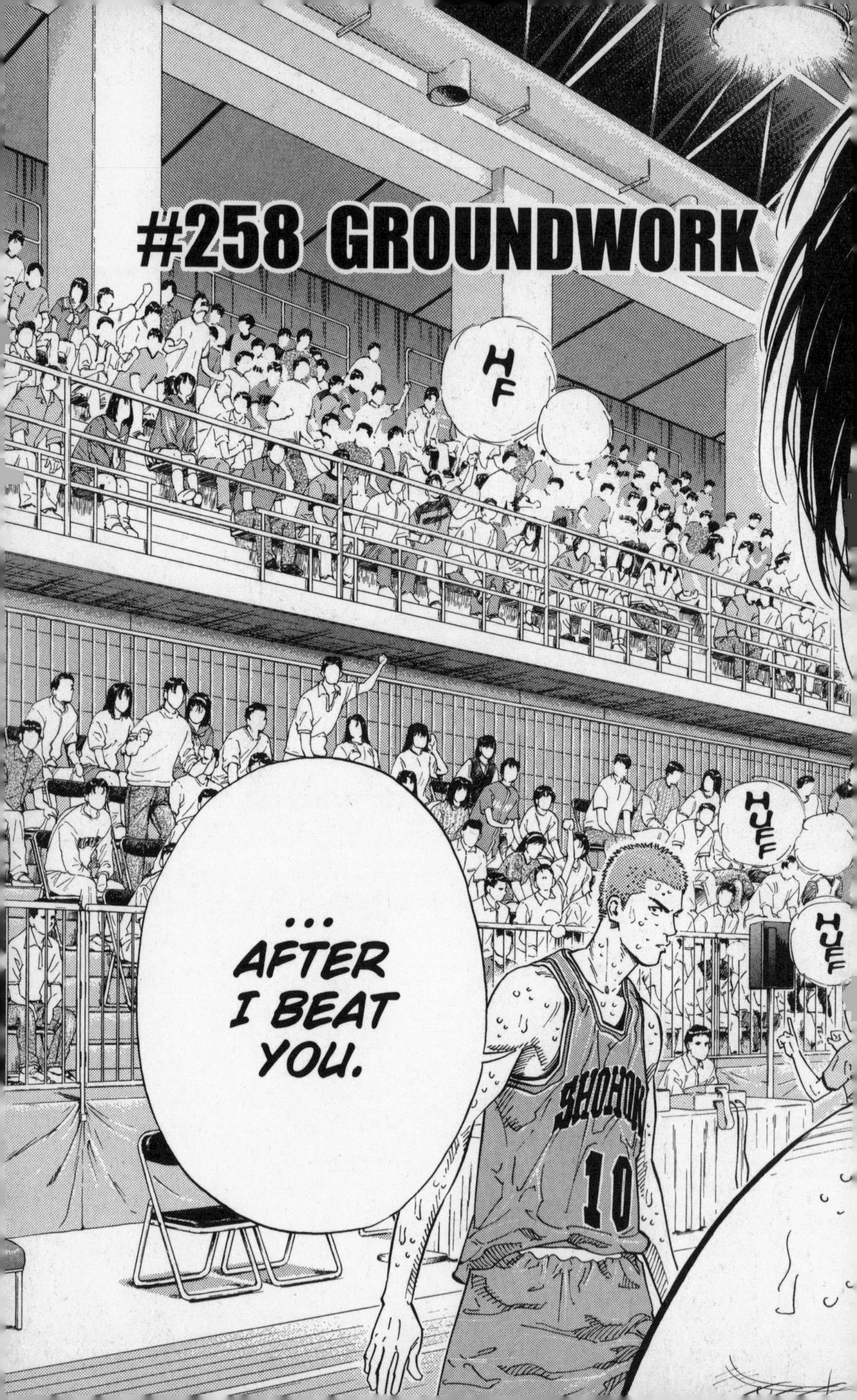
HF
HUFF
HUFF
... AFTER I BEAT YOU.
SHOHOKU
10

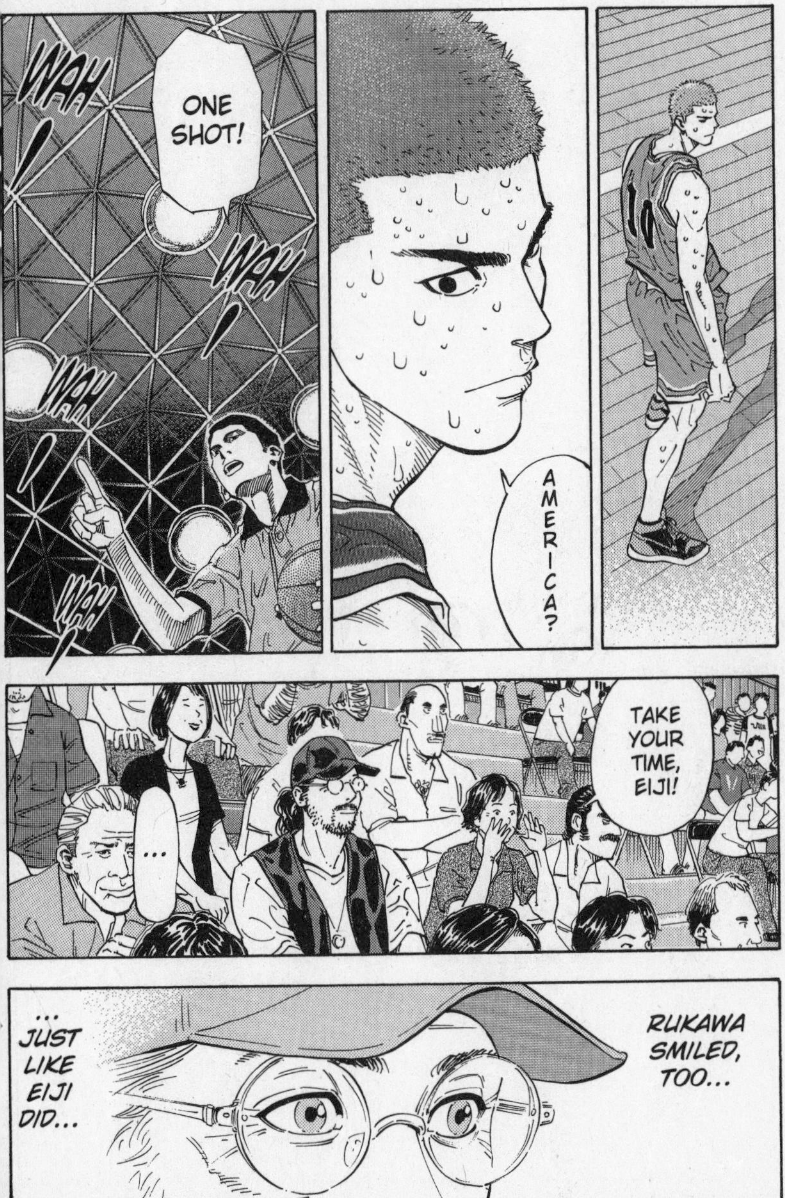
AMERICA?
ONE SHOT!
WAH!
WAH!
WAH!
WAH!
WAH!
TAKE YOUR TIME, EIJI!
...
RUKAWA SMILED, TOO...
... JUST LIKE EIJI DID...

READ THIS WAY

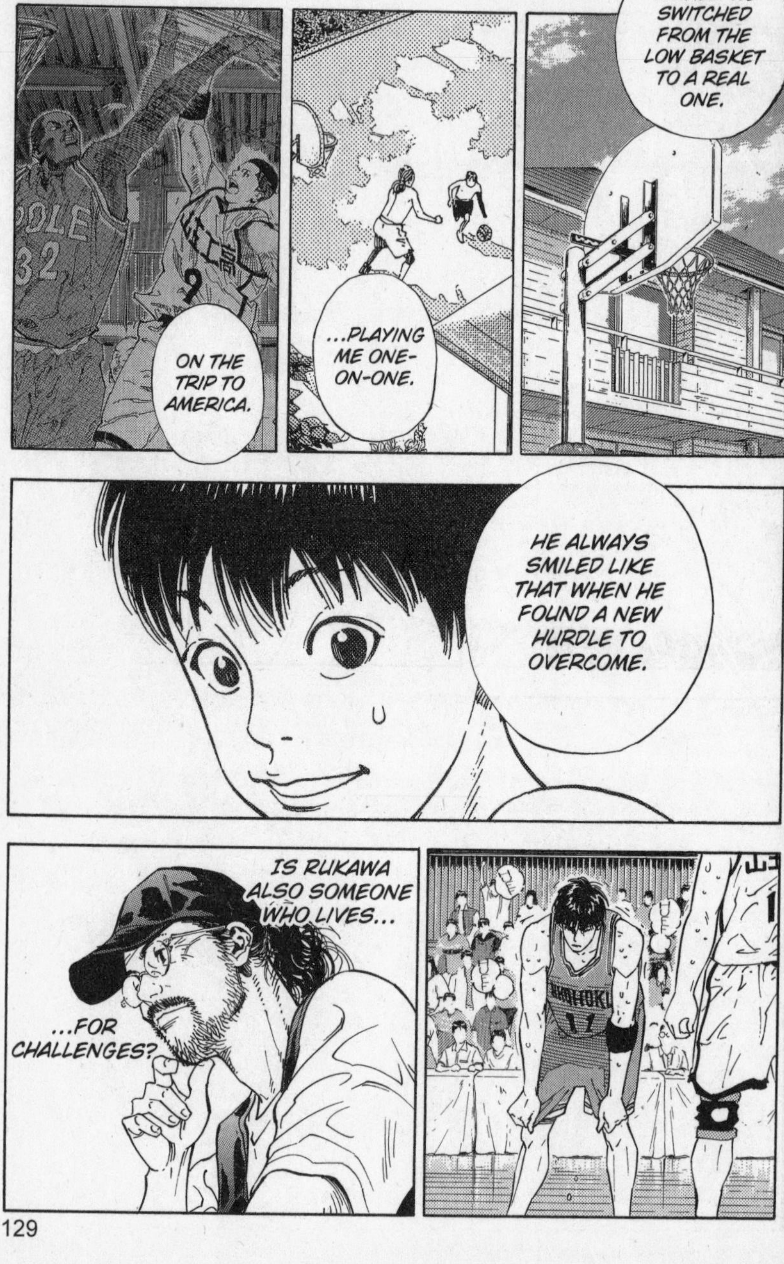
...WHEN WE SWITCHED FROM THE LOW BASKET TO A REAL ONE.
...PLAYING ME ONE-ON-ONE.
ON THE TRIP TO AMERICA.
HE ALWAYS SMILED LIKE THAT WHEN HE FOUND A NEW HURDLE TO OVERCOME.
IS RUKAWA ALSO SOMEONE WHO LIVES...
...FOR CHALLENGES?

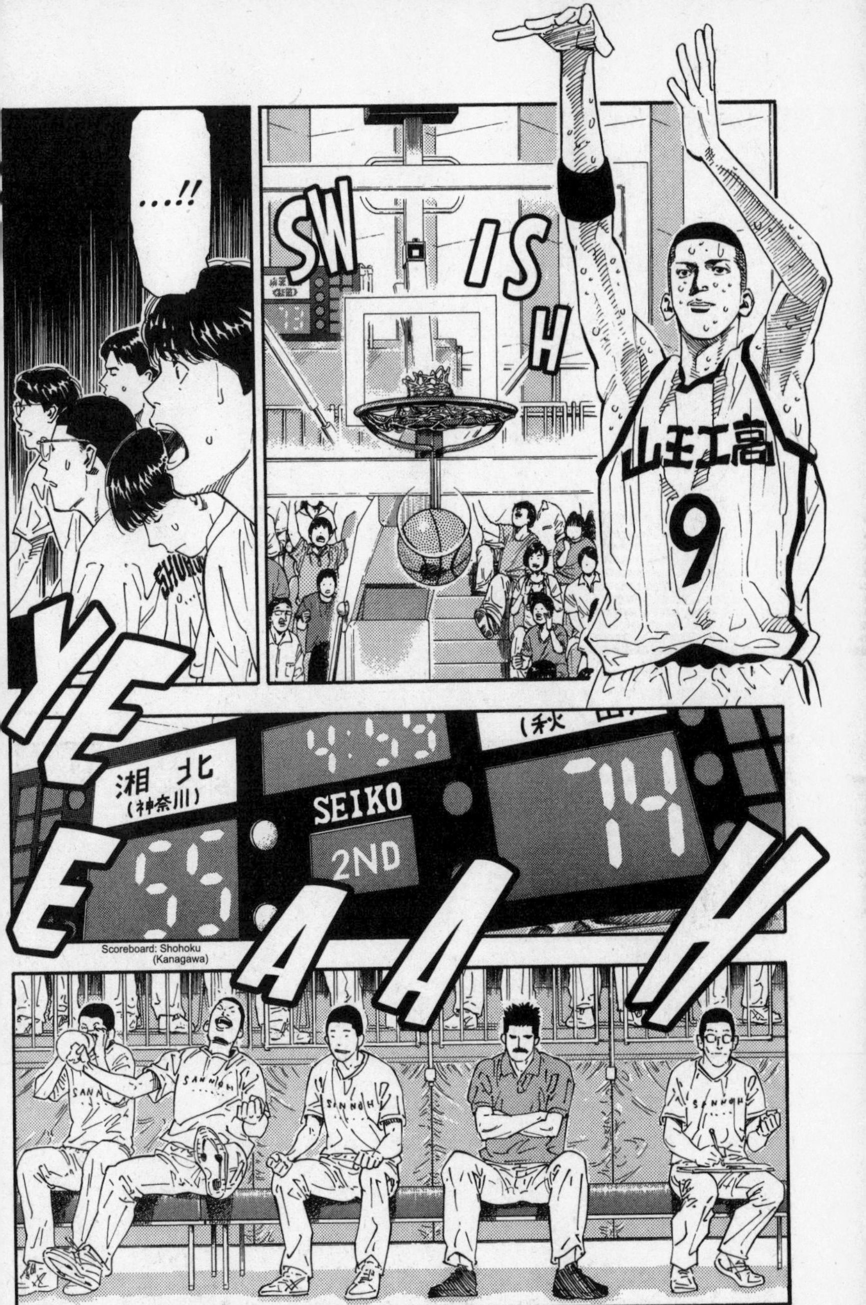
山王工高
9
SWISH
...!!
YEEAAAH
湘北
(神奈川)
4:59
SEIKO
2ND
55
74
Scoreboard: Shohoku (Kanagawa)

READ THIS WAY

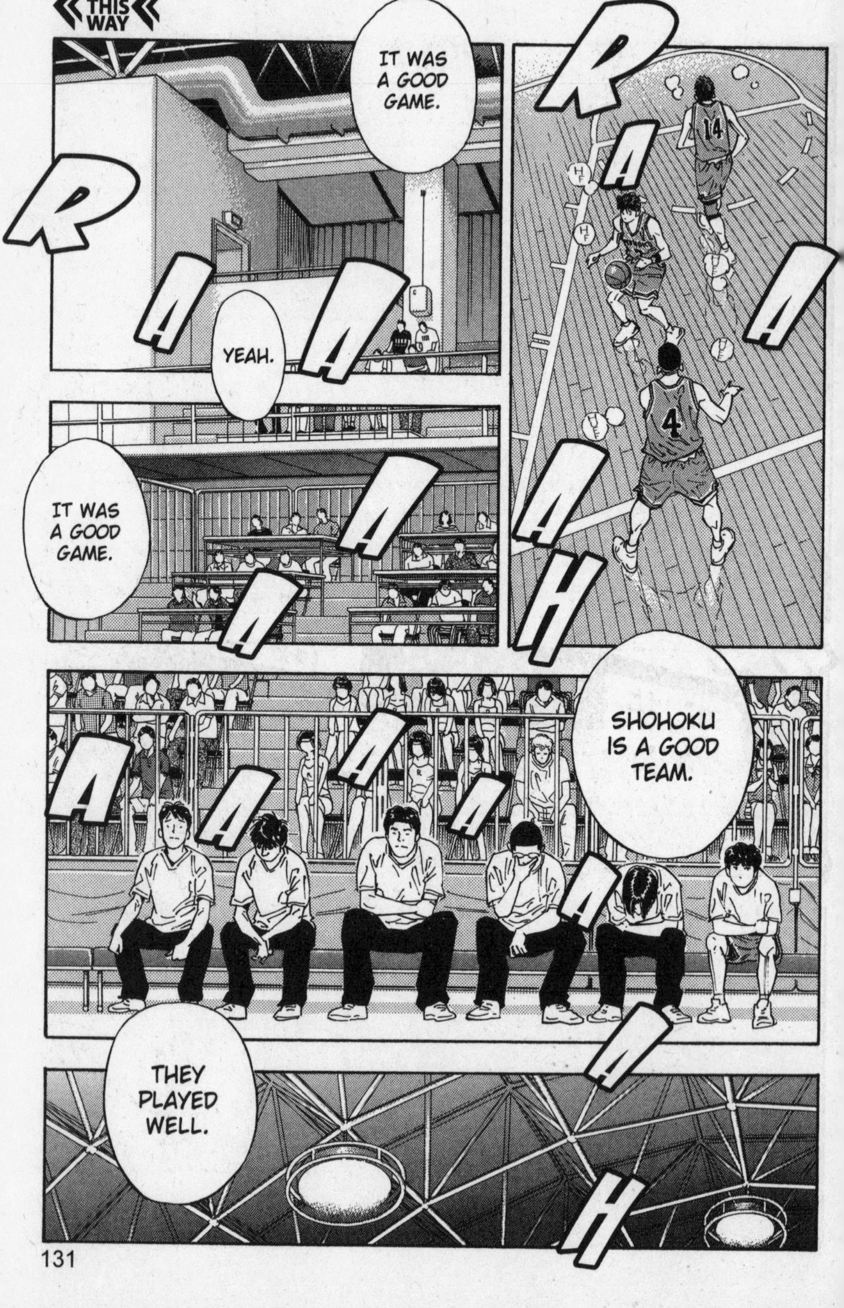
RAAAH
IT WAS A GOOD GAME.
YEAH.
IT WAS A GOOD GAME.
RAAAAAAAAAAH
SHOHOKU IS A GOOD TEAM.
THEY PLAYED WELL.

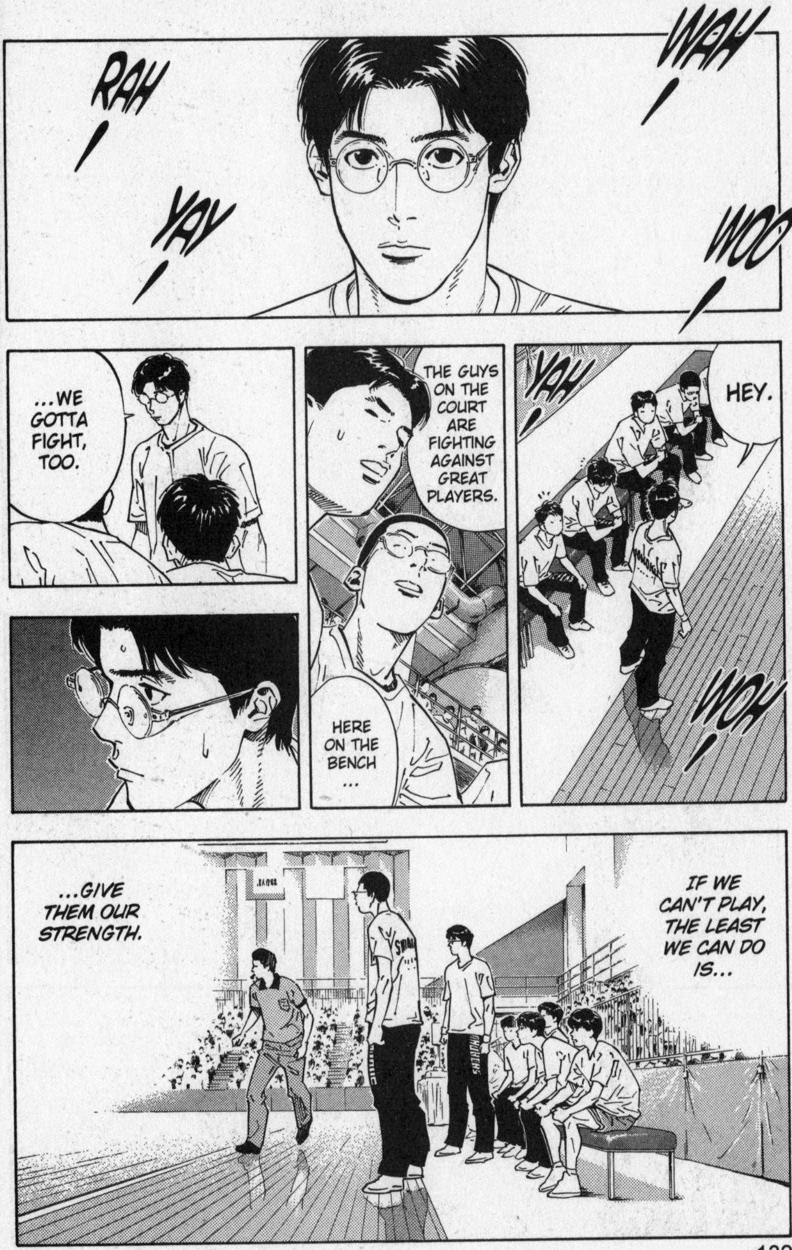
WAH!
RAH!
WOO!
YAY!
YAH!
HEY.
WOH!
THE GUYS ON THE COURT ARE FIGHTING AGAINST GREAT PLAYERS.
HERE ON THE BENCH...
...WE GOTTA FIGHT, TOO.
IF WE CAN'T PLAY, THE LEAST WE CAN DO IS...
...GIVE THEM OUR STRENGTH.

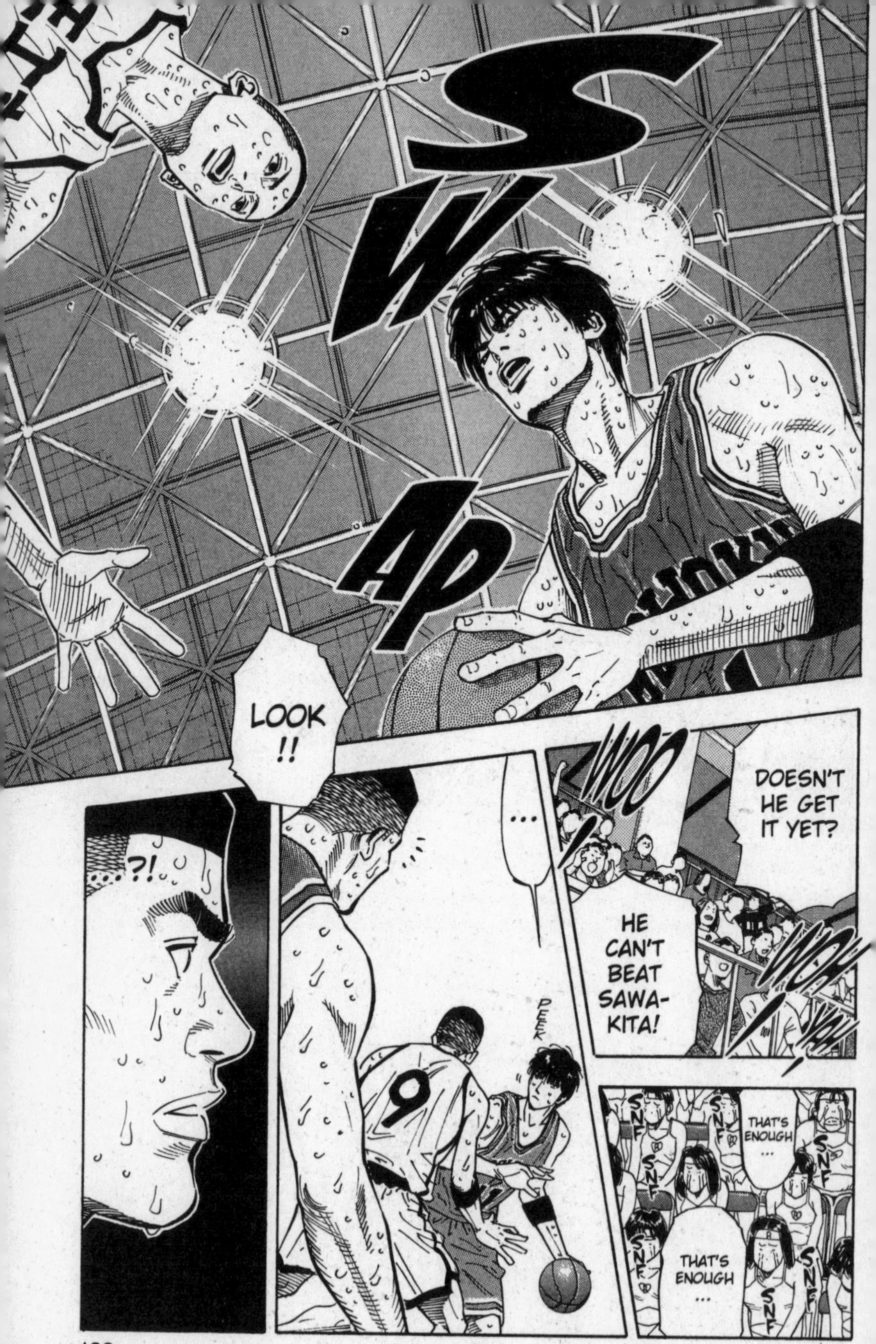
SWAP
LOOK !!
WOOO
DOESN'T HE GET IT YET?
HE CAN'T BEAT SAWA-KITA!
WOH
THAT'S ENOUGH ...
THAT'S ENOUGH ...
...
PEEK
...?!

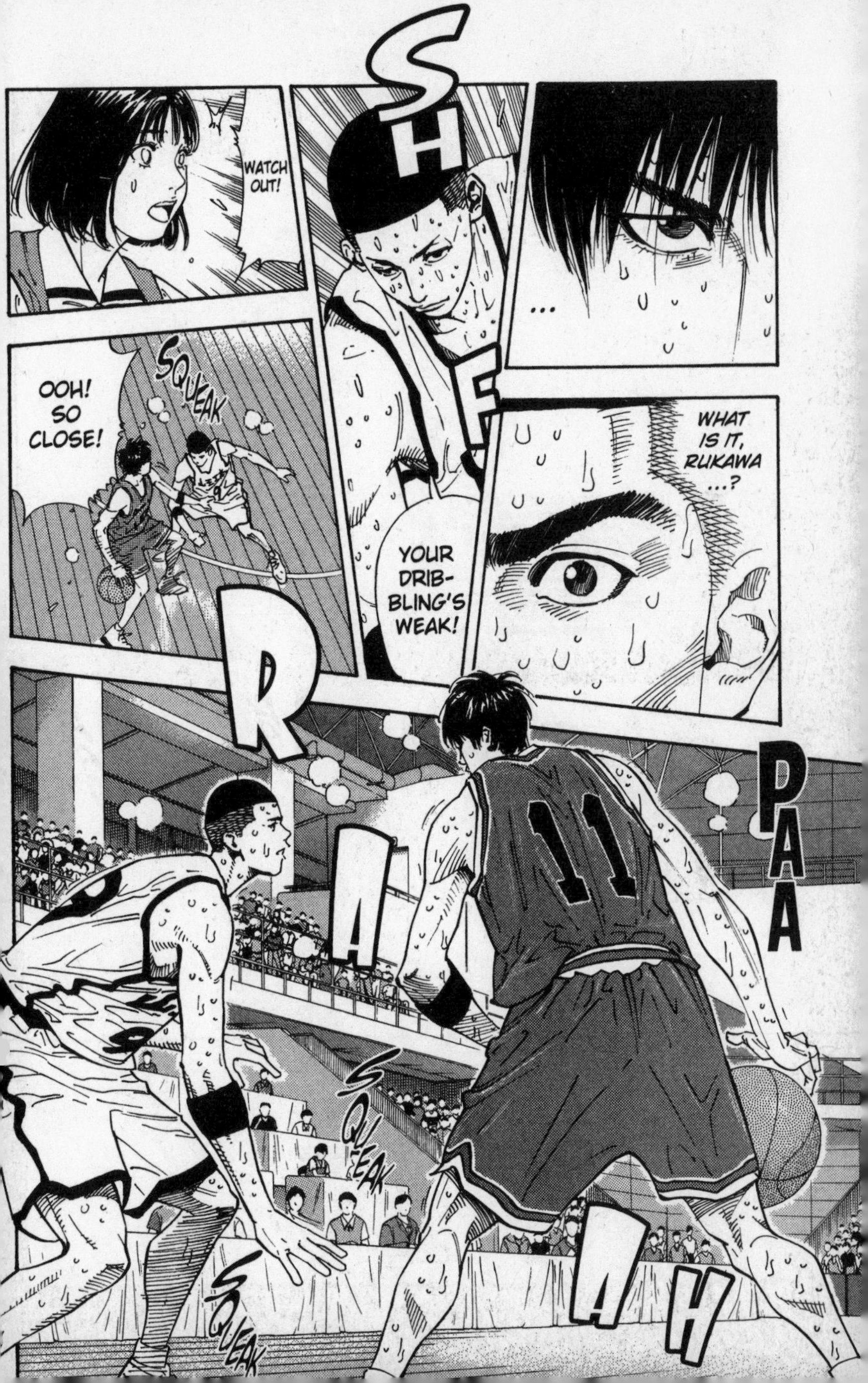
...
WHAT IS IT, RUKAWA ...?
SH
F
YOUR DRIB-BLING'S WEAK!
WATCH OUT!
OOH! SO CLOSE!
SQUEAK
PAA
R
A
A
H
SQUEAK
SQUEAK

READ THIS WAY

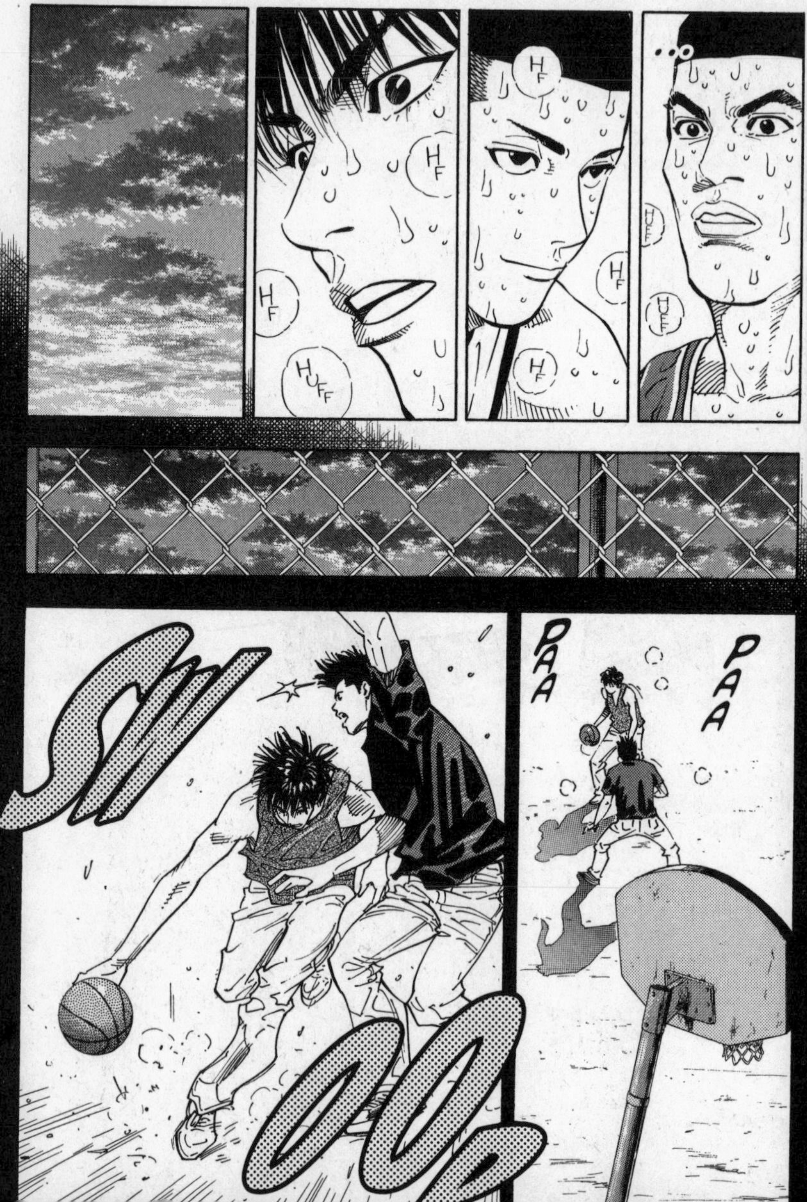
HUFF
HUFF
HF
HF
HF
HF
HF
HUFF
PAA
PAA

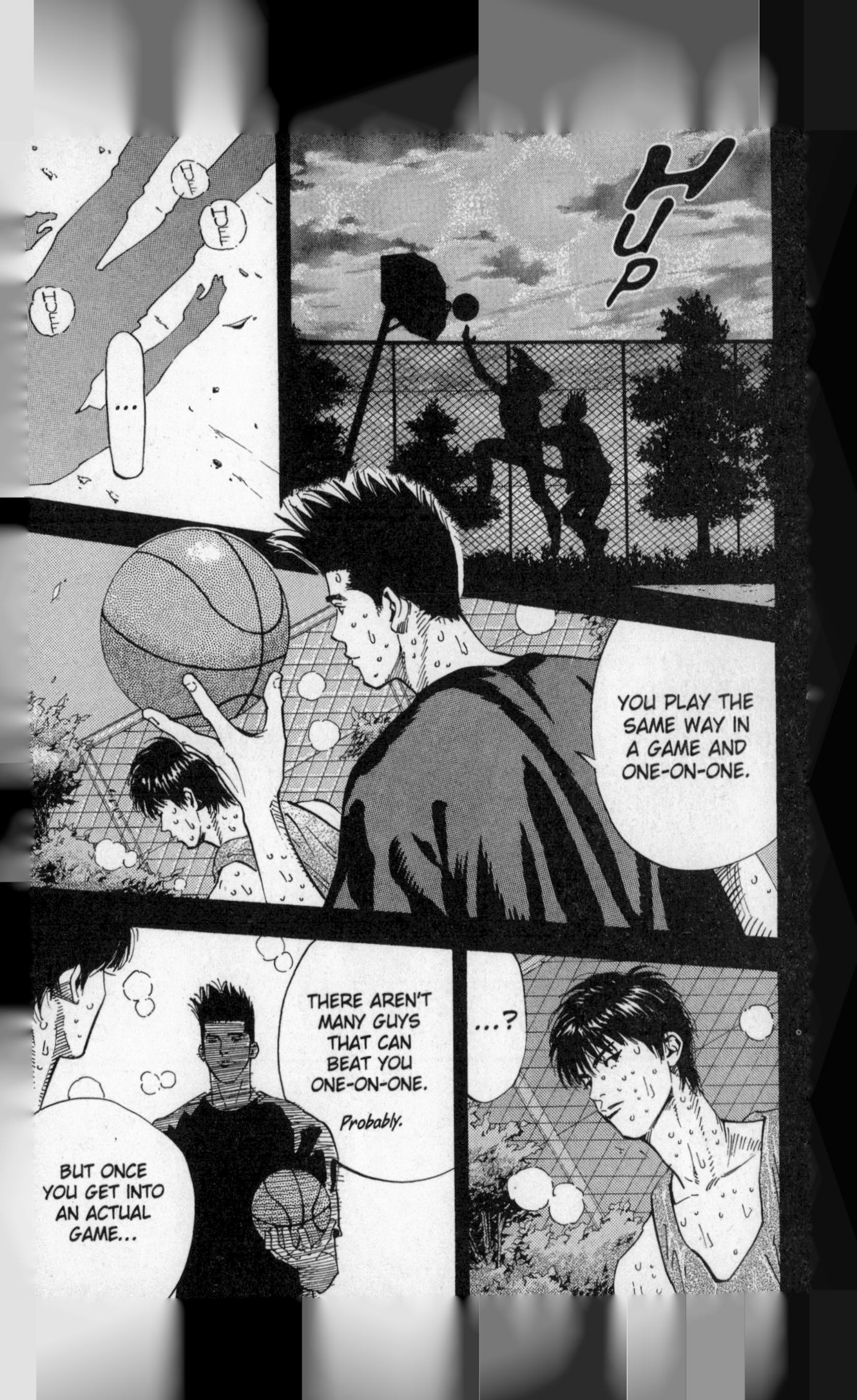
HUP
HUFF
HUFF
HUFF
...
YOU PLAY THE SAME WAY IN A GAME AND ONE-ON-ONE.
...?
THERE AREN'T MANY GUYS THAT CAN BEAT YOU ONE-ON-ONE.
Probably.
BUT ONCE YOU GET INTO AN ACTUAL GAME...

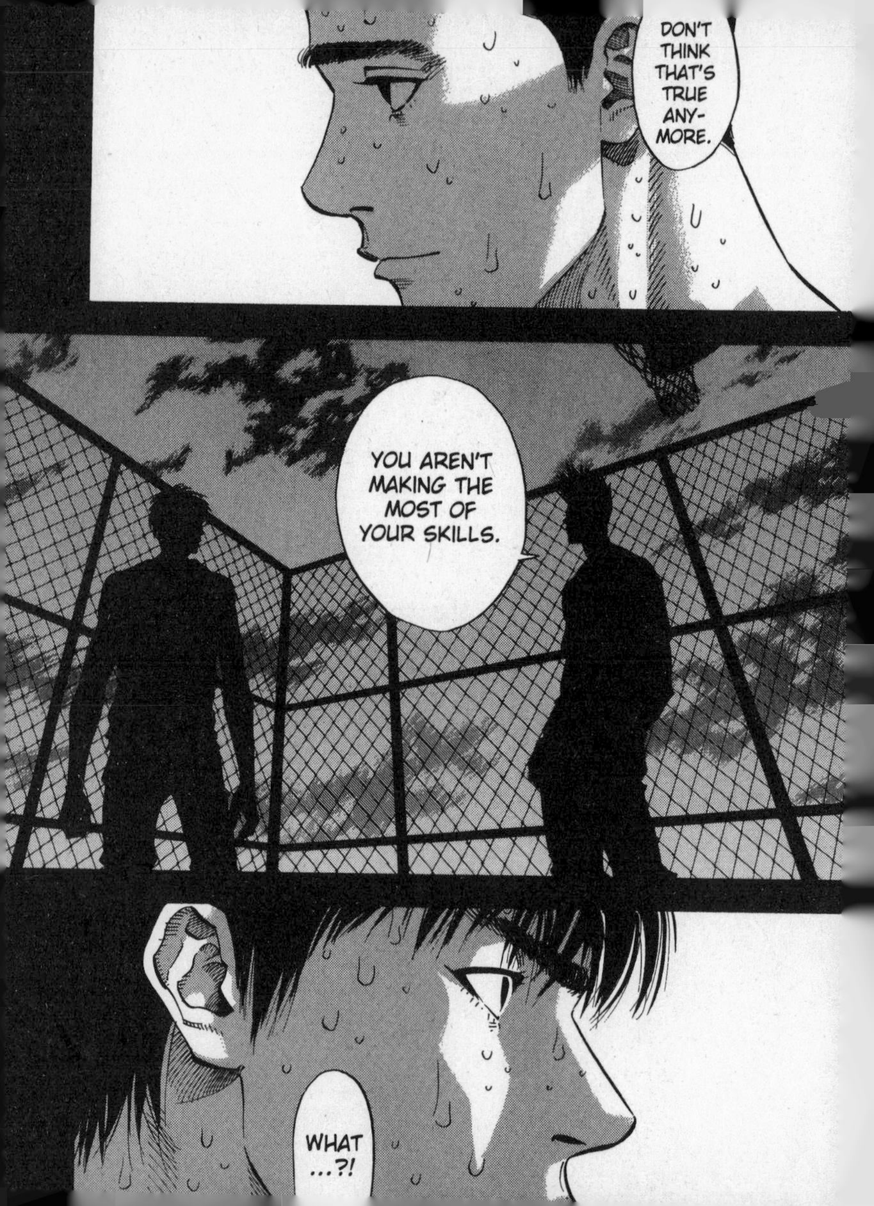
DON'T THINK THAT'S TRUE ANY-MORE.
YOU AREN'T MAKING THE MOST OF YOUR SKILLS.
WHAT ...?!

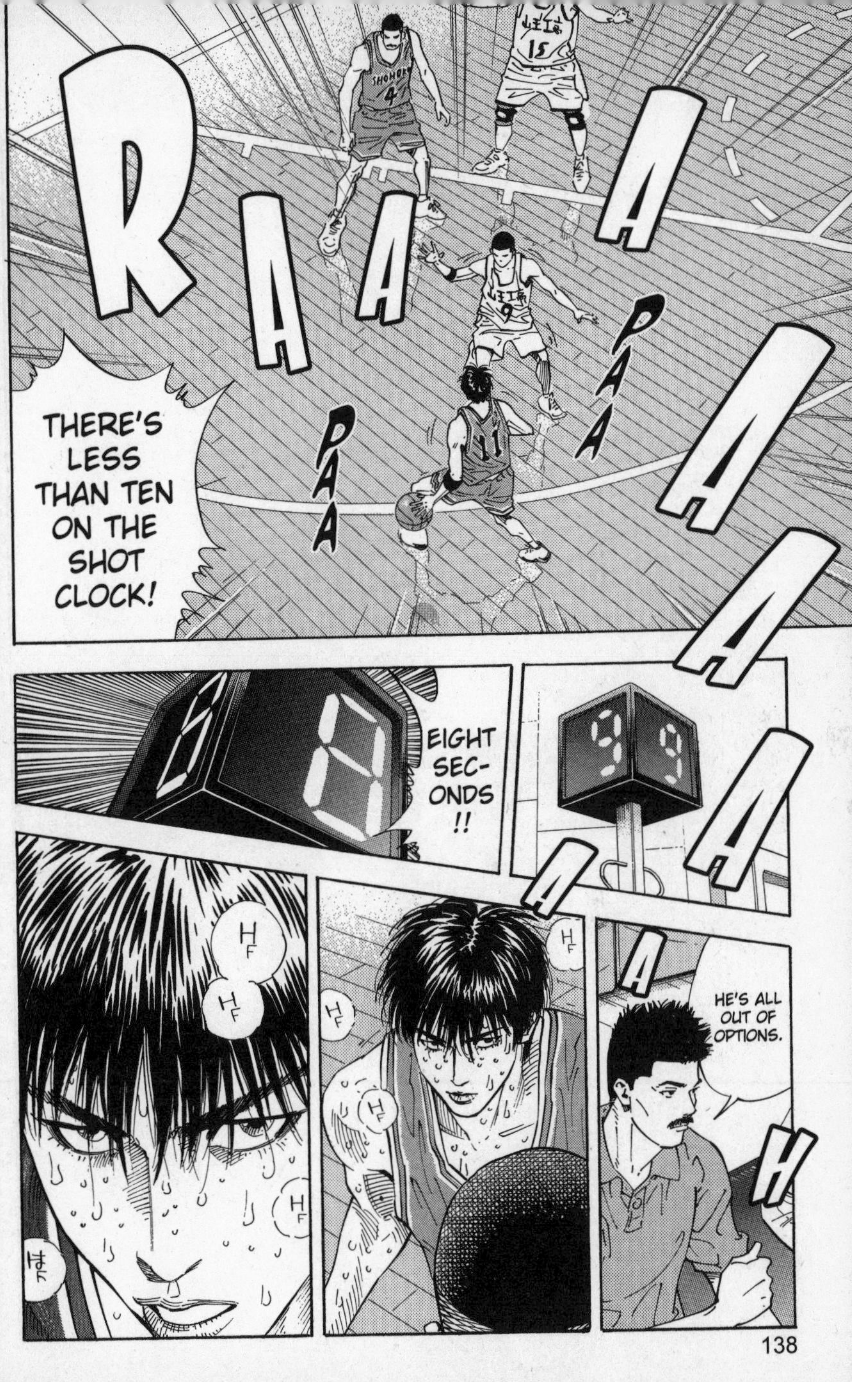
RAAAAAAAAAAH
THERE'S LESS THAN TEN ON THE SHOT CLOCK!
PAAA
PAAA
EIGHT SEC-ONDS!!
HE'S ALL OUT OF OPTIONS.
HF
HF
HF
HF
HF
HF

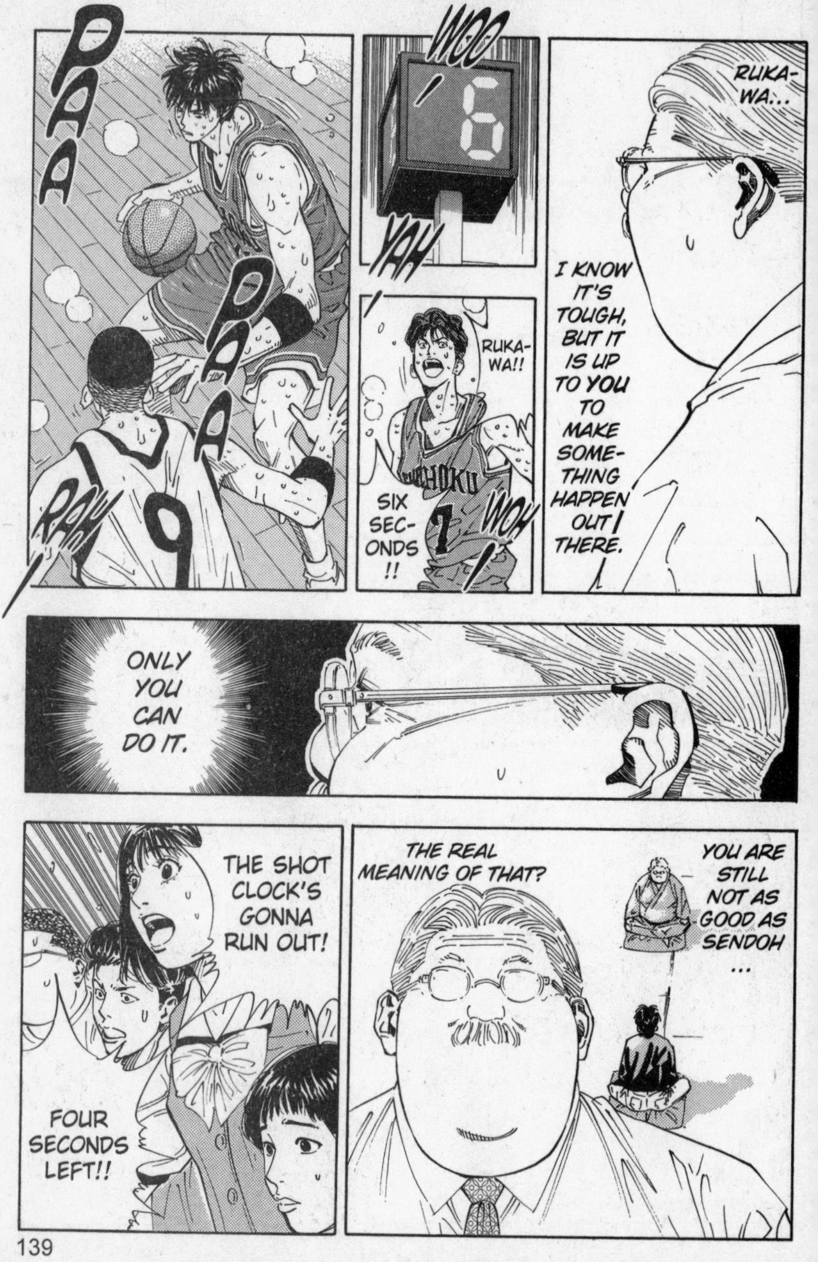
RUKA-WA...
I KNOW IT'S TOUGH, BUT IT IS UP TO YOU TO MAKE SOME-THING HAPPEN OUT THERE.
WOO-
6
YAH
RUKA-WA!!
SIX SEC-ONDS!!
WOH
PAAA
PAAA
RAH
ONLY YOU CAN DO IT.
YOU ARE STILL NOT AS GOOD AS SENDOH...
THE REAL MEANING OF THAT?
THE SHOT CLOCK'S GONNA RUN OUT!
FOUR SECONDS LEFT!!

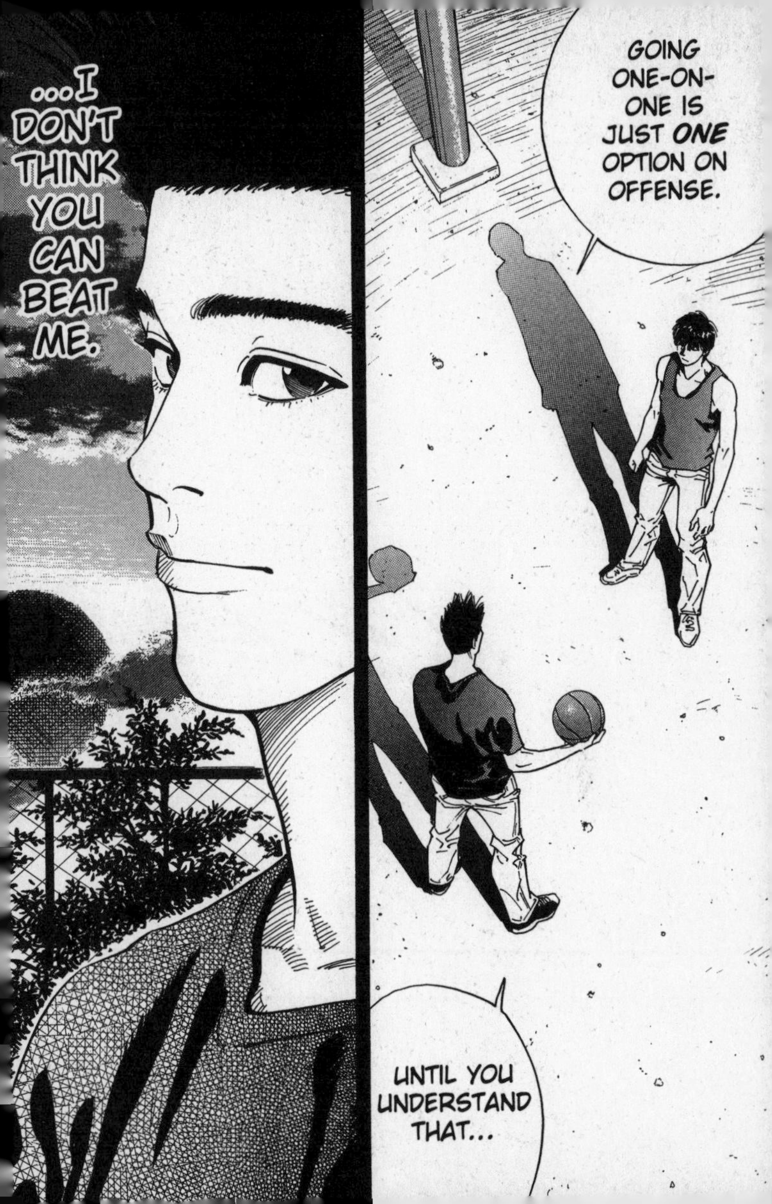
GOING ONE-ON-ONE IS JUST **ONE** OPTION ON OFFENSE.
UNTIL YOU UNDERSTAND THAT...
...I DON'T THINK YOU CAN BEAT ME.

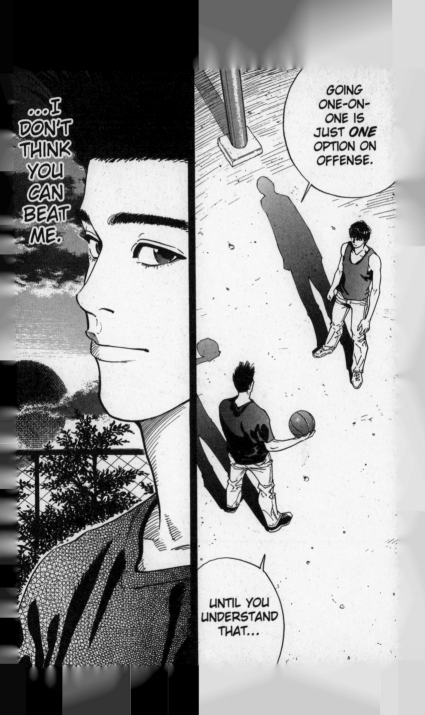

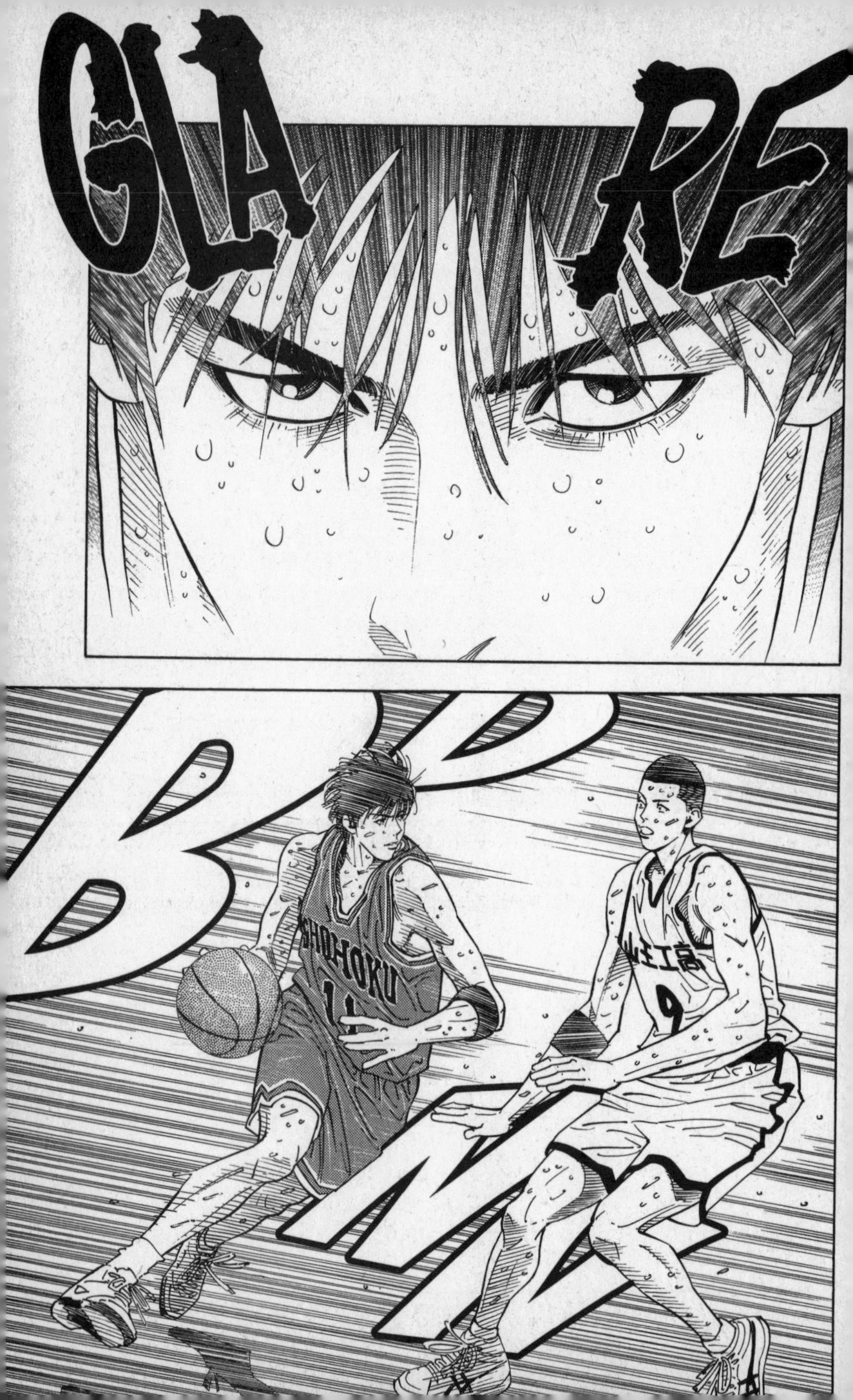
GLARE
SHOHOKU
11
9

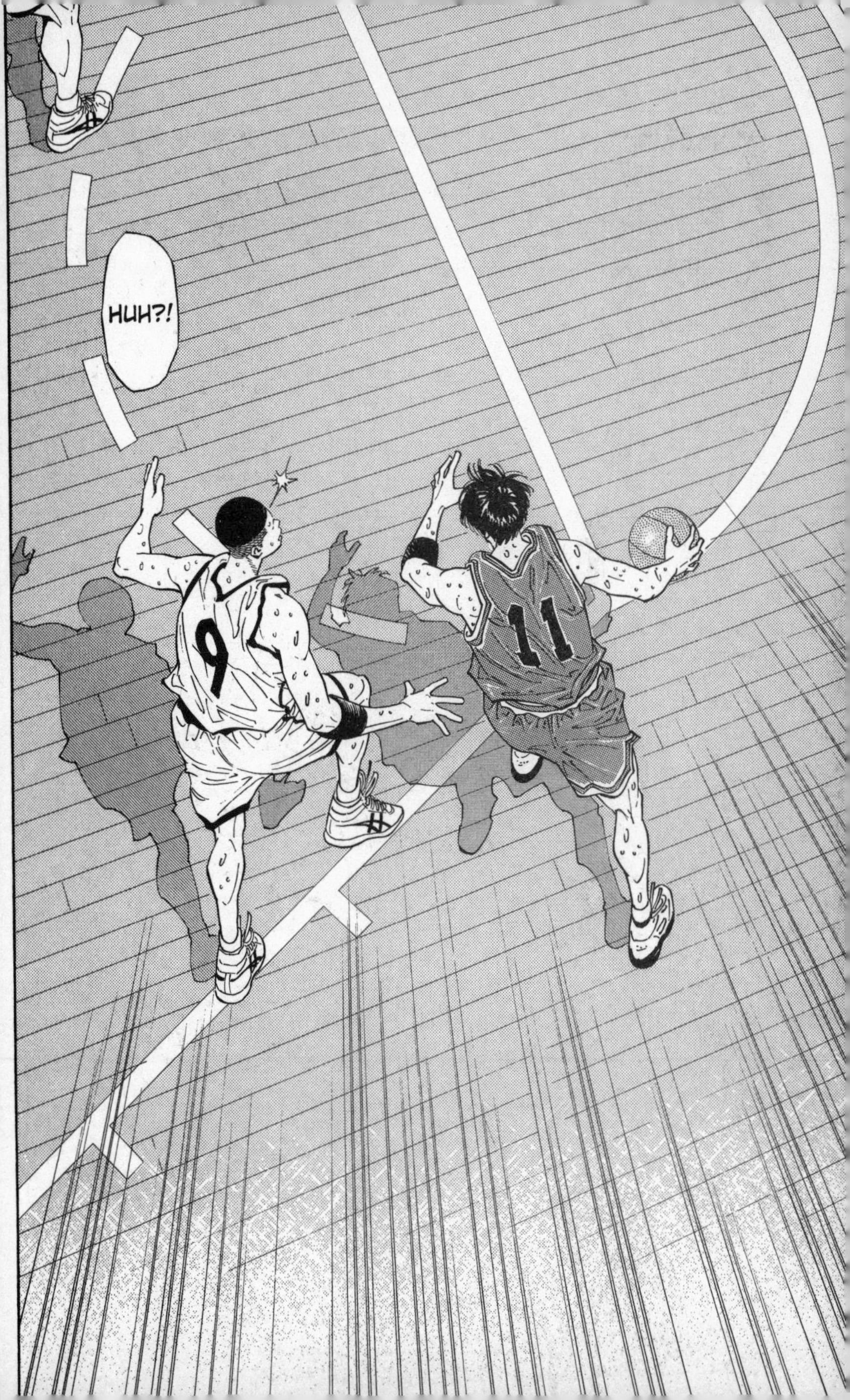
HUH?!

READ THIS WAY

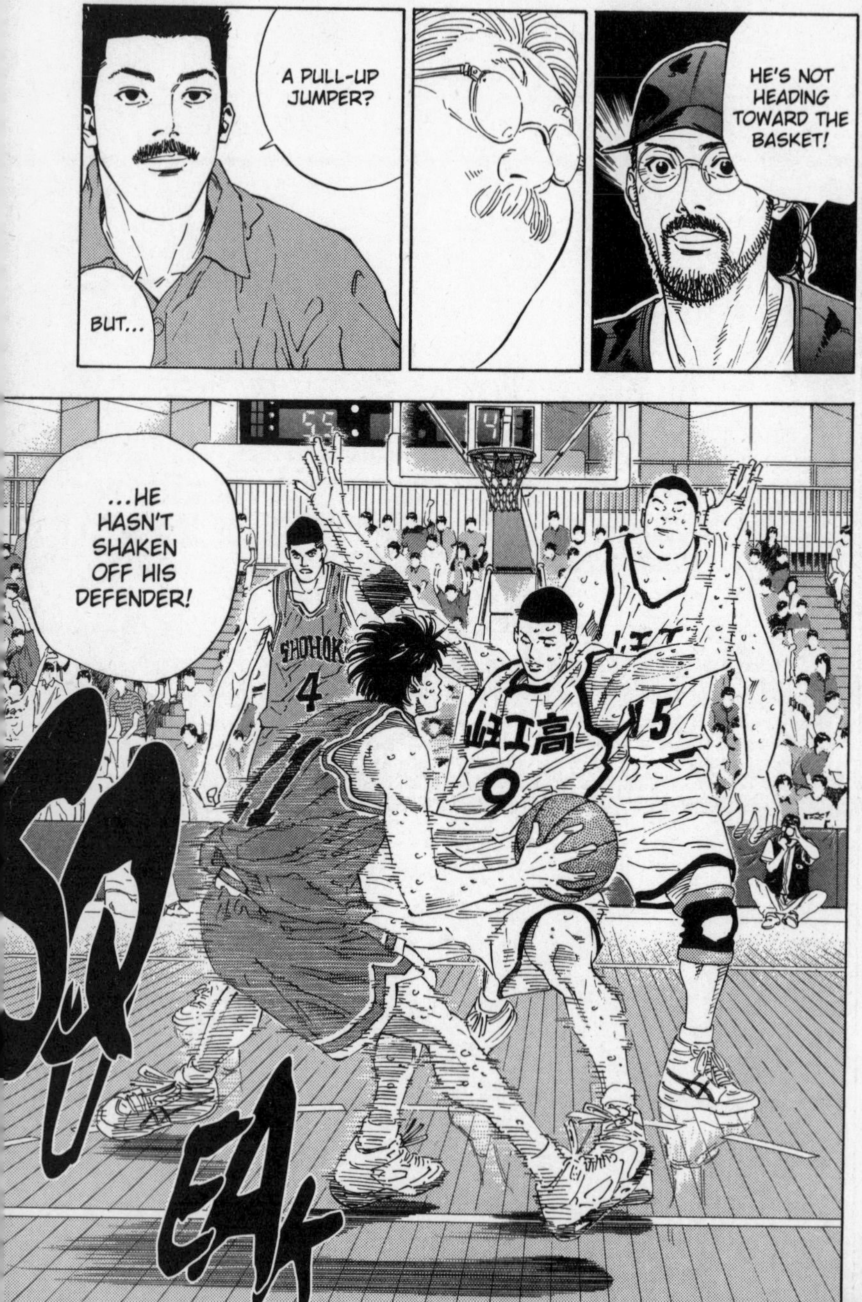
HE'S NOT HEADING TOWARD THE BASKET!
A PULL-UP JUMPER?
BUT...
...HE HASN'T SHAKEN OFF HIS DEFENDER!
SQUEAK

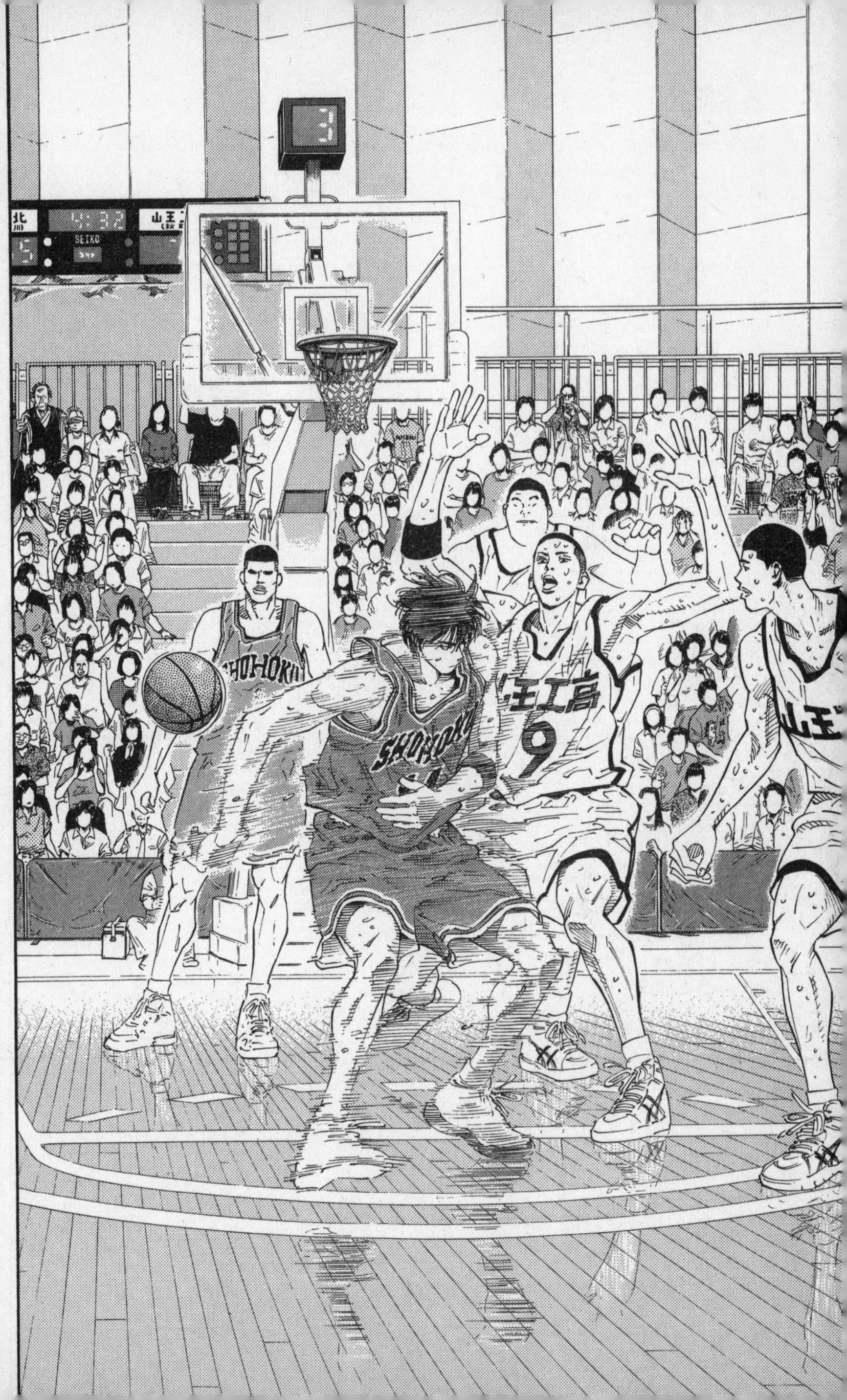
SHOHOKU
山王工高
9

READ THIS WAY

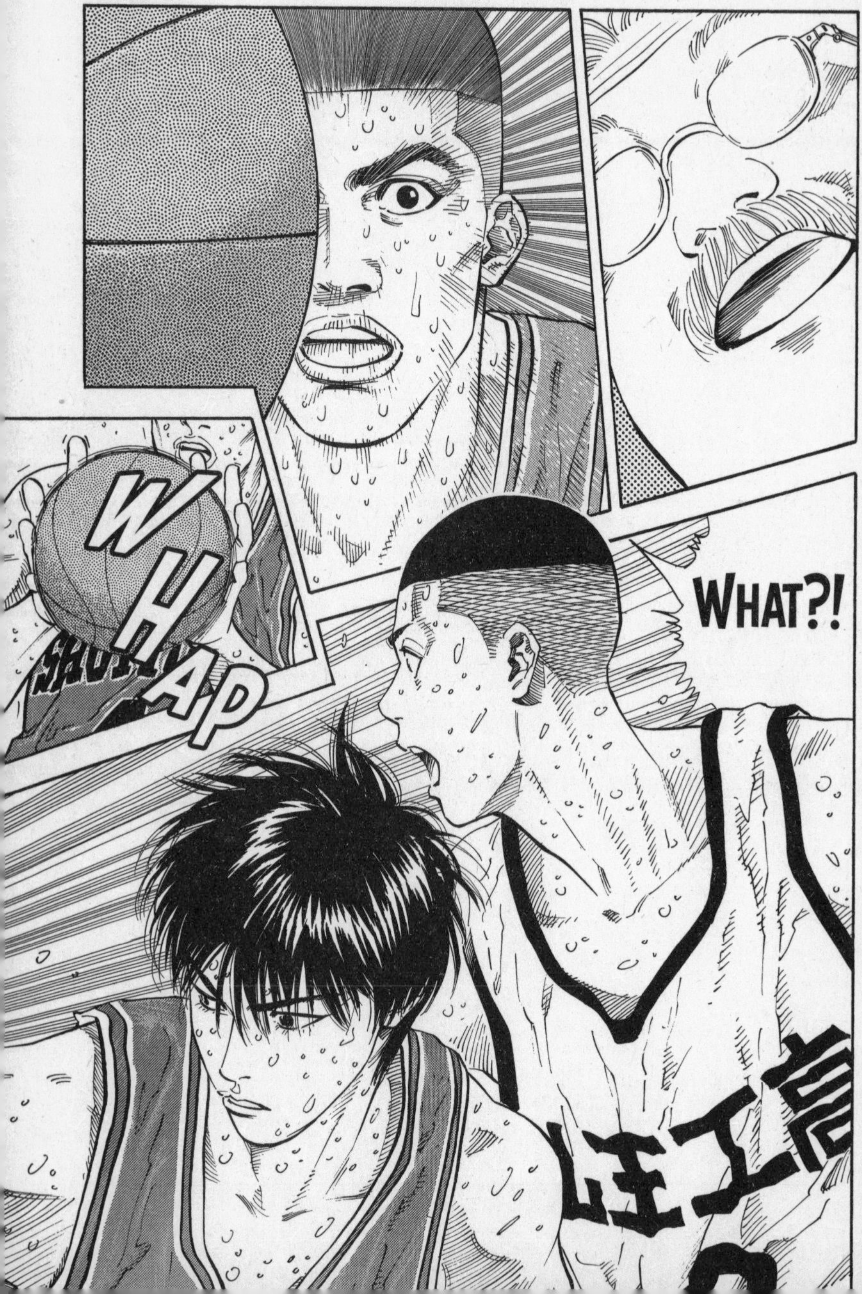
WHAP
WHAT?!

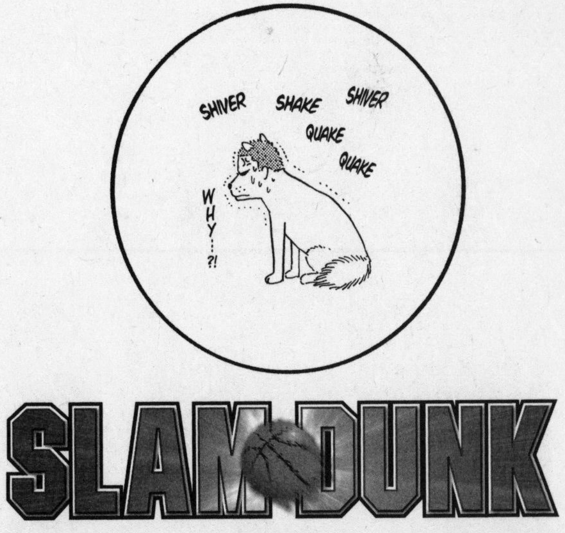
SHIVER
SHAKE
SHIVER
QUAKE
QUAKE
WHY...?!

#259 GROUNDWORK 2

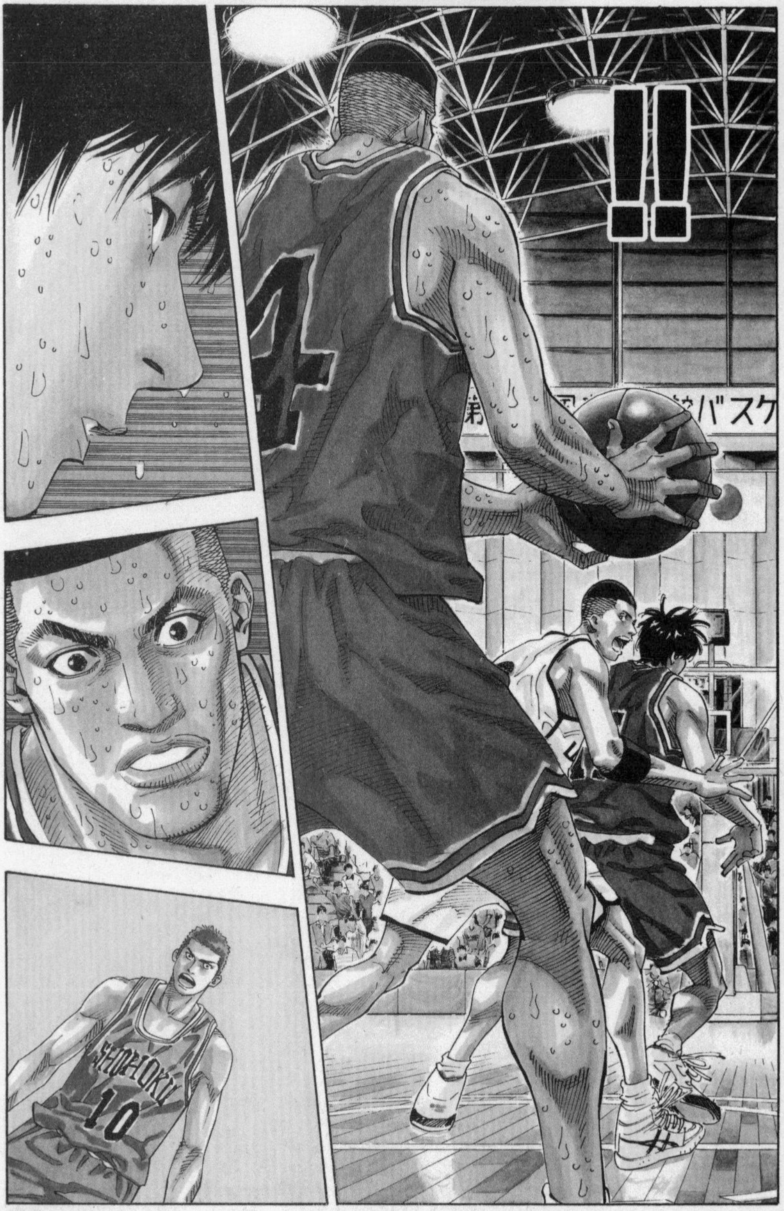
!!

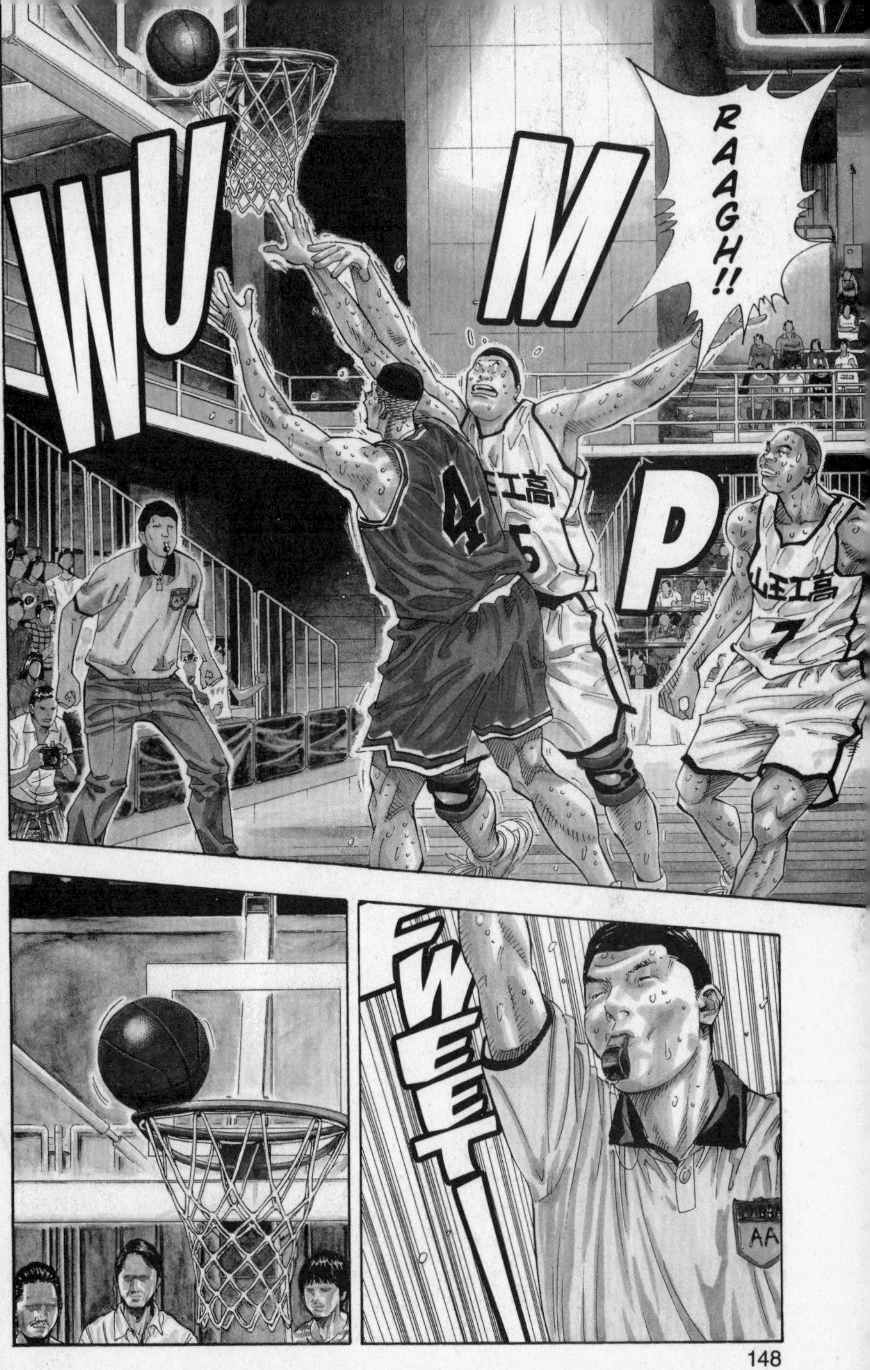
RAAGH!!
WUMP
山王工高
山王工高
TWEET

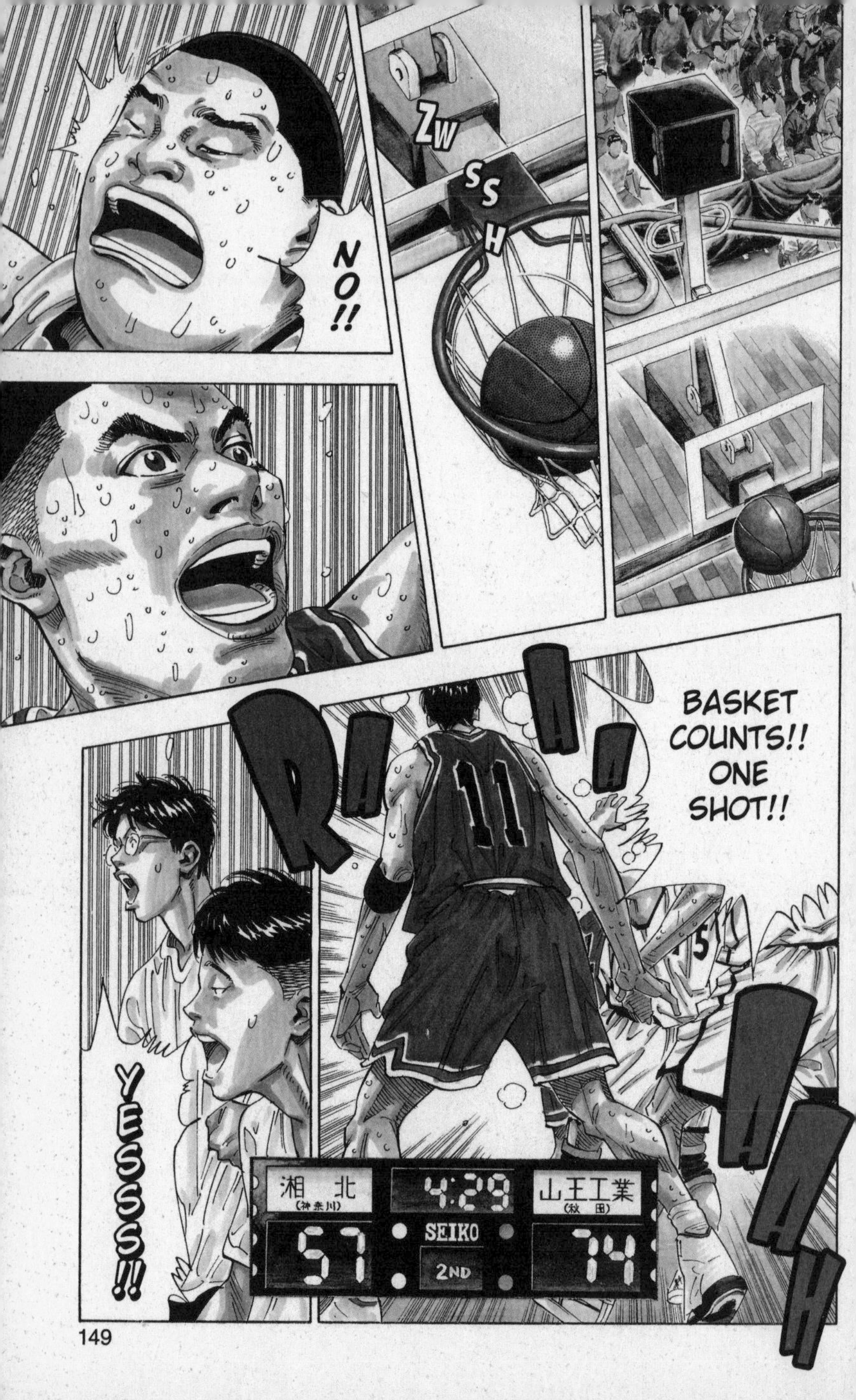
ZWSSH
NO!!
BASKET COUNTS!! ONE SHOT!!
RAAAAAAAAAH
YESSS!!
湘北
(神奈川)
4:29
山王工業
(秋田)
57
SEIKO
2ND
74

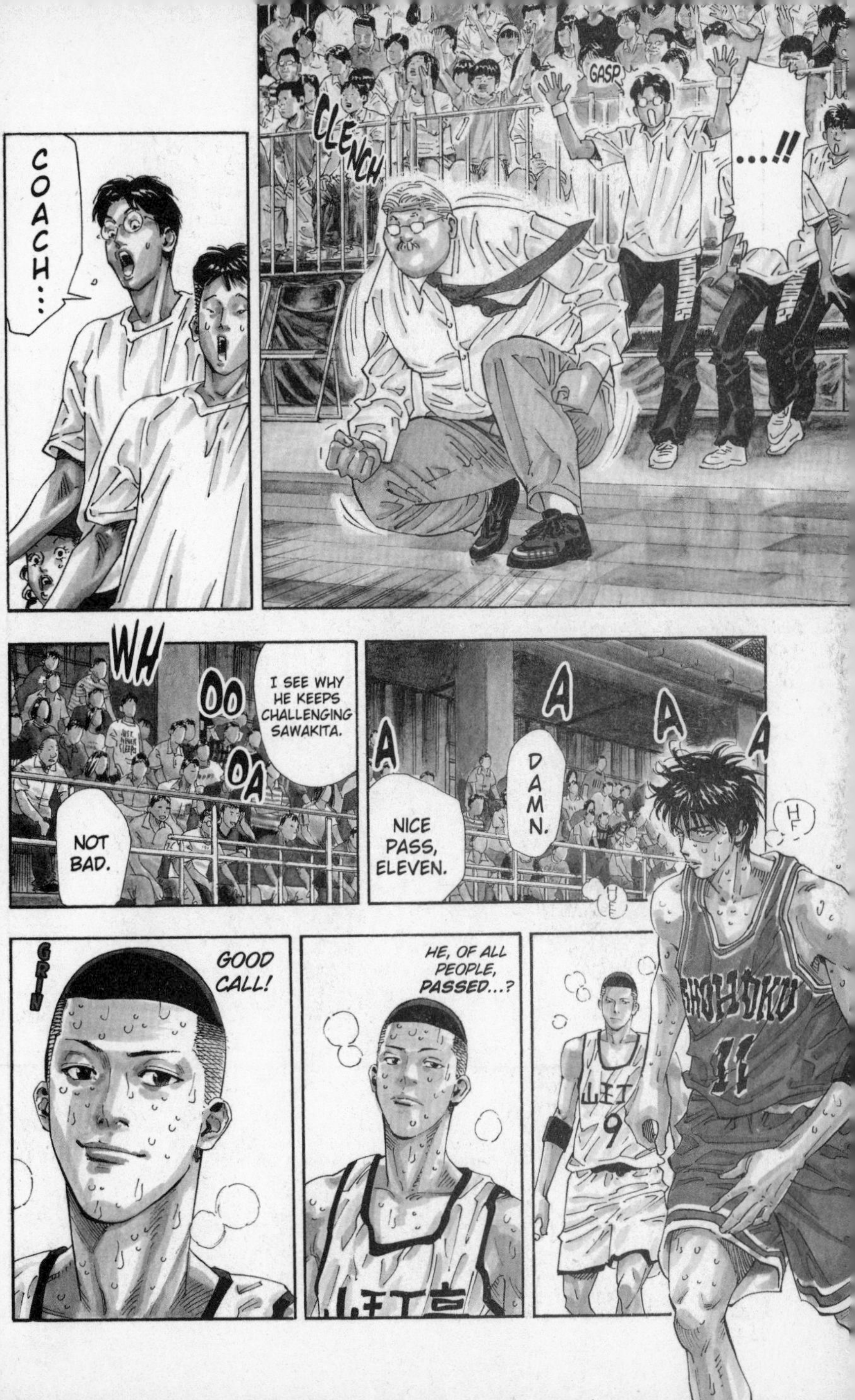
...!!
GASP
CLENCH
COACH...
A A A A
HF
DAMN.
NICE PASS, ELEVEN.
WHOOOA
I SEE WHY HE KEEPS CHALLENGING SAWAKITA.
NOT BAD.
SHOHOKU
11
9
HE, OF ALL PEOPLE, PASSED...?
GOOD CALL!
GRIN

READ THIS WAY

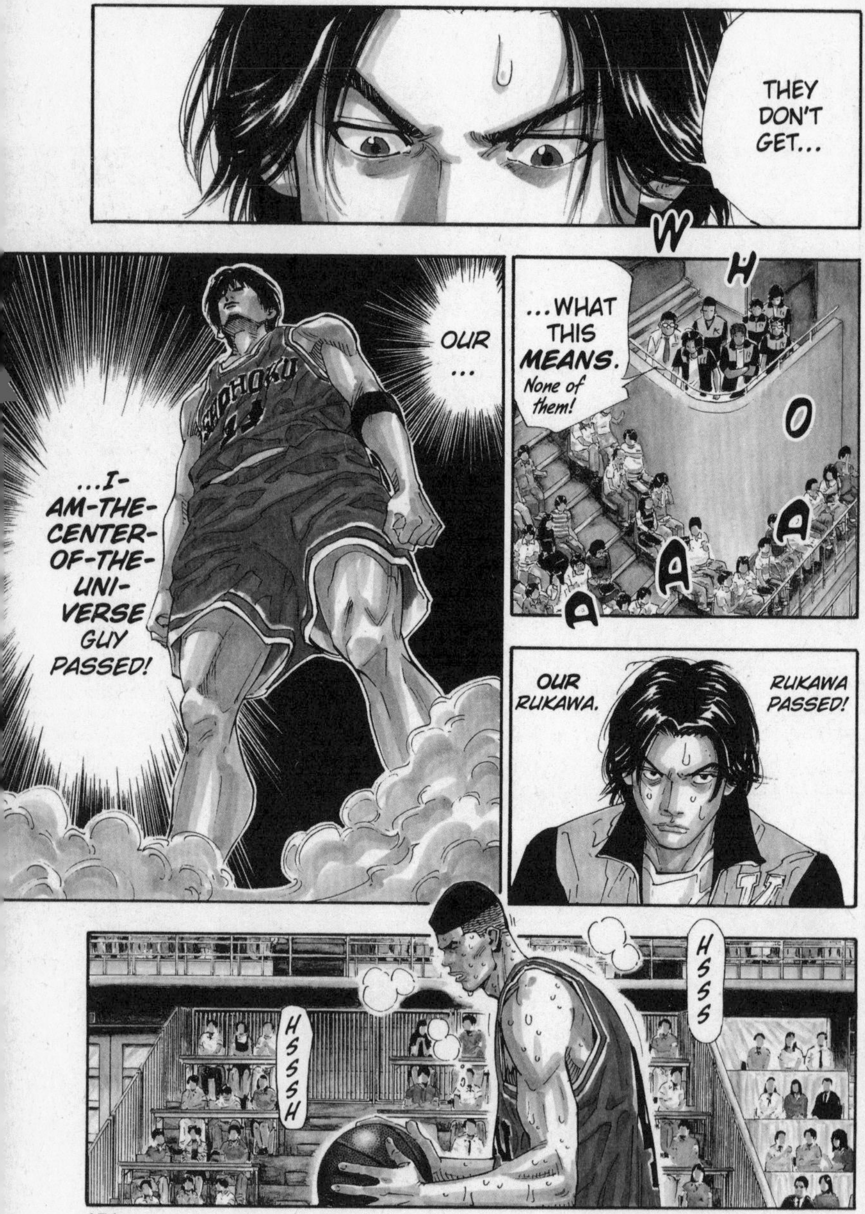
THEY DON'T GET...
WHOAAA
...WHAT THIS MEANS. None of them!
RUKAWA PASSED!
OUR RUKAWA.
OUR...
...I-AM-THE-CENTER-OF-THE-UNI-VERSE GUY PASSED!
HSSS
HSSSH

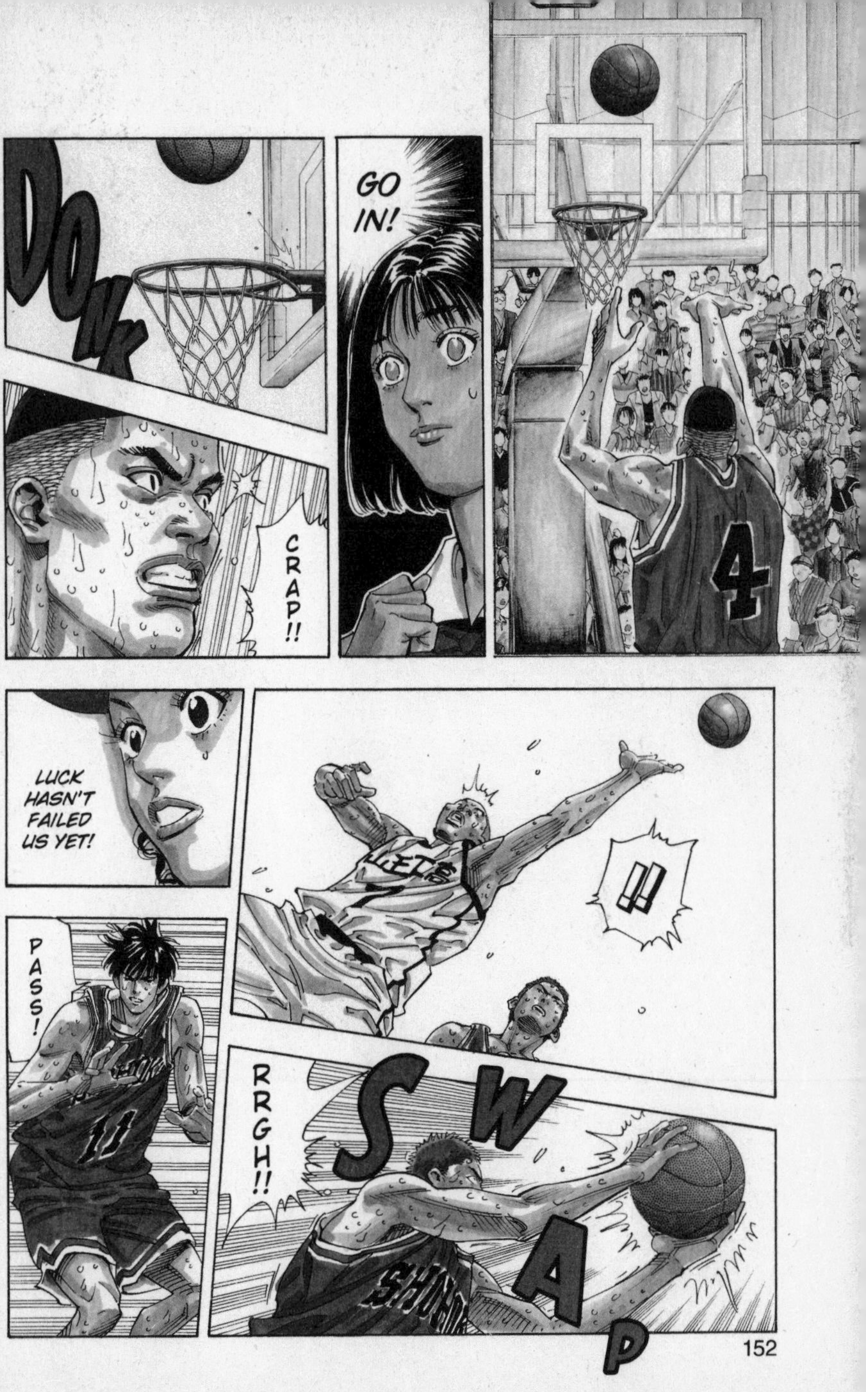
GO IN!
DONK
CRAP!!
!!
LUCK HASN'T FAILED US YET!
RRGH!!
SWAP
PASS!

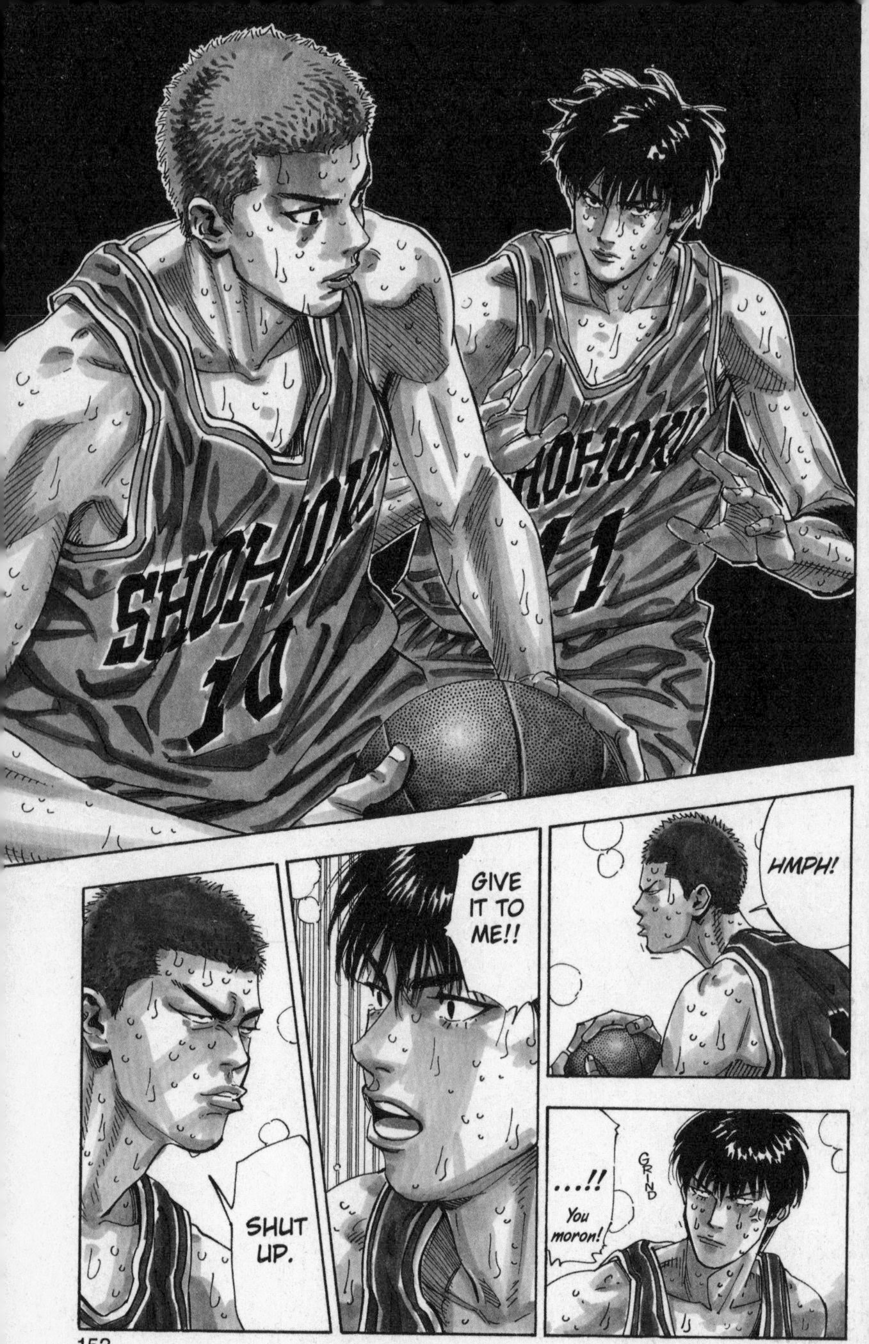
HMPH!
GRIND
...!!
You moron!
GIVE IT TO ME!!
SHUT UP.

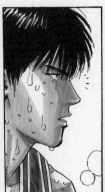

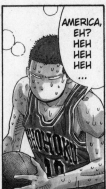

AMERICA, EH? HEH HEH HEH ...

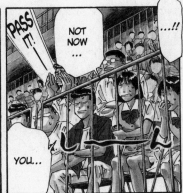

PASS IT!

NOT NOW ...

...!!

YOU...

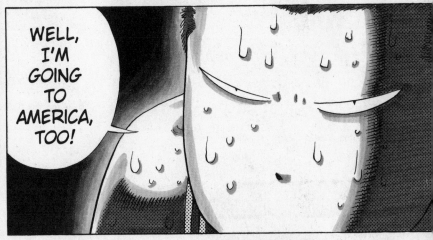

WELL, I'M GOING TO AMERICA, TOO!

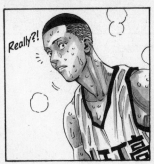

Really?!

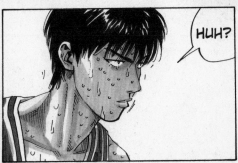

HUH?

154

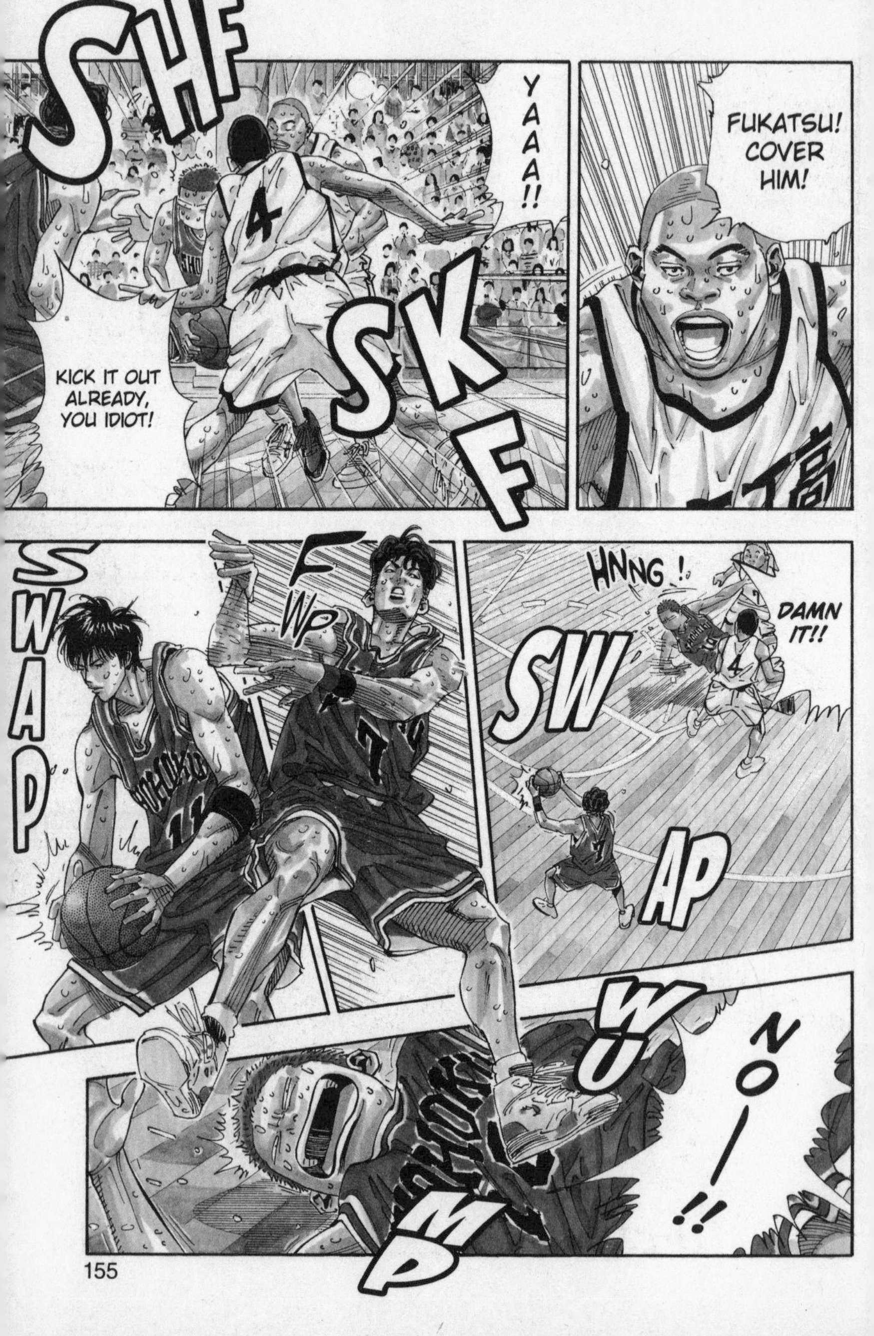
FUKATSU! COVER HIM!
YAAAA!!
SHF
SK
F
KICK IT OUT ALREADY, YOU IDIOT!
HNNG!
DAMN IT!!
SW
AP
F
WP
SWAP
NO—!!
WU
MP

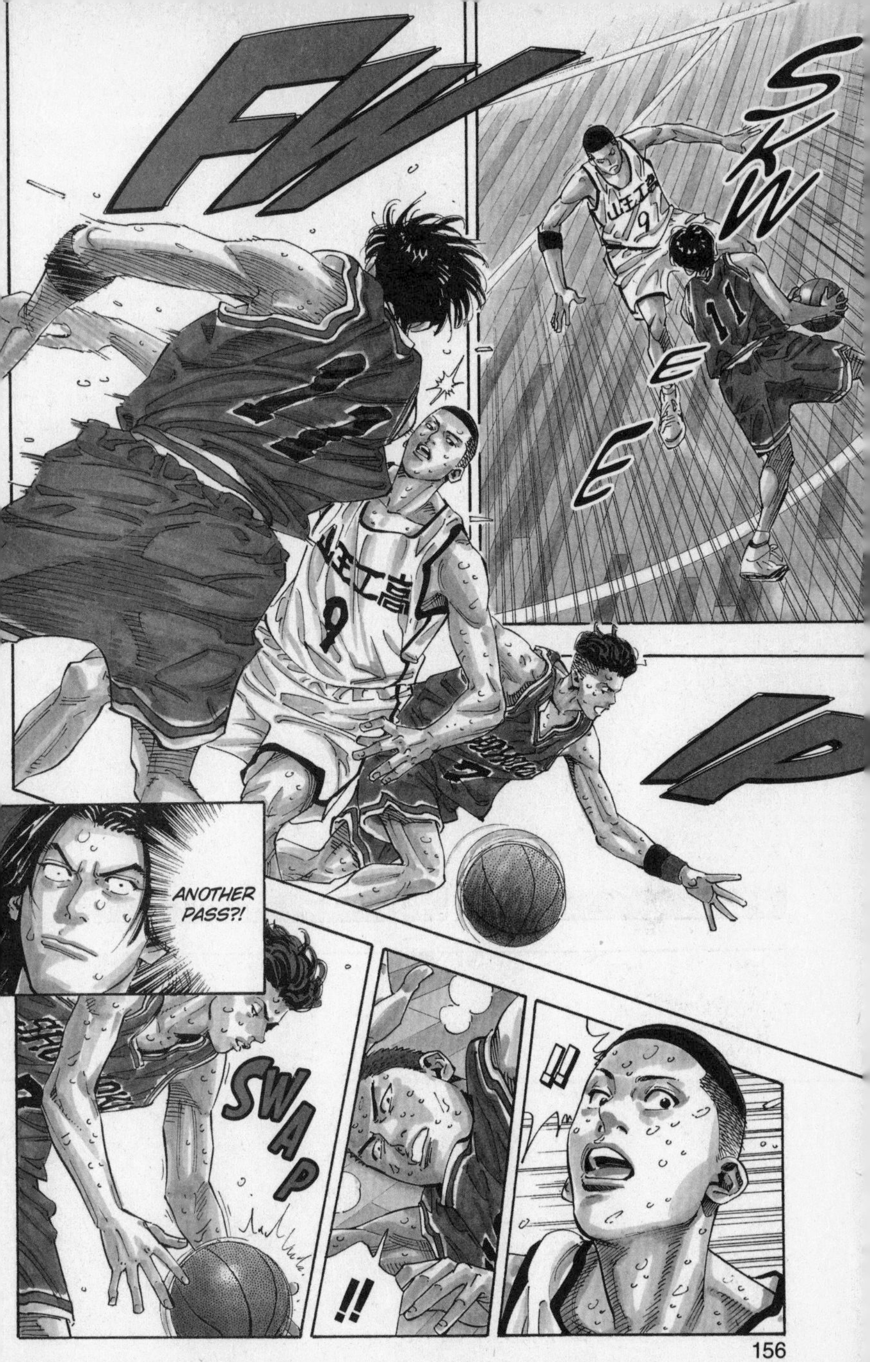
SKWEEE
FW
P
ANOTHER PASS?!
!!
!!
SWAP

READ THIS WAY

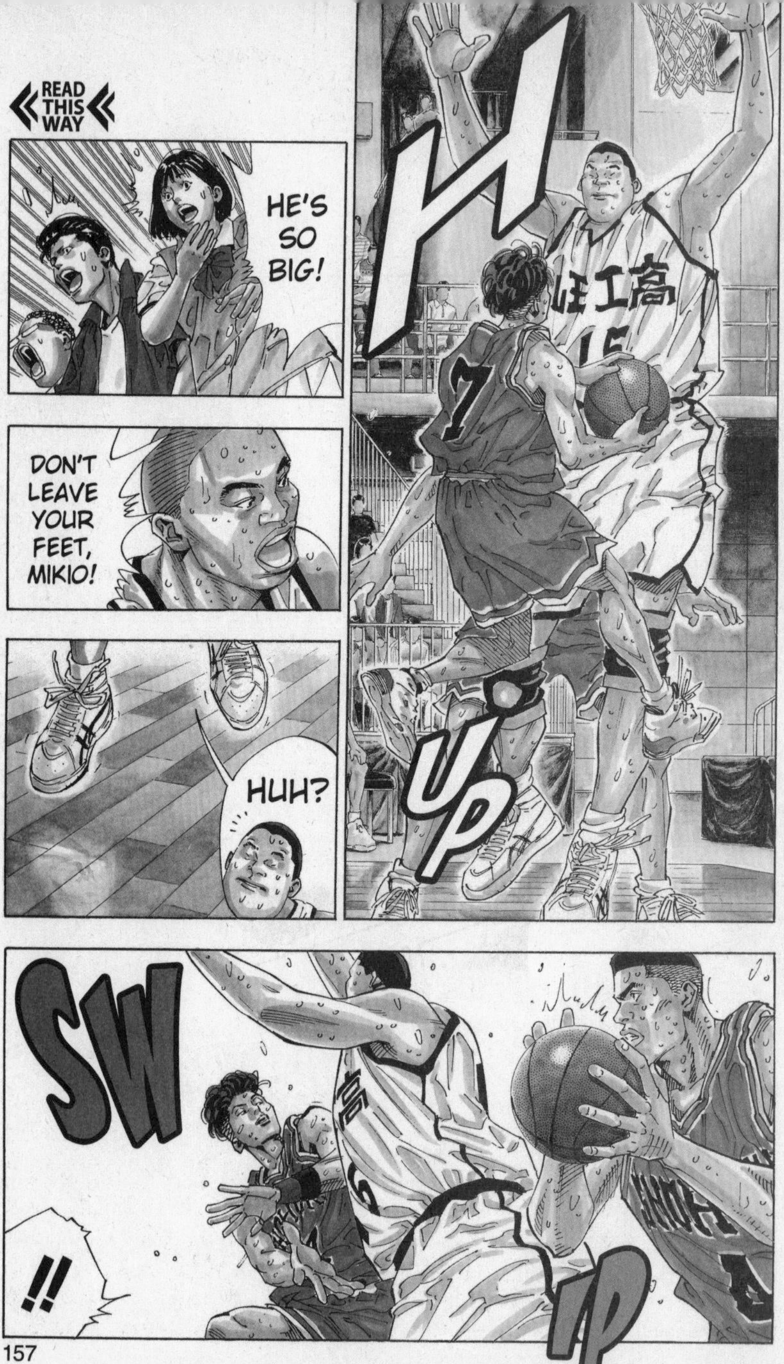
H
UP
HE'S SO BIG!
DON'T LEAVE YOUR FEET, MIKIO!
HUH?
SW
IP
!!

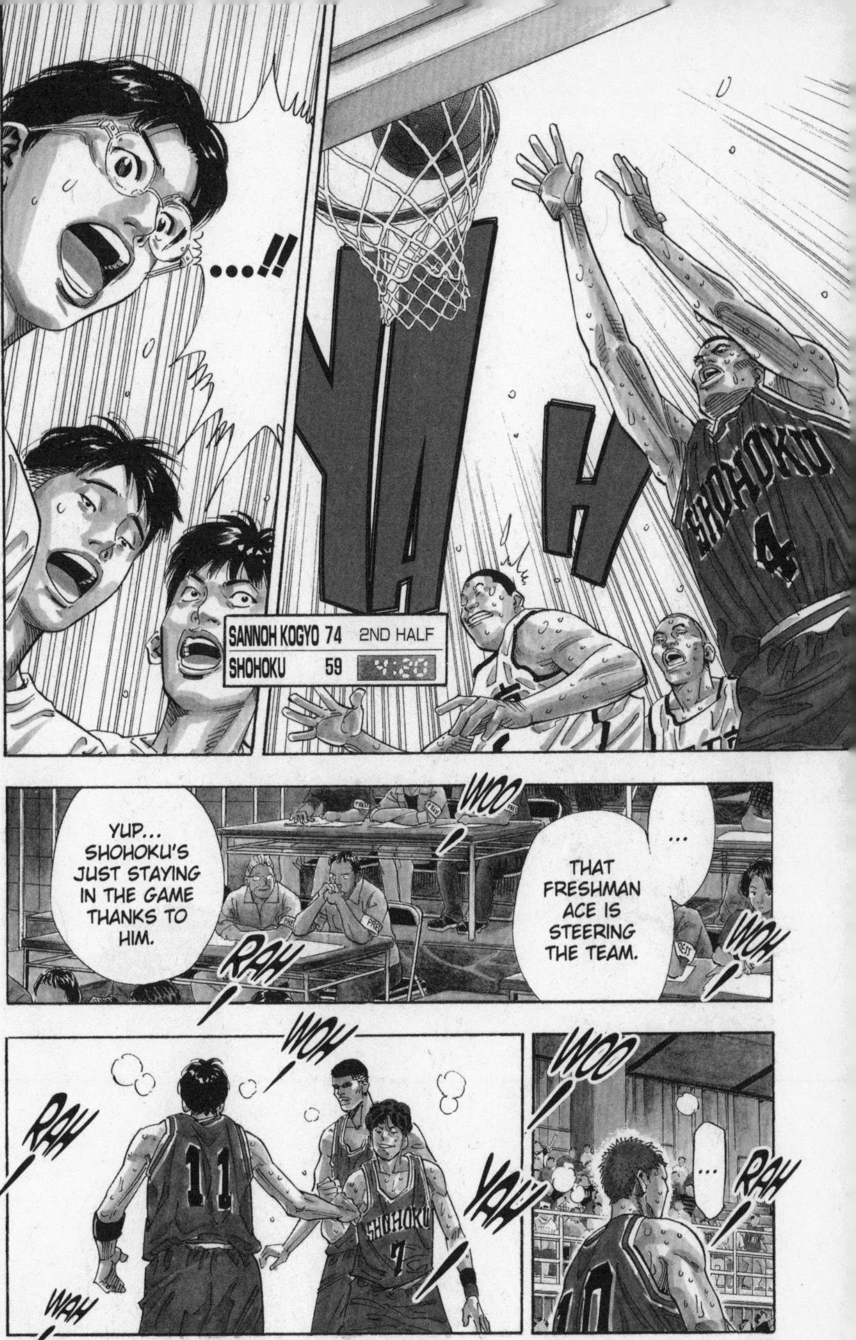
SANNOH KOGYO 74 2ND HALF
SHOHOKU 59
...!!
WOO!
...
THAT FRESHMAN ACE IS STEERING THE TEAM.
WOH!
YUP... SHOHOKU'S JUST STAYING IN THE GAME THANKS TO HIM.
RAH!
WOO!
...
RAH!
YAH!
WOH!
RAH!
WAH!

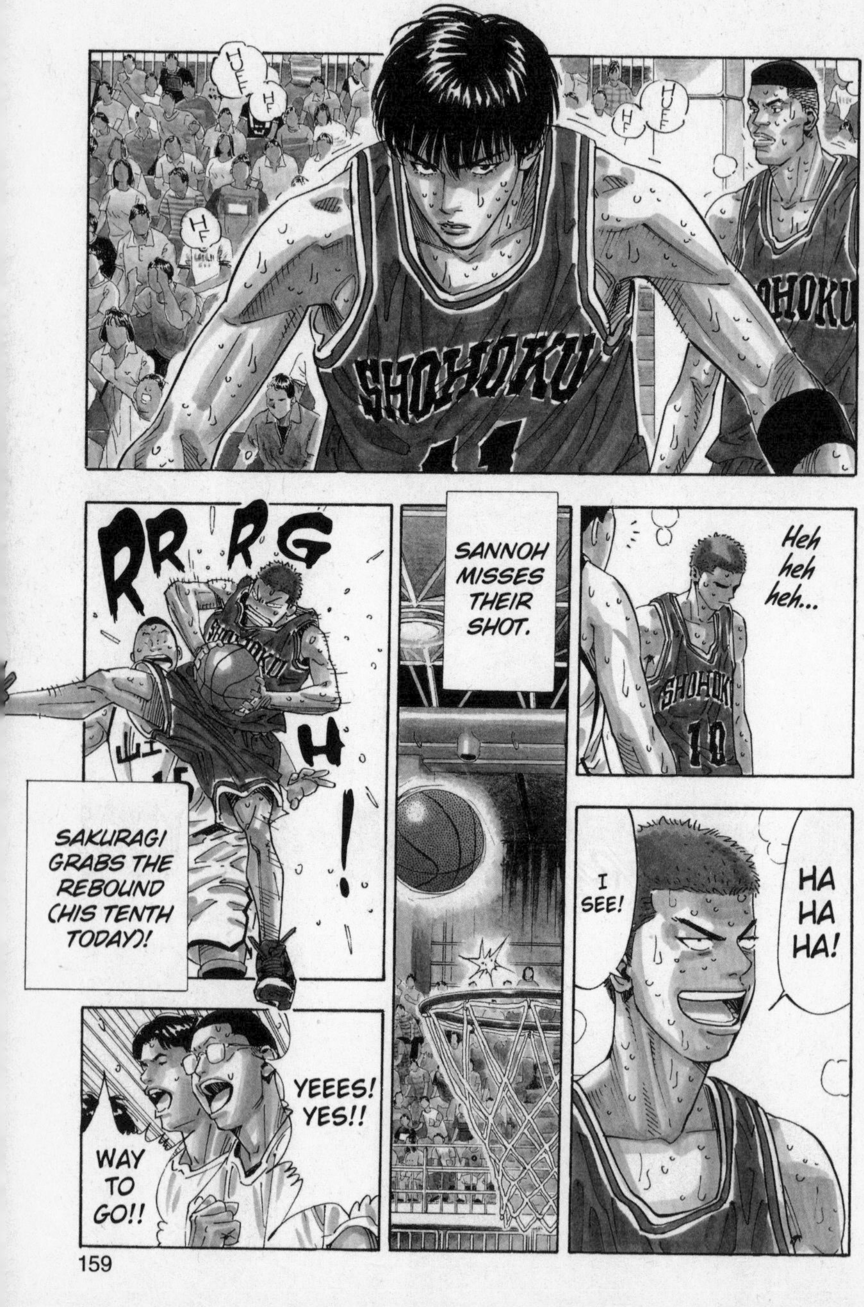
HUFF
HF
HUFF
HF
HF
Heh heh heh...
HA HA HA!
I SEE!
SANNOH MISSES THEIR SHOT.
RRRGH!
SAKURAGI GRABS THE REBOUND (HIS TENTH TODAY)!
YEEES! YES!!
WAY TO GO!!

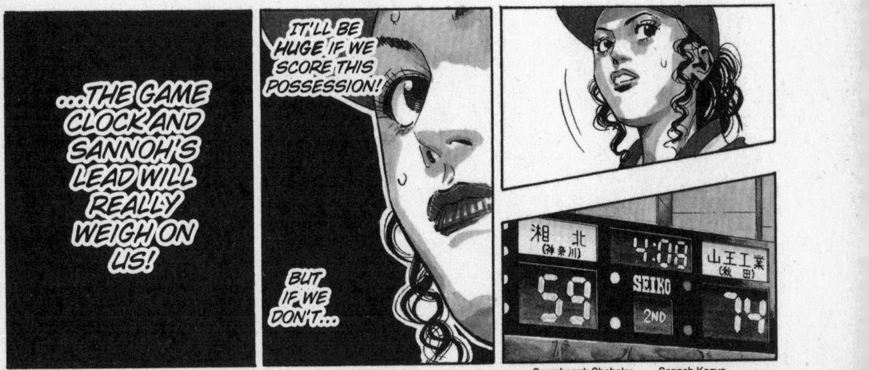
湘北 (神奈川)
4:08
山王工業 (秋田)
59
SEIKO
2ND
74
IT'LL BE HUGE IF WE SCORE THIS POSSESSION!
BUT IF WE DON'T...
...THE GAME CLOCK AND SANNOH'S LEAD WILL REALLY WEIGH ON US!

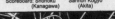

Scoreboard: Shohoku (Kanagawa) Sannoh Kogyo (Akita)

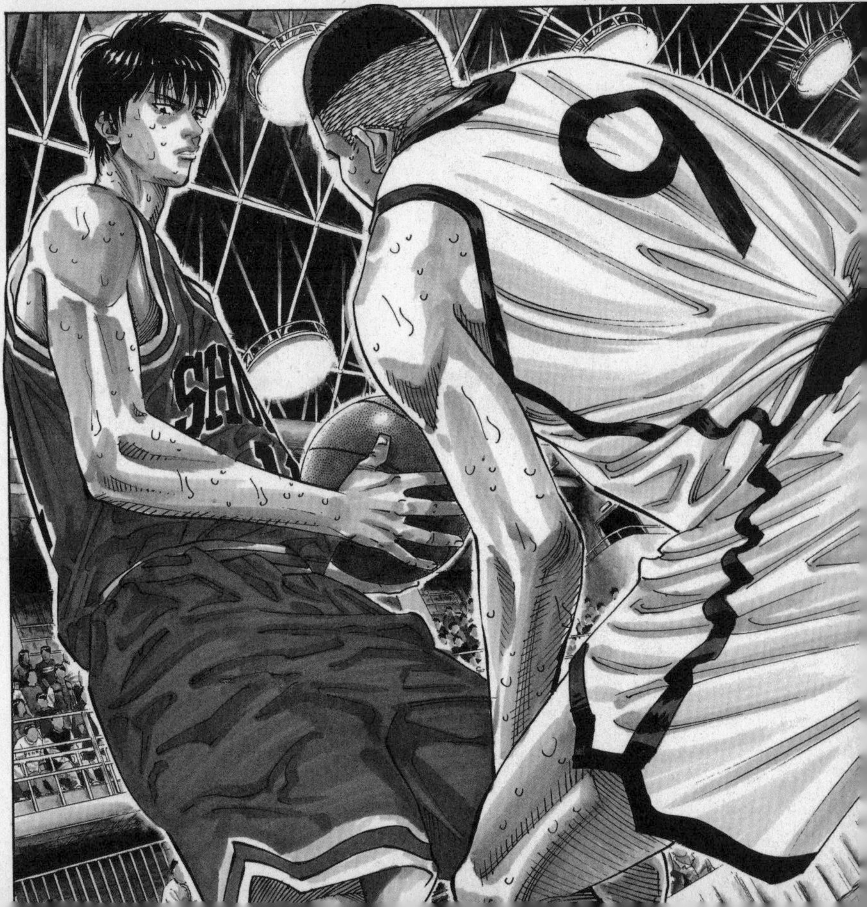

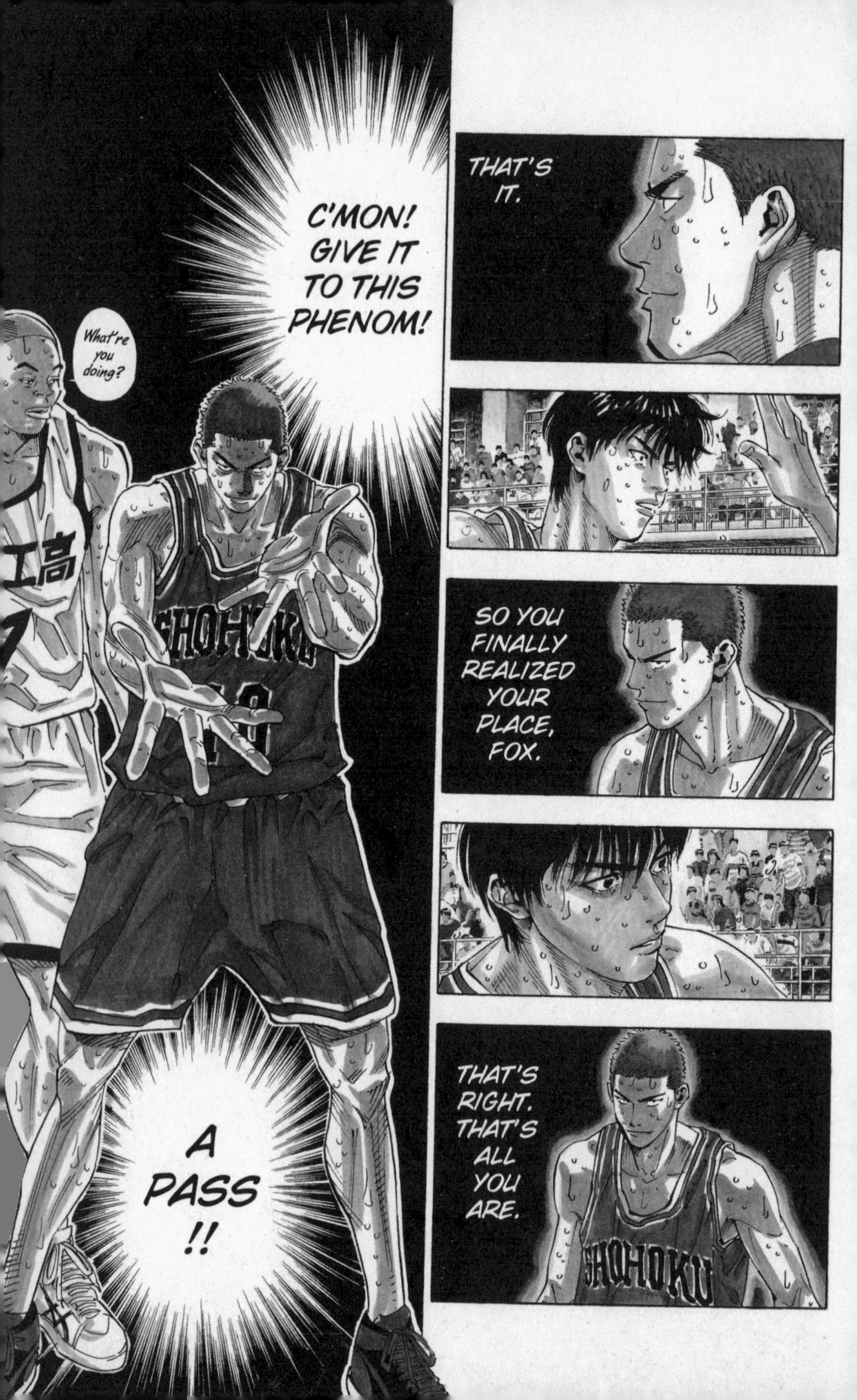
THAT'S IT.
SO YOU FINALLY REALIZED YOUR PLACE, FOX.
THAT'S RIGHT. THAT'S ALL YOU ARE.
C'MON! GIVE IT TO THIS PHENOM!
What're you doing?
A PASS !!

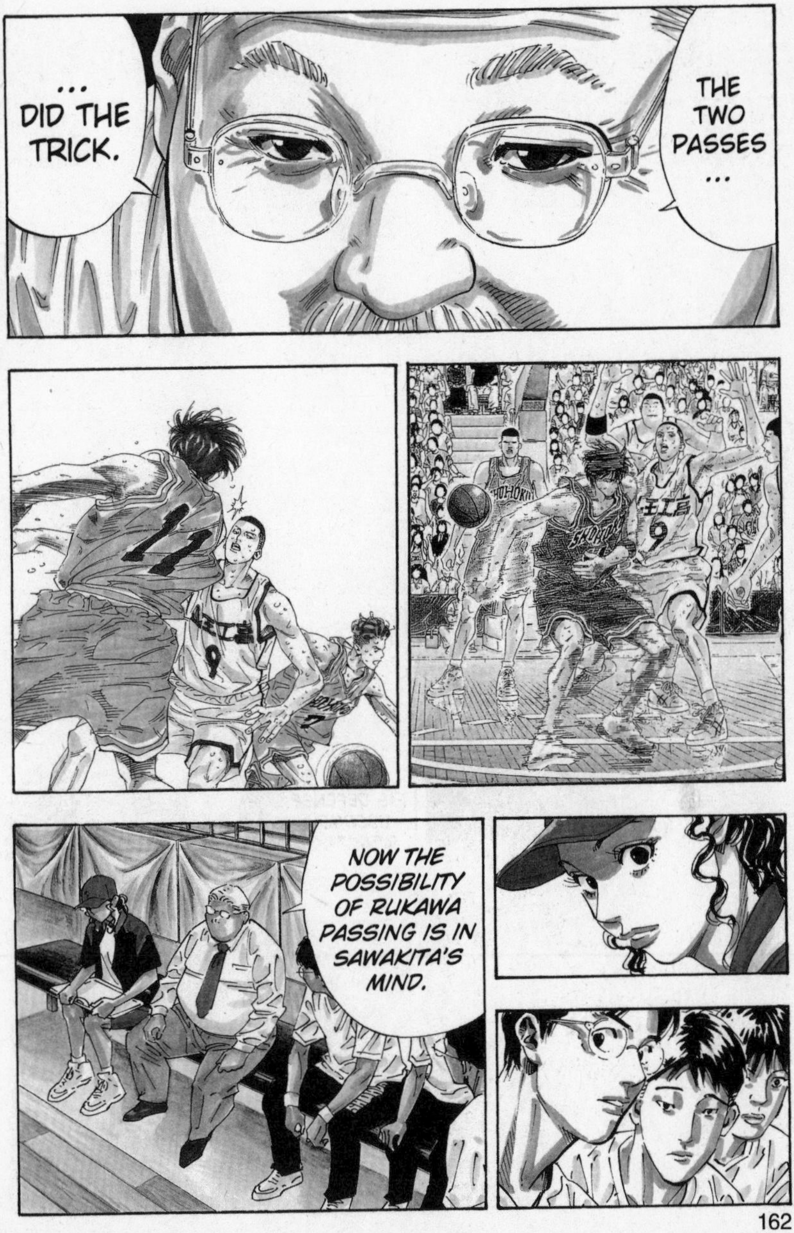
THE TWO PASSES...
...DID THE TRICK.
NOW THE POSSIBILITY OF RUKAWA PASSING IS IN SAWAKITA'S MIND.

READ THIS WAY

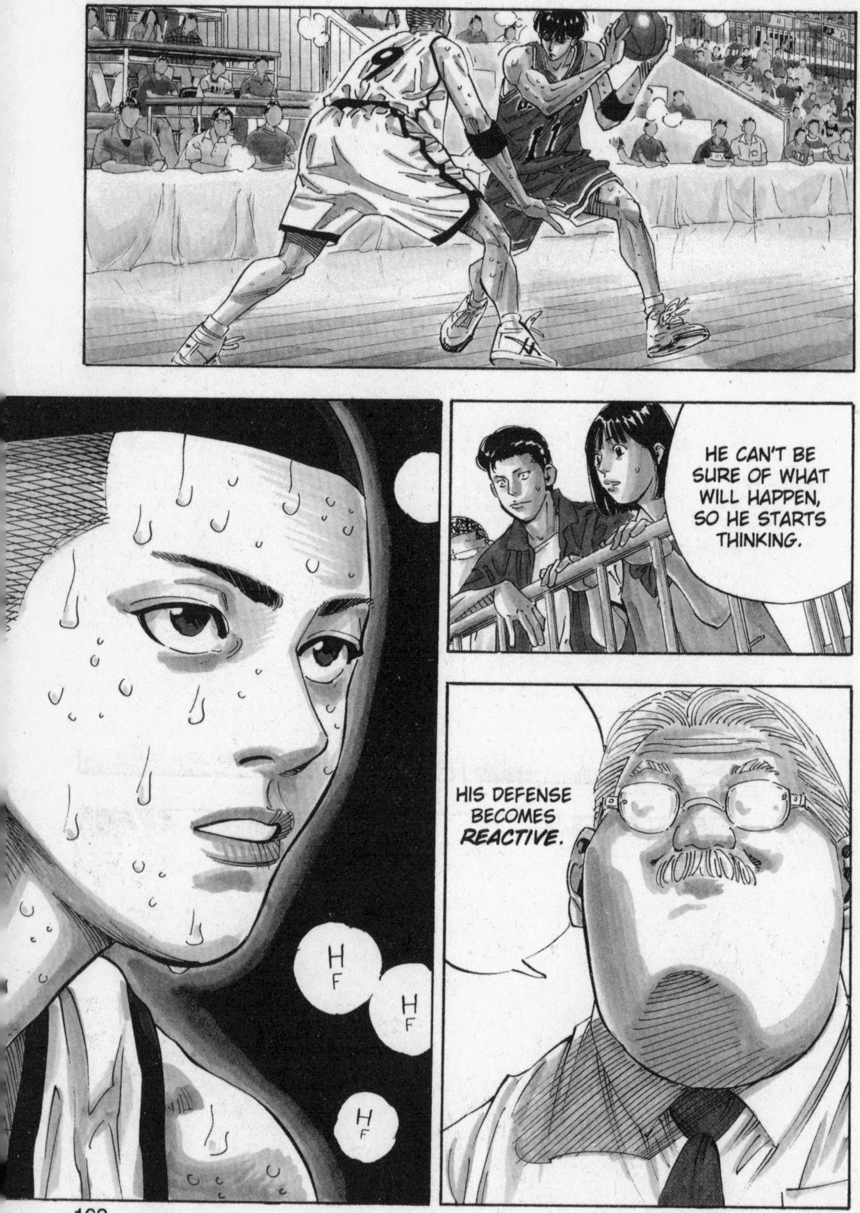
HE CAN'T BE SURE OF WHAT WILL HAPPEN, SO HE STARTS THINKING.
HIS DEFENSE BECOMES *REACTIVE*.
HF
HF
HF

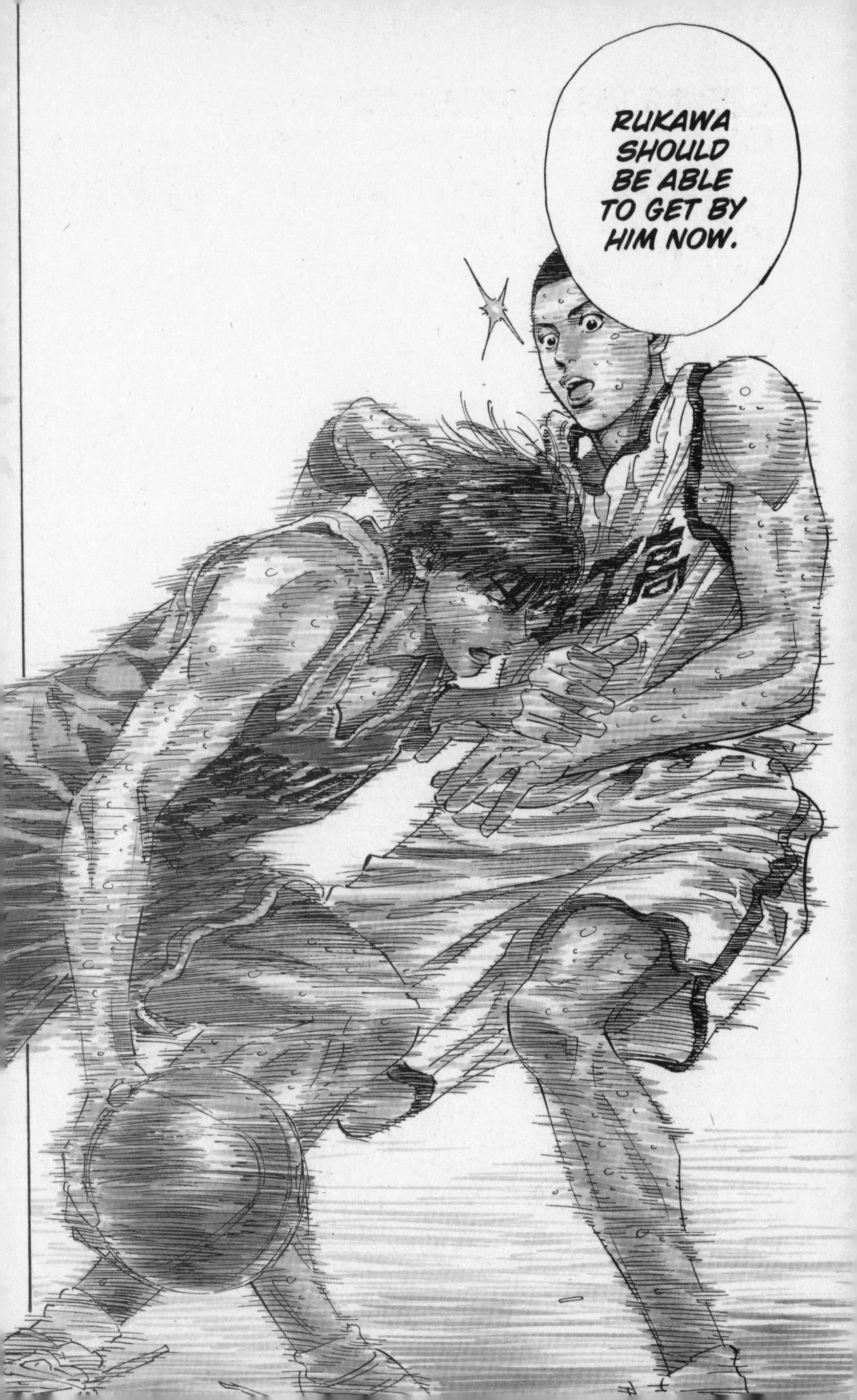
RUKAWA SHOULD BE ABLE TO GET BY HIM NOW.

DEBTS MUST BE REPAID IMMEDIATELY

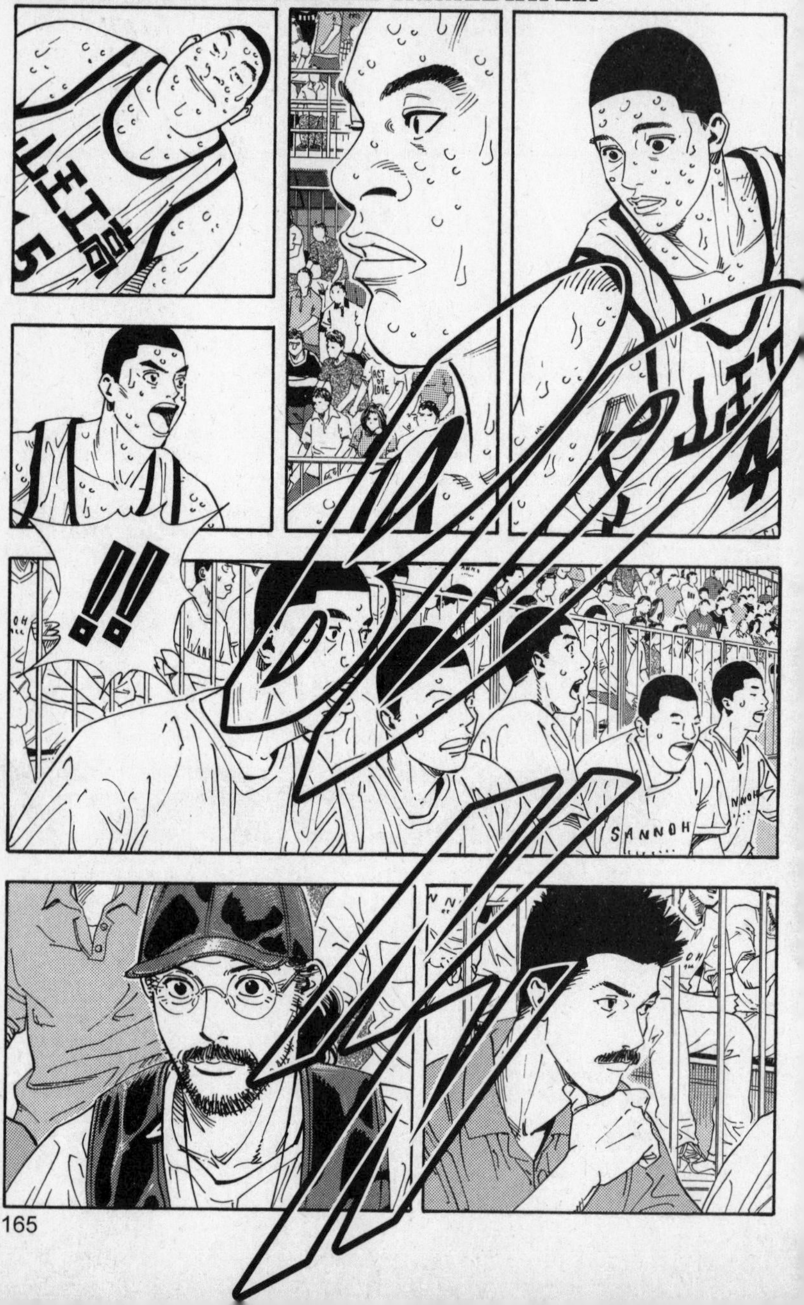
!!

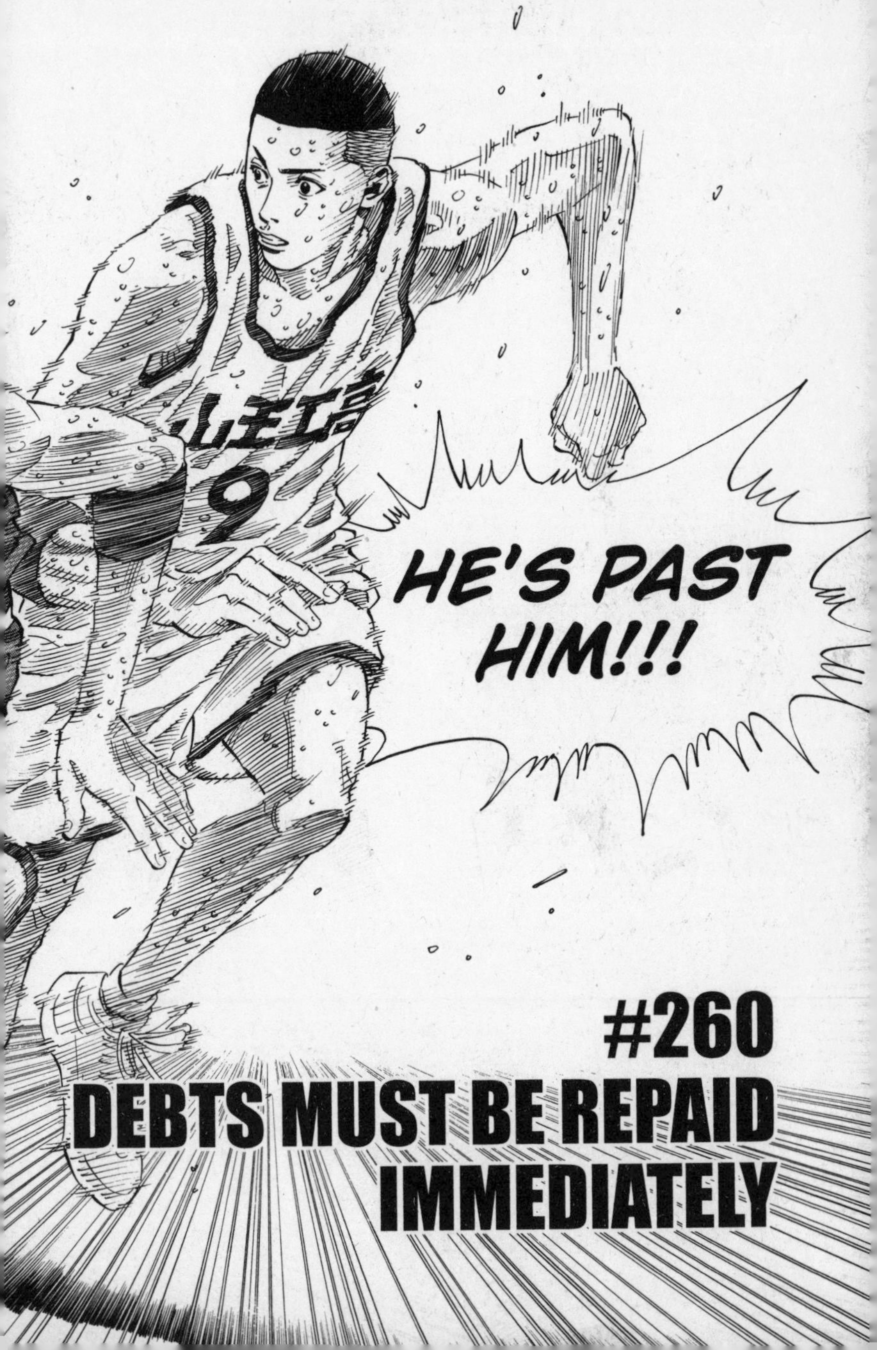
HE'S PAST HIM!!!

#260
DEBTS MUST BE REPAID IMMEDIATELY

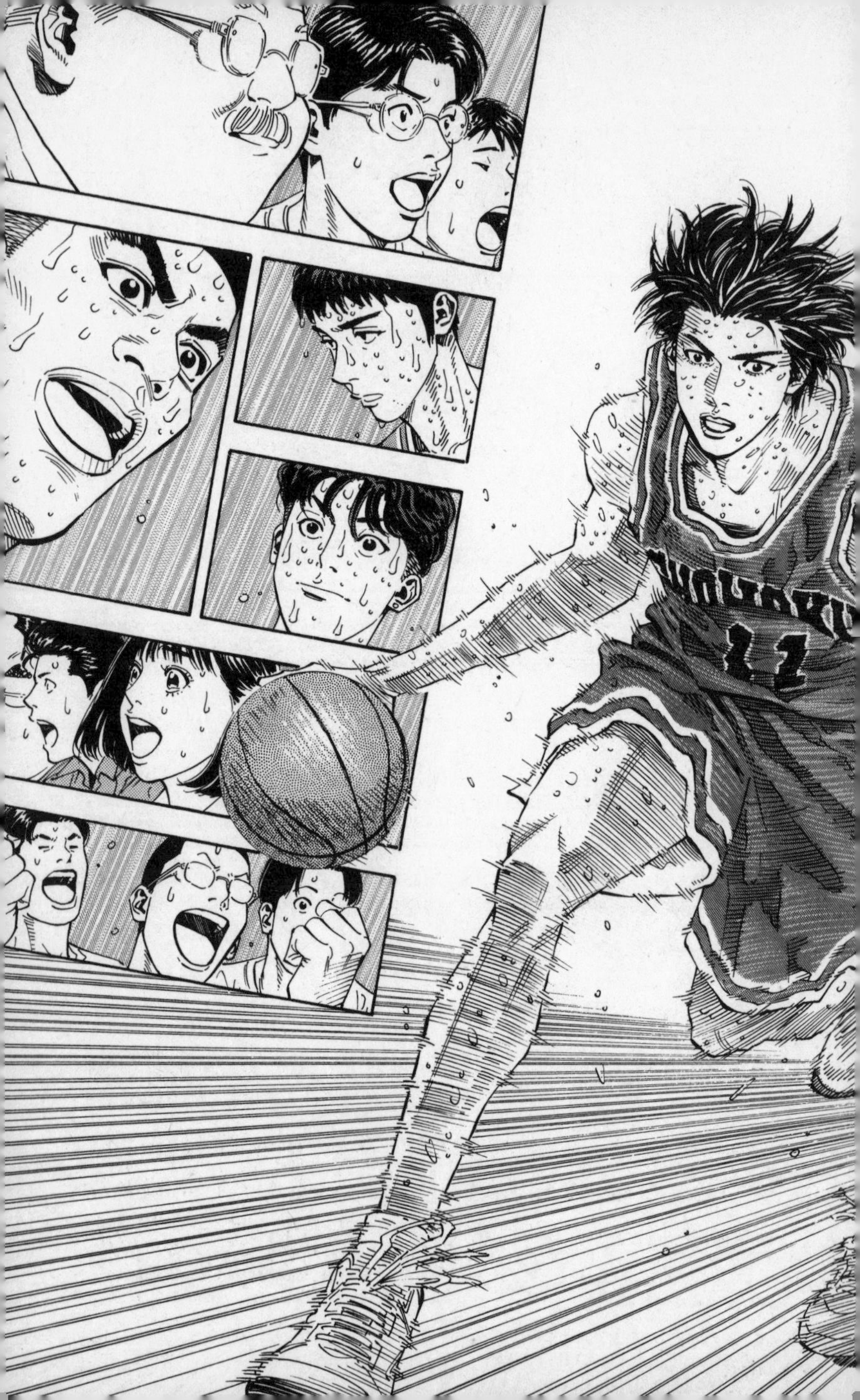

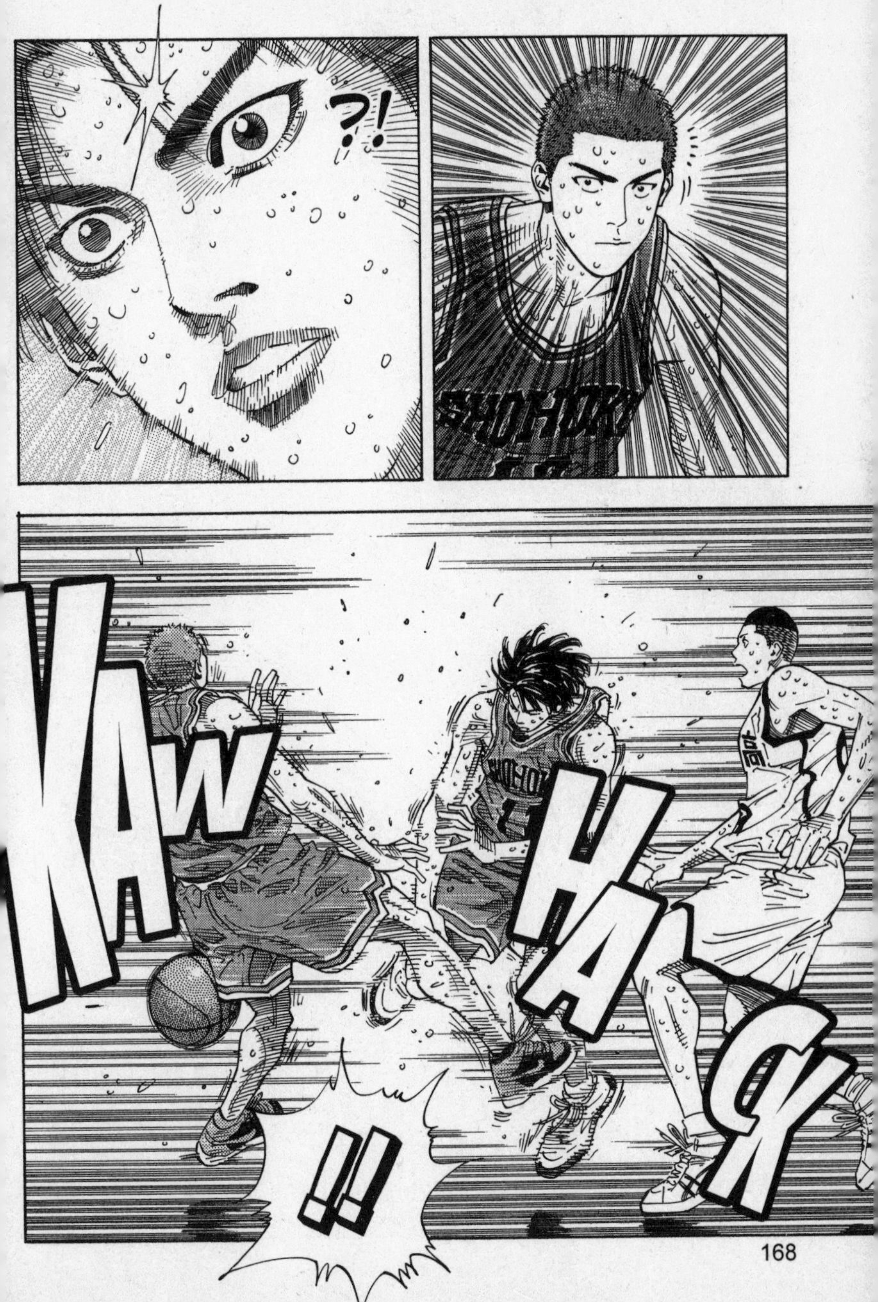
?!
KAW
HAACK
!!

READ THIS WAY

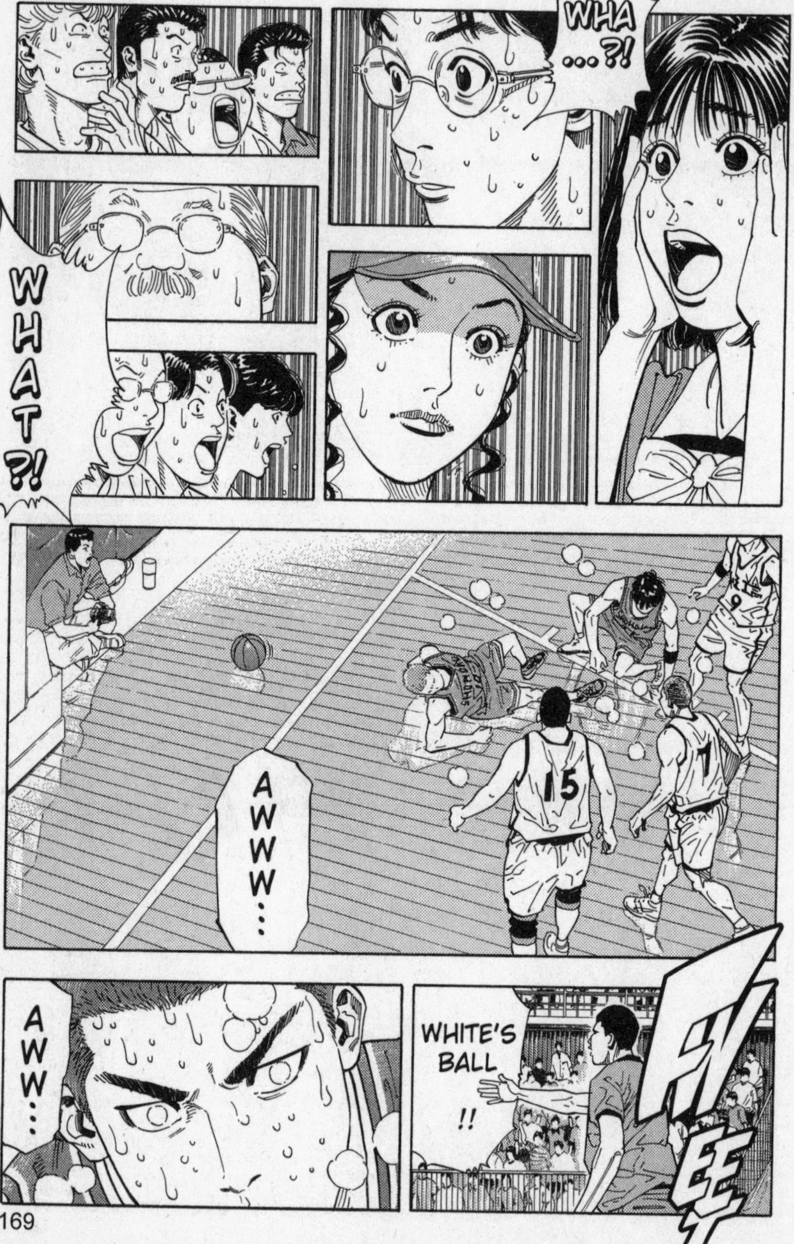
WHA...?!
WHAT?!
AWWW...
WHITE'S BALL
!!
FWEET
AWW...

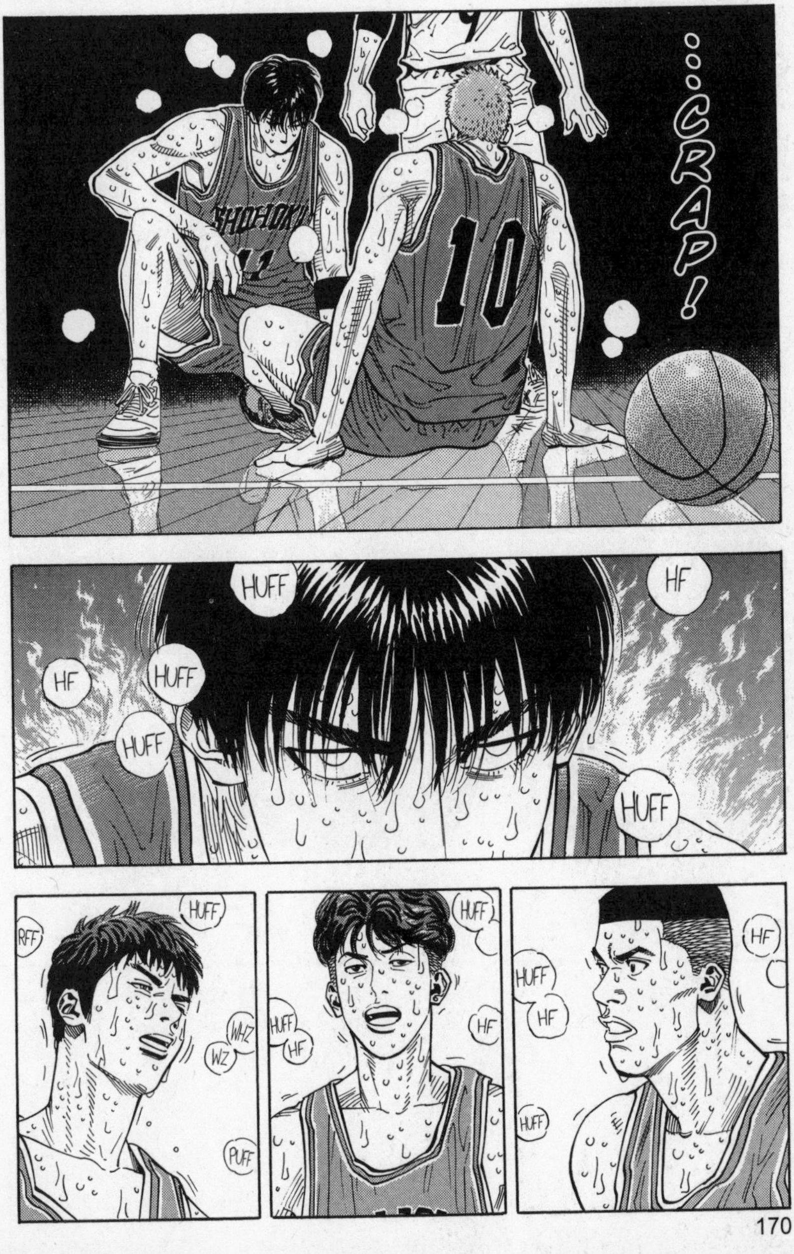
...CRAP!
HF
HUFF
HUFF
HF
HUFF
HUFF
HF
HUFF
HF
HUFF
HUFF
HF
HUFF
HF
HUFF
RFF
WHZ
WZ
PUFF

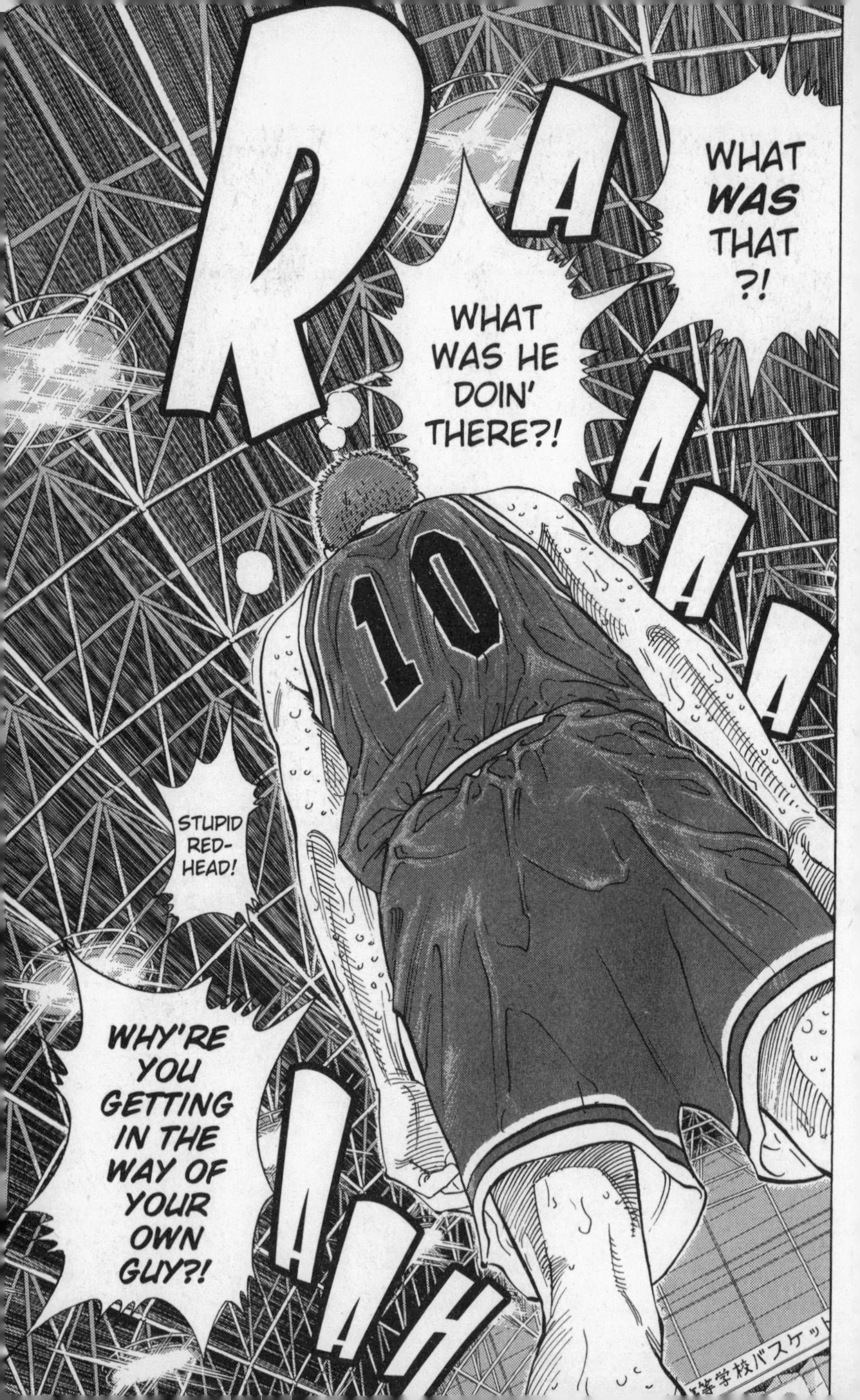
WHAT WAS THAT?!
WHAT WAS HE DOIN' THERE?!
RAAAAAAAH
STUPID RED-HEAD!
WHY'RE YOU GETTING IN THE WAY OF YOUR OWN GUY?!

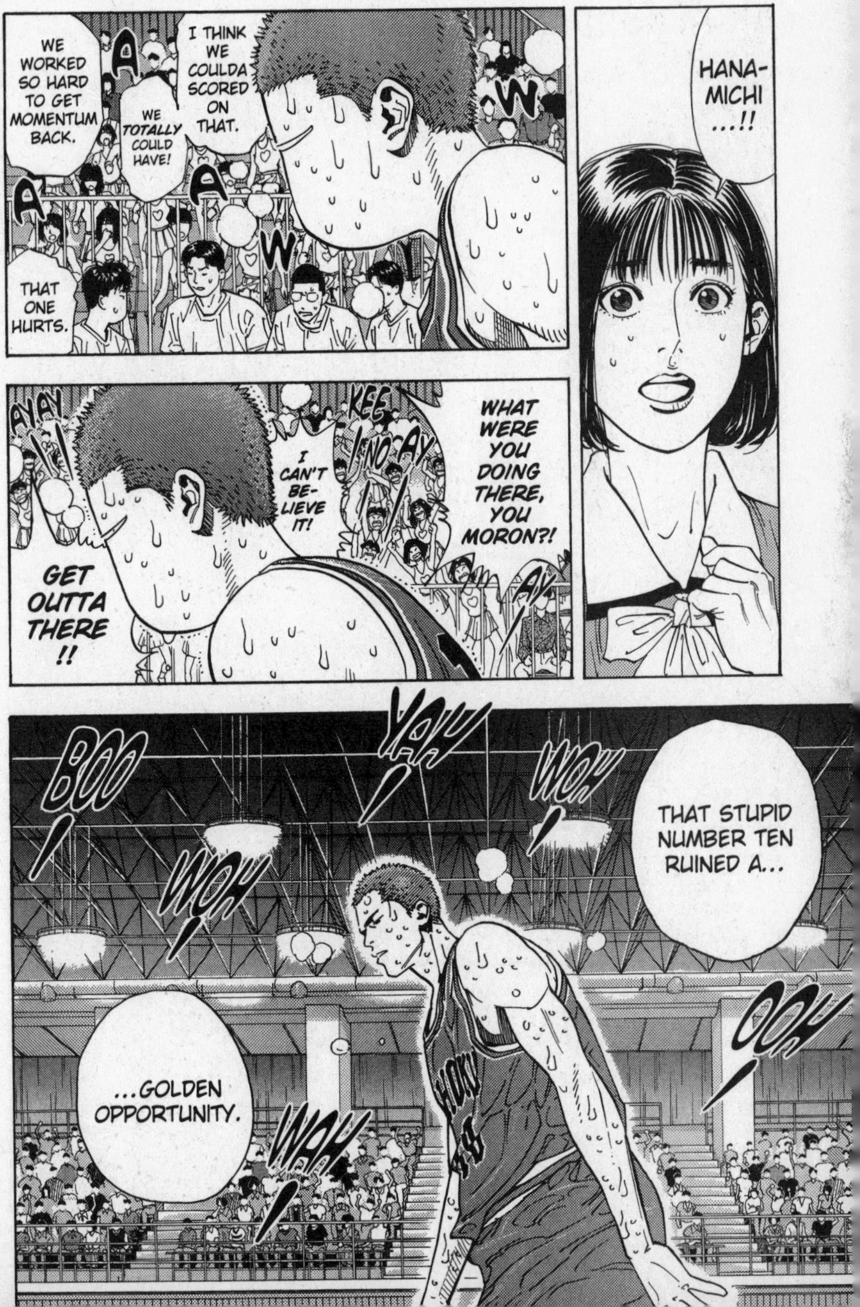
HANA-MICHI ...!!
I THINK WE COULDA SCORED ON THAT.
WE TOTALLY COULD HAVE!
WE WORKED SO HARD TO GET MOMENTUM BACK.
AW
AA
THAT ONE HURTS.
WHAT WERE YOU DOING THERE, YOU MORON?!
KEE
NO AY
I CAN'T BE-LIEVE IT!
AYAY!
GET OUTTA THERE!!
YAH!
WOH!
BOO!
THAT STUPID NUMBER TEN RUINED A...
WOH!
OOH!
...GOLDEN OPPORTUNITY.
WAH!

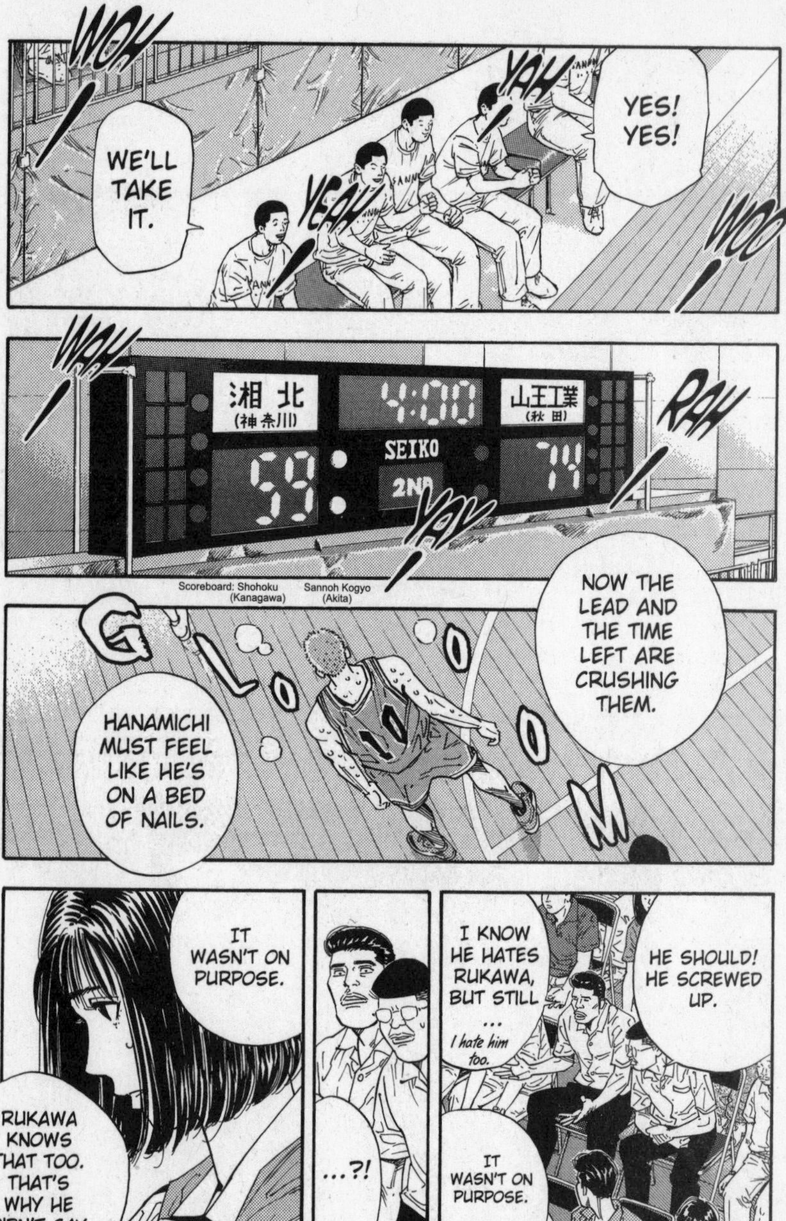
YES! YES!
WOO!
YAH!
WE'LL TAKE IT.
WOH!
YEAH!
RAH!
湘北 (神奈川)
4:00
山王工業 (秋田)
SEIKO
59
2ND
74
YAY!
WAH!
Scoreboard: Shohoku (Kanagawa) Sannoh Kogyo (Akita)
NOW THE LEAD AND THE TIME LEFT ARE CRUSHING THEM.
GLOOM
HANAMICHI MUST FEEL LIKE HE'S ON A BED OF NAILS.
HE SHOULD! HE SCREWED UP.
I KNOW HE HATES RUKAWA, BUT STILL...
I hate him too.
IT WASN'T ON PURPOSE.
...?!
IT WASN'T ON PURPOSE.
RUKAWA KNOWS THAT TOO. THAT'S WHY HE DIDN'T SAY ANYTHING.

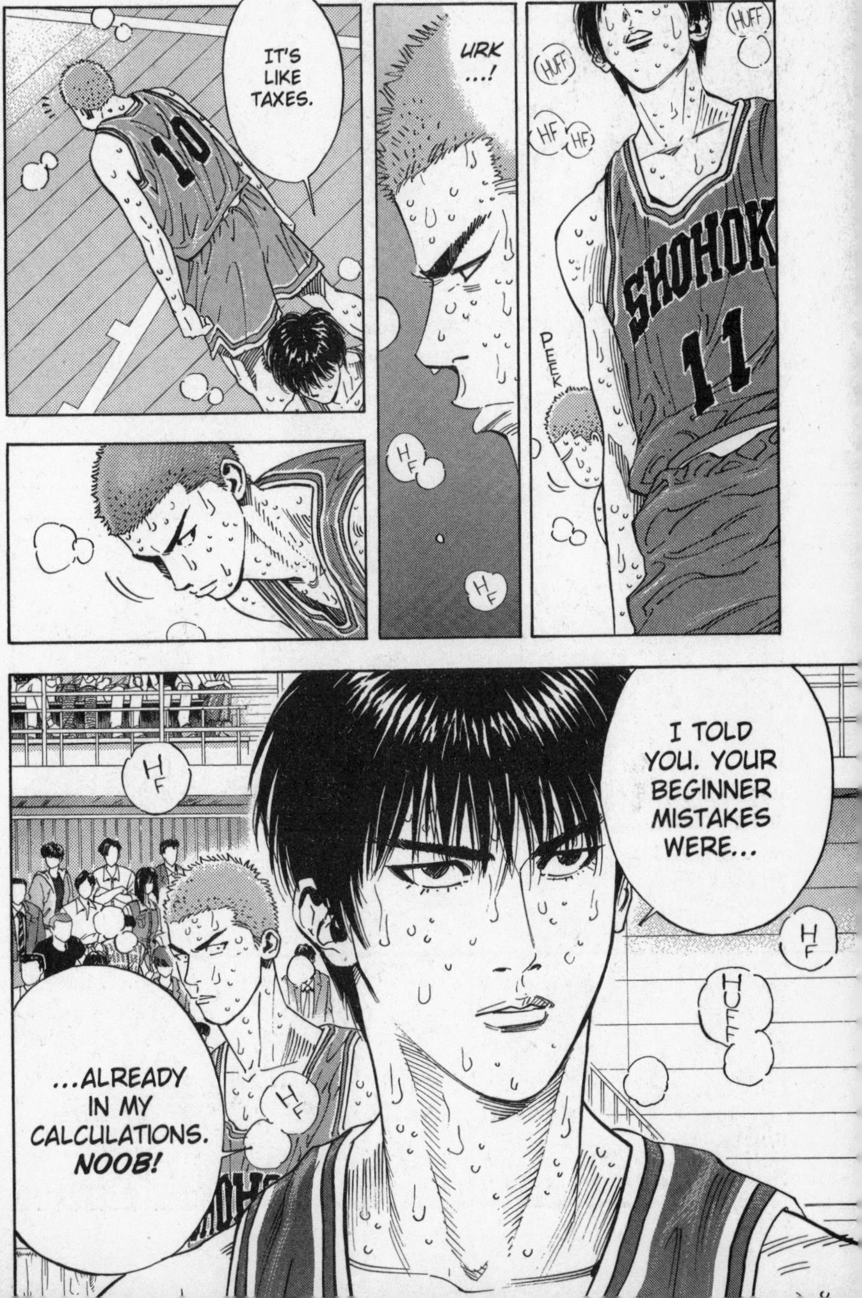
HUFF
HUFF
HF
HF
PEEK
URK ...!
HF
HF
IT'S LIKE TAXES.
I TOLD YOU. YOUR BEGINNER MISTAKES WERE...
HF
HUFF
HF
HF
...ALREADY IN MY CALCULATIONS. *NOOB!*

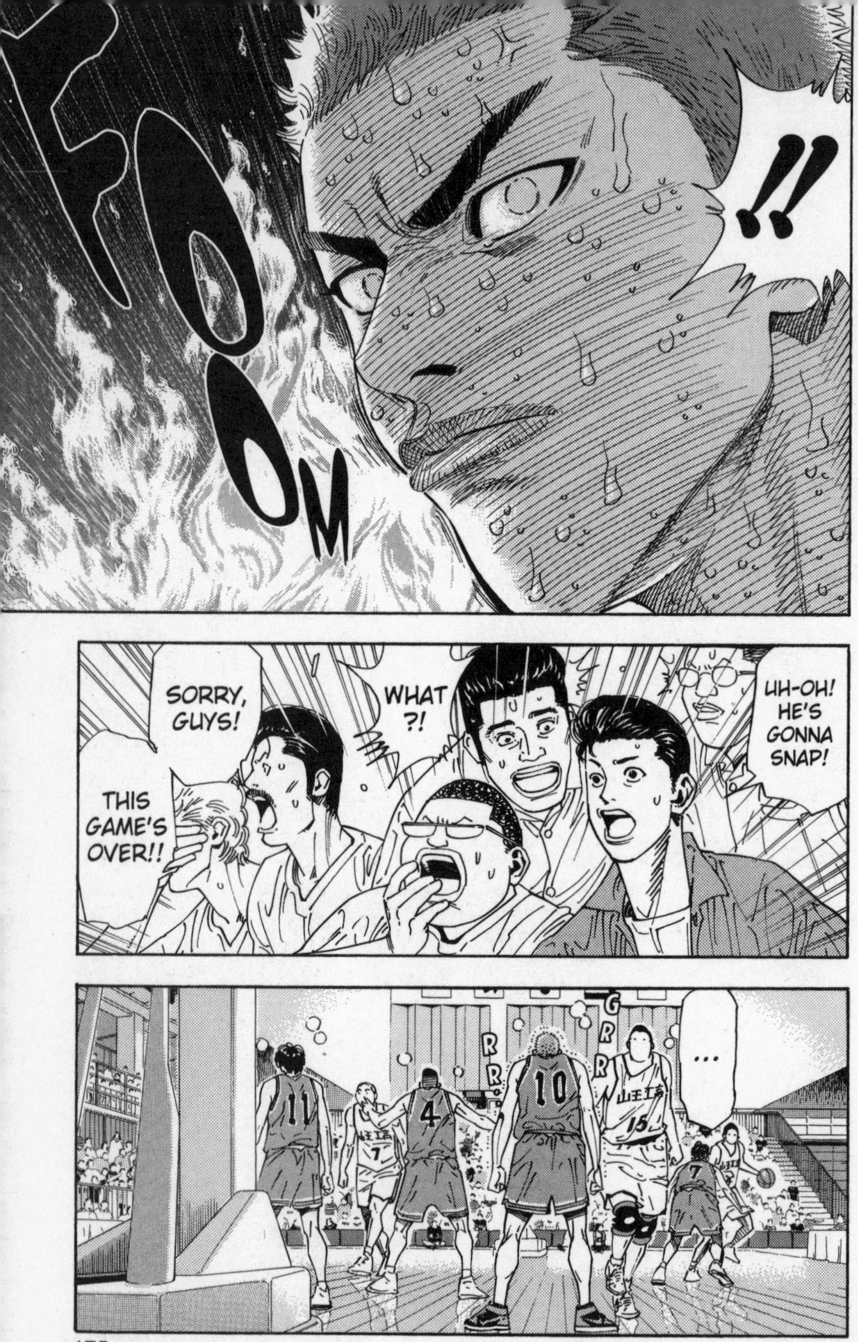
!!
FOOOM
UH-OH! HE'S GONNA SNAP!
WHAT?!
SORRY, GUYS!
THIS GAME'S OVER!!
...
GRR
RRR

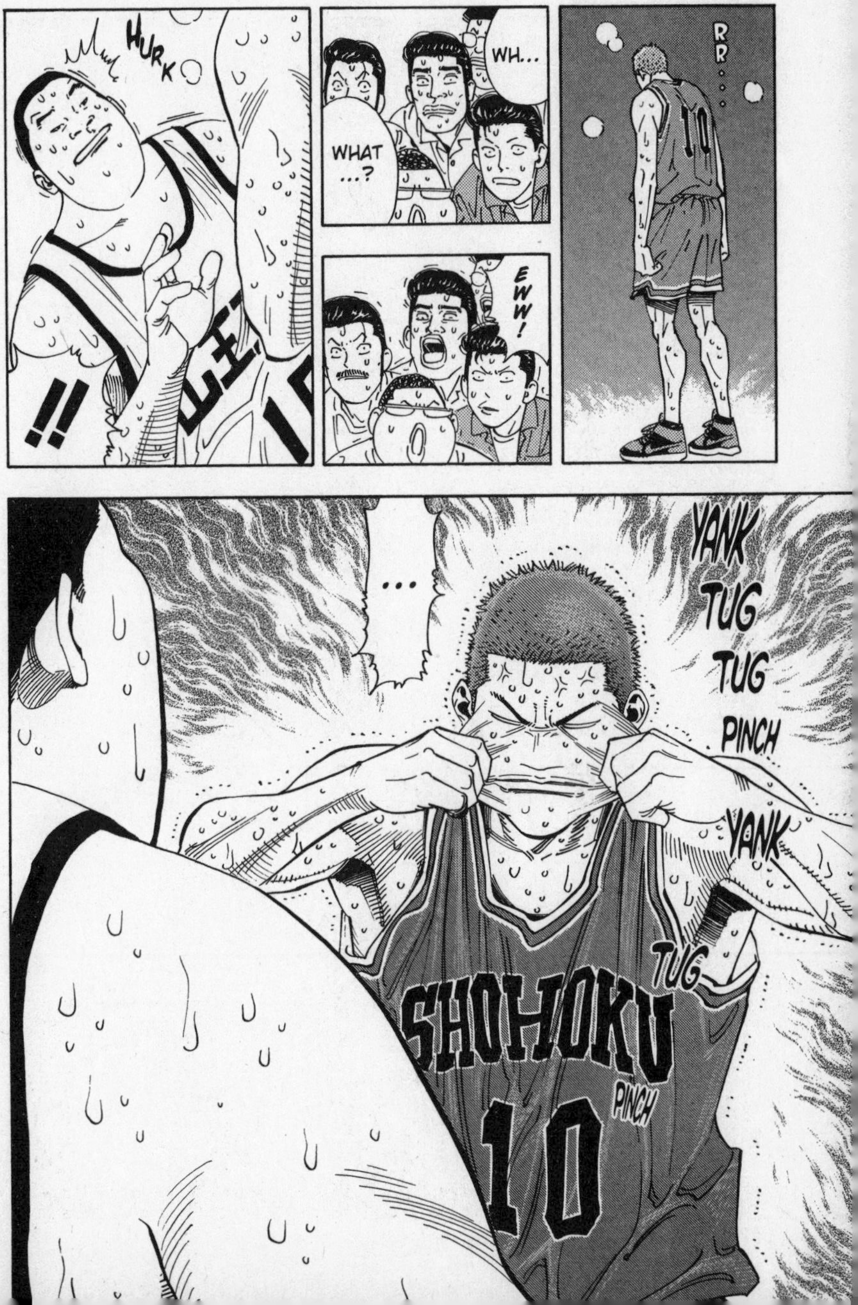
RR...
WH...
WHAT ...?
EWW!
HURK
!!
...
YANK
TUG
TUG
PINCH
YANK
TUG
SHOHOKU
10
PINCH

READ THIS WAY

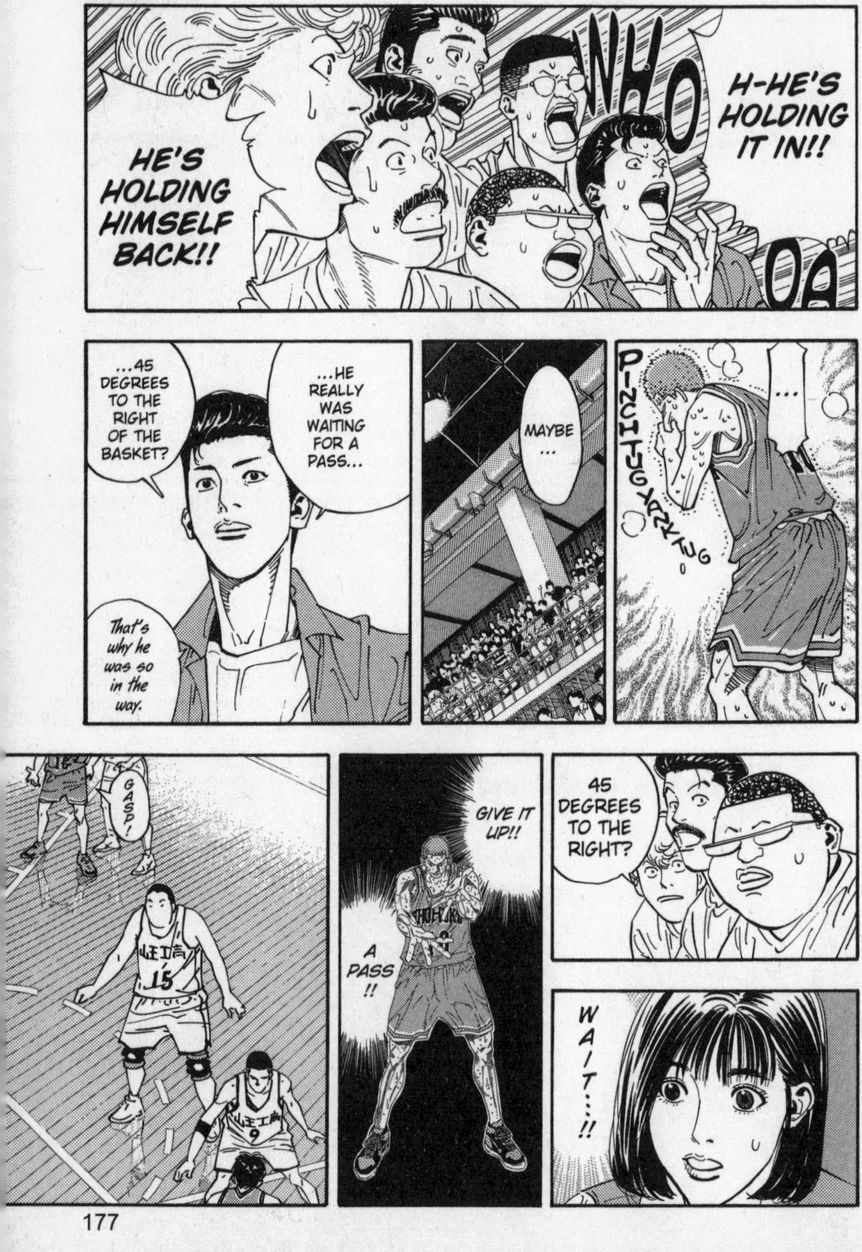
H-HE'S HOLDING IT IN!!
WHOOA
HE'S HOLDING HIMSELF BACK!!
...
PINCH TUG YANK TUG
MAYBE ...
...HE REALLY WAS WAITING FOR A PASS...
...45 DEGREES TO THE RIGHT OF THE BASKET?
That's why he was so in the way.
45 DEGREES TO THE RIGHT?
WAIT...!!
GIVE IT UP!!
A PASS!!
GASP!

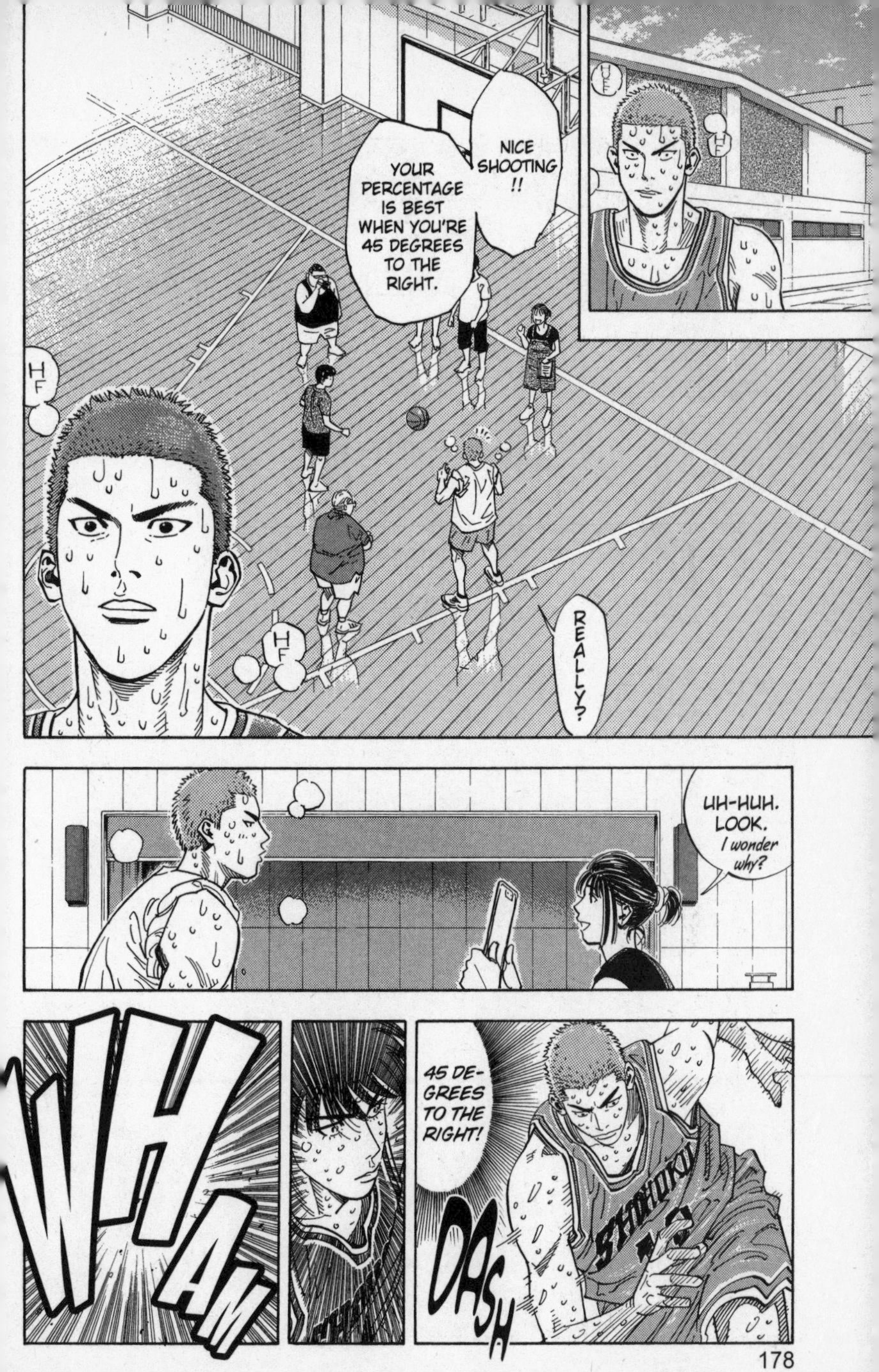
HUF
HF
NICE SHOOTING !!
YOUR PERCENTAGE IS BEST WHEN YOU'RE 45 DEGREES TO THE RIGHT.
REALLY?
HF
HF
UH-HUH. LOOK. I wonder why?
45 DE-GREES TO THE RIGHT!
DASH
WHAM

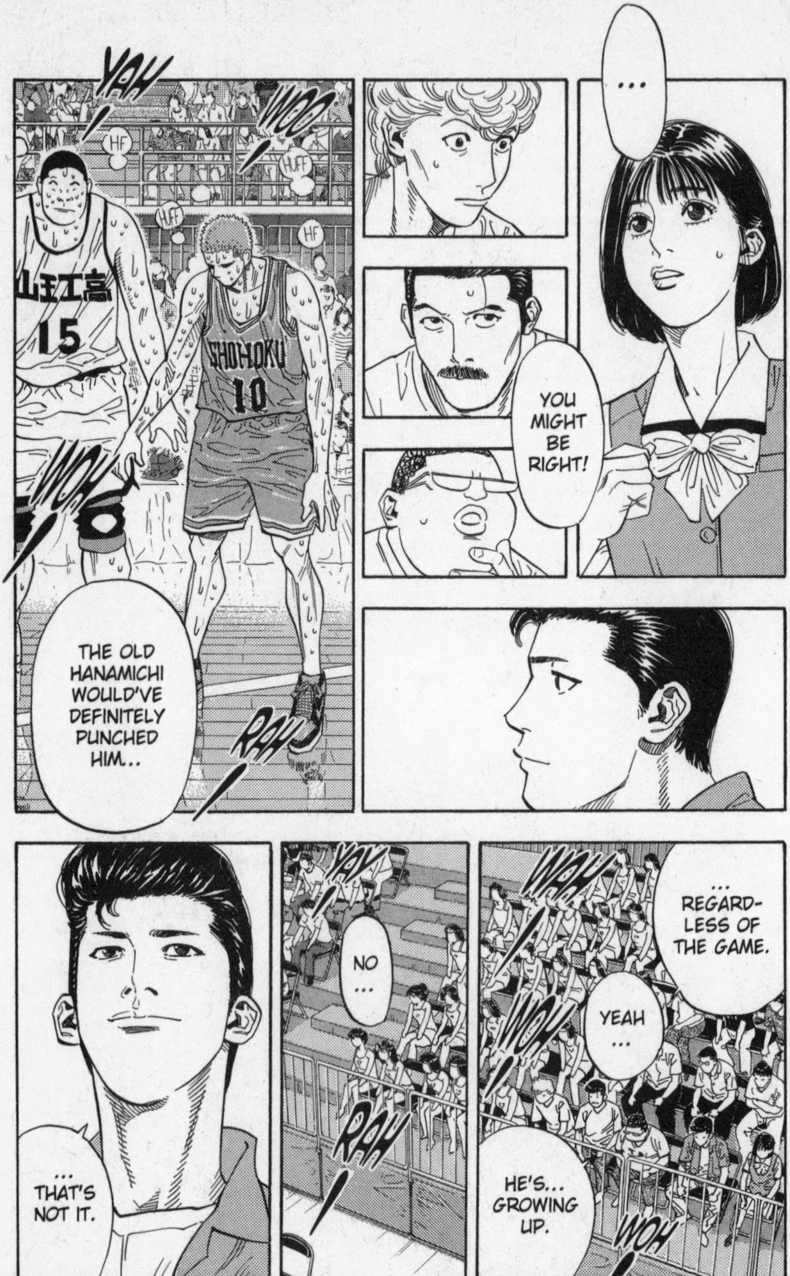
...
YOU MIGHT BE RIGHT!
YAH!
WOO!
HF
HUFF
HUFF
HF
WOH!
THE OLD HANAMICHI WOULD'VE DEFINITELY PUNCHED HIM...
RAH!
WAH!
...REGARDLESS OF THE GAME.
WOW!
YEAH...
HE'S... GROWING UP.
WOH!
YAY!
NO...
RAH!
...THAT'S NOT IT.

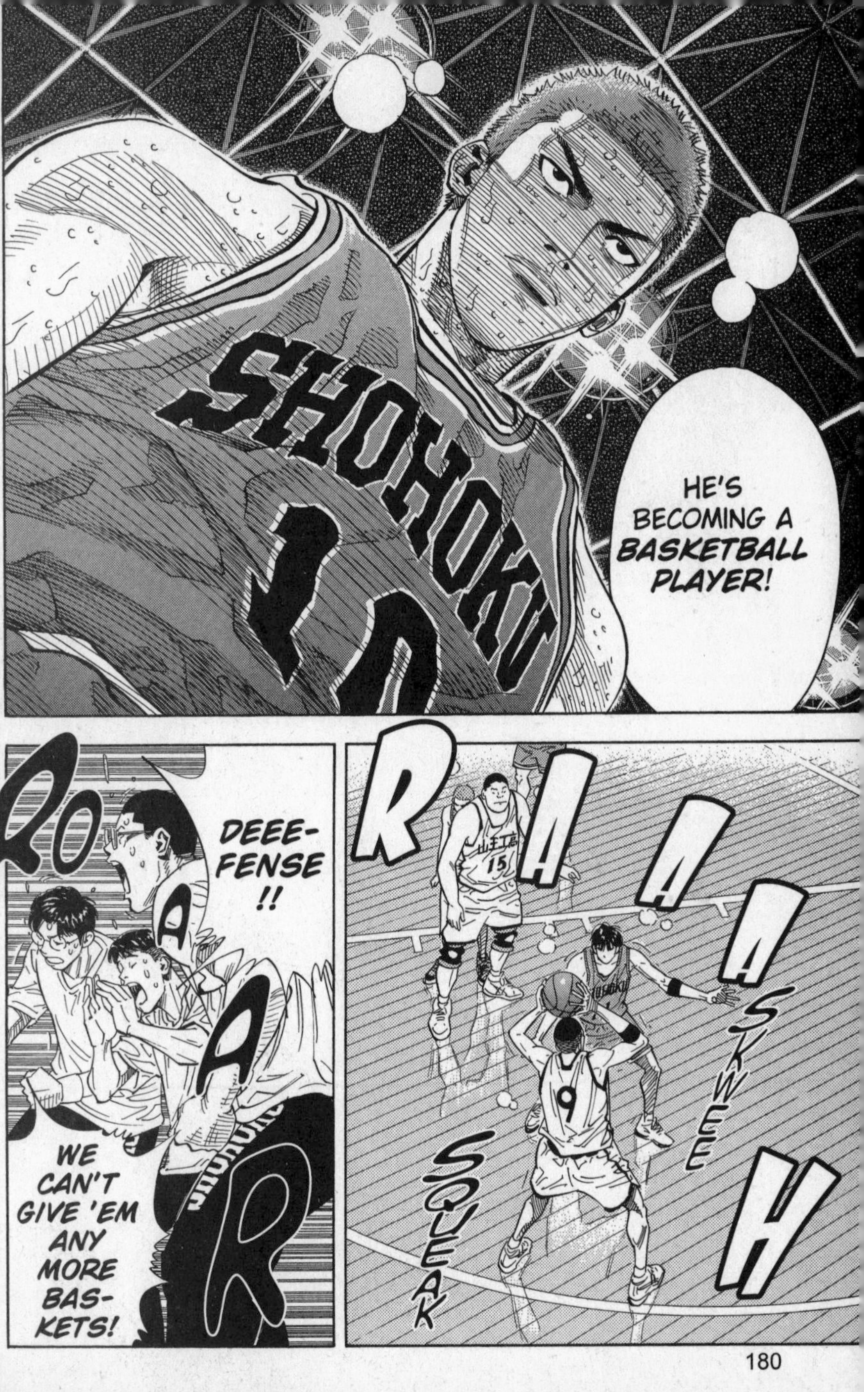
HE'S BECOMING A BASKETBALL PLAYER!
RAAAAH
SKWEE
SQUEAK
ROAAAR
DEEEE-FENSE!!
WE CAN'T GIVE 'EM ANY MORE BAS-KETS!

READ THIS WAY

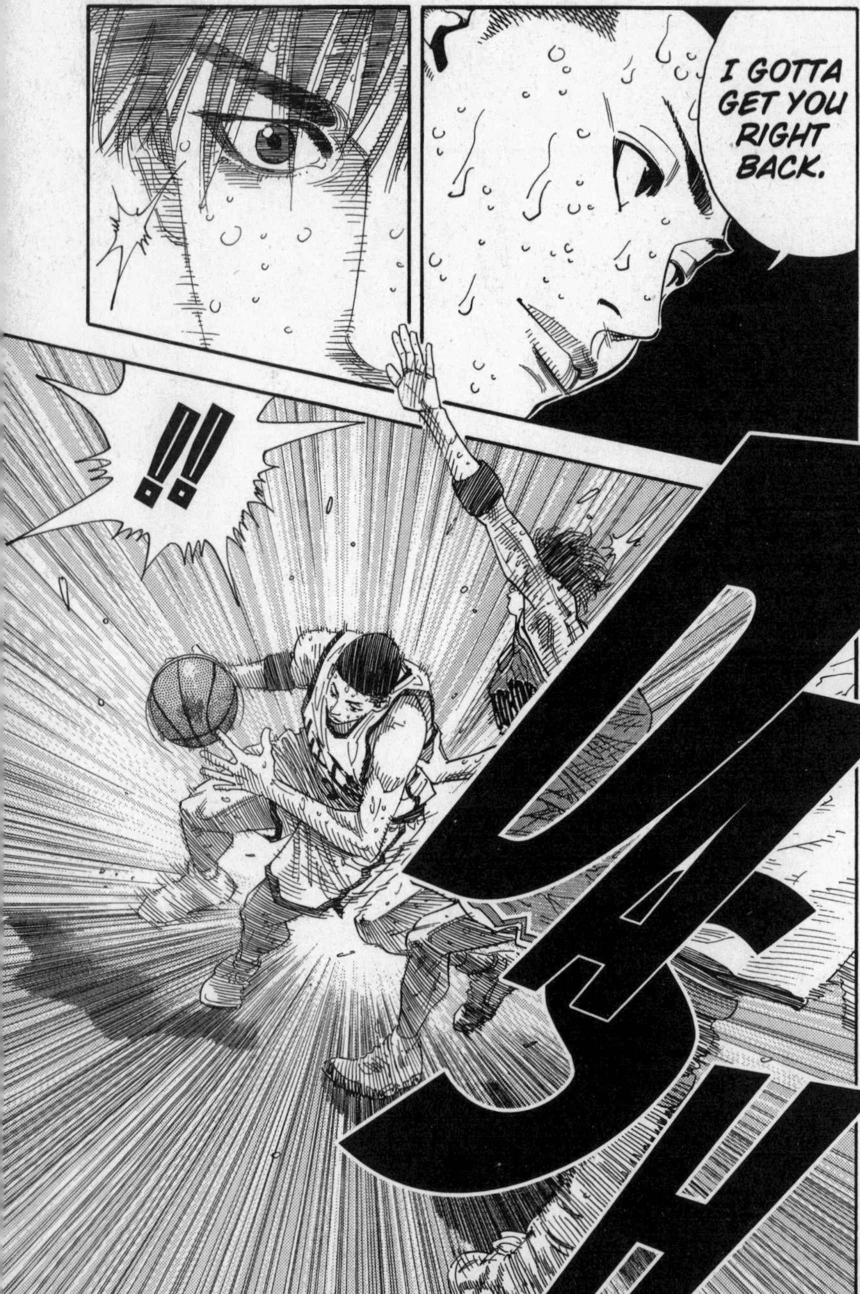
I GOTTA GET YOU RIGHT BACK.
!!

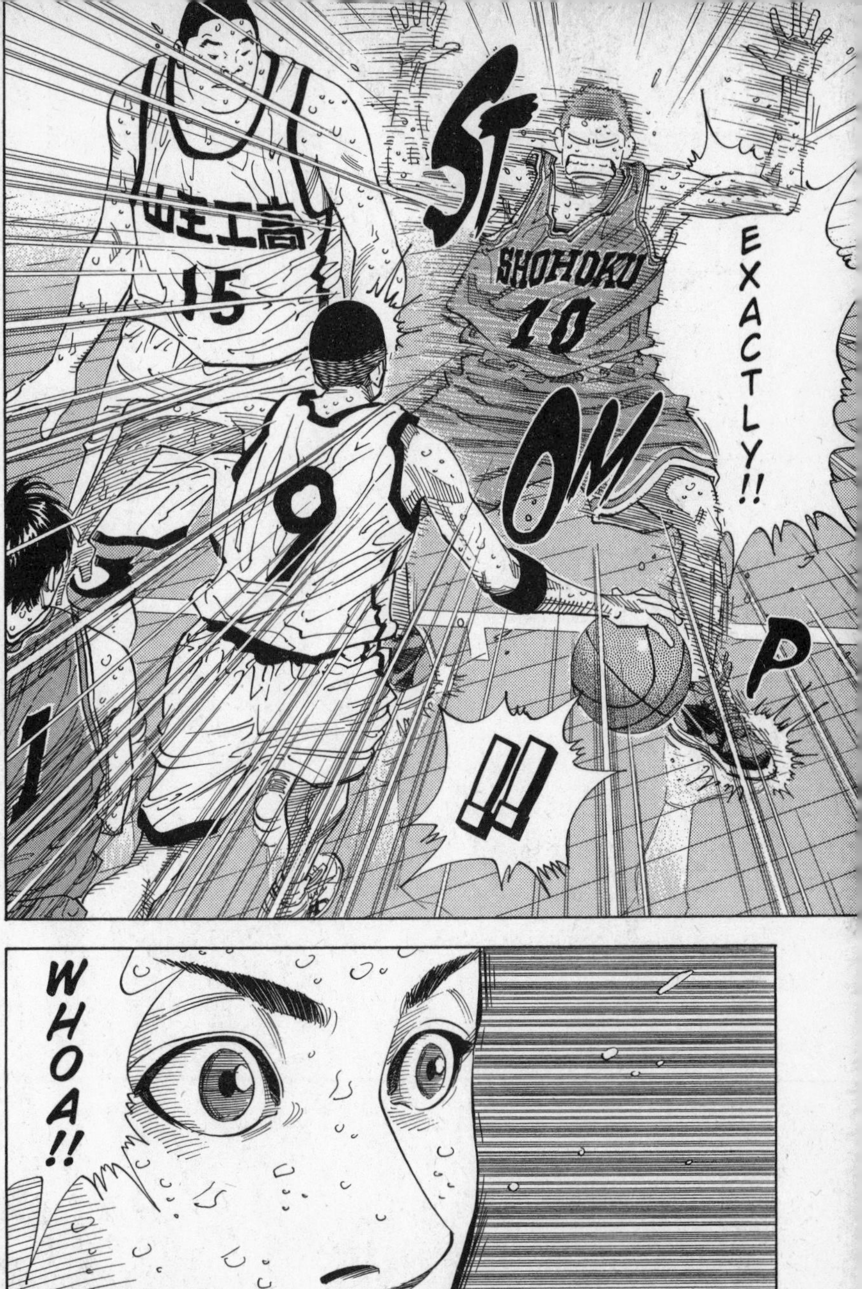
EXACTLY!!
STOMP
!!
WHOA!!

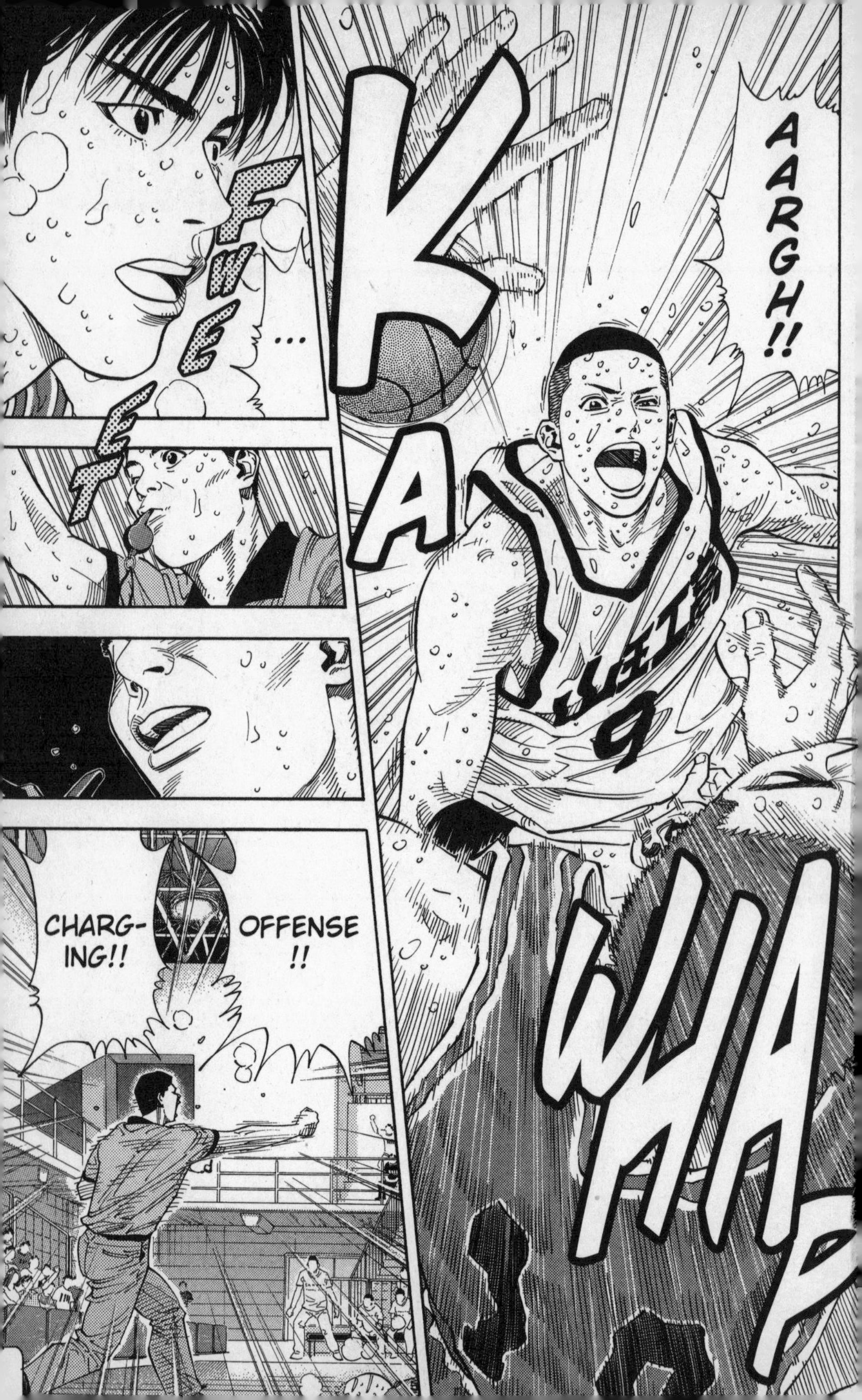
KA
AARGH!!
WHAP
FWEEET
...
OFFENSE!!
CHARG-ING!!

Coming Next Volume

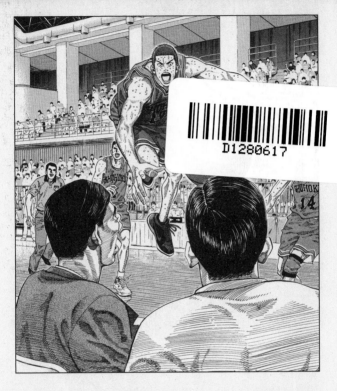

The second half is winding down and Shohoku is working harder than they ever have before to close the seemingly insurmountable lead Sannoh has over them. Rukawa has found something inside him and continues to evolve as a player, and Sakuragi is totally in his own zone. But will pushing themselves beyond their limits lead Shohoku to victory or ruin?

ON SALE OCTOBER 2013

ML 8/2013